The UCAS Guide to getting into

LAW

For entry to university and college in 2013

378.41

Published by: UCAS Rosehill New Barn Lane Cheltenham GL52 3LZ

Produced in conjunction with GTI MEDIA LTD

© UCAS 2012

UCAS, a company limited by guarantee, is registered in England and Wales number: 2839815
Registered charity number: 1024741 (England and Wales) and SC038598 (Scotland)

UCAS reference number: PU035013
Publication reference: 12_046
ISBN: 978-1-908077-16-5
Price £15.99

We have made all reasonable efforts to ensure that the information in this publication was correct at time of publication. We will not, however, accept any liability for errors, omissions or changes to information since publication. Wherever possible any changes will be updated on the UCAS website (www.ucas.com).

UCAS and its trading subsidiary, UCAS Media Limited, accept advertising for publications that promote products and services relating to higher education and career progression. Revenue generated by advertising is invested by UCAS in order to enhance our applications services and to keep the cost to applicants as low as possible. Neither UCAS nor UCAS Media Limited endorse the products and services of other organisations that appear in this publication.

Further copies available from UCAS (p&p charges apply):

Contact Publication Services PO Box 130 Cheltenham GL52 3ZF

email: publicationservices@ucas.ac.uk or fax: 01242 544806

For further information about the UCAS application process go to www.ucas.com.

If you need to contact us, details can be found at www.ucas.com/about_us/contact_us

UCAS QUALITY AWARDS

Contents

> CONTENTS

Foreword

THINKING ABOUT LAW?

Finding the higher education course that's right for you at the right university or college can take time and it's important that you use all the resources and guides available to you in making this key decision. We at UCAS have teamed up with LawCareers.Net to provide you with *The UCAS Guide to getting into Law* to show you how you can progress from being a student to careers in law. You will find key information on what the subject includes, entry routes and real-life case studies on how it worked out for others.

Once you know which subject area you might be interested in, you can use the listings of all the full-time higher education courses in art and design to see where you can study your subject. The course entry requirements are listed so you can check if getting in

would be achievable for you. There's also advice on applying through UCAS, telling you what you need to know at each stage of the application process in just six easy steps to starting university or college.

We hope you find this publication helps you to choose and make your application to a course and university or college that is right for you.

On behalf of UCAS and LawCareers.Net, I wish you every success in your research.

Mary Curnock Cook, Chief Executive, UCAS

Find **your career in** law

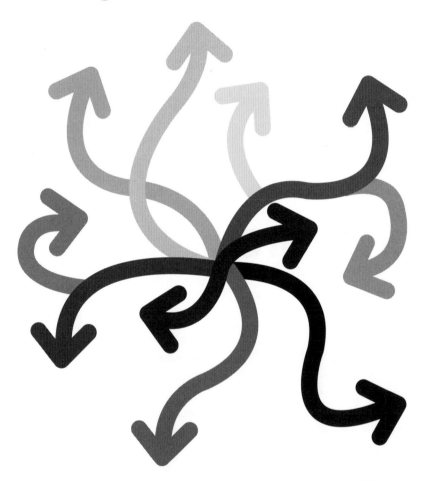

Law Careers.Net

Follow LawCareers.Net

Introducing law

What do lawyers do...

Law is entwined with almost every aspect of our society - from the age at which you can take your driving test, to the speed at which you can drive when you pass it; from the minimum wage you can expect to earn in a new job, to the rights you have should you lose it. This is reflected by the breadth of the legal profession.

The first thing to know is that the profession has two branches – you can become either a solicitor or a barrister (known as advocates in Scotland). For more on which strand might suit youbetter, see 'Solicitor or Barrister' (page 16) but read on for a broad description of what each type of lawyer might do.

SOLICITORS

Solicitors give advice and assistance on matters of law. Specifically, they are the first point of contact for people and bodies (ie, members of the public, companies and charities) seeking skilled legal advice and representation. Most solicitors work as part of a departmental team in private practice, while others work in central and local government, orin-house (ie, they work in a legal department within a company or organisation, such as Shell or the BBC).

Day to day
While solicitors are found in a variety of areas of law, the fundamentals of the job remain largely the same. These include:

- meeting clients, finding out their needs and establishing how they can help
- taking instruction from clients, researching relevant areas of law and proposing courses of action
- drafting letters, contracts and other legal documents
- acting on behalf of clients in negotiations, and occasionally representing them at tribunals or in court.

A CAREER IN LAW?

Here are a few facts you should know if you want to work in the legal profession.

- You don't need to take an undergraduate law degree to become a lawyer – see Entry routes on page 51
- Admissions tutors and legal recruiters look for good grades, and for excellent communication and problem-solving ability – see The career for you? on page 15
- Qualifying as a solicitor or barrister takes five to eight years and combines full-time study, and vocational and practical training – see Entry routes on page 51
- Most barristers are self-employed and about three-quarters of solicitors work in private practice – see Solicitor or Barrister on page 16

Client care

Every step of the above list will require intense interaction with a client who is depending on his/her solicitor to help with a matter that's of great significance to them. Indeed, many solicitors find that the relationships they develop with clients are the most rewarding part of the job.

High street solicitors take the duty of care they owe those they serve very seriously – it is an essential and often emotionally demanding part of, for instance, personal injury and family law cases.Meanwhile, a solicitor at a city firm assisting a multinational company on a takeover bid will need to know their client's business and marketplace inside out to advise on both legal and commercial issues.

Career progression

Being a solicitor is a tough but rewarding job. Many of those entering the profession work their way up through the ranks from newly qualified solicitor to associate to partner, often at the same firm. They become experts in their field, and are asked for advice by clients and for comment by journalists.

But that route is not the only way. Increasingly, firms are adapting the traditional hierarchy so that those who feel more comfortable lower down the ladder aren't left short-changed by staying there. Meanwhile, some solicitors jump the fence to work for the in-house legal departments of companies or the Government Legal Service.

BARRISTERS

Barristers offer advice on specific legal issues and are on the front line, representing clients in court. They receive their information and instructions through a client's solicitor. When not appearing in court, they work in chambers where they prepare their court cases and arguments.

Day to day

Again, although barristers work in a huge variety of areas of law, the fundamental elements of the job remain largely the same. These include:

- advising clients on the law and the strength of their case, usually following lots of research and writing an 'opinion'
- holding 'conferences' with clients to discuss their case
- representing clients in court, including presenting the case, cross-examining witnesses and summation
- negotiating settlements with the other side.

Client care

Initially a barrister is instructed by a solicitor on behalf of his/her client, so it may be that there is more interaction with the solicitor than with the client. Solicitors have good working relationships with barristers and they are likely to know or be able to find out the most suitable barrister to deal with a particular case. So in some ways, the solicitor-barrister relationship is as, if not more, important than the relationship between client and barrister.

In many cases, barristers are able to give advice on a case simply by looking at the papers and never meeting the client. However, in more complex matters, and certainly those which will be going to court, it will usually be necessary to have a conference or consultation with the client.

Career progression

Having been called the Bar, a barrister is then known formally as a 'junior'. He or she remains a junior until such time as he or she is made a Queen's Counsel (QC), otherwise known as 'silk'. A QC is a senior barrister, of at least 10 years' practice, who is regarded as having outstanding ability. They are normally instructed in very serious or complex cases. Most senior judges once practised as QCs.

Only a small proportion of barristers become QCs (about 10%) and, as such, the majority will remain juniors for their entire careers. Worth noting is that after 10 years as a junior, and not having been appointed a QC, they will be known formally as a 'senior junior' (rather confusingly!).

PERKS OF THE JOB

In the thick of things

Lawyers have the opportunity to work with interesting people and businesses on projects vital to everyday existence. They may also be involved with exciting ground-breaking or precedent-setting work. They are often at the centre of a web of other professionals such as bankers, social workers, accountants and civil servants.

Risk resistant

When other professions such as banking or IT ease off on recruitment during an economic downturn, law stays relativelybuoyant. Certain practice areas thrive during boom times, but others, such as family law, insolvency and litigation, do well no matter how the city is faring.

Well paid

Average starting salaries for solicitors vary enormously depending on the type of firm you go to. Heading to a firm with large corporate clients? Expect to be well paid from day one. Off to take on legal aid work? You're looking at a more modest salary. For barristers, life at the commercial and chancery Bar offers lucrative work and large pupillage awards, whereas criminal barristers need several years' experience before matching their counterparts in top solicitors' firms.

STATISTICS

SOLICITORS

- As of July 2010, there were around 150,000 on the solicitors' roll.
- Around three quarters of solicitors in England and Wales are in private practice, with the remainder working in commerce/industry or in the public sector.
- Women now make up over 45% of the profession.
- At least 11% of solicitors with practising certificates are from ethnic minority backgrounds.

Source: Law Society: Trends in the solicitors' profession

BARRISTERS

- As of December 2010, there were 12,420 self-employed barristers (around 1,400 of whom are QCs). There were nearly 3,000 employed barristers (eg, at the CPS and GLS).
- Nearly two thirds of barristers work in London, although other urban hotspots include Birmingham and Manchester.
- Women make up around 50% of pupils and around a third of practising barristers.   Source: Bar Council

WHAT DO LAWYERS SAY?

'If you're thinking about this as a career, you need to jump in with both feet because it requires total commitment.'
Colin Werriner, GDL student, page 40

'The best part of the job is that every day is different, and it's always interesting. You certainly meet some characters in this job!'
Kieran Brand, barrister, page 42

'You can't always control what's going to happen but that's just part of the job, and the trade-off is that you're not stuck in a boring 9:00-5:00 job.'
Lorraine McLinn, litigation solicitor, page 44

'The key is to be prepared to ask all the questions that no-one else will ask in case they look silly. I quite often ask for things to be explained in "Fisher Price language"!'
Lucy Garrett, commercial barrister, page 46

'We are a client-focused firm and there is a real emphasis on having a clear strategy to achieve client goals, while at the same time it is a necessity of the work to pay close attention to detail. Being trained to succeed at both is challenging and rewarding.'
Matt Marshall, trainee solicitor, page 48

THE UK LEGAL SYSTEM

At the heart of the UK legal system is a hierarchical court structure, split into civil and criminal courts. In the civil courts, organisations and individuals may bring cases against each other for a range of legal issues, such as breach of contract, discrimination, human rights, unfair dismissal and data protection. In the criminal courts, the Crown prosecutes the accused in cases such as murder, domestic violence and child abuse.

England, Wales and Northern Ireland

Criminal cases (and a few civil cases) are normally heard in the magistrates' courts. They usually deal only with cases which arise in their own area. There is no jury - rather, a panelof three magistrates (or justices of the peace) hear each case, decide whether the defendant is innocent and guilty, and if guilty, decide on a sentence.

The county courts are where civil cases are heard. The judge presides on his or her own, and deals with cases that include divorce hearings, personal injury claims, and landlord and tenant disputes.

The High Court deals with civil cases and hears appeals in criminal cases. It has three divisions; Family, Queen's Bench and Chancery. The Court of Appeal deals with civil and criminal appeals in England and Wales, whereas in Northern Ireland, there can be a rehearing of a county court case in the High Court and an appeal from there to the Court of Appeal.

In October 2009 the Supreme Court replaced the House of Lords as the highest court of appeal in the United Kingdom. Its 12 justices hear appeals on points of law. However, if the point at issue is covered by EU law, the case may be referred to the European Court of Justice in Luxembourg for a guide on interpretation. The case is then sent back to the national court to make a ruling.

Scotland

In the civil system, the lowest courts are the sheriff courts, which are in most districts in Scotland, The sheriff is usually a qualified solicitor or advocate. The Court of Session, which is in Edinburgh, is the highest civil court in Scotland. Litigants can then appeal to the Supreme Court (as above).

Criminal cases dealing with minor offences, such as being drunk and disorderly, are heard in the justice of the peace courts. The sheriff courts can hear some criminal cases (eg, theft or assault), while the High Court of the Justiciary hears the most serious criminal cases (eg, murder or rape). It is also the final court of appeal for all criminal cases.

www.ucas.com

at the heart of connecting people to higher education

Save with UCAS Card

If you're in Year 12, S5 or equivalent and thinking about higher education, sign up for the **FREE** UCAS Card to receive all these benefits:

- information about courses and unis
- expert advice from UCAS
- exclusive discounts for card holders

UCAS

Register today at
www.ucas.com/ucascard

The
career
for you?

Solicitor or barrister?

SOLICITOR	BARRISTER
Mostly employed in private law firms, so receives regular monthly salary	Mostly self-employed, so receives irregular (but often substantial) fees
Works mainly with the public and barristers	Works mainly with solicitors and other barristers
Office-based	Chambers and court-based
Engages more in ongoing advisory and one-to-one client work	Engages more in one-off advocacy - ie, court cases
Aspires to partner - ie, part ownership of firm and entitlement to a percentage of its profits. In 2010 nearly 50% of all male solicitors in private practice were partners, compared with only around 20% of women	Aspires to Queen's Counsel (QC) - ie, a top barrister, normally instructed in very serious/complex cases. Only about 10% of barristers make it
Solicitors Regulation Authority sets minimum annual salary for trainees; in 2011-12, it was £18,590 (London) and £16,650 (outside London). Many firms pay considerably more: a first-year trainee at a large City firm could earn around £37,000, rising to £65,000 on qualification	Bar Standards Board requires that all pupils must be paid no less than £12,000 per annum. Many earn much more - upwards of £45,000 in some instances

Which kind of lawyer could you be?

One of the most fundamental questions you must address when considering a career in the law is whether to become a solicitor or a barrister. Simply put, a barrister appears in court, while a solicitor works in a law firm. The term 'lawyer' applies to both.

However, the differences aremuch more complex. Some say it comes down to being an individualist (barrister) or a team player (solicitor). While it is true that a barrister is almost always self-employed and bound to other barristers only by convenience, and a solicitor may be just one worker in a law firm of thousands of people, in reality, the situation is less black and white. Barristers are often involved in teamwork and some solicitors may spend many hours on their own in a backroom drafting documents.

This decision as to which strand suits you best rests on a number of factors concerning your abilities,

temperament and - dare we say it - financial circumstances. Here's a general guide to some factors which may help you decide.

Academic performance

Fantastic academic results are the ideal underpinnings of every legal career. You will generally find a pretty close correlation between the best academic scores and the best (or at least the best-paying) jobs in the legal profession. It may be slightly more important for the Bar as it is smaller and consequently even more selective. The Bar is also probably rather more weighted to the traditional universities, to which the Oxbridge-heavy tenant lists at many chambers testify (the Bar is doing its best to address this bias, however).

Positions of responsibility

Again, having been the head prefect is an impressive achievement whichever strand you choose. However, positions of responsibility are concerned with keeping hierarchies in order and thus could be described as management training. For this reason they may be better valued by firms of solicitors.

Sporting prowess

Even stevens on this one. Sporting prowess implies drive, teamwork and organisational skills. Some sports may lend themselves better to one branch of the profession or the other (eg, team sports for would-be solicitors and individual sports for the Bar), but really all are good for both.

Acting/performing

These are highly relevant skills for both branches of the profession. You will be in the business of conveying information and ideas whether you are a solicitor or barrister. However, the courtroom side of a barrister's work is a direct application of these attributes, so the Bar may value them slightly higher.

Commercial/business know-how

Whatever you do in the law you will, at some level, be involved in running a business - be it as a small cog in a huge firm or as a self-employed person in sole practice or at the Bar. Furthermore, you will often be working to assist the businesses of others. Firms of solicitors no longer provide purely legal advice, but are employed as business advisers with an eye on overall strategy. Barristers are more typically 'hired hands' for advocacy or for preparing highly specific legal opinions.

Legal work experience

At trainee or pupil level, nobody expects you to know the law inside out. What they do expect is for you to have a relatively sophisticated grasp of the profession, its activities and its rhythms, as a way of showing that you have thought sensibly about why you want to become a lawyer. One of the best ways of doing this is to find a law (or law-related) environment in which you can learn what it's all about.

Eloquence

As we saw above, the ability to communicate is the fundamental tool of the trade. The better you are at communicating, the better lawyer you will be. But different methods of communication may be required; for example, while barristers may spend more time talking to experts, solicitors may be more often speaking to clients and lay people.Again, the fact a barrister is regularly standing up and talking in court means this skill is more important at the Bar.

Sociability

The law is a sociable profession in which you can expect to meet large numbers of people from all walks of life. Crucially, you must be able to get on with your clients and other lawyers with whom you work. The legal community is intimate and occasionally incestuous; it helps to be able to fit in and get on. Yes, there are legendary curmudgeons lurkingaround (particularly at the Bar), but don't think it's advisable to become one of them. If you become a barrister, you'll need social skills to stay onside with the clerks – they decide whether you work or not!

Self-reliance

You'll need a fair amount of self-reliance and self-belief whatever you do in law. The solicitor generally has a more definite career structure, but after a certain point (especially towards partnership),it's dog eat dog. As a barrister, though, you are literally on your own. It's your career and you've got to make it happen, make the most of it and deal with the quiet times. If you need more structure, then think again.

Intellectual curiosity

In reality, the area of law in which you end up will be the greatest driver of the intellectual content of your work. However, if you want to be a really serious analyst and provider of opinions on heavyweight points of law, then the Bar may be for you - especially as the 'backroom boys' at firms of solicitors are considered to be a dying breed.

Finances

Quite clearly, it is right and proper that a career in the law should be available to all. That said, the relevant training (especially at postgraduate level) means that it is not uncommon for individuals to finish the LPC or BPTC with over £40,000-worth of debt. Before you rack up this kind of bill, be realistic about your job prospects.

Enthusiasm for dressing up

Do you like wearing tights? Gowns? Wigs? Do you feel that panto should be staged all year round? The Bar values sartorial tradition above virtually any calling and the outfits reflect this. Solicitors' dress is, by contrast, dull, dull, dull (even on Fridays).

Commitment to social justice

There remain many commendable organisations and individuals in the legal profession who work tirelessly to beat injustice and ensure that right prevails. Furthermore, the grandest and greatest may well be involved in something socially useful (usually trumpeted all round town as 'pro bono'), but don't be fooled; the law is an industry like any other and should be treated as such.

Which area?

Only those outside the profession see law as one profession or general career path. Those inside it know that there is a whole range of options and career choices once you've made your decision between solicitor and barrister.

This section outlines some of the main areas of practice in which you can specialise, as either solicitor or barrister.But first – the word "practice". In the legal profession, you "practise" law – which means that you are a legal practitioner, not that you have to practise being a lawyer in the same way that you have to practise a musical instrument. Similarly, areas of law are called "practice areas".

And one further thing to note – while the following list of different practice areas may appear distinct on paper, in realitythere is some crossover. A company buying another company may require advice on everything

from structuring assets to redrafting employment contracts to selling premises.

Here follows just a small selection of the vast array of practice areas out there

CORPORATE/COMMERCIAL

Commercial and corporate solicitors advise on complex transactions and act for businesses of all sizes, from international corporations to small start-ups. General company law work involves advising on company directors' rights and responsibilities, company board meetings, memoranda and articles of association, and shareholders' rights. Corporate transactional work concerns mergers and acquisitions, demergers and restructurings, joint ventures, takeovers, privatisations, initial public offerings (IPOs) and new issues of shares.

Barristers in this field normally only become involved to help resolve disputes between businesses, for example were a takeover has gone wrong.

Upside?

Lawyers in this area are among the most highly paid in the profession, with opportunities for international travel and the chance to work with big-name clients.

Downside?

Weekend work and all-nighters are not uncommon when working on a deal, so be prepared to sacrifice your social/family life at times.

Client example

Multinational company, Big Brand, seeks advice from its solicitor on merging with a competitor, Little Brand.

CRIME

Criminal lawyers – both solicitors and barristers – advise and represent their clients in court, on criminal charges that can range from minor motoring misdemeanours to more serious crimes, including murder. Barristers may be called on to act for either the defence or the prosecution. A guilty plea can be dealt within a couple of days (or less), while a more complex casecan take months to just come to trial.

Upside?

The unpredictability of not knowing what case will be next is exciting, and the satisfaction to the defending side of a non-guilty verdict can't be beat.

Downside?

The late nights, holidays and weekends spent at the police station, and the often very short notice given to prepare a case.

Client example

Peter Pettythief has been arrested for breaking and entering. His lawyer is off down to the police station to advise him and work on his defence.

EMPLOYMENT

As a solicitor, you'll be working on contentious work such as disputes that end up in employment tribunals or in the high court. You may also advise on non-contentious work, such as drafting contracts of employment or advising on working hours and family-friendly policies such as maternity leave. Your client could be the employer or employee. As a barrister, you will be appearing on behalf of your client in either a tribunal or court, often in different parts of the country – travel is often required.

Upside?

The human element to your work can be very rewarding – you may find yourself helping your client resolve a personally very difficult situation.

Downside?

People are relying on your success, which can lead to tremendous lows if things go against you in court.

Client example

Brenda Bossyboots is facing a claim of harassment which she denies. She seeks advice from her lawyer on how to defend the claim and assess her chances of success if it goes to tribunal.

FAMILY

Family lawyers deal with all legal matters relating to marriage, separation, divorce, cohabitation and legal issues relating to children (eg, maintenance and access arrangements, and adoption both in the UK and internationally). Family law also encompasses financial negotiations, inheritance issues and prenuptial contracts. Some family law cases involve substantial assets and complex financial arrangements, or high-profile cases with well-known personalities.

Family law developments are very much driven by changes in society, and although the role of a family law solicitor calls for an astute legal mind, you also need 'softer' skills such as tact, sympathy and to be non-judgemental.

Upside?
With regular client contact, you can build great relationships and are often instrumental in improving a difficult situation for your client.

Downside?
Clients in a painful period of their lives may be unreasonable or demanding, and the emotional demands on you may be draining.

Client example
Divorced Dan is seeking advice from his family law solicitor on a new contact order so that he can see his children more often.

HUMAN RIGHTS

In recent years, human rights law has become a popular choice for both students and practitioners. The introduction of the Human Rights Act 1998 incorporated human rights law, public law and EU law into English law, and made the European Convention on Human Rights directly enforceable in ournational courts.This practice area is incredibly wide-ranging and includes immigration and asylum cases, privacy cases affecting celebrities, and international law issues. Clients may range from low-income refugees and prisoners through to large news organisations and government departments.

Upside?
The work is topical and interesting – often newsworthy – and your success can make a huge difference to both your client and society as a whole.

Downside?
It can be hard to persuade clients that not every wrong perpetrated against them is a breach of their human rights!

Client example
Scruffy Student was involved in a recent protest and feels he was badly treated by the police and falsely imprisoned. He is seeking advice from a human rights lawyer as to whether he has a claim for police misconduct.

INTELLECTUAL PROPERTY

This involves protecting the exploitation of intellectual ideas, normally by the way of copyright, trademarks and patents. IP lawyers advise on issues ranging from commercial exploitation to infringement disputes, and agreements that deal either exclusively with IP or with IP rights in the wider context of larger commercial transactions. For example, issues include securing copyright in a hit song or contesting a 'copycat' logo. This is a very technical field so it suits lawyers who enjoy ferreting around in legal documents for minute points of law on which to build a case. Clients range from inventors looking to protect an idea to huge multinational companies.

Upside?
The law is constantly trying to keep pace with changes in technology, which makes it dynamic and exciting.

Downside?
It is a fiendishly technical and difficult area of law, which can lead to protracted cases – sometimes taking more than a year even to get to court.

Client example
Pharma Co has developed a new drug that will cure the common cold. It consults its IP lawyer on how to protect the formula from its competitors and how to register it in various jurisdictions.

PRIVATE CLIENT

Private client lawyers advise on all aspect of the financial affairs of clients, most of whom are high net-worth individuals. The core work involves advising on capital gains tax, inheritance tax planning, setting up lifetime trusts and preparing wills. Some clients have more specialist needs – for example, landowners might include farmers with thousands of acres seeking advice on how to structure their business, or owners of historic estates open to the public who need advice on protecting their heritage assets.

Private client lawyers also handle a wide range of charity work, advising on specific charity law issues as well as on commercial and property matters that affect charitable organisations and the establishment of charities.

Upside?
You're likely to get to know clients well probably over many years and become a vital support to them and their families.
Downside?
The law itself is extremely complex and some may find the sedate pace a disappointment.
Client example
Mr and Mrs Bagsofcash have gone to see their private client solicitor to get help setting up a trust for their children and restructuring their tax arrangements.

TAX

Virtually all commercial transactions have tax implications. Accordingly, corporate tax is one of the most important practice areas for any major law firm. Working in corporate tax involves advising on the most tax-efficient means of acquiring, relinquishingor restructuring assets, negotiating and documenting the transaction, and ensuring the smooth completion of the resulting deal. On the contentious side, corporate tax lawyers advise on all aspects of tax litigation and investigations, negotiate with tax authorities and conduct litigation in the civil courts.

Tax lawyers are responsible for small discrete pieces of work for a lot of different transactions, as opposed to other areas where you may do a lot of work on one big deal at a time.

Upside?
The pay is generous and the academic nature of the area means that you spend a lot of your time doing research and exercising your brain.
Downside?
New tax rules and legislation are constantly being introduced, so staying on top of things can be a challenge.
Client example
Fabulous FoundationsIncis seeking advice from its tax lawyer on whether it can avoid paying 4% stamp duty land tax on a large housing development.

Other areas not mentioned above, but which might catch your eye and require further research, include banking, competition, construction, environment, EU, insolvency, insurance, personal injury, property, shipping, sportand TMT (technology media and telecommunications).

Alternative paths

Nobody ever said that having a law degree confines you to life as a lawyer – far from it, in fact. There are many alternatives to becoming a solicitor or barrister, and routes to qualification other than the standard training contract or pupillage. Employers will value the skills you have learned through your legal training, such as the ability to research, collect and analyse large amounts of information, and to create a logical argument and reasoned conclusion from a set of facts. The ability to communicate clearly with the public and the profession alike is another sought-after skill. Discretion and a first-class memory are alsohighly valued in the general career market.

Read on to see whether any of these alternative careers and/or routes to law tickles your fancy.

ALTERNATIVE PROFESSIONS

Accountancy and taxation

Many accountancy firms recruit law students to specialise in tax work because, arguably, there are few differences between the job of a tax accountant and a tax lawyer. In addition, some large accountancy firms have launched their own law firms.Accountancy exams are tough but the potential rewards – both professional and financial – are excellent. A move into accountancy also offers the opportunity to branch out into other careers with positions in industry, management and consultancy.

Finance

Banks are keen to recruit law graduates, as are building societies, insurance companies, stockbrokers and related professions. Those who thrive in a competitive and high-pressure environment may find a financial services or City career attractive and well worth investigating. Most of the leading financial institutions offer summer work placement programmes, which are a good starting point for you to explore this as a career option.

Civil service

There are opportunities throughout the civil service, some of which are particularly appropriate to holders of a law degree. Law graduates may wish to pursue a career in the Home Office, the Ministry of Justice, the diplomatic service or the Foreign Office.HM Revenue & Customs employs tax inspectors and those with a proven ability to understand the intricacies of tax law are especially suited to such jobs. It is worth investigating the Civil Service Fast Stream, an accelerated training scheme for graduates.

Other professions to consider include specialisms within the **media, police, the European Commission, conveyancing** or **court reporting**.

ALTERNATIVE QUALIFICATION OPPORTUNITIES

In-house lawyers

Approximately 2,500 companies and non-governmental organisations in the United Kingdom employ around 7,000 lawyers to work in-house. The main characteristic of the in-house role is that lawyers deal exclusively with their employer's legal business. This close involvement enables the lawyers to develop detailed knowledge of all aspects of their employer's business and provide advice that is in tune with the employer's commercial needs. Most in-house lawyers agree that this close working relationship is the most satisfying feature of such work.

Common to most in-house legal departments is a requirement to draft and maintain up-to-date standard contract and policy documents. In-house lawyers may also be involved in planning business strategies with commercial colleagues and negotiating the terms of deals with customers or other lawyers. Other responsibilities could involve advising on the supply of goods and services, leases, mortgages, mergers and acquisitions, and cooperation agreements for research, production, distribution or marketing, as well as litigation stemming from disputes arising from any of these activities.

Government Legal Service

The Government Legal Service (GLS) is the organisational name for the legal teams of about 30 central government departments, agencies and public bodies which between them employ over 2,000 qualified lawyers. The teams provide a comprehensive range of legal services to the government of the day.

The work carried out by lawyers in the GLS covers virtually all aspects of the law relating to the private sector (eg, advisory services, litigation and prosecution), as well as a wide range of specialisms (eg, company/commercial, charity, criminal, social security, land, property and trust laws). In addition, the GLS has unique responsibilities of national and international importance, including drafting subordinate legislation, instructing parliamentary counsel on primary legislation and advising ministers on policy or constitutional matters.

Crown Prosecution Service

The Crown Prosecution Service (CPS) is the largest legal employer in England and Wales with around 2,800 lawyers who conduct criminal prosecutions on behalf of the crown.Crown prosecutors weigh up evidence and public interest factors in all cases and decide those which should be heard by the courts. They also advise the police on matters relating to criminal cases. CPS caseworkers assist prosecutors in case management as well as attending court, dealing with post-court administration, assessing professional fees and liaising with witnesses and other organisations within the criminal justice system.

Other roles to consider include advisers at **law centres** or **Citizens Advice**, or as a **magistrates'** or **justices' clerk**.

ALTERNATIVE ROUTES INTO LAW

Paralegals

Many non-law graduates get work as paralegals. The standing of paralegals is rising, with paralegals now able to become partners and seek junior judicial office. Most paralegals specialise in one type of law - commonly personal injury, family, criminal, conveyancing, debt recovery, probate or commercial law – so most vacancies are in these practice areas. Paralegals sometimes carry out solicitor-level work. As such, some firms offer training contracts to their paralegals, while others may reduce the length of the standard training contract.

ILEX legal executive

The Institute of Legal Executives (ILEX) represents over 22,000 individuals who are employed in various legal institutions in the United Kingdom, including private practice law firms, local government and commerce and industry. ILEX legal executives are qualified lawyers who have at least five years' experience of working under the supervision of a solicitor and who have passed the ILEX exams.

Their daily work is similar to that of solicitors. Depending on his or her area of specialisation, a legal executive may be called on to brief barristers, advise a party to a matrimonial dispute, draft a will or draw up documentation for the formation of a company. Legal executives are qualified lawyers but not qualified solicitors, although recent developments mean that legal executive lawyers are eligible for judicial appointments and partnerships in legal disciplinary practices.

Chartered secretaries

Chartered secretaries work as company secretaries and in other senior positions in companies, charities, local government, educational institutions and trade bodies. They are qualified in company law, accounting, corporate governance, administration, company secretarial practice and management. They are trained to deal with regulation, legislation and best practice, and to ensure effective operations.

Finances

How do we put this? Training to be a lawyer isn't cheap. The reality is that if you have to pay for all your university tuition fees and vocational courses, you could incur debts of many tens of thousands of pounds. And it's not just course fees that have to be taken into account – there are also the hidden costs of books, accommodation, food, transport and at least one good suit! This is a huge financial investment with no guarantee of a training contract or pupillage at the end of it.

DOING THE SUMS

With increased tuition fees coming in from 2012, you could be looking at paying up to £9,000 per year for your undergraduate studies. But that's just the beginning. In 2010-11 Graduate Diploma in Law (GDL) course fees were as much as £9,400.Fees for theLegal Practice Course (LPC) and the Bar Professional Training Course (BPTC) were even higher, with the LPC costing as much as £13,550 and the BPTC up to £16,885.These fees represent the upper limits of what you can expect to pay, but the courses are always a significant financial undertaking - especially given the rising cost of living.

So with that in mind, how do you go about financing your study? Thankfully, there is a variety of options. At undergraduate level, and assuming you're not relying on the bank of mum and dad, government-funded loans are provided by the Student Loans Company. You can get a loan for tuition fees (covering the full amount) and living costs (the amount will vary depending on where you're studying and whether you live independently or at home). The loans are repayable only after graduation and only when you are earning more than £21,000 per annum. Go to **www.ucas.com/students/ studentfinance** to find out more.

At the postgraduate stage, for those lucky students who secure a training contract or pupillage before they begin their GDL/LPC/BPTC training, sponsoring firms or chambers may pay (some) fees and/or a maintenance grant. However, most students have little choice but to finance their own way through this stage and careful financial planning is therefore essential. Sponsorship, local authority grants, bursaries, college access funds and loans are all worth looking into.

CASH BACK

And the good news is that once you're a bona fide trainee or pupil, you'll start receiving some income. The Solicitors Regulation Authority sets the minimum salaries that trainees should be paid, and in 2011-12, these were fixed at £18,590 for those in London and £16,650 for those outside of London. However, many firms pay considerably more! For instance, a first-year trainee at a large international firm can currently expect to earn around £37,000 – rising to a whopping £65,000 on qualification. Equally, while the Bar Standards Board requires that all pupils must be paid no less than £12,000 per annum, many earn much more – more than £45,000 in some cases.

Future of the profession

The legal profession, like any other, is subject to change brought about by new governments, fluctuating market conditions, landmark decisions in case law, and much more.

We don't pretend to have a crystal ball, but here are a few hot topics that are of direct interest to those of you thinking about a legal career and which highlight a profession in a state of flux.

LEGAL SERVICES ACT

Without a doubt, the coming into force on 6 October 2011 of the Legal Services Act 2007 has changed the English and Welsh legal profession forever. The aim of the act is to simplify regulatory arrangements in the legal services market, to provide common standards, and to increase competition and choice for consumers. The most high-profile provision is the introduction of alternative business structures (ABS), which allow lawyers to form partnerships with non-lawyers, accept outside investment and operate under external ownership. The Solicitors Regulation Authority (SRA) began accepting applications for ABS licences on 3 January 2012 and, as of mid-February, it had received around 120 applications, from law firms such as Irwin Mitchell and other companies, including BT and the Co-op.

Other ground-breaking ABS developments included the provisional acquisition in February 2012 of a significant stake by investment firm Duke Street in the Parabis Group, a leading legal services provider. The transaction was valued at between £150 million and £200 million. In another first, Australian firm Slater & Gordon agreed to buy PI specialists Russell Jones & Walker (RJW) for £53.8 million, subject to SRA approval of the new firm's ABS licence.

The arrival of ABS has been a long time coming, and the profession is divided on whether it's a positive development or not. Many lawyers feel the new regime will create more opportunity, while others fear that high-street solicitors could become an endangered species.In a speech in January 2012, Law Society President John Wotton addressed key issues regarding the present and future of the legal profession, predicting that smaller, traditional firms would still be able to remain competitive: "ABS have no magic bullet in competitive terms. I have no doubt that well-managed firms will continue to thrive in the more competitive legal markets of the future, and it will be no mean feat for new ABS entrants to displace them."

WORK-BASED LEARNING

The SRA's two-year work-based learning (WBL) pilot came to an end in 2010. The pilot was designed to assess whether the traditional training contract should be replaced by a model that would improve quality and access, and looked at different ways of assessing competence in trainees and paralegals.

A report on the pilot was published by Middlesex University in June 2011 and concluded that the pilot had been successful in its approach to assuring quality. The report made a number of recommendations, including the need for further work on the skills and attributes for qualifying as a solicitor.

In February 2012 the SRA appointed a research company to conduct a final evaluation of the pilot until June 2012. The findings and report will be fed into the legal education and training review- on which more below…

LEGAL EDUCATION AND TRAINING REVIEW

The three main legal regulators – theSRA, the Bar Standards Board (BSB) and the Institute of Legal Executives Professional Standards –have joined forces to review legal education and training. The aim is to ensure that ethical standards and levels of competence of those delivering legal services are sufficient to secure a high standard of client service, and to support public interest and the rule of law. More specifically, the review is looking at:

- the educational requirements placed on individuals entering the sector and their regulatory function
- the requirements for continuing education for individuals and entities
- the requirements placed on those delivering approved education.

The review is underway and is due to be completed by December 2012. There will be a conference in July 2012 to expand on the key issues identified by its research team. While it's going to take some time for any changes to filter through to practical application, its comprehensive nature and buy-in from all the regulatory bodies means that this will definitely impact on the way all would-be lawyers are trained.

LEGAL AID CUTS

No surprise given the economic climate, but the world of legal aid remains unsettled, underfunded and under pressure. The government announced controversial plans in November 2010 to cut legal aid funding by around £350 million by 2014-15. A wide range of cases will no longer be covered by the legal aid system – including immigration, employment, medical malpractice and personal injury – and fees paid to lawyers in civil and family cases will be cut by 10%.

Many commentators and lawyers have noted the serious impact the reforms will have on access to justice for poorer members of society, with the Law Society, the Junior Lawyers Division, senior judges and social welfare organisations criticising the plans. Publication of the bill introducing the proposals in June 2011 further inflamed sectors of the profession. The Law Society called the Legal Aid, Sentencing and Punishment of Offenders Bill an "attack on access to justice"and said that it "will not deliver the claimed financial savings and risks denying access to justice to all but the well-off".Human Rights charities Liberty and Justice agreed.

Significantly, in December 2012 Justice Minister Ken Clarke announced that he was postponing some of the reforms that were due to be implemented in October 2012, delaying them instead until 2013. Among other vocal opponents, Lord Justice Jackson had criticised the cuts in September 2011, and called for a government rethink. The future remains uncertain for both those reliant on legal aid and their legal aid lawyers.

ADMISSIONS TESTS

There has been much talk of introducing admissions (or 'aptitude') tests for students at all levels. In February 2011 the University of Manchester signed up to the National Admissions Test for Law (LNAT) - an aptitude test developed by a consortium of UK universities to assess candidates' potential for studying law at undergraduate level. Universities already using LNAT as part of their law admissions process include the universities of Birmingham, Bristol, Durham, Nottingham and Oxford, King's College London and University College London. See page 97 for more information about LNAT.

The Law Society commissioned research to investigate introducing an aptitude test for entry to the LPC, and published the report in February 2011. It concluded not to pursue the introduction of a test, but "welcomes the report as a contribution to the debate" and will be feeding it into the education and training review (as above).

Kaplan Law School announced in October 2010 that it would be the first provider to introduce an aptitude test for its GDL and LPC students, but its trailblazing was rather undermined when in February 2011 the SRA shot the plan down in flames, with a curt statement: 'The SRA has not validated any LPC proposals which feature aptitude testing as part of the admissions arrangements.'

Meanwhile, the BSB ran a pilot aptitude test for the Bar Professional Training Course (BPTC), which showed a good correlation between test performance and success on the course. The test is pending final approval, but if approved will be taken by BPTC applicants aiming to begin the course in September 2013. The test is designed to identify unsuitable candidates before they embark on the significant financial outlay of the BPTC.

DIVERSITY

Diversity and access to the profession is never far from the minds of decision-makers in firmsand chambers – both in terms of who and how they recruit, and who they retain. The requirements of full disclosure may soon force change: the Legal Services Board (LSB) announced in August 2011 that firms and chambers will be required to publish internal diversity and social mobility data on their websites. Anonymised information relating to the socio-economic background, age, race and gender of their workforce, as well as information about disabilities, will be required to be disclosed. The LSB also expects that from 2012, the majority of law firms and chambers will be obliged to carry out and publish regular surveys into the make-up of their workforce.

Organised jointly by the Law Society, the Bar Council and ILEX, the bi-annual Minority Lawyers Conference in April2011 celebrated the achievements of black and minority ethnic (BME) lawyers, and highlighted the issues facing the profession in a year of both challenge and opportunity. Conference co-chair Sundeep Bhatia said that 2011 "represents a watershed year", with many BME firms facing tough challenges with the introduction of ABS and government cuts.

Not forgetting life at the Bar, in February 2011 the Bar Council launched a new website, Become-a-barrister.com, which aims to promote social mobility in the profession and dispel the pervasive myth that the career is only open to those from privileged backgrounds. The site features a short film about diversity, and a section profiling practising and aspiring barristers from a wide range of backgrounds.

UCΛS

Confused about courses?

Indecisive about institutions?

Stressed about student life?

Unsure about UCAS?

Frowning over finance?

Help is available at
www.ucasbooks.com

Professional bodies

that people who work in the area are fully trained and meet ethical guidelines. They generally have regulatory roles, making sure that members of the profession are able to work successfully in their jobs without endangering lives or abusing their position. For example, the Solicitors Regulation Authority and the Bar Standards Board (on which more below) both handle complaints against solicitors/barristers from members of the public.

Those jobs that require extensive training and learning, such as law, are likely to have bodies with a regulatory focus. Many professional bodies offer student membership - sometimes free or with reduced fees. Membership can be extremely valuable as a source of advice, information and resources.

Professional bodies in the field of law include the following:

Law Society
www.lawsociety.org.uk
The Law Society is the representative body for solicitors in England and Wales. It influences the development of effective law and supports solicitors in their day-to-day work. Among other things, it negotiates with and lobbies the profession's regulators, the government and others, and offers training and advice. It aims "to help, protect and promote solicitors across England and Wales".

Bar Council
www.barcouncil.org.uk
The Bar Council is the governing body for the Bar. Its role is to promote and improve the services and functions of the Bar, and to represent the interests of the Bar on all matters relating to the profession. Its principal objectives include, among other things, to:represent the Bar as a modern and forward-looking profession; maintain and enhance professional

standards; regulate education and training for the profession; and combat discrimination and disadvantage at the Bar.

Solicitors Regulation Authority
www.sra.org.uk

The Solicitors Regulation Authority (SRA) is the independent regulatory body of the Law Society of England and Wales. It regulates solicitors, registered foreign lawyers, registered European lawyers, trainees, students and firms in England and Wales in the public interest. It is responsible for: protecting consumers by setting qualification standards;monitoring training organisations' performance;setting and monitoring compliance with the rules of professional conduct;providing authoritative guidance; andadministering the roll of solicitors.

Bar Standards Board
www.barstandardsboard.org.uk

The Bar Standards Board regulates barristers in England and Wales in the public interest. It is responsible for setting the education and training requirements for becoming a barrister; setting continuing training requirements to ensure that barristers' skills are maintained throughout their careers; setting standards of conduct for barristers; monitoring the service provided by barristers to assure quality; and handling complaints against barristers and taking disciplinary or other action where appropriate.

Institute of Legal Executives
www.ilex.org.uk

The Institute of Legal Executives (ILEX) is the professional body representing and regulating around 22,000 qualified and trainee legal executive lawyers. The role of a legal executive lawyer is so similar to that of a solicitor that the average client is unlikely to be able to distinguish between them. In fact, many legal

executive lawyers supervise solicitors. The difference is that a legal executive is a qualified lawyer who is trained to specialise as an expert in a particular area of law, whereas solicitors have a broader, more general legal training.

Other notable legal bodies include:

Bar of Northern Ireland
www.barlibrary.com

Faculty of Advocates (Scotland)
www.advocates.org.uk

Institute of Barristers' Clerks
www.ibc.org.uk

Institute of Chartered Secretaries and Administrators
www.icsa.org.uk

Institute of Paralegals(for non-lawyers doing legal work)
www.instituteofparalegals.org

Junior Lawyers Division
http://juniorlawyers.lawsociety.org.uk/

Law Commission (consultation and reform)
www.lawcom.gov.uk

Law Society of Northern Ireland
www.lawsoc-ni.org

Law Society of Scotland
www.lawscot.org.uk

London Young Lawyers Group
www.lylg.org.uk

Graduate destinations

Law
HESA Destination of Leavers of Higher Education Survey

Each year, comprehensive statistics are collected on what graduates are doing six months after they complete their course. The survey is co-ordinated by the Higher Education Statistics Agency (HESA) and provides information about how many graduates move into employment (and what type of career) or further study and how many are believed to be unemployed.

The full results across all subject areas are published by the Higher Education Careers Service Unit (HECSU) and the Association of Graduate Careers Advisory Services (AGCAS) in *What Do Graduates Do?*, which is available from **www.ucasbooks.com**.

	Law
In UK employment	38.4%
In overseas employment	1.4%
Working and studying	10.7%
Studying in the UK for a higher degree	6.4%
Studying in the UK for a teaching qualification	0.5%
Undertaking other further study or training in the UK	26.4%
Studying overseas	0.6%
Not available for employment, study or training	3.6%
Assumed to be unemployed	6.8%
Other	5.3%

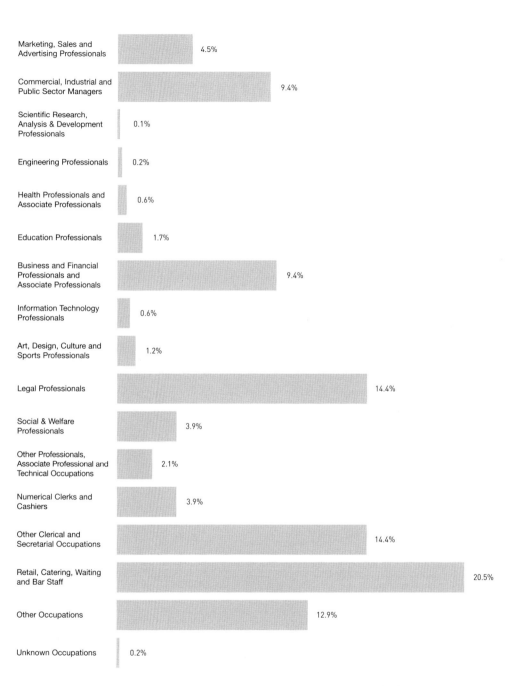

Marketing, Sales and Advertising Professionals — 4.5%

Commercial, Industrial and Public Sector Managers — 9.4%

Scientific Research, Analysis & Development Professionals — 0.1%

Engineering Professionals — 0.2%

Health Professionals and Associate Professionals — 0.6%

Education Professionals — 1.7%

Business and Financial Professionals and Associate Professionals — 9.4%

Information Technology Professionals — 0.6%

Art, Design, Culture and Sports Professionals — 1.2%

Legal Professionals — 14.4%

Social & Welfare Professionals — 3.9%

Other Professionals, Associate Professional and Technical Occupations — 2.1%

Numerical Clerks and Cashiers — 3.9%

Other Clerical and Secretarial Occupations — 14.4%

Retail, Catering, Waiting and Bar Staff — 20.5%

Other Occupations — 12.9%

Unknown Occupations — 0.2%

Reproduced with the kind permission of HECSU/AGCAS, What Do Graduates Do? 2011.
All data comes from the HESA Destinations of Leavers of Higher Education Survey 2009/10

Connect with us...

 www.facebook.com/ucasonline

 www.twitter.com/ucas_online

 www.youtube.com/ucasonline

Case studies

A WORLD OF LAWYERS

Still not sure whether you want to work in law? Perhaps you don't know if being a barrister is your cup of tea or whether life as a solicitor takes your fancy. Read the following profiles to see where the world of work has taken recent graduates in the legal profession and beyond.

GDL Student

COLIN WARRINER

Route into law:

A levels – History, English Literature, French (2003); BA (Hons) History – University of Oxford (2006)

MSt History- University of Oxford (2007); GDL – BPP Law School, London (2012)

WHY LAW?

After university, I worked for a few years in both legal publishing and in policy. I decided to convert to law because I was attracted by the intellectual challenge and I wanted to do something that was more stimulating and varied than the work I was doing.

WHAT DOES YOUR COURSE INVOLVE?

The GDL is essentially a condensed run-through of the academic law subjects. All the main topics you'd get in a law degree are covered, so constitutional, EU, criminal, tort, contract, land, and equity and trusts law. You cover what are normally termed 'black-letter law' subjects, so it's not the practical side of things, but rather the theoretical underpinnings of what you'll be doing as a lawyer.

CAN YOU DESCRIBE A RECENT PIECE OF WORK THAT WAS PARTICULARLY INTERESTING OR CHALLENGING?

We recently had to do some coursework on EU law with a very tight word limit. It was challenging to include all the information necessary to provide a complete answer and not go over the limit. It was an extreme exercise in brevity! I've never had to be so brief before; I had to shave out every single unnecessary word.

We also get to do an independent research exercise, which is a longer bit of coursework on a choice of 21 topics which aren't normally covered during the GDL. It's a chance for me to study in depth an area of law that I'm interested in practising, which is intellectual property.

WHAT DO YOU MOST/LEAST ENJOY ABOUT YOUR COURSE AND WHY?

I'm relieved to find that, by and large, law as a subject is very interesting. In fact, even the less interesting stuff isn't actually boring! But what's hard is the sheer volume of material that you have to cover during the year. No one topic is so difficult that you wouldn't be able to understand it if you worked through it, but you sometimes don't have the time. You have to race through things – it can feel like you're trying to drink from a fire hose! Even though I went into it with open eyes, I still find it overwhelming.

WHAT SKILLS/STRENGTHS DO YOU NEED TO DO WELL AS A LAW STUDENT?

The ability to focus is very important; you need to be able to shut out distractions. A good memory helps as well! You are called on to memorise vast amounts of information, quickly. As the GDL is increasingly focused on practising law, you need good analytical skills, even at this stage – applying the law to situations in a practical way and thinking laterally is essential.

COLIN'S TOP TIPS:

I know that it's easier said than done, but if you do have a training contract lined up before you start the GDL, it does make life a lot easier. It's not impossible to go on to get a training contract during or after the course – lots of people do – but knowing that a firm is paying for it and you don't have to worry about making applications does take the pressure off. With that in mind, getting practical experience such as vacation schemes is essential.

Also, if you're thinking about this as a career, you need to jump in with both feet because it requires total commitment. But it's not the end of the world if you don't do it immediately after your undergraduate degree. I've waited a few years, and I don't feel that I'm at a disadvantage.

Barrister

Maidstone Chambers, Maidstone, Kent

KIERAN BRAND

Route into law:
A-Levels – English, History, Sociology (2001-2003); LLB – University of Greenwich (2006);
BVC – BPP Law School, London (2007)

WHY LAW?

I was first attracted to the profession by the Jim Carey film, *Liar Liar!* More seriously though, I was influenced by the work experience I undertook during my GCSEs. I spent two interesting weeks with a firm and attended a magistrate's court. My interest in the law took off from there.

WHAT DOES YOUR JOB INVOLVE?

I mainly work in criminal law, which means that I'm in court almost every day. When a crime has been committed and the accused has been charged, a solicitor will be instructed to represent him/her and prepare the case. The solicitor will then instruct the barrister to represent the client in court. Solicitors can act in the magistrate's court and more are doing so in the crown court, but the advocacy side of things remains the speciality of barristers.

CAN YOU TELL ME ABOUT A RECENT PIECE OF WORK THAT WAS PARTICULARLY INTERESTING OR REPRESENTATIVE OF THE SORT OF THING YOU COMMONLY DEAL WITH?

The best part of the job is that every day is different, and it's always interesting. Recently I was appealing a restraining order at the Court of Appeal. The order prevented a young man from going to his own home because he had burgled his neighbour's house. That was an interesting day, to say the least. More recently I worked on a trial in which a chef at a well-known restaurant chain was accused of sexually assaulting a waitress. You certainly meet some characters in this job!

WHAT DO YOU MOST/LEAST ENJOY ABOUT YOUR CAREER AND WHY?

The variety is obviously a big plus. I enjoy being in court every day and all that working in court entails. The only real downside is that, because barristers are usually self-employed (unless you work in-house for a company), there isn't the reassurance of a regular, fixed income.

WHAT SKILLS/STRENGTHS DO YOU NEED TO SUCCEED AS A LAWYER?

You need confidence and the ability to think on your feet – certainly in criminal law. You will also need to be personable and able to deal with people from all walks of life.

WHAT IS THE ONE THING YOU WISH YOU'D KNOWN ABOUT BEING A LAWYER BEFORE YOU STARTED?

I think people perceive barristers to be very wealthy, which was also my first impression (thanks *Liar Liar!*), but life at the criminal bar in particular can actually be very tough financially. As I've said, there is no regular salary because barristers are self-employed. The government's cutting of legal aid also means that my work is not as financially rewarding as is depicted on TV. You can certainly earn a very decent living, but there's also some reliance on the overdraft at times!

KIERAN'S TOP TIPS:

Hard work throughout your time in school is essential. The process of getting your foot in the door of the profession is so competitive that academic results inevitably have a big influence on your chances of success. It's also important to get as much work experience as you can.

Solicitor – litigation

Ashurst LLP

LORRAINE MCLINN

Route into law:

Alevels – English Literature, History and Biology (2002); LLB – University of Newcastle (2005)

LLM – Durham University (2006); LPC – BPP Law School, London (2007)

WHY LAW?

I had the perception that it was an interesting and stable career. When I was studying for my A levels, I shadowed a barrister and did some work experience in a firm, as well as getting involved with the Bar National Mock Trial Competition, so I'd had some good exposure to the profession. I also felt that even if I didn't end up in practice, at the very least a strong law degree would be a good, transferable qualification to have.

WHAT DOES YOUR JOB INVOLVE?

I'm in the dispute resolution department at Ashurst, so we are generally either defending a client against a claim issued against them or pursuing a claim on their behalf. This may be via the traditional litigation route or via another form of 'alternative dispute resolution', such as arbitration or mediation. If a case doesn't settle, we may end up in court (or a tribunal). Either way, I am involved in speaking to witnesses, putting together witness statements, gathering evidence, attending client meetings, drafting and reviewing documents, and scrutinising the other side's documents. The adversarial nature of what we do certainly seems closer to the sort of lawyering you see on TV - rather than, say, structured finance or tax law!

CAN YOU TELL ME ABOUT A RECENT PIECE OF WORK THAT WAS PARTICULARLY INTERESTING OR REPRESENTATIVE OF THE SORT OF THING YOU COMMONLY DEAL WITH?

I'm part of an ongoing bribery case, which has had lots of exciting twists and turns over the past year. We're defending a company that is accused of being involved in large-scale bribery and corruption, and is linked to civil and criminal investigations in the UK and the US. We've been advising the company throughout the whole process, including on how to deal with dawn raids, accompanying directors to police interviews, and giving employment law advice on how to dismiss particular individuals. It's been amazingly exciting! That's the great thing about contentious work– you're never going to be bored because every case is different.

WHAT DO YOU MOST/LEAST ENJOY ABOUT YOUR CAREER AND WHY?

I love the team I work with. The partners are great – they're real characters, who are bright and inspiring! The hours are less fun. You sometimes have to cancel plans at the last minute, which can mean letting family and friends down. You can't always control what's going to happen but that's just part of the job, and the trade-off is that you're not stuck in a boring 9:00-5:00 job.

WHAT SKILLS/STRENGTHS DO YOU NEED TO SUCCEED AS A LAWYER?

You've got to like challenging, intellectually stimulating work, and you've got to be organised and efficient. As you become more senior, it's increasingly important to have good client relationship skills. Problem solving is crucial – you've got to devise the best strategy for defending your client – and you've got to have a thirst for an argument!

There's no one type of personality, though – everyone I work with is very different, but we combine our skills well. Some are classic bookworms, some are great at client-facing work, and some are really good analysts. As long as you're smart and prepared to work hard, the profession can accommodate all types of people.

WHAT IS THE ONE THING YOU WISH YOU'D KNOWN ABOUT BEING A LAWYER BEFORE YOU STARTED?

There's a perception that it's glamorous, especially if your impression is based on what you see on TV, but 95% of the time, you're just getting the job done. I'll always remember what a partner said to me when I was doing work experience – he likened lawyers to ducks on the water; we have to portray to the client that everything's calm and we're just gliding along, but underneath the water, the legs are kicking away furiously!

LORRAINE'S TOP TIPS:

Work experience is very important. I found it relatively easy to organise at school – you'd be surprised at how keen firms are to have you if you offer your services for free! At university, get involved with mooting, go to every possible law fair and presentation, and speak to everyone you can.

Commercial barrister
(Construction law) – 10 years' call

Keating Chambers, London

LUCY GARRETT

Route into law:

A levels – French, German and English Literature (1995); BA (hons) English Language and Literature – University of Manchester (1998); GDL – Manchester Metropolitan University, (2000)

WHY LAW?

After a gap year post-university, I found out about the Bar and thought it sounded like the only job I could imagine myself doing.

WHAT DOES YOUR JOB INVOLVE?

I'm a specialist practitioner in construction law, a niche area of commercial law. It covers disputes about anything you can build, from a building to a road to a ship or any kind of infrastructure. And these days it also includes IT software projects, as they're also about putting individual bits together in the right way to reach a solution. The same contractual issues come up regardless of what's being built – for example, an employer changes its mind about something, a contractor underbids for a project, or technical things go wrong and cause delay.

The real joy of commercial law comes from the intellectual challenge – every contract is different and there is a new problem in every case. All of my cases involve technical issues, so a large part of my job is being taught about buildings by an engineer or an architect, or how to build a bridge or lay a road. It's absolutely fascinating; I don't have a technical background, but that has made no difference to my ability to cross examine an expert witness. The key is to be prepared to ask all the questions that no-one else will ask in case they look silly. I quite often ask for things to be explained in "Fisher Price language"! I was never interested in science at school so if you'd told me then that I would be asking an engineer how concrete sets, and interested in the answer, I wouldn't have believed you.

WHAT DO YOU MOST/LEAST ENJOY ABOUT YOUR CAREER AND WHY?

The best bit is the advocacy and the cross examination – I don't think there's a barrister in the land who would disagree! I'm in full-blown trials relatively rarely, especially as I get more senior, but when I am, they tend to last for several weeks or months. When I was working on the Wembley litigation, we were in trial for three months. I also do lots of substantial interim work in court, such as major applications which might last a couple of days.

The long hours are hard, but I always think that you can choose between an easy and boring job that is 9:00-5:00, or a stimulating and challenging job where the hours are long. The Bar is the best job in the world – I love it.

WHAT SKILLS/STRENGTHS DO YOU NEED TO SUCCEED AS A LAWYER?

As a commercial barrister, it's not just about being academically brilliant; you need to be focused and analytical, and have lots of common sense. You must understand the commercial realities related to the issue and give not only a legal answer, but also advice on whether it's worth fighting for from a commercial perspective. You need to be able to translate the black-letter law advice into the practical situation: you're dealing with real people and their businesses, and they need straightforward advice in relation to a live project. You also need to be confident (maybe even a bit bossy!). Even when you're junior, you're in charge of running the case so you have to decide what to do and the buck stops with you. You need to be calm and confident when dealing with solicitors and hard-headed businessmen alike.

WHAT IS THE ONE THING YOU WISH YOU'D KNOWN ABOUT BEING A LAWYER BEFORE YOU STARTED?

That it is so much more brilliant being self-employed than I could have imagined. The independence of working outside a hierarchy, not having a boss, being in charge of when you arrive and leave, and sorting out your own deadlines is great. It's like being a grown-up at work as well as in your life!

LUCY'S TOP TIPS:

First, if you want to be a barrister, get a first-class degree.

Second, don't do a law degree. The academic study of law is so different to law in practice that it's better to do a degree in a subject that you know you like and will enjoy, which will mean you are more likely to get a First (see previous tip!).

Trainee solicitor

Bond Pearce

MATT MARSHALL

A levels –Maths, Psychology, Business Studies (2002) and AS level law and computer science (2000); Law and economics - Keele University (2005); LPC – University of the West of England (2009)

WHY LAW?

I was attracted by the intellectual challenge. Although I was more focused on maths at school, I enjoyed articulating arguments and felt that I was more suited to a career in the law. Nonetheless, I have certainly benefitted from an understanding of economics and business as there is a strong focus on commercial awareness in modern law firms.

WHAT DOES YOUR JOB INVOLVE?

I'm currently in my first seat as a trainee in the professional risks team of the insurance department. My role is to assist fee earners with a wide range of tasks. I have had plenty of opportunity to practice drafting various litigation documents, including witness statements, letters of claim, letters of response, settlement offers, applications and cost schedules – almost every element of the litigation process. It's a thriving department, with a strong reputation, so there's a constant stream of work and plenty of opportunity.

CAN YOU TELL ME ABOUT A RECENT PIECE OF WORK THAT WAS PARTICULARLY INTERESTING OR REPRESENTATIVE OF THE SORT OF THING YOU COMMONLY DEAL WITH?

One of the most interesting aspects of the professional risks team is the focus on strategy. I have been given the opportunity to attend various mediations while in the seat. The first mediation I attended involved four separate parties. From listening to opening statements, it appeared that there was no possibility of settlement. It was fascinating to follow each party's tactics throughout the day, to observe the mediator challenging each party's case and to eventually reach a compromise that was acceptable to all present.

WHAT DO YOU MOST/LEAST ENJOY ABOUT YOUR CAREER AND WHY?

I most enjoy the stimulus and intellectual challenge. We are a client-focused firm and there is a real emphasis on having a clear strategy to achieve client goals, while at the same time it is a necessity of the work to pay close attention to detail. Being trained to succeed at both is challenging and rewarding.

As mentioned, I have spent my first seat working for clients who are defending claims of negligence. A far less enjoyable aspect of the job is dealing with the occasional 'interesting' litigant in person! Our focus is trying to achieve sensible commercial outcomes for our client, whereas sometimes the litigant in person doesn't share the same agenda. It does add another dimension to the job though!

WHAT SKILLS/STRENGTHS DO YOU NEED TO SUCCEED AS A LAWYER?

You need a willingness to take on a challenge. I am aware that some trainees worry that they'll be used as an extra resource for administrative tasks, but usually the reverse is true – at Bond Pearce, trainees are expected to engage with the work and apply themselves from day one.

WHAT IS THE ONE THING YOU WISH YOU'D KNOWN ABOUT BEING A LAWYER BEFORE YOU STARTED?

The large number of non-law graduates who go into law. Law firms actively recruit non-law graduates, as they like to have a balance of law and non-law graduates. Having knowledge and interests outside of law really helps when building relationships with colleagues and clients. Not having an undergraduate law degree should not deter you from pursuing a career in law.

MATT'S TOP TIPS:

Work experience is one of the most important things you can do, so go to open days and, if possible, get on a vacation scheme. That will give you two weeks to showcase yourself and what you've got to offer. I did the vacation scheme at Bond Pearce, and was offered a paralegal job and a training contract shortly after.

You should also get in touch with the graduate recruitment teams at the firms you're interested in to find out who their ideal candidate is. You will invest a lot of time in the application form (if you're doing it properly!),so there is no point in dedicating your time to it if you're not a good match for that particular firm. Target only those firms that are right for you, and then find out everything you can about what they offer, what you can offer themand whether you feel that you will fit in.

Entry routes

Entry routes

Routes to qualification

There are clearly defined paths to becoming a fully
qualified solicitor, barrister or legal executive. Each of
the first two involves three steps:

1. Academic stage
2. Vocational stage
3. Practical stage.

Stage 1 is the same for would-be solicitors
and barristers, whereas stages 2 and 3 are different,
see page 53. Legal executives must complete an
academic stage and a qualifying employment stage, see
page 59.

Solicitor and barrister

1. ACADEMIC STAGE

This is the first step on the road to becoming a lawyer and these years really do count. It's important to get good grades to show a hard-working attitude. There are two ways to complete this stage...

LLB

The first is by completing a qualifying undergraduate law degree. This must contain the seven foundations of legal practice: public, criminal, contract, tort, property, equity and trusts, and EU law (see box below for more detail).It must also be validated by the Solicitors Regulation Authority. A law degree is typically three years long, although as of 2012 it is possible to do a two-year undergraduate degree at two private institutions, The College of Law and BPP Law School.

This route gives you the opportunity to go into the subjects in significant depth, and hopefully fit in some all-important work experience.

Assessment: A mixture of exams and coursework.
Fees: Up to £9,000 per annum.
Institutions: There are nearly 100 institutions and other providers that offer qualifying law degrees in the UK (see course listings section of this book, page 147).

Non-law degree and GDL

The second way is to do any non-law undergraduate degree,which usually takes three years,followed by the Graduate Diploma in Law (GDL), which is normally one year (or two years part-time). The GDL again concentrates on the seven foundations of legal practice; when combined with your non-law degree, you end up with the equivalent of a law degree. This route gives you the chance to do an undergraduate degree in a subject of particular academic interest and potentially be more well-rounded (and possibly more attractive to potential employers).

Assessment (GDL): A mixture of exams and coursework.
Fees: Up to £9,400 (2012).
Institutions: There are currently around 40 institutions which teach the GDL (see course listings section of this book, page 147).

2. VOCATIONAL STAGE

You're almost there! But first you need to do the Legal Practice Course (solicitors) or the Bar Professional Training Course (barristers) to learn how to be a lawyer in practice...

LPC (solicitor)
Like the GDL, there are part-time and full-time options available, but distance learning options are more limited because of the LPC's emphasis on learning by doing. It focuses not on learning by rote, but on the mastering of practical skills, and the emphasis is on workshops, continuous assessment, independent research and group discussions. The course also permits a certain amount of specialisation through a range of optional subjects. And some colleges have specialist legal aid or corporate streams, while a small number of major firms have created bespoke LPCs in conjunction with particular law schools.

Changes implemented in 2010 mean that the LPC is now modular. Stage 1 covers the core subjects oflitigation, property, business, professional conduct and regulation, taxation, wills and the administration of estates. This stage also teaches students specific skillssuch as advocacy, drafting and writing, interviewing and advising, problem solving and legal research. This stage is completed at law school.

It is now possible to complete Stage 2 during your training contract (on which more below), should you wish to do so. This stage consists of electives from a range of subjects in private and corporate client work, including commercial law and practice, employment, intellectual property, consumer, housing, family and immigration.

Assessment: A mixture of exams and coursework.
Fees: Up to £13,550 (2012).
Institutions: There are around 34 institutions, offering around 11,000 places between them.

BPTC (barrister)
The full-time BPTC is a one-year course; the part-time course takes two years. There are admission requirements, namely that (i) students must hold at least a 2.2 degree (either in law, or non-law plus the GDL), and (ii) if English is not your first language, you must gain a score of at least 7.5 in all subjects of the British Council's IELTS test.In addition, the Bar Standards (BSB)has run a pilot aptitude test for the BPTC, which is pending final approval. If approved, it will be taken by BPTC applicants aiming to begin the course in September 2013.

The BPTC teaches the following skills: case work; legal research; written; opinion-writing; interpersonal; conference; resolution of disputes out of court; and advocacy.The main areas of knowledge taught on the BPTC are civil litigation and remedies, criminal litigation and sentencing, evidence, professional ethics. Students are then allowed to choose two optional subjects, from areas that include family, intellectual property, company and employment law.

Assessment: Mix of exams, videoed practical exercises and multi-choice tests.
Fees: Up to £16,885 (2012).
Institutions: There are nine institutions, offering around 1,700 places between them.

3. PRACTICAL STAGE

Congratulations! You've got your feet under the desk and you're earning a proper salary. Find out what it means to be a trainee (solicitor) or a pupil (barrister)...

Trainee (solicitor)

The training contract is a two-year employment contract with a law firm or other approved organisation, akin to an apprenticeship. The two years provide an opportunity for trainees to put into practice all the knowledge and skills they have acquired so far, with the firm assessing the trainee's suitability for retention upon completion of the training period.

The training contract format varies between firms. Most operate a 'seat' system, in which trainees spend six months in four different departments. This gives trainees exposure to different practice areas so that they can make an informed choice as to their preferred qualification area. Trainees must be exposed to at least three practice areas and both contentious (ie, where there is a dispute between two parties, such as somebody suing a sports club over an accident on possibly faulty equipment) and non-contentious (ie, where there is no dispute, such as in conveyancing when both parties are wanting to move house). In some firms, trainees may also have the opportunity to spend a seat in an overseas office or on secondment to a client.

What trainees learn during the training contract will depend on the type of firm and its solicitors, but most trainees will be involved with drafting, writing and researching, with everything being checked by a qualified solicitor.Clearly, the practice areas covered as a trainee working at a commercial firm in the city are going to differ from those experienced by a trainee at provincial high-street firms.

Trainees are assessed continuously throughout their training contract. Almost without exception, firms have a three- and six-monthly appraisal for each training contract seat. In this way trainees get good feedback about their performance both during and after a seat, and get to have their say about anything they're not 100% happy with.

Pupil (barrister)

Pupillage is essentially a year-long apprenticeship, whereby pupils practise under the guidance and supervisionof a 'pupil supervisor' - a junior barrister of at least five years' experience. Pupils are required by the Bar Council to obtain sufficient practical experience of advocacy, conferences and negotiation, as well as legal research and the preparation of drafts and opinions.

The year is divided into two six-month periods known as 'sixes'. The first six is spent shadowing and assisting the pupil supervisor. This involves attending court and case conferences, undertaking research, doing background reading and drafting documents. Thus, a pupil gains insight into how a case is prepared and argued, how a competent practitioner responds to developments as they occur and how agreed tactics can be changed.

The second six sees a pupil take his or her first steps as a professional practitioner. Pupils are permitted to undertake their own cases for clients, under supervision. Inevitably, much of this work involves straightforward cases, but there is always the chance that an important or ground-breaking case may arise.

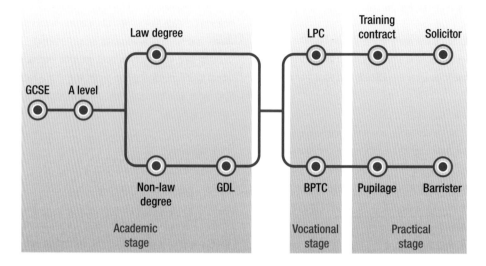

Law degree · LPC · Training contract · Solicitor

GCSE · A level

Non-law degree · GDL · BPTC · Pupilage · Barrister

Academic stage · Vocational stage · Practical stage

To research postgraduate law courses, visit Course Search at **www.ukpass.ac.uk**

SEVEN FOUNDATIONS OF LEGAL PRACTICE

Contract - Whether signing away your spare time for an evening job or buying a train ticket, you'll have entered into a contract at some point. This module covers how they are made, how they work – and what the options are when they go pear-shaped.

Tort - Slip or fall? Car accident not your fault? 'Tort' means civil wrong and refers to people or companies seeking compensation when something's gone awry. This could be you falling over in the street or the implications of a freight ship sinking.

Criminal - The defendant cries: "Not guilty, your honour!" Whether that's true or not, you have to be confident about the complexities of criminal law, considering ethical issues, as well as what the law actually says.

Equity and trusts - With equity, the law's conscience really kicks in. You'll learn how the courts enforce obligations such as agreeing to act as a trustee for a child, as well as about trusts and equity in a commercial context.

European Union - Here's a good conversation topic: how far does EU law influence the UK legal system? The module also covers how EU principles regulate trade across the continent.

Property - There's a mountainous volume of law relating to land. You'll need to study issues of ownership, registered land, mortgages and leases, as well as things with intriguing names such as easements and covenants.

Public - It's a free country, right? Here you'll find out about the curious relationship between the government and the people, as well as how state institutions relate to each other and how the law protects human rights.

QUALIFYING AS A SOLICITOR

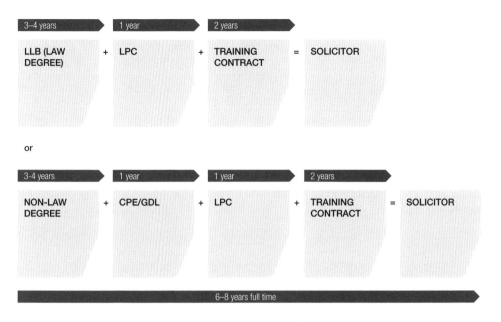

3–4 years	1 year	2 years		
LLB (LAW DEGREE)	+ LPC	+ TRAINING CONTRACT	= SOLICITOR	

or

3-4 years	1 year	1 year	2 years	
NON-LAW DEGREE	+ CPE/GDL	+ LPC	+ TRAINING CONTRACT	= SOLICITOR

6–8 years full time

SOLICITOR – HOW TO APPLY

APPLYING FOR	APPLY THROUGH	APPLY BY
Undergraduate law degree	UCAS Apply online – see **www.ucas.com** and click on Apply	15 October for University of Oxford and University of Cambridge; 15 January for other universities and colleges
CPE or GDL	The Central Applications Board for full-time courses. Online applications preferred See **www.lawcabs.ac.uk** For part-time courses, apply direct to institutions	
LPC	For full-time courses, apply through the Central Applications Board. Online applications preferred See **www.lawcabs.ac.uk** For part-time courses, apply direct to institutions	
Training contract	Directly to individual firms of solicitors Check out their websites, online recruitment sites and LawCareers.Net for advertisements	Deadlines vary from firm to firm (the majority have 31 July as their deadline).

QUALIFYING AS A BARRISTER

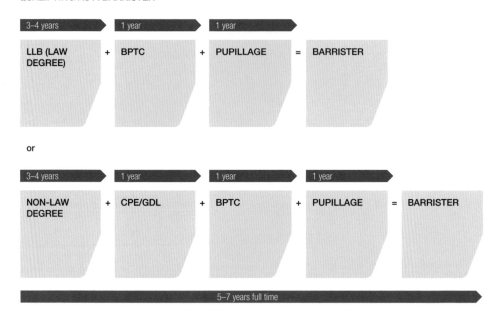

or

BARRISTER – HOW TO APPLY

APPLYING FOR	APPLY THROUGH	APPLY BY
Undergraduate law degree	UCAS Apply online – see **www.ucas.com** and click on Apply	15 October for University of Oxford and University of Cambridge;15 January for other universities and colleges
CPE or GDL	The Central Applications Board for full-time courses. Online applications preferred See **www.lawcabs.ac.uk** For part-time courses, apply direct to institutions	
BPTC	**www.barprofessionaltraining.org.uk** Online applications only	Beginning or mid-January
Pupillage	Either through the Pupillage Portal (the online pupillage application system) at **www.pupillages.com** for two-thirds of chambers, or directly to the remaining third of chambers, who don't recruit through the Pupillage Portal. ALL pupillage vacancies are advertised on the Pupillage Portal site	End April for summer season pupillages; end September for autumn season pupillages

Legal executive

A legal executive is a qualified lawyer who is trained to specialise as an expert in a particular area of law. Importantly, you do not have to do an undergraduate degree to become a legal executive.

Fully qualified and experienced legal executive lawyers are able to undertake many of the legal activities that solicitors do, and often supervise solicitors and other legal staff. They will have their own clients and can represent clients in court. Although legal executives can be involved in a wide range of areas of law, the most common areas of specialism are:

- conveyancing - the legal side of buying and selling property
- family - advising on divorces/separation and matters affecting children
- crime - defending and prosecuting people accused of crimes

- company and business law - advising clients on legislation that affects their business such as tax, contract and employment law
- litigation - where a client is in dispute with another party (eg, an individual, company or local authority)
- probate - dealing with wills, trusts and inheritance tax
- personal injury - handling accident claims.

TRAINING

The Chartered Institute of Legal Executives (CILEx) is the professional body representing and regulating around 22,000 qualified and trainee legal executive lawyers. There are two routes to becoming a legal executive lawyer, depending on whether you hold a qualifying law degree or not.

Without a degree:
An individual will need to take the full ILEX route, which is comprised of the Level 3 ILEX qualification (set at A level standard) and the Level 6 ILEX qualification (equivalent to an honours degree). This will typically take four years to complete part-time, although time scales can be flexible according to personal and professional needs, and it is possible to do it full time in two years.

With a degree:
If you have a law degree, you can take the Graduate Fast-Track Diploma, which takes nine months to complete, parttime.

With both routes, a five-year qualifying period of employment must be completed (working as a paralegal while studying counts towards this). If you have already done the Legal Practice Course (LPC) or the Bar Professional Training Course (BPTC), then you will be exempt from all the CILEx qualifications and will just need to complete your qualifying employment period.

At the end of this, you become an CILExFellow and are qualified as a legal executive. If you decide to go on to become a solicitor, it is possible that you may be exempt from the training contract requirements, but this is at the discretion of the Solicitors Regulation Authority.

For more on CILEx and training to become a legal executive lawyer, visit **www.ilex.org.uk**.

Scotland and Northern Ireland

Lawyers are trained differently in the various parts of the United Kingdom. Here follows a brief explanation of what happens in Scotland and Northern Ireland.

SCOTLAND

Over the last few years, legal education and training in Scotland has undergone a major review. A number of changes came into force in September 2011, including replacing the current LLB with a Foundation Programme, and renaming the Diploma in Legal Practice and the traineeship as 'Professional Education and Training Stage 1 and 2' (PEAT 1 and PEAT 2), respectively. Both PEAT 1 and PEAT 2 are described in more detail below, but they essentially cover the vocational study (PEAT 1) and practical training (PEAT 2) elements of becoming a solicitor or barrister.

For more detailed information, visit **www.lawscot.org.uk**.

Undergraduate study

It is possible to study an LLB at 10 universities in Scotland. The ordinary degree takes three years, while the honours degree takes four. There are also accelerated degree options, which can be taken if you have a non-law first degree. Students on the Scottish law degree at the University of Dundee can take enough English law modules to achieve a dual-qualified law degree, enabling them to progress to qualification in England and Wales or in Scotland.

For those who do not wish to do an LLB, it is possible to do a three-year, pre-diploma training contract with a qualified Scottish solicitor, at the end of which you sit the Law Society of Scotland's professional exams. During the three years you must receive training in various prescribed areas.

Vocational study

All those who intend to practise as a solicitor or advocate (the Scottish equivalent of a barrister in England and Wales or Northern Ireland) must complete PEAT 1 (formerly the Diploma in Professional Legal Practice). This is a seven-month course currently offered at sevenScottish universities. The course teaches knowledge and skills necessary for working life, with an emphasis on practical application and much of the teaching carried out by practising lawyers.

Training
Solicitors

To qualify as a solicitor, individuals must complete PEAT 2, a two-year training contract. Trainees are usually paid by the training firm as per agreed rates set by the Law Society of Scotland. Trainees must complete a logbook and have regular quarterly reviews. After six months of the contract, trainees must attend a Professional Competence Course. Trainees are normally paid at least the minimum recommended by the Law Society of Scotland - £15,965 for a first year and £19,107 for a second year(2011 figures).

It is possible to be admitted as a solicitor after one year of training, but normally, at the end of the two years – and provided all conditions have been met – the trainee is admitted as a fully qualified solicitor.

Advocates (Barristers)

The body that administers the Scottish Bar is the Faculty of Advocates. Having completed PEAT 1 (the diploma), a trainee advocate (or 'intrant') must undertake a 21-month period of paid training in a solicitors' office (as for a trainee solicitor above, although slightly shorter), followed by a nine-month period 'devilling' as an unpaid pupil to an advocate. The trainee must then pass an exam set by the Faculty of Advocates in evidence, practice and procedure. At this stage, he or she is admitted as an advocate. Prospective students should note that a law degree from an English university will not form part of the qualification process in Scotland. Nor will a Scottish law degree be recognised by the Law Society of England and Wales as part of their qualification process. If you train in, say, Scotland, you'll have to retrain to practise in England, Wales or Northern Ireland, and the same applies for movement in the opposite direction – unless you are a graduate of the special dual-qualified degree on offer at the University of Dundee.

For more details see **www.lawscot.org.uk** and **www.advocates.org.uk**.

NORTHERN IRELAND

Undergraduate study

Law degrees are offered at Queen's University Belfast (QUB) and the University of Ulster in Northern Ireland. However, law degrees from a number of other institutions in England, Wales and Ireland are also accepted as qualifying law degrees for the purposes of passing on to the next stage, apprenticeship.

Non-law graduates must study the two-year master's in legal science at QUB before they can progress to their apprenticeship.

Vocational study/training
Solicitors

The vocational study and practical training aspects that are found separately in England, Wales and Scotland are combined in Northern Ireland. Trainee solicitors must undertake a two-year apprenticeship under a supervising solicitor, called a 'master'. The practical component comes first, with a four-month period of office-based training. This is followed by one year studying for the Certificate of Professional Studies at the Institute of Professional Legal Studies at QUB or the Graduate School of Professional Legal Education at the University of Ulster. This is then followed by a further eight months of office-based work.

There is a reciprocal arrangement whereby English qualified solicitors may transfer to Northern Ireland without having to take any further qualifications or examinations. The procedure is simply to complete an application form, supply proofs asked for in the necessary form and pay a fee. However, Scottish solicitors are required to take further examinations and a period of apprenticeship before they can be admitted in Northern Ireland.

Barristers

Trainee barristers must undertake the one year, full-time Degree of Barrister-at-Law at the Institute of Professional Legal Studies at QUB. They are then called to the Bar, but before they can practise, must enter into one year of pupillage with a practising barrister of not less than seven years' standing.

For more details see **www.lawsoc-ni.org** and **www.barlibrary.com**.

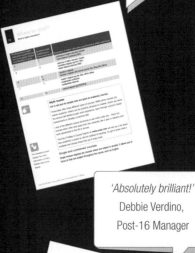

How to succeed

Research and sources of advice

This is the crucial first step on the road to a legal career - research, research and more research. You're working hard to get good grades, but if you really want to make it in the competitive world that is law, you need to have spent time learning about the profession and the players within it.

Here is a brief rundown of a few places you can look and some practical steps to take that will set you on the right path. It's not exhaustive – part of this exercise is about showing your initiative and going further than your peers, so consider this a jumping-off point...

LEARNING ABOUT FIRMS/CHAMBERS

LawCareers.Net (LC.N)
www.lawcareers.net
This is a one-stop shop for information and advice on what it means to be a lawyer, how you go about becoming one and much more. It is one of the most sophisticated resources available to tomorrow's lawyers, today. Sections include news (updated daily), the Oracle (answering tricky questions), deadline timetable, diary of events, feature articles, blogs and much more. You can also sign up for the newsletter, LC.N Weekly, which contains topical information and is delivered for free to your inbox every week. If you're serious about law, LC.N should be your constant companion.

The right tools for the job

Getting a job in the legal profession is like a massive competition between you and many other candidates to win a prize that will change your life. Like any competition, there are rules, strategies and tactics that you can follow to maximise your chances. In fact, there are a number of rules that, if you do not follow them, will probably consign you to failure. "What are these rules?" and "Where can I find them?", we hear you cry. Fear not – help is at hand. **www.LawCareers.Net** is a website that is designed to give you the insights, information and advice that will give you the best chance of victory.

LawCareers.Net has grown and developed for well over a decade, continually looking to provide and present information in the most effective way. Let's look at what it contains:

Authoritative information and advice - The nuts and bolts of what lawyers do, the different types of law and lawyers, and how to become one. Our core editorial steers you through the process of understanding how you might fit into the legal world.

A comprehensive directory of employers and legal educators - With over 1,250 organisations listed in its directory, **LawCareers.Net** introduces you to all those who might offer you a job. There is no other list with this range or sophistication.

Continuously updated news, features, profiles, advice, blogs, diary, Facebook, tweets and a weekly newsletter along with other crucial background information - The successful candidate needs all the background, nuance and insight he/she can muster. Our subscription email, LC.N Weekly, highlights the best of the continually updated content. **LawCareers.Net** provides new information daily

MyLC.N: a specially designed suite of practical tools to boost your effectiveness - Every LawCareers.Net user has access to a personal 'MyLC.N' account. MyLC.N offers expert practical support in the search for a job, allowing users to save and manage their research and analyse their experiences to see if they have the skills for success.

Using **LawCareers.Net** is both simple and essential. As the most popular resource available, most successful candidates use it - can you afford not to?

www.LawCareers.Net

The Training Contract & Pupillage Handbook
www.tcph.co.uk

LC.N's printed sister publication, the handbook is produced in association with the Law Society and features details of over 1,000 firms offering training contracts and all sets of chambers that offer pupillages - the only comprehensive list available to students. The handbook also contains extensive information on the legal profession. This is essential reading, and is available from university careers service and at law fairs.

Client guides

Online and in print, Legal 500 and Chambers UK Guideare the key players in the client guide category. They review the strengths and strategies of law firms and barristers' chambersin the UK. The guides are compiled by researchers who speak to firms'/chambers' clients (and rivals), and thenrank the firms/chambersin terms of their strength in particular practice areas. They are useful if you already have an idea of the sort of law you'd like to practice (eg, family, commercial or employment law) and want to find out which firms are the movers and shakers in that field.

Chambers also publishes a student guide, which contains the ever-useful "True Picture" section, giving an insight into various firms, straight from the horses' mouths – ie, the trainees who work there.

Pupillage Portal
www.pupillages.com

This website is where you apply for a pupillage in England and Wales, but it also has useful information about the chambers that offer pupillages, FAQs and a page of useful links to other Bar-related bodies and organisations where you can get relevant work experience.

Firms' and chambers' websites

It seems obvious, but you should certainly be checking out the websites of those firms/chambers you've learnt a bit about and are interested in. Although you may have to wade through a certain amount of marketing and PR puffery, most firms/chambers include useful information about who they are as a firm, the things they consider important, recent work they've been involved in, profiles of those who work there, and details of their graduate recruitment processes.

You might also like to check out these other student-oriented publications and websites: TARGETjobs Law, Prospects and Lex 100.

LEGAL PRESS

As with any industry, the legal profession has its own specialist publications. The following list – just a small selection of some of the more well-known publications – is the place where you can start to get a sense of the profession as a whole: the issues that occupy it, the big names and the big clients. Read on…

The Lawyer/Lawyer2B
www.thelawyer.com

The Lawyer is essential reading to get a broad view of what's happening in law. Perhaps most importantly, it has a sister publication/website aimed specifically at law students and trainees, called Lawyer2B.

Legal Week
www.legalweek.com

One of the big names in the legal press, this weekly magazine is best used online, where it puts up news stories every day. You can even sign up to its daily newsletter, which provides a round-up of its biggest stories.

Law Gazette
www.lawgazette.co.uk
The Law Society's weekly magazine is full of news, comment, job ads and feature articles related to the profession, both topical and editorial.

RollOnFriday
www.rollonfriday.com
RollOnFriday offers an irreverent (but insightful) take on the profession. It's the place to go for somelight-hearted analysisif everywhere else is feeling a little dry and humourless.

There are also several very good blogs, from trainees and pupils up to senior solicitors and QCs. Some of the best include. BabyBarista (**www.babybarista.com**), Charon QC (**charonqc.wordpress.com**), Ashley Connick (**ashleyconnick.wordpress.com**), Legal Cheek (**www.legalcheek.com**) and Legal Bizzle (**legalbizzle.wordpress.com**).

PRACTICAL RESEARCH

So you've done lots of reading — excellent work. Now, you need to get out into the real world and do some interacting with live human beings! This advice best applies when you have started your university degree, but they do say that forewarned is forearmed…

Law fairs
The university law fair may be the first contact youhave with lots of firms, chambers and postgraduate providers – and all in one conveniently placed location; the university campus. Even when you're in your first year, and thus a year away from applying for training contracts/pupillage, it is still important that you attend to start to get a feel for the legal landscape. Firms and some chambers will bring representatives, recruitment brochures and goodies, so it is worth your while heading along. Before you arrive, spend a bit of time checking out which firms are there, identifying those that are of particular interest to you, and preparing a few sensible questions to ask. Recruiters remember keen students, so be one of them.

Presentations
Again, a lot of firms reach out to students on campus and you should be among those reaching back. Firms' presentations and workshopsare a chance for you to shine, either by asking pertinent questionsor having a chat with a firm's representative. It will also give you another chance to get a sense of whether this firm might be somewhere you can imagine yourself working in years to come, or if not, it can help you hone your criteria for where you can imagine yourself.

Work experience
Relevant work experience is absolutely essential if you want to get a training contract or pupillage. You need to get some practical work experience in a firm or chambers, be that through a formal work placement or vacation scheme (ie, the schemes run by firms, for which you must formally apply) or mini-pupillage (ie, the formal schemes run by barristers' chambers) or more informally, by approaching firms on an ad hoc basis. It's the best possible way to find out what really happens at a law firm/chambers, and you will have the chance to impress future employers. Also, it's never too early to start – you should begin trying to amass some experience early in your university career or even before you start.

Careers service
Use this very valuable resource! Either at school or at university, these are professionally trained people who are there to help you. You'd be foolish to ignore their expertise. Go and have a chat about what you think you might be looking for, get CV and application help, do some practice interviews and see what they have in their library of printed and online materials. They're there for you – use them!

Self-analysis

KNOW THYSELF!

If there is one piece of research that can be described as essential to success in establishing a career in law, it is research into yourself. You are the commodity that you are putting in front of recruiters and asking them to buy into. If you do not know exactly what you are selling and what you have to offer, then you are unlikely to succeed in getting a career which is a good match to your talents and personality.

Armed with information about what it means to be a lawyer, you now need to work out if law is right for you. In other words, is a legal career a good match for your skills and personal qualities? Here are a few questions to ask yourself (and answer honestly) before deciding:

- When you think of your future, in what kind of environment do you see yourself working (eg, an office, outdoors, high-pressure or regular routine)?
- What are your favourite hobbies and what is it about them that you enjoy (eg, 'I enjoy playing football; specifically, being part of a team and studying the statistics of the game')?
- What are your favourite subjects and what is it about them that you enjoy (eg, problem-solving, practical elements or intellectually stimulating)?
- What do you dislike about the other subjects you're studying?
- Which aspects of your work experience have you most enjoyed?

As for particular skills and qualities that are highly valued by recruiters at law firms, and indeed those that are essential to be an effective law student, the following are key – how many of them describe you?

- Academic ability
- Attention to detail
- Enthusiasm and energy
- Good judgement
- Precise written and oral communication skills, including accurate grammar and punctuation
- Commercial awareness (ie, an appreciation of issues that affect clients)
- Problem-solving ability
- Strong people skills, to build rapport with clients and other professionals
- Self-motivation and self-confidence
- Ability to work as part of a team
- Genuine interest in a legal career.

One way to get things started is to use the MySelf tool, available on **www.lawcareers.net**. MySelf offers you a structured way to identify the skills you possess that are desirable to employers.

In brief, you take an individual experience - be it academic (eg, special project), extracurricular (eg, volunteering or hobbies) or work experience (eg, part-time job) - and you score it against six core competencies(intellectual ability;enthusiasm/drive/ motivation/resilience; accuracy/attention to detail; teamwork/leadership; commercial awareness; and communication skills). Once submitted, all analysed experiences are grouped together in a grid for future use and action – the analysis will be a useful tool as you clarify your ideas and refine your options.

Interview technique

There are two stages to a successful interview. First is the preparation and second is the way you conduct yourself at the interview itself. By taking some time to consider both stages you can confidently approach the law firm/chambers you're hopingto work in, knowing that you're about to deliver a fine interview.

PREPARATION

One of the most common reasons for failure at interview is poor preparation, so spending some time on this could make all the difference. Remember that an interview is a two-way process. It is an opportunity for the firm to find out more about you and for you to find out whether this is a place you want to work. Start with what they might want from you.

Your application has obviously aroused their interest, so go back to that first. Analyse it in the three main areas: academic life, work experience and extracurricular activity. Ask yourself why you made the choices you did, what you have gained from your experiences in terms of skills and personal development, and whether you would have done anything differently.

If you have an academic result that seems out of step with other results, or you have some other issue like illness or bereavement, think in advance about how you want to present that to the interviewer in a way that won't make you anxious or upset. Honesty is certainly the best policy here - if less than impressive grades were a result of things going temporarily astray, you should state this, but explain that things are now back on track.

Spend some time looking for clues to questions in your application. If you have been a keen and committed member of a sports team, part of a rather off-the-wall club or society, or have travelled during a gap year, then you might reasonably expect the interviewer to pick up on those points. Even if you feel that you haven't done anything wildly exciting, clearly something made them interested enough to invite you to interview, so what was it?

One of the things you can confidently expect them to want to know is why you have decided on a career in law. If you are going to be convincing, you need to be able to demonstrate that you understand what a solicitor or barrister actually does and you have considered the different practice areas. For example, if you are applying to a commercial law firm, do you know what the role of the solicitor is in business and can you show that you are commercially aware?

Further, it is important that you take time to read the newspapers, particularly the law sections, to keep up with current events. No interviewer will ever go for anything too obscure but they might reasonably expect you to be interested enough to follow major stories in the press. If you are interested in commercial law you should read the business sections as well.

The firm/chambers will also want to establish why you applied to them in particular, so research them thoroughly. They will only expect you to know what is available to you, but if you know nothing about them as a firm you are unlikely to impress! You need to be looking at the firm's/chambers' own website, with particular focus on the 'About Us', 'News' and 'Recent Deals' sections. It may also be useful to do a search on some of the legal press websites to see what comes up in relation to that particular firm/chambers.

So that's their agenda. Now what's yours? If you are trying to find out whether this is a place you want to work, there will be questions you want to ask and they will expect you to ask them. Think about this before the interview rather than during it!

The final part of your preparation should be to give some thought to what you are going to wear. You don't need to rush out to Armani, but you do need to be recognisable as a future solicitor.Many recruiters mention less-than-suitable clothing as being seriously distracting and not a good idea!

ON THE DAY

If you have prepared thoroughly for an interview, it shouldn't be too nerve-wracking when you get to the interview itself. And while a few nerves can work in your favour, as you use the adrenalin to make you that little bit sharper, if you suffer badly, you should think about getting some advice from a careers adviser on techniques for overcoming the problem.

Throughout an interview, your interviewer will be trying to assess how good you will be with clients. This is a key issue in any law firm and it is very important that you demonstrate an appropriate level of confidence at your interview. Make eye contact, smile and listen carefully to what is being said. Make sure that you sit comfortably - don't perch, don't slouch! Your body language will say a lot about your confidence.

Remember that this is a two-way process so it is important to have a conversation with your interviewer. The interviewer will set the course of that conversation, but don't make it hard work for them. Monosyllabic answers are not going to work. It is also important not to get so carried away that the interviewer finds it hard to get a word in. Be enthusiastic about what you have achieved and be interesting to talk to.

Many people worry about how to deal with difficult or unexpected questions. It is OK to take a minute to consider your answer to a question, but don't allow long silences to develop. If you really don't know how to answer a question, it is better to say so with a smile and allow the interview to move on.

Every interviewer has their own style of interviewing and you may find that all your careful preparation has been for nothing. It has been known for a keen rugby fan to spend the entire interview discussing rugby with a candidate who listed rugby as their main interest. The key is not to panic and feel cut adrift simply because the interview is not what you expected. Be prepared to think on your feet and give it your best shot.

Allow plenty of time to get to your interview and aim to get there at least 15 minutes before so that you have time to gather your thoughts. There is nothing more likely to cause panic and anxiety than the fear that you are going to be late. This will also give you a chance to go to the bathroom and check your appearance - spinach in your teeth or newsprint all over your forehead (true story!) can be distracting for an interviewer, and take away from all the interesting things you might have to say.

Don't forget - you should remember that you are being assessed constantly from the time you arrive at reception to the time you leave so it is important not to let your guard down. If you are being shown around by a current trainee or pupil, it is not wise to confide in them things you would not say to the interviewer. If you are offered lunch with other candidates and trainees/pupils, be careful what you say and avoid any alcohol that might be offered. Having said that, don't feel you have to be someone you're not. Try and relax and be yourself as much as possible.

Lastly, a top student tip on training contract interviews - if you are given coffee, don't touch the chocolate biscuits. The chocolate melts a little as it rests on the saucer against the cup and you can guarantee that someone will want to shake your hand just as you realise you have chocolate all over your fingers.

Application technique: training contract and pupillage

Online application forms are now the most common method of applying to law firms and chambers. The internet and database technologies have made the business of applying for a job quicker than ever before, but don't let that lull you into a false sense of security. The online application form is a formal business document and it should command your time and attention. You are in a competitive race to win funding and support from an organisation that does not know you yet - surely that is deserving of time and effort? Here follows a whistle-stop tour of issues of security, spam and embarrassing mistakes...

RESEARCH

Many candidates want to apply to as many law firms as they possibly can - interest in the actual firm and work environment is sometimes not even a consideration. But this is not just a job application; it's about where you are going to spend at least two years of your life. Two years in a working environment that you do not enjoy, with work you find dull, would be awful, so take the time to think about where you want to work and do thorough research.

Online application technology and innovations such as MyLocker (a function created jointly by LawCareers.Net and Apply4Law) make the business of applying quicker, but don't fall into the trap of thinking that they make it easy and subsequently bet on too many horses! MyLocker allows you to store key information about yourself in a central hub and then use this data across participating Apply4Law application forms. The hope is that this will allow you to spend more time focusing on the longanswer questions of the application form, which should help firms identify which candidates have really done their research. But be warned: an ill-researched, ill-considered and rushed application form will stick out like a sore thumb, so be sure to do your research and take plenty of time.

FEELING SECURE?

It's amazing what you can find out about yourself on the internet, and the furore surrounding Facebook's privacy settings opens up a good debate about web security and how we can all protect our information online. Web security is rarely thought about, especially in relation to online applications. This is strange considering the amount of personal detail that you will enter into an application form.

Online application forms can be secured using encryption technology so make sure you know what to look out for before you enter your personal details. Encrypted secure websites generally have some or all of the following features:

- They have "https" in the URL (eg, https://www.apply4law.com).
- They display a padlock logo.
- They have security certificates, which verify the website's owners and confirm the use of secure sockets layer technology to keep your data safe.

SPAMALOT

Suitable contact details are a basic - but essential - part of a successful application. Most firms send correspondence via email, so it is important to choose an account that you have long-term access to. Bear in mind that an academic email account will be closedas soon as you leave the institution.

To ensure that you do not miss any email correspondence, alter your junk filter settings to allow emails from the firms to which you are applying, and regularly check your emails. Firms are unlikely to look kindly on a candidate missing an interview because their email account had expired.

WHAT NOT TO DO

It may be fun to giggle at the hideous mistakes made by applicants, but thousands of applications are wasted every year by a lack of attention to detail, so it pays not to be too smug. Here are a handful of common mistakes.

Txt spk ok 4 txtin
The Bible may have been translated into text speak, but law firms generally communicate with their clients in full sentences. Text language sticks out like a sore thumb and is best avoided.

It's an App, but not as we know it!
Completing online application forms on your iPhone, iPad, Blackberry or equivalent is just inadvisable. Such applications are easy to spot as they tend to be littered with typos and missing sections, and display a general lack of attention to detail.

I CAN'T HEAR YOU
Don't fill your application with unnecessary capital letters. It displays a lack of grammatical knowledge and it makes it look like you are SHOUTING! Equally, the inappropriate use of lower-case letters makes it look as if your approach is casual.

The dangers of cut and paste
Beware: if you plan to cut and paste answers from Word in order to spell check what you write, remember that it's no replacement for good, honest proofing.

Boasting of your "excellen eye for deetail" is unlikely to impress; claiming you want to work for completely the wrong firm will mean your application is binned.

Sexybeast@yahoodid.com seeks training contract

Fun email addresses are fine for contacting your friends but they are inappropriate when it comes to applying to law firms. It is not hard to generate sensible email accounts and it is worth it in the long run!

Deadlines

Online application forms are automatically withdrawn at the deadline. If you are applying at the last minute, remember to check the time as well as the date of the deadline. A firm will see the exact time at which your application is submitted - does one minute to midnight look impressive?

HOW TO IMPRESS

Online applications are deceptively easy to complete - in fact, you need to plan your approach to them every bit as carefully as to your UCAS application. In particular you should:

- read all the instructions carefully and review the application form as a whole before you start;
- work out what your main strengths are and where you will include them on the application form

- give full answers to every section - all the questions will have been asked for a reason
- avoid making statements without backing them up - simply claiming to be "an excellent team player" is weak in comparison to saying: "I demonstrated my skills within a team when I worked for the university radio station"
- check your application as many times as you can bear and then ask your friends to check it
- be aware of the deadline and submit your application well before it
- make the firm aware of any significant developments up until the deadline by adding information through the online application home page or by contacting the firm directly
- keep a copy of your application - you'll want to review it if invited to interview.

GOOD LUCK!

The application form is a golden opportunity to market yourself to your prospective employer. Firms and chambers invest a lot of time and money in their recruits and therefore it often helps to view your application as a business request for funding. Remember, it ain't over 'til the fat lady sings (or the deadline passes).

What others say...

These are extracts from case studies in previous editions of this book. They give some insights into the experiences and thoughts of people who were once in the same position as you.

Ayla Dogruyol - family solicitor

Ayla found law school really interesting and enjoyable, but advises anyone considering this career to speak to people in the profession and their university careers adviser, to do some work experience and apply for vacation schemes. "You can also go to your local magistrate's court and sit on a case, or perhaps try and arrange to shadow the legal clerk. Law is such a vast area, from criminal through to corporate, so that you need to access as many different areas so you can find out what interests you. You also need good communication, because you're dealing with clients all the time, and good time-keeping. This is especially important in litigation, when you're managing lots of different cases and you've to keep on top of court deadlines – and family law is litigious!"

Eleanor Searley – barrister, criminal law

Eleanor's degree was in music, and she says: 'What I enjoyed most was being in the spotlight and under pressure to perform. Jury trials provide the same level of adrenaline and excitement. I also really enjoyed the analysis part of my degree, but that wouldn't really be a large part of a career as a professional musician... I felt that being a barrister combined the best bits of performance and analysis in one career. I also wanted to work in an area that was client focused because I enjoy the human interest.'

'The best bits are the variety – every day is different so you never get stuck in a rut; the responsibility – the decisions you take or the performance you give matters; and the independence – being self-employed is great.'

Alistair Rattray – trainee solicitor

Alistair qualified in IT and worked initially in industry, which he says gave him the chance 'to see the legal aspects of business. I discussed the various options with solicitors and barristers and decided that the types of work and the teamwork opportunities available to solicitors were more appealing.'

'I'm given a great deal of responsibility, ranging from drafting and negotiating documents directly with other solicitors and serving papers in Court, right through to managing cases from start to finish. One of the primary functions of a solicitor is problem-solving and I enjoy helping clients face and overcome the various challenges that they meet.'

Zoe Rotheram – trainee solicitor

Zoe was attracted to the law by the sheer variety, and the fact that it is relevant to everyday life and is always changing, so will never be a dull or predictable field in which to work. She has found the reality lives up to her expectations: "Being a trainee, it varies massively depending on the department you are in. AT the moment, I am sitting in the Corporate Department, so my work generally involves assisting other fee-earners with their work and helping the team as a whole. That work might involve research; drafting, amending or checking a document; liaising with clients and attending client meetings; or putting together document lists and bibles (copies of the sets of documents signed in a deal with are grouped together and distributed to the parties to the deal).

"The one thing I wish I'd known before I began is the amount of stigma attached to the job, namely that all lawyers are 'bad eggs', which is often frustrating. But it is up to us to disprove this through being personable and performing well, while achieving the right results for our clients."

Donald Lilly – barrister, commercial and chancery law

Donald was attracted by the clear career path of law and advises aspirant lawyers to 'be methodical. Within the time constraints, make sure you have done everything you can to see the problem from every angle. That way, you will be less surprised.'

Kate Herbert – barrister, civil law

Kate took A levels in English, economics, history and general studies, and AS level theatre studies. The most useful thing you can do as a student to find out if you would like to be a barrister is to get experience. This would be best achieved by doing a few mini-pupillages in different areas of law.

'This is a job where you take on a lot of pressure and responsibility from a young age. You have to make decisions in split seconds, so it is important to trust your own judgment.'

Kerry Blake – solicitor, Crown Prosecution Service

Kerry always wanted to understand why cases on the news involving legal troubles turned out the way they did. It didn't take her long to realise she wanted to specialise in criminal law. 'Reading some of the files can be difficult when there are upsetting or disturbing details and photographs. I have dealt with this aspect with the help of more experienced people in my team and by keeping up to date with the case for further

developments and the eventual outcome of a trial.
I have also learnt to expect the unexpected.'

Kerry advises applicants to 'get involved! In my second
year at university I took part in a mooting competition,
arguing a case in a mock courtroom. This kind of
activity will improve your public speaking and boost your
confidence, which is something examiners and
employers will look for.'

Edmund White – GDL student

Both Edmund's parents are barristers so law was
always on the radar, but the moment he finally decided
that law was for him was during some successful work
experience. The thing he regrets however, is "not doing
some formal vacation schemes, as I think that definitely
helps you decide what type of working environment
would suit you as well as helping you when it comes to
applying for firms. Obviously, it also helps if yo've got a
training contract before you start the GDL, especially
from a financial point of view, as many firms pay for the
GDL and Legal Practice Course (LPC).

"The GDL is based around the seven core subjects and
involve lectures and a number of workshops. We also
have two pieces of coursework, which generally go
beyond the set syllabus.

"There are times when it can be a bit boring, as there is
a certain amount of law that we must learn, and we just
have to sit down and get on with it. But the really
encouraging thing is that the times when we're required
to act more like solicitors – ie applying the law to
factual scenarios – are the bits I'm most enjoying."

Edmund says it is really important to get your name
about. "Network like a demon; it helps a lot. For
example, at university law fairs, recruiters to prefer you

to come and talk with confidence and ask good
questions. Don't just go and grab all the free stuff.
Make an effort to get people's cards, and follow up with
an email, perhaps asking some more questions. All the
applications I completed asked whether I knew anyone
at the firm, so to be able to say 'yes' can do you any
harm. And when answering the inevitable question of
'Why this firm?', to be able to say that you've spoken to
people and formed a good perception of the firm goes a
long way."

Oliver Jeffries – associate solicitor

Oliver studied languages and has always enjoyed
discussion and argument. In his view law is all about
'the way we regulate our society – from the rights of
employees or liability in a car crash to the level of
social support given by the government.'

'Working in law can be challenging and the hours can
be long, but the pay and perks are above average and
you will have the opportunity to work with some of the
best people and do some work that is really interesting.
Personally, I think enjoying my job makes the occasional
long hours worth it.'

Ben Witherall – trainee solicitor

Born into a family of lawyers, Ben has gone far afield in
his pursuit of learning, studying European, international
and comparative law and studying at law school for six
months in the United States. 'If you decide to do an
LLB, think carefully about which types of law you want
to study during your degree as this will give you a good
idea of what sort of solicitor you might want to be in the
future. Remember that involvement in extra-curricular
activities will help distinguish you from competing
candidates.'

It all starts now...

Having performed some healthy self-analysis (see page 70), if you do decide that a career as a lawyer is the way forward for you, there are a few things you should be doing over the coming months. Here is a brief, and not exhaustive, checklist to get you started and help focus your attention.

Course listings starting on page 147 and university prospectuses and websites).

- Read the business pages of the general press to improve your commercial awareness.
- Read some of the legal press (see 'Research and sources of advice', page 66).
- Talk to your careers adviser at school about degree options.
- Get some practical work experience at a law firm, barristers' chambers or legal advice centre.

- Work hard at your academic studies. Good grades are essential!
- Talk to friends, parents, acquaintances - anyone with a connection to the legal profession.
- Think about the kinds of extracurricular things you can do to make yourself into a well-rounded candidate.
- Consider whether you want to become a solicitor, barrister or advocate (Scotland).
- Research universities and degree subjects (see Course listings starting on page 147 and university prospectuses and websites).

Applicant journey

SIX EASY STEPS TO UNIVERSITY AND COLLEGE

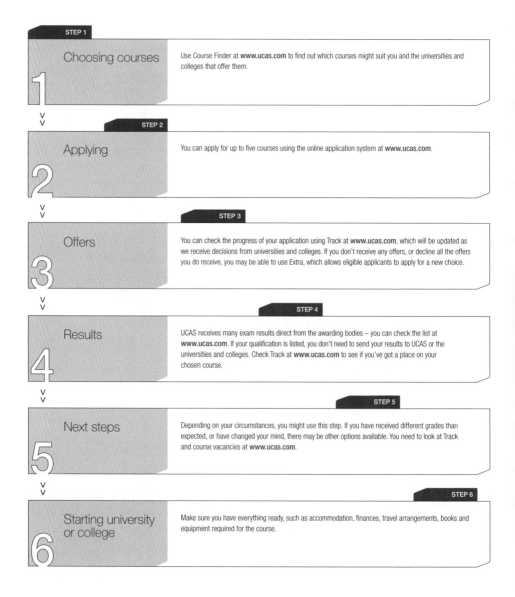

STEP 1

Choosing courses

Use Course Finder at **www.ucas.com** to find out which courses might suit you and the universities and colleges that offer them.

STEP 2

Applying

You can apply for up to five courses using the online application system at **www.ucas.com**.

STEP 3

Offers

You can check the progress of your application using Track at **www.ucas.com**, which will be updated as we receive decisions from universities and colleges. If you don't receive any offers, or decline all the offers you do receive, you may be able to use Extra, which allows eligible applicants to apply for a new choice.

STEP 4

Results

UCAS receives many exam results direct from the awarding bodies – you can check the list at **www.ucas.com**. If your qualification is listed, you don't need to send your results to UCAS or the universities and colleges. Check Track at **www.ucas.com** to see if you've got a place on your chosen course.

STEP 5

Next steps

Depending on your circumstances, you might use this step. If you have received different grades than expected, or have changed your mind, there may be other options available. You need to look at Track and course vacancies at **www.ucas.com**.

STEP 6

Starting university or college

Make sure you have everything ready, such as accommodation, finances, travel arrangements, books and equipment required for the course.

Choosing courses

1

Step 1 – Planning your application for law

Planning your application is the start of your journey to finding a place at a university or college.

This section will help you decide what course to study and how to choose a university or college where you'll enjoy living and studying. Find out about qualifications, degree options, how they'll assess you, and coping with the costs of higher education.

ENTRY REQUIREMENTS

NB: This section covers routes into law from A levels. (An additional, longer route to becoming a solicitor is available through the Institute of Legal Executives (ILEX), See page 59 and **www.ilex.org.uk**.)

WHICH SUBJECTS?

Newsflash – you **don't** have to study law at A level (A2 level) or even at undergraduate level to become a solicitor or barrister. In fact, some law courses positively prefer students not to have studied law at A level, as they find they have to get students to 'unlearn' what they think they already know!

Similarly, almost all law recruiters – both barristers' chambers and firms of solicitors – welcome recruits who have taken a non-law degree, especially if the first degree is in a subject of relevant interest, eg modern languages for EU or corporate solicitors. Gap years are also of interest, as legal recruiters want to hire 'rounded' people who can relate to the world in which they'll be working.

However, although they don't require law at A level, most university law departments will look for subjects that reflect the rigour and skills required on a law degree. This means they're mostly looking for academic subjects, for example English or history, which will provide evidence of making logical arguments and strong written communication skills so essential to a career in law. The only subject not accepted as a valid A level by most law schools is general studies.

WHICH GRADES?

While the subject you've studied may not be quite so important, grades most certainly are. Competition for places in the top law schools is becoming more intense each year, so AAB at A level is a common entry grade requirement for the leading law schools today.

REMEMBER

You don't have to study law at university to become a lawyer, but this book focuses on studying a law degree. You can study a non-law degree of your choosing and then take a postgraduate conversion course. See **Entry routes** on page 51.

UCAS CARD

At its simplest, the UCAS Card scheme is the start of your UCAS journey. It can save you a packet on the high street with exclusive offers to UCAS Card holders, as well as providing you with hints and tips about finding the best course at the right university or college. If that's not enough you'll also receive these benefits:

- frequent expert help from UCAS, with all the essential information you need on the application process
- free monthly newsletters providing advice, hints, tips and exclusive discounts
- tailored information on the universities and courses you're interested in
- and much more

If you're in Year 12, S5 or equivalent and thinking about higher education for autumn 2013, sign up for your FREE UCAS Card today to receive all these benefits at **www.ucas.com/ucascard**.

www.ucas.com

at the heart of connecting people to higher education

Choosing courses

1

Choosing courses

USE COURSE FINDER AT WWW.UCAS.COM TO FIND OUT WHICH COURSES MIGHT SUIT YOU, AND THE UNIVERSITIES AND COLLEGES THAT OFFER THEM.

Use the UCAS website – www.ucas.com has lots of advice on how to find a course. Go to the students' section of the website for the best advice or go straight to Course Finder to see all the courses available through UCAS. Our map of the UK at **www.ucas.com/students/choosingcourses/choosinguni/map/** shows you where all the universities and colleges are located.

Watch UCAStv – at **www.ucas.tv** there are videos on How to choose your course and Attending events as well as case studies from students talking about their experience of finding a course at university or college.

Attend UCAS conventions – UCAS conventions are held throughout the UK. Universities and colleges have exhibition stands where their staff offer information about their courses and institutions. Details of when the conventions are happening are shown at **www.ucas.com/conventions**.

Look at websites and prospectuses – universities and colleges have prospectuses and course-specific leaflets on their undergraduate courses. Your school or college library may have copies or go to the university's website to download a copy or ask them to send one to you.

Go to university and college open days – most institutions offer open days to anyone who wants to attend. See the list of universities and colleges on **www.ucas.com** and the UCAS open days publication (see the Essential Reading chapter) for information on when they are taking place. Aim to visit all of the universities and colleges you are interested in before you apply. It will help with your expectations of university life and make sure the course is the right one for you.

League tables – these can be helpful but bear in mind that they attempt to rank institutions in an overall order reflecting the views of those that produce them. They may not reflect your views and needs. Examples can be found at **www.thecompleteuniversityguide.co.uk**, **www.guardian.co.uk/education/universityguide**, **www.thetimes.co.uk** (subscription service) and **www.thesundaytimes.co.uk** (subscription service). See page 93 for more information about leaue tables.

Do your research – speak and refer to as many trusted sources as you can find. Talk to someone already doing the job you have in mind. The section on 'Which area?' on page 20 will help you identify the different areas of law you might want to enter.

> 1 | Choosing courses

Choosing your institution

Different people look for different things from their university or college course, but the checklist on the next page sets out the kinds of factors all prospective students should consider when choosing their university. Keep this list in mind on open days, when talking to friends about their experiences at various universities and colleges, or while reading prospectuses and websites.

TOP TIP

Don't be afraid to pick up the phone – university and college admissions officers welcome enquiries directly from students, rather than careers officers phoning on your behalf. It shows you're genuinely interested and committed to your own career early on.

WHAT TO CONSIDER WHEN CHOOSING YOUR LAW COURSE

Location	Do you want to stay close to home? Would you prefer to study at a city or campus university or college?
Grades required	Use the Course Finder facility on the UCAS website, **www.ucas.com**, to view entry requirements for courses you are interested in. Also, check out the university or college website or call up the admissions office. Some institutions specify grades required, eg AAB, while others specify points required, eg 340. If they ask for points, it means they're using the UCAS Tariff system, which awards points to different types and levels of qualification. For example, an A grade at A level = 120 points; a B grade at A level = 100 points. The full Tariff tables are available on pages 122-131 and at **www.ucas.com**.
Employer links	Ask the course tutor or department about links with employers, especially for placements or work experience.
Graduate prospects	Ask the careers office for their list of graduate destinations.
Cost	Ask the law admissions office about variable tuition fees and financial assistance, especially at popular university law departments.
Law or non-law degree?	Is there another subject that you enjoy, that you could study first, that might actually help give you an edge in employers' eyes?
Degree type	Do you want to study law on its own (single honours degree) or 50/50 with another subject (joint) or as one of a few subjects (combined degree)? If you opt for a joint or combined course, check that it's still a qualifying law degree, ie that you won't need to do a conversion course.
Teaching style	How many lectures and tutorials per week, amount of one-to-one work, etc?
Course assessment	Can you see yourself writing lots of essays and doing filmed mock trials?
Facilities for students	Check out the law library and computing facilities, and find out if there is a careers adviser dedicated to law.
'Fit'	Even if all the above criteria stack up, this one relies on gut feel – go and visit the institution if you can and see if it's 'you'.

Choosing courses

1

League tables

The information that follows has been provided by Dr Bernard Kingston of The Complete University Guide.

eague tables are worth consulting early in your research and perhaps for confirmation later on. But never rely on them in isolation – always use them alongside other information sources available to you. Universities typically report that over a third of prospective students view league tables as important or very important in making their university choices. They give an insight into quality and are mainly based on data from the universities themselves. Somewhat confusingly, tables published in, say, 2012 are referred to as the 2013 tables because they are aimed at applicants going to university in that following year. The well known ones - *The Complete University Guide*, *The Guardian*, *The Times*, and *The Sunday Times* - rank the institutions and the subjects they teach using input measures (eg entry standards), throughput measures (eg student : staff ratios) and output measures (eg graduate prospects). Some tables are free to access whilst others are behind pay walls. All are interactive and enable users to create their own tables based on the measures important to them.

The universities are provided with their raw data for checking and are regularly consulted on methodology. But ultimately it is the compilers who decide what measures to use and what weights to put on them. They are competitors and rarely consult amongst themselves. So, for example, *The Times* tables differ significantly from *The Sunday Times* ones even though both newspapers belong to the same media proprietor.

Whilst the main university rankings tend to get the headlines, we would stress that the individual subject tables are as least as important, if not more so, when deciding where to study. All universities, regardless of their overall ranking, have some academic departments that rank highly in their subjects. Beware also giving much weight to an institution being a few places higher or lower in the tables – this is likely to be of little significance. This is particularly true in the lower half of the main table where overall scores show considerable bunching.

Most of the measures used to define quality come from hard factual data provided by the Higher Education Statistics Agency (HESA) but some, like student satisfaction and peer assessment, are derived from surveys of subjective impressions where you might wish to query sample size. We give a brief overview of the common measures here but please go to the individual websites for full details.

- **Student satisfaction** is derived from the annual National Student Survey (NSS) and is heavily used by *The Guardian* and *The Sunday Times*.
- **Research assessment** comes from a 2008 exercise (RAE) aimed at defining the quality of a university's research (excluded by *The Guardian*).
- **Entry standards** are based on the full UCAS Tariff scores obtained by new students.
- **Student : staff ratio** gives the number of students per member of academic staff.
- **Expenditure figures** show the costs of academic and student services.
- **Good honours** lists the proportion of graduates gaining a first or upper second honours degree.
- **Completion** indicates the proportion of students who successfully complete their studies.

- **Graduate prospects** usually reports the proportion of graduates who obtain a graduate job – not any job – or continue studying within six months of leaving.
- **Peer assessment** is used only by *The Sunday Times* which asks academics to rate other universities in their subjects.
- **Value added** is used only by *The Guardian* and compares entry standards with good honours.

All four main publishers of UK league tables (see Table 1) also publish university subject tables. *The Complete University Guide* and *The Times* are based on four measures: student satisfaction, research quality, entry standards and graduate destinations. *The Sunday Times* uses student satisfaction, entry standards, graduate destinations, graduate unemployment, good degrees and drop-out rate, while *The Guardian* uses student satisfaction (as three separate measures), entry standards, graduate destinations, student-staff ratio, spend per student and value added. This use of different measures is one reason why the different tables can yield different results (sometimes very different, especially in the case of *The Guardian* which has least in common with the other tables).

League tables compiled by *The Complete University Guide* (**www.thecompleteuniversityguide.co.uk**) and *The Guardian* (**www.guardian.co.uk**) are available in spring, those by *The Times* (**www.thetimes.co.uk**) and *The Sunday Times* (**www.thesundaytimes.co.uk**) in the summer.

Table 1 – measures used by the main publishers of UK league tables

	Universities	Measures	Subjects	Measures
The Complete University Guide	116	9	62	4
The Guardian	119	8	46	8
The Sunday Times	122	8	39	6
The Times	116	8	62	4

THINGS TO WATCH OUT FOR WHEN READING SUBJECT LEAGUE TABLES

- The tables make no distinction between universities which offer courses that are accredited by the Solicitors Regulation Authority and those which do not.

WHO PUBLISHES LAW LEAGUE TABLES?

- All four league tables include data for law.

UCAS

Confused about courses?

Indecisive about institutions?

Stressed about student life?

Unsure about UCAS?

Frowning over finance?

Help is available at
www.ucasbooks.com

> Choosing courses

> 1

How will they choose you?

ADMISSIONS TESTS

Students applying to some courses are required to sit an admissions test as part of the application process. The tables on page 98-99 give details of some of the law courses that use admissions tests as part of their selection criteria. This is not a definitive list, so check the entry requirements for your chosen course(s) on Course Finder on the UCAS website, or contact the university or college for the most up-to-date information on their admissions tests. An up-to-date list of tests can be found on **www.ucas.com/students/choosingcourses/admissions/**.

Admissions tests are a way to manage application numbers for high-demand courses by helping to differentiate fairly between well-qualified applicants. They can widen access and participation in higher education as they measure academic potential without being influenced by educational background.

Admissions tests broaden and complement other selection criteria as they often assess aptitude and reasoning rather than achievement and recall.

Admissions tests do not generally require additional teaching, although applicants should familiarise themselves with a specimen paper beforehand. Check with the test centre about what type of preparation is required. It is usually the applicant's own responsibility to ensure they are entered for a test by the closing date. Some tests are taken at the applicant's school or college, others require applicants to sit the test at a test centre or at the university or college as part of an interview day. Overseas applicants may not be required to sit an admissions test – check with the course provider.

LNAT

Such is the level of competition for places on some law courses that a number of university law departments now require applicants to sit a standardised entry test as part of their selection criteria. Why? The test helps universities to make fairer choices among the many highly qualified applicants who want to join their undergraduate law programmes, and is also a possible aid to widening participation by helping to identify academic potential.

NATIONAL ADMISSIONS TEST FOR LAW (LNAT)	
Which universities require it?	University of Birmingham University of Bristol Durham University University of Glasgow King's College London (University of London) The National University of Ireland, Maynooth (mature candidates only) University of Manchester University of Nottingham University of Oxford University College London (University of London) Check the LNAT website for the latest information – **www.lnat.ac.uk**
What does it involve?	A 2¼ hour on-screen written test centres under exam conditions, comprising two sections: 95 minutes – 42 multiple-choice questions to assess your critical reasoning. It tests how well you analyse and interpret data and make logical deductions from passages of text. 40 minutes – essay (on a choice of subjects).
Where is the test held?	In one of a global network of test centres throughout the UK and abroad. See the LNAT website – **www.lnat.ac.uk**.
How much does it cost	For UK and EU centres £50. For centres outside EU £70. Bursaries are available for candidates in need of financial support.
How can I prepare?	This test does NOT assess your legal knowledge, so swotting up on the law of tort won't get you very far. Instead, it aims to assess your aptitude for law, by testing your written communication and logical thinking, so any practice you can get writing essays to weigh up pros and cons of issues and come to a logical conclusion is useful. You can also check out the sample tests, (which are available as an executable test or as a document that can be printed out) with answer key and commentary, and the advice given in the Preparation section on the LNAT website.
Where can I get more info?	**www.lnat.ac.uk/lnat-preparation.aspx**

LNAT COURSE DETAILS

UNIVERSITY/COLLEGE	COURSE	CODE	NOTES
University of Birmingham (B32)	LLB Law	M100	Candidates for University of Birmingham must sit the LNAT by 20 January 2013.
	LLB Law with Business Studies	M1N1	
	LLB Law with French (4 years)	MR11	
	LLB Law with German (4 years)	MR12	
University of Bristol (B78)	LLB Law	M100	Candidates for University of Bristol must sit the LNAT by 20 January 2013.
	LLB Law and French (4 years)	MR11	
	LLB Law and German (4 years)	MR12	
Durham University (D86)	LLB Law	M101	Candidates for Durham University must sit the LNAT by 20 January 2013.
	BA Law with Foundation	M102	
University of Glasgow (G28)	LLB Law	M114	Candidates for University of Glasgow must sit the LNAT by 20 January 2013.
	LLB Law with French Language	M1R1	
	LLB Law with French Legal Studies	M121	
	LLB Law with German Language	M1R2	
	LLB Law with German Legal Studies	M122	
	LLB Law with Italian Language	M1R3	
	LLB Law with Italian Legal Studies	M1M9	
	LLB Law with Spanish Language	M1R4	
	LLB Law with Spanish Legal Studies	M123	
	LLB Law/Business Economics	MN11	
	LLB Law/Business and Management	MN12	
	LLB Law/Economic and Social History	MV13	
	LLB Law/Economics	ML11	
	LLB Law/English Literature	MQ13	
	LLB Law/Gaelic Language	MQ15	
	LLB Law/History	MV11	
	LLB Law/Philosophy	MV15	
	LLB Law/Politics	ML12	
King's College London (University of London) (K60)	LLB Law	M100	Candidates for King's College London must sit the LNAT by 16 January 2013.
	LLB Law with German Law	M122	
	LLB English Law and French Law (LBB Honours)	M121	
	LLB Politics, Philosophy and Law	LM21	
	English Law and Hong Kong Law	M190	

UNIVERSITY/COLLEGE	COURSE	CODE	NOTES
National University of Ireland, Maynooth†	BCL Law and Arts BBL Business and Law LLB Bachelor of Laws	MH115 (BCL*) MH406 (BBL*) MH119*	
University of Manchester	LLB Law LLB Law with Criminology BA Law with Politics	M100 M1M9 M1L2	Candidates for University of Manchester must sit the LNAT by 20 January 2013.
The University of Nottingham (N84)	BA Law BA Law with German BA Law with French BA Law with Spanish LLB Senior Status Bachelor of Law with Honours	M100 M1R2 M1R1 M1R4 M101	Candidates for University of Nottingham must sit the LNAT by 20 January 2013.
University of Oxford (O33)	BA Law BA Law with Spanish Law BA Law with Italian Law BA Law with French Law BA Law with German Law BA Law with European Law	M100 M194 M193 M191 M192 M190	Candidates for the University of Oxford are required to register and book a test slot by 5 October 2012 and to sit the LNAT by 20 October 2012
University College London (University of London) (U80)	LLB Law LLB Law with Advanced Studies (4 years) LLB Law with Another Legal System (4 years) LLB Law with French Law (4 years) LLB Law with German Law (4 years) LLB Law with Hispanic Law (4 years) LLB English and German Law LLB and LLB Baccalaureus Legum (4 years)	M100 M101 M102 M141 M142 M144 M146	Candidates for University College London must sit the LNAT by 20 January 2012.

Further information can be found on the LNAT website, **www.lnat.ac.uk.** Candidates are advised to check the 2012 LNAT website (which will be launched in summer 2012) for up-to-date information on courses, deadlines etc. For entry in 2012/13 or deferred entry in 2014 LNAT registration begins on 1 August 2012, and LNAT testing starts on 1 September 2012.

†This is not a UCAS member institution. Check **www.nuim.ie** for information on how to apply. *Mature candidates only. Candidates should consult the LNAT website for deadlines at **www.lnat.ac.uk/lnat-registration/law-admissions-test.aspx**.

CAMBRIDGE LAW TEST

Most Cambridge colleges require applicants for law to take the Cambridge Law Test, which is designed to provide an assessment of your potential for their law course. In most cases applicants will take the test when they are in Cambridge for interview. The college dealing with your application will contact you about the arrangements if they are using it. There is no need for you to register for this test and there is no fee.

Further information about the test, including specimen questions and answers, is available on the Faculty of Law website: **www.law.cam.ac.uk/admissions/cambridge-law-test.php**.

wondering how much higher education costs?

need information about student finance?

Visit www.ucas.com/students/studentfinance and find sources for all the information on student money matters you need.

With access to up-to-date information on bursaries, scholarships and variable fees, plus our online budget calculator. Visit us today and get the full picture.

www.ucas.com/students/studentfinance

Choosing courses
1

The cost of higher education

The information in this section was up-to-date when this book was published. You should visit the websites mentioned in this section for the very latest information.

THE COST OF STUDYING IN THE UK

As a student, you will usually have to pay for two things: tuition fees for your course, which for most students do not need to be paid for up front, and living costs such as rent, food, books, transport and entertainment. Fees charged vary between courses, between universities and colleges and also according to your normal country of residence, so it's important to check these before you apply. Course fee information is supplied to UCAS by the universities and is displayed in Course Finder at **www.ucas.com**.

STUDENT LOANS

The purpose of student loans from the Government is to help cover the costs of your tuition fees and basic living costs (rent, bills, food and so on). Two types are available: a tuition fee loan to cover the tuition charges and a maintenance loan to help with accommodation and other living costs. Both types of student loan are available to all students who meet the basic eligibility requirements. Interest will be charged at inflation plus a fixed percentage while you are studying. In addition, many other commercial loans are available to students studying at university or college but the interest rate can vary considerably. Loans to help with living costs will be available for all eligible students, irrespective of family income.

Find out more information from the relevant sites below:

England: Student Finance England –
www.direct.gov.uk/studentfinance

Northern Ireland: Student Finance Northern Ireland –
www.studentfinanceni.co.uk

Scotland: Student Awards Agency for Scotland –
www.saas.gov.uk

Wales: Student Finance Wales –
www.studentfinancewales.co.uk or
www.cyllidmyfyrwyrcymru.co.uk

BURSARIES AND SCHOLARSHIPS

- The National Scholarships Programme gives financial help to students studying in England. The scheme is designed to help students whose families have lower incomes.
- Students from families with lower incomes will be entitled to a non-repayable maintenance grant to help with living costs.
- Many universities and colleges also offer non-repayable scholarships and bursaries to help students cover tuition and living costs whilst studying.
- All eligible part-time undergraduates who study for at least 25% of their time will be able to apply for a loan to cover the costs of their tuition, which means they no longer have to pay up front.

There will be extra support for disabled students and students with child or adult dependants. For more information, visit the country-specific websites listed above.

TOP TIP

Before you choose your institution, make sure you find out about the bursaries they offer. Some are likely to be more generous than others, and this may make the difference between a financially comfortable or uncomfortable time.

```
┌─────────────────────────────────┐
│        Choosing courses         │
│  ┌─┐                            │
│  │ │                            │
│ ─┘ │                            │
│    │                            │
└────┴────────────────────────────┘
```

Choosing courses

1

International students

APPLYING TO STUDY IN THE UK

Deciding to go to university or college in the UK is very exciting. You need to think about what course to do, where to study, and how much it will cost. The decisions you make can have a huge effect on your future but UCAS is here to help.

HOW TO APPLY

Whatever your age or qualifications, if you want to apply for any of the 35,000 courses listed at 300 universities and colleges on the UCAS website, you must apply through UCAS at **www.ucas.com**. If you are unsure, your school, college, adviser, or local British Council office will be able to help. Further advice and a video guide for international students can be found on the non-UK section of the UCAS website at **www.ucas.com/international**.

If you already have a degree from your own country, you will probably have to take a conversion course in English law. Most British Council offices will have information and advice about entry to UK law schools.

Students may apply on their own or through their school, college, adviser, or local British Council if they are registered with UCAS to use Apply. If you choose to use an education agent's services, check with the British Council to see if they hold a list of certificated or registered agents in your country. Check also on any charges you may need to pay. UCAS charges only the application fee (see below) but agents may charge for additional services.

How much will my application cost?

If you choose to apply to more than one course, university or college you need to pay UCAS £23 GBP when you apply. If you only apply to one course at one university or college, you pay UCAS £12 GBP.

WHAT LEVEL OF ENGLISH?

UCAS provides a list of English language qualifications and grades that are acceptable to most UK universities and colleges, however you are advised to contact the institutions directly as each have their own entry requirement in English. For more information go to **www.ucas.com/students/wheretostart/ nonukstudents/englangprof**.

INTERNATIONAL STUDENT FEES

If you study in the UK, your fee status (whether you pay full-cost fees or a subsidised fee rate) will be decided by the UK university or college you plan to attend. Before you decide which university or college to attend, you need to be absolutely certain that you can pay the full cost of:

- your tuition fees (the amount is set by universities and colleges, so contact them for more information – visit their websites where many list their fees. Fee details will also be included on Course Finder on **www.ucas.com** from mid-July.)
- the everyday living expenses for you (and your family) for the whole time that you are in the UK, including accommodation, food, gas and electricity bills, clothes, travel and leisure activities.
- books and equipment for your course
- travel to and from your country.

You must include everything when you work out how much it will cost. You can get information to help you do this accurately from the international offices at universities and colleges, UKCISA (UK Council for International Student Affairs) and the British Council. There is a useful website tool to help you manage your money at university – **www.studentcalculator.org.uk.**

Scholarships and bursaries are offered at some universities and colleges and you should contact them for more information. In addition, you should check with your local British Council for additional scholarships available to students from your country who want to study in the UK.

LEGAL DOCUMENTS YOU WILL NEED

As you prepare to study in the UK, it is very important to think about the legal documents you will need to enter the country.

Everyone who comes to study in the UK needs a valid passport, details of which will be collected either in your UCAS application or later through Track. If you do not yet have a passport, you should apply for one as soon as possible. People from certain countries also need visas before they come into the UK. They are known as 'visa nationals'. You can check if you require a visa to travel to the UK by visiting the UK Border Agency website and selecting 'Studying in the UK', so please check the UK Border Agency website at **www.ukba.homeoffice.gov.uk** for the most up-to-date guidance and information about the United Kingdom's visa requirements.

When you apply for your visa you need to make sure you have the following documents:

- A confirmation of acceptance for studies (CAS) number from the university or college where you are going to study. The university or college must be on the UKBA Register of Sponsors in order to accept international students.
- A valid passport.
- Evidence that you have enough money to pay for your course and living costs.
- Certificates for all qualifications you have that are relevant to the course you have been accepted for and for any English language qualifications.

You will also have to give your biometric data.

Do check for further information from your local British Embassy or High Commission. Guidance information for international students is also available from UKCISA and from UKBA.

ADDITIONAL RESOURCES

There are a number of organisations that can provide further guidance and information to you as you prepare to study in the UK:

- British Council
  www.britishcouncil.org
- Education UK (British Council website dealing with educational matters)
  www.educationuk.org
- English UK (British Council accredited website listing English language courses in the UK)
  www.englishuk.com
- UK Border Agency (provides information on visa requirements and applications)
  www.ukvisas.gov.uk
- UKCISA (UK Council for International Student Affairs)
  www.ukcisa.org.uk
- Directgov (the official UK government website)
  www.direct.gov.uk
- Prepare for Success
  www.prepareforsuccess.org.uk

Applying

2

Step 2 – Applying

You apply through UCAS using the online application system, called Apply, at **www.ucas.com**. You can apply for a maximum of five choices, but you don't have to use them all if you don't want to. If you apply for fewer than five choices, you can add more at a later date if you want to. But be aware of the course application deadlines (you can find these in Course Finder at **www.ucas.com**).

IMPORTANT DATES FOR 2012 ENTRY	
Early June 2012	UCAS Apply opens for 2013 entry registration.
Mid-September 2012	Applications can be sent to UCAS.
15 October 2012	Application deadline for the receipt at UCAS of applications for all medicine, dentistry, veterinary medicine and veterinary science courses and for all courses at the universities of Oxford and Cambridge.
15 January 2013	Application deadline for the receipt at UCAS of applications for all courses except those listed above with a 15 October deadline, and some art and design courses with a 24 March deadline.
25 February 2013	Extra starts (see page 120 for more information about Extra).
24 March 2013	Application deadline for the receipt at UCAS of applications for art and design courses except those listed on Course Finder at **www.ucas.com** with a 15 January deadline.
31 March 2013	If you apply by 15 January, the universities and colleges should aim to have sent their decisions by this date (but they can take longer).
9 May 2013	If you apply by 15 January, universities and colleges need to send their decisions by this date. If they don't, UCAS will make any outstanding choices unsuccessful on their behalf.
30 June 2013	If you send your application to us by this date, we will send it to your chosen universities and colleges. Appliocations received after this date are entered into Clearing (see page 134 for more information about Clearing).
3 July 2013	Last date to apply through Extra.
August 2013 (date to be confirmed)	Scottish Qualifications Authority (SQA) results are published.
15 August 2013	GCE and Advanced Diploma results are published (often known as 'A level results day'). Adjustment opens for registration (see page 135 for more information about Adjustment).

DON'T FORGET...

Universities and colleges guarantee to consider your application only if we receive it by the appropriate deadline. Check application deadlines for your courses on Course Finder at **www.ucas.com**.

If you send it to UCAS after the deadline but before 30 June 2013, universities and colleges will consider your application only if they still have places available.

Applying

2

How to apply

You apply online at **www.ucas.com** through Apply – a secure, web-based application service that is designed for all our applicants, whether they are applying through a UCAS-registered centre or as an individual, anywhere in the world. Apply is:

- **easy to access** – all you need is an internet connection
- **easy to use** – you don't have to complete your application all in one go: you can save the sections as you complete them and come back to it later
- **easy to monitor** – once you've applied, you can use Track to check the progress of your application, including any decisions from universities or colleges. You can also reply to your offers using Track.

Watch the UCAStv guide to applying through UCAS at **www.ucas.tv**.

APPLICATION FEE

For 2013 entry, the fee for applying through UCAS is £23 for two or more choices and £12 for one choice.

DEFERRED ENTRY

If you want to apply for deferred entry in 2014, perhaps because you want to take a year out between school or college and higher education, you should check that the university or college will accept a deferred entry application. Occasionally, tutors are not happy to accept students who take a gap year, because it interrupts the flow of their learning. If you apply for deferred entry, you must meet the conditions of any offers by 31 August 2013 unless otherwise agreed by the university or college. If you accept a place for 2014 entry and then change your mind, you cannot reapply through us in the 2014 entry cycle unless you withdraw your original application.

APPLYING THROUGH YOUR SCHOOL OR COLLEGE

1 GET SCHOOL OR COLLEGE 'BUZZWORD'

Ask your UCAS application coordinator (may be your sixth form tutor) for your school or college UCAS 'buzzword'. This is a password for the school or college.

2 REGISTER

Go to **www.ucas.com/students/apply** and click on **Register/Log in to use Apply** and then **register**. After you have entered your registration details, the online system will automatically generate a username for you, but you'll have to come up with a password and answers to security questions.

3 COMPLETE SEVEN SECTIONS

Complete all the sections of the application. To access any section, click on the section name at the left of the screen and follow the instructions. The sections are:

Personal details – contact details, residential status, disability status

Additional information – only UK applicants need to complete this section

Student finance – UK students can share some of their application details with their student finance company. Finance information is provided for other EU and international applicants.

Choices – which courses you'd like to apply for

Education – your education and qualifications

Employment – eg work experience, holiday jobs

Statement – see page 112 for personal statement advice.

Before you can send your application you need to go to the **View all details** screen and tick the **section completed** box.

4 PASS TO REFEREE

Once you've completed all the sections, send your application electronically to your referee (normally your form tutor). They'll check it, approve it and add their reference to it, and will then send it to UCAS on your behalf.

USEFUL INFORMATION ABOUT APPLY

- Important details like date of birth and course codes will be checked by Apply. It will alert you if they are not valid.
- We strongly recommend that the personal statement and reference are written in a word-processing package and pasted in to Apply.
- If you want to, you can enter European characters into certain areas of Apply.
- You can change your application at any time before it is completed and sent to UCAS.
- You can print and preview your application at any time. Before you send it you need to go to the **View all details** screen and tick the **section completed** box.
- Your school, college or centre can choose different payment methods. For example, they may want us to bill them, or you may be able to pay online by debit or credit card.

NOT APPLYING THROUGH A SCHOOL OR COLLEGE

If you're not currently studying, you'll probably be applying as an independent applicant rather than through a school, college or other UCAS-registered centre. In this case you won't be able to provide a 'buzzword', but we'll ask you a few extra questions to check you are eligible to apply.

If you're not applying through a UCAS-registered centre, the procedure you use for obtaining a reference will depend on whether or not you want your reference to be provided through a registered centre. For information on the procedures for providing references, visit **www.ucas.com/students/applying/howtoapply/reference**.

INVISIBILITY OF CHOICES

Universities and colleges cannot see details of the other choices on your application until you reply to any offers or you are unsuccessful at all your choices.

You can submit only one UCAS application in each year's application cycle.

APPLICATION CHECKLIST

We want this to run smoothly for you and we also want to process your application as quickly as possible. You can help us to do this by remembering to do the following:

✓ check the closing dates for applications – see page 108
✓ check the student finance information at **www.ucas.com/students/studentfinance/** and course fees information in Course Finder at **www.ucas.com**
✓ start early and allow plenty of time for completing your application – including enough time for your referee to complete the reference section
✓ read the online instructions carefully before you start
✓ consider what each question is actually asking for – use the 'help'
✓ pay special attention to your personal statement (see page 112) and start drafting it early
✓ ask a teacher, parent, friend or careers adviser to review your draft application – particularly the personal statement
✓ if you get stuck, watch our videos on YouTube where we answer your frequently asked questions on completing a UCAS application at **www.youtube.com/ucasonline**
✓ if you have extra information that will not fit on your application, send it direct to your chosen universities or colleges after we have sent you your Welcome letter with your Personal ID – don't send it to us
✓ print a copy of the final version of your application, in case you are asked questions on it at an interview.

Applying

2

The personal statement

Next to choosing your courses, this section of your application will be the most time-consuming. It is of immense importance as many universities and colleges make their selection relying solely on the information in the UCAS application, rather than interviews and admissions tests. The personal statement can be the deciding factor in whether or not they offer you a place. If it is an institution that interviews, your statement could be the deciding factor in whether you get invited for interview.

Keep a copy of your personal statement – if you are called for interview, you will almost certainly be asked questions based on it.

Tutors will look carefully at your exam results, actual and predicted, your reference and your personal statement. Remember, they are looking for reasons to offer you a place – try to give them every opportunity to do so!

A SALES DOCUMENT

The personal statement is your opportunity to sell yourself, so do so. The university or college admissions tutor wants to get a rounded picture of you to decide whether you will make an interesting member of the university or college both academically and socially. They want to know more about you than the subjects you are studying at school.

HOW TO START

At **www.ucas.com** you'll find several tools to help you write a good personal statement.

- Personal statement timeline, to help you do all your research and plan your statement over several drafts and checks.
- Personal statement mind map, which gives you reminders and hints on preparation, content and presentation, with extra hints for mature and international applicants.
- Personal statement worksheet, which gets you to start writing by asking relevant questions so that you include everything you need. You can also check your work against a list of dos and don'ts.

Include things like hobbies and work experience, and try to link the skills you have gained to the type of course you are applying for. Describe your career plans and goals. Have you belonged to sports teams or orchestras or held positions of responsibility in the community? Try to give evidence of your ability to undertake higher level study successfully by showing your commitment and maturity. If you left full-time education a while ago, talk about the work you have done and the skills you have gathered or how you have juggled bringing up a family with other activities – that is solid evidence of time management skills. Whoever you are, make sure you explain what appeals to you about the course you are applying for.

WHAT ADMISSIONS TUTORS LOOK FOR	WHAT TO TELL THEM
<ul><li>Your reasons for wanting to take this subject in general and this particular course.</li><li>Your communication skills – not only what you say but how you say it. Your grammar and spelling must be perfect.</li><li>Relevant experience – practical things you've done that are related to your choice of course.</li><li>Evidence of your teamworking ability, leadership capability, independence.</li><li>Evidence of your skills, for example: IT skills, empathy and people skills, debating and public speaking, research and analysis.</li><li>Other activities that show your dedication and ability to apply yourself and maintain your motivation.</li></ul>	<ul><li>Why you want to do this subject – how you know it is the subject for you.</li><li>What experience you already have in this field – for example work experience, school projects, hobbies, voluntary work.</li><li>The skills and qualities you have as a person that would make you a good student, for example anything that shows your dedication, communication ability, academic achievement, initiative.</li><li>Examples that show you can knuckle down and apply yourself, for example running a marathon or your Extended Project.</li><li>If you're taking a gap year, why you've chosen this and (if possible) what you're going to do during it.</li><li>About your other interests and activities away from studying – to show you're a rounded person. (But remember that it is mainly your suitability for the particular course that they're looking to judge.)</li></ul>

For law courses admissions tutors are particularly looking for evidence of an analytical approach to your reading and writing; evidence that you are capable of understanding abstract concepts and can apply them to the real world in a logical manner; a commitment to the subject and realistic expectations of your career options.

Visit **www.ucas.tv** to view the video to help guide you through the process and address the most common fears and concerns about writing a personal statement.

WORK EXPERIENCE

How much does it count? Ask any law admissions tutor or legal recruiter about the importance of work experience on a candidate's application and they'll all agree – work experience shows a real, rather than theoretical, interest in the legal profession. An absence of work experience might lead tutors to question your commitment to your choice of career.

Work experience will not only give you a real insight into the work of a solicitor or barrister, it will also give you valuable examples of the skills you have to offer.
As part of the application process, you'll be asked to write a personal statement setting out which subject you'd like to study, why you'd like to study it, and what skills and experience you bring that would make you a great student for the course. This is where your work experience will help you stand out.

Unfortunately for sixth formers, most of the formal work experience schemes offered by chambers and firms of solicitors are aimed at undergraduates (see the table on the next page). However, there are still some alternative work experience routes for the dedicated A level student, including taster days and introductory courses offered by universities and colleges, volunteering at your local Citizens' Advice Bureau or community advice centre, or work placements in a firm of solicitors organised by your school or college.

WORK EXPERIENCE SCHEMES FOR LAW UNDERGRADUATES

	BARRISTERS	SOLICITORS
Scheme	Mini-pupillages	Work placement schemes Vavation schemes
Typical tasks	Attending court Drafting legal opinions Researching litigation Sitting in on client conferences	Shadowing a solicitor Researching legal points Drafting letters Attending client meetings
Duration	Typically 3–5 days in barristers' chambers; it's now the norm for law students to do several mini-pupillages in different chambers and sectors	1–4 weeks in a firm of solicitors; most common are summer vacation schemes, but many firms also run schemes in the Christmas and Easter university breaks
How to apply	**www.pupillages.com** offers a list of organisations that operate mini-pupillages, but you'll still have to apply to chambers directly	Check out the individual law firms' websites and write directly to them - most have online forms to fill in
Note	Some chambers now operate assessed mini-pupillages, in which participants are given a task, eg drafting an opinion, which is formally assessed, and which may be used as part of their assessment for a full pupillage at a later date.	Firms are not obliged to pay trainees on vacation placements, though most now do. Rates range from around £100–£300 per week (of those firms that pay!)

If you have only non-legal work experience, it will still be useful to include it in any applications you make. The trick is to pull out the professional and personal skills you have developed that are relevant to the work of a barrister or solicitor.

> Offers

3

Step 3 – Offers

Once we have sent your application to your chosen universities and colleges, they will all consider it independently and tell us if they can offer you a place. Some universities and colleges will take longer to make decisions than others. You may be asked to attend an interview, sit an additional test or provide a piece of work, such as an essay, before a decision can be made.

INTERVIEWS

Many universities (particularly the more popular ones, running competitive courses) use interviews as part of their selection process. Universities will want to find out why you want to study your chosen course at their institution, and they want to judge whether the course is suitable for you and your future career plans. Interviews also give you an opportunity to visit the university and ask any questions you may have about the course or their institution.

If you are called for interview, the key areas they are likely to cover will be:

- evidence of your academic ability
- your capacity to study hard
- your commitment to a law career, best shown by work experience
- your awareness of current issues in the news that may have an impact on your chosen field of study, for example new Acts of Parliament or EU directives
- your logic and reasoning ability.

A lot of the interview will be based on information on your application, especially your personal statement. See page 112 for tips about the personal statement.

SAMPLE INTERVIEW QUESTIONS

- How would you feel about defending a known criminal or dealing with a conflict of interest? (To explore your approach to 'ethical' issues.)
- Do you enjoy public speaking or debating? (One for the would-be barristers.)
- What do you think of the changes to employment law, etc? (To test your awareness of what's going on in your chosen field.)

Whenever a university or college makes a decision about your application, we record it and let you know. You can check the progress of your application using Track at **www.ucas.com**. This is our secure online service which gives you access to your application, using the same username and password you used when you applied. You use it to find out if you have been invited for an interview or need to provide an additional piece of work, and you can check to see if you have received any offers. Whenever there is any change in your application status, we email you to advise you to check Track

TYPES OF OFFER

Universities can make two types of offer: conditional or unconditional.

Conditional offer

A conditional offer means the university or college will offer you a place if you meet certain conditions – usually based on exam results. The conditions may be based on Tariff points (for example, 300 points from three A levels), or specify certain grades in named subjects (for example, A in English, B in philosophy, C in history).

Unconditional offer

If you've met all the academic requirements for the course and the university or college wants to accept you, they will make you an unconditional offer. If you accept this you'll have a definite place.

However, for both types of offer, there might be other requirements, such as medical or financial conditions, that you need to meet before you can start your course.

REPLYING TO OFFERS

When you have received decisions for all your choices, you must decide which offers you want to accept. You will be given a deadline in Track by which you have to make your replies. Before replying, get advice from family, friends or advisers, but remember that you're the one taking the course so it's your decision.

Firm acceptance

- Your firm acceptance is your first choice - this is your preferred choice out of all the offers you have received. You can have only one firm acceptance.
- If you accept an unconditional offer, you are entering a contract that you will attend the course, so you must decline any other offers.
- If you accept a conditional offer, you are agreeing that you will attend the course at that university or college if you meet the conditions of the offer. You can accept another offer as an insurance choice.

Insurance acceptance

- If your firm acceptance is a conditional offer, you can accept another offer as an insurance choice. Your insurance choice can be conditional or unconditional and acts as a back-up, so if you don't meet the conditions for your firm choice but meet the conditions for your insurance, you will be committed to the insurance choice. You can only have one insurance choice.
- The conditions for your insurance choice would usually be lower than your firm choice.
- You don't have to accept an insurance choice if you don't want one, but if you do need to be certain that it is an offer that you would accept.

For more information watch our video guides How to use Track, Making sense of your offers, and How to reply to your offers at **www.ucas.tv**.

WHAT IF YOU HAVE NO OFFERS?

If you have used all five choices on your application and either received no offers, or decided to turn down any offers you have received, you may be eligible to apply for another choice through Extra. Find out more about Extra on page 120.

If you are not eligible for Extra, in the summer you can contact universities and colleges with vacancies in Clearing. See page 134 for more information.

Connect with us...

 www.facebook.com/ucasonline

 www.twitter.com/ucas_online

 www.youtube.com/ucasonline

Offers

3

Extra

Extra allows you to make additional choices, one at a time, without having to wait for Clearing in July. It is completely optional and free, and is designed to encourage you to continue researching and choosing courses if you are holding no offers. You can search for courses available through Extra on Course Finder at **www.ucas.com**. The Extra service is available to eligible applicants from 24 February to early July 2012 through Track at **www.ucas.com**.

WHO IS ELIGIBLE?

You will be eligible for Extra if you have already made five choices and:

- you have had unsuccessful or withdrawal decisions from all five of your choices, or
- you have cancelled your outstanding choices and hold no offers, or

- you have received decisions from all five choices and have declined all offers made to you.

HOW DOES IT WORK?

We contact you and explain what to do if you are eligible for Extra. If you are eligible a special Extra button will be available on your Track screen. If you want to use Extra you should:

- tick the **Available in Extra** box in the Study Options section when looking for courses on Course Finder
- choose one that you would like to apply for and enter the details on your Track screen.

When you have chosen a course the university or college will be able to view your application and consider you for a place.

WHAT HAPPENS NEXT?

We give the universities and colleges a maximum of 21 days to consider your Extra application. During this time, you cannot be considered by another university or college. If you have not heard after 21 days you can apply to a different university or college if you wish, but it is a good idea to ring the one currently considering you before doing so. If you are made an offer, you can choose whether or not to accept it.

If you accept any offer, conditional or unconditional, you will not be able to take any further part in Extra.

If you are currently studying for examinations, any offer that you receive is likely to be an offer conditional on exam grades. If you already have your examination results, it is possible that a university or college may make an unconditional offer. If you accept an unconditional offer, you will be placed. If you decide to decline the offer or the university or college decides they cannot make you an offer, you will be given another opportunity to use Extra, time permitting. Your Extra button on Track will be reactivated.

Once you have accepted an offer in Extra, you are committed to it in the same way as you would be with an offer through the main UCAS system. Conditional offers made through Extra will be treated in the same way as other conditional offers, when your examination results become available.

If your results do not meet the conditions and the university or college decides that they cannot confirm your Extra offer, you will automatically become eligible for Clearing if it is too late for you to be considered by another university or college in Extra.

If you are unsuccessful, decline an offer, or do not receive an offer, or 21 days have elapsed since choosing a course through Extra, you can use Extra to apply for another course, time permitting.

ADVICE

Do the same careful research and seek guidance on your Extra choice of university or college and course as you did for your initial choices. If you applied to high-demand courses and institutions in your original application and were unsuccessful, you could consider related or alternative subjects or perhaps apply for the subject you want in combination with another. Your teachers or careers advisers or the universities and colleges themselves can provide useful guidance. Course Finder at **www.ucas.com** is another important source of information. Be flexible, that is the key to success.

But you are the only one who know how flexible you are prepared to be. Remember that even if you decide to take a degree course other than law, you can take the postgraduate route into the profession.

Visit **www.ucas.tv** to watch the video guide on how to use Extra.

```
Offers
3
```

The Tariff

Finding out what qualifications are needed for different higher education courses can be very confusing.

The UCAS Tariff is the system for allocating points to qualifications used for entry to higher education. Universities and colleges can use the UCAS Tariff to make comparisons between applicants with different qualifications. Tariff points are often used in entry requirements, although other factors are often taken into account. Information on Course Finder at **www.ucas.com** provides a fuller picture of what admissions tutors are seeking.

The tables on the following pages show the qualifications covered by the UCAS Tariff. There may have been changes to these tables since this book was printed. You should visit **www.ucas.com** to view the most up-to-date tables.

FURTHER INFORMATION?

Although Tariff points can be accumulated in a variety of ways, not all of these will necessarily be acceptable for entry to a particular higher education course. The achievement of a points score therefore does not give an automatic entitlement to entry, and many other factors are taken into account in the admissions process.

The Course Finder facility at **www.ucas.com** is the best source of reference to find out what qualifications are acceptable for entry to specific courses. Updates to the Tariff, including details on how new qualifications are added, can be found at **www.ucas.com/students/ucas_tariff/**.

HOW DOES THE TARIFF WORK?

- Students can collect Tariff points from a range of different qualifications, eg GCE A level with BTEC Nationals.
- There is no ceiling to the number of points that can be accumulated.
- There is no double counting. Certain qualifications within the Tariff build on qualifications in the same subject. In these cases only the qualification with the higher Tariff score will be counted. This principle applies to:
    - GCE Advanced Subsidiary level and GCE Advanced level
    - Scottish Highers and Advanced Highers
    - Speech, drama and music awards at grades 6, 7 and 8.
- Tariff points for the Advanced Diploma come from the Progression Diploma score plus the relevant Additional and Specialist Learning (ASL) Tariff points. Please see the appropriate qualification in the Tariff tables to calculate the ASL score.
- The Extended Project Tariff points are included within the Tariff points for Progression and Advanced Diplomas. Extended Project points represented in the Tariff only count when the qualification is taken outside of these Diplomas.
- Where the Tariff tables refer to specific awarding organisations, only qualifications from these awarding organisations attract Tariff points. Qualifications with a similar title, but from a different qualification awarding organisation do not attract Tariff points.

HOW DO UNIVERSITIES AND COLLEGES USE THE TARIFF?

The Tariff provides a facility to help universities and colleges when expressing entrance requirements and when making conditional offers. Entry requirements and conditional offers expressed as Tariff points will often require a minimum level of achievement in a specified subject (for example, '300 points to include grade A at A level chemistry', or '260 points including SQA Higher grade B in mathematics').

Use of the Tariff may also vary from department to department at any one institution, and may in some cases be dependent on the programme being offered.

In July 2010, UCAS announced plans to review the qualifications information provided to universities and colleges. You can read more about the review at **www.ucas.com/qireview**.

The following qualifications are included in the UCAS Tariff. See the number on the qualification title to find the relevant section of the Tariff table.

1   AAT NVQ Level 3 in Accounting
2   AAT Level 3 Diploma in Accounting (QCF)
3   Advanced Diploma
4   Advanced Extension Awards
5   Advanced Placement Programme (US and Canada)
6   Arts Award (Gold)
7   ASDAN Community Volunteering qualification
8   Asset Languages Advanced Stage
9   British Horse Society (Stage 3 Horse Knowledge & Care, Stage 3 Riding and Preliminary Teacher's Certificate)
10 BTEC Awards (NQF)
11 BTEC Certificates and Extended Certificates (NQF)
12 BTEC Diplomas (NQF)
13 BTEC National in Early Years (NQF)
14 BTEC Nationals (NQF)
15 BTEC QCF Qualifications (Suite known as Nationals)
16 BTEC Specialist Qualifications (QCF)
17 CACHE Award, Certificate and Diploma in Child Care and Education
18 CACHE Level 3 Extended Diploma for the Children and Young People's Workforce (QCF)
19 Cambridge ESOL Examinations
20 Cambridge Pre-U
21 Certificate of Personal Effectiveness (COPE)
22 CISI Introduction to Securities and Investment
23 City & Guilds Land Based Services Level 3 Qualifications
24 Graded Dance and Vocational Graded Dance
25 Diploma in Fashion Retail
26 Diploma in Foundation Studies (Art & Design; Art, Design & Media)
27 EDI Level 3 Certificate in Accounting, Certificate in Accounting (IAS)
28 Essential Skills (Northern Ireland)
29 Essential Skills Wales
30 Extended Project (stand alone)
31 Free-standing Mathematics
32 Functional skills
33 GCE (AS, AS Double Award, A level, A level Double Award and A level (with additional AS))
34 Hong Kong Diploma of Secondary Education (from 2012 entry onwards)
35 ifs School of Finance (Certificate and Diploma in Financial Studies)
36 iMedia (OCR level Certificate/Diploma for iMedia Professionals)
37 International Baccalaureate (IB) Diploma
38 International Baccalaureate (IB) Certificate
39 Irish Leaving Certificate (Higher and Ordinary levels)
40 IT Professionals (iPRO) (Certificate and Diploma)
41 Key Skills (Levels 2, 3 and 4)
42 Music examinations (grades 6, 7 and 8)
43 OCR Level 3 Certificate in Mathematics for Engineering
44 OCR Level 3 Certificate for Young Enterprise
45 OCR Nationals (National Certificate, National Diploma and National Extended Diploma)
46 Principal Learning Wales
47 Progression Diploma
48 Rockschool Music Practitioners Qualifications
49 Scottish Qualifications
50 Speech and Drama examinations (grades 6, 7 and 8 and Performance Studies)
51 Sports Leaders UK
52 Welsh Baccalaureate Advanced Diploma (Core)

Updates on the Tariff, including details on the incorporation of any new qualifications, are posted on **www.ucas.com**.

UCAS TARIFF TABLES

1

AAT NVQ LEVEL 3 IN ACCOUNTING	
GRADE	TARIFF POINTS
PASS	160

2

AAT LEVEL 3 DIPLOMA IN ACCOUNTING	
GRADE	TARIFF POINTS
PASS	160

3

ADVANCED DIPLOMA

Advanced Diploma = Progression Diploma plus Additional & Specialist Learning (ASL). Please see the appropriate qualification to calculate the ASL score. Please see the Progression Diploma (Table 47) for Tariff scores

4

ADVANCED EXTENSION AWARDS	
GRADE	TARIFF POINTS
DISTINCTION	40
MERIT	20

Points for Advanced Extension Awards are over and above those gained from the A level grade

5

ADVANCED PLACEMENT PROGRAMME (US & CANADA)	
GRADE	TARIFF POINTS
Group A	
5	120
4	90
3	60
Group B	
5	50
4	35
3	20

Details of the subjects covered by each group can be found at www.ucas.com/students/ucas_tariff/tarifftables

6

ARTS AWARD (GOLD)	
GRADE	TARIFF POINTS
PASS	35

7

ASDAN COMMUNITY VOLUNTEERING QUALIFICATION	
GRADE	TARIFF POINTS
CERTIFICATE	50
AWARD	30

8

ASSET LANGUAGES ADVANCED STAGE			
GRADE	TARIFF POINTS	GRADE	TARIFF POINTS
Speaking		Listening	
GRADE 12	28	GRADE 12	25
GRADE 11	20	GRADE 11	18
GRADE 10	12	GRADE 10	11
Reading		Writing	
GRADE 12	25	GRADE 12	25
GRADE 11	18	GRADE 11	18
GRADE 10	11	GRADE 10	11

9

BRITISH HORSE SOCIETY	
GRADE	TARIFF POINTS
Stage 3 Horse Knowledge & Care	
PASS	35
Stage 3 Riding	
PASS	35
Preliminary Teacher's Certificate	
PASS	35

Awarded by Equestrian Qualifications (GB) Ltd (EQL)

10

BTEC AWARDS (NQF) (EXCLUDING BTEC NATIONAL QUALIFICATIONS)			
GRADE	TARIFF POINTS		
	Group A	Group B	Group C
DISTINCTION	20	30	40
MERIT	13	20	26
PASS	7	10	13

Details of the subjects covered by each group can be found at www.ucas.com/students/ucas_tariff/tarifftables

11

BTEC CERTIFICATES AND EXTENDED CERTIFICATES (NQF) (EXCLUDING BTEC NATIONAL QUALIFICATIONS)					
GRADE	TARIFF POINTS				
	Group A	Group B	Group C	Group D	Extended Certificates
DISTINCTION	40	60	80	100	60
MERIT	26	40	52	65	40
PASS	13	20	26	35	20

Details of the subjects covered by each group can be found at www.ucas.com/students/ucas_tariff/tarifftables

12

BTEC DIPLOMAS (NQF) (EXCLUDING BTEC NATIONAL QUALIFICATIONS)			
GRADE	TARIFF POINTS		
	Group A	Group B	Group C
DISTINCTION	80	100	120
MERIT	52	65	80
PASS	26	35	40

Details of the subjects covered by each group can be found at www.ucas.com/students/ucas_tariff/tarifftables

UCAS TARIFF TABLES

13

BTEC NATIONAL IN EARLY YEARS (NQF)						
GRADE	TARIFF POINTS	GRADE	TARIFF POINTS	GRADE	TARIFF POINTS	
Theory				Practical		
Diploma		Certificate		D	120	
DDD	320	DD	200	M	80	
DDM	280	DM	160	P	40	
DMM	240	MM	120			
MMM	220	MP	80			
MMP	160	PP	40			
MPP	120					
PPP	80					

Points apply to the following qualifications only: BTEC National Diploma in Early Years (100/1279/5); BTEC National Certificate in Early Years (100/1280/1)

14

BTEC NATIONALS (NQF)					
GRADE	TARIFF POINTS	GRADE	TARIFF POINTS	GRADE	TARIFF POINTS
Diploma		Certificate		Award	
DDD	360	DD	240	D	120
DDM	320	DM	200	M	80
DMM	280	MM	160	P	40
MMM	240	MP	120		
MMP	200	PP	80		
MPP	160				
PPP	120				

15

BTEC QUALIFICATIONS (QCF) (SUITE OF QUALIFICATIONS KNOWN AS NATIONALS)					
EXTENDED DIPLOMA	DIPLOMA	90 CREDIT DIPLOMA	SUBSIDIARY DIPLOMA	CERTIFICATE	TARIFF POINTS
D*D*D*					420
D*D*D					400
D*DD					380
DDD					360
DDM					320
DMM	D*D*				280
	D*D				260
MMM	DD				240
		D*D*			210
MMP	DM	D*D			200
		DD			180
MPP	MM	DM			160
			D*		140
PPP	MP	MM	D		120
		MP			100
	PP		M		80
				D*	70
		PP	D		60
			P	M	40
				P	20

16

BTEC SPECIALIST (QCF)			
GRADE	TARIFF POINTS		
	Diploma	Certificate	Award
DISTINCTION	120	60	20
MERIT	80	40	13
PASS	40	20	7

UCAS TARIFF TABLES

17

CACHE LEVEL 3 AWARD, CERTIFICATE AND DIPLOMA IN CHILD CARE & EDUCATION

AWARD		CERTIFICATE		DIPLOMA	
GRADE	TARIFF POINTS	GRADE	TARIFF POINTS	GRADE	TARIFF POINTS
A	30	A	110	A	360
B	25	B	90	B	300
C	20	C	70	C	240
D	15	D	55	D	180
E	10	E	35	E	120

18

CACHE LEVEL 3 EXTENDED DIPLOMA FOR THE CHILDREN AND YOUNG PEOPLE'S WORKFORCE (QCF)

GRADE	TARIFF POINTS
A*	420
A	340
B	290
C	240
D	140
E	80

19

CAMBRIDGE ESOL EXAMINATIONS

GRADE	TARIFF POINTS
Certificate of Proficiency in English	
A	140
B	110
C	70
Certificate in Advanced English	
A	70

20

CAMBRIDGE PRE-U

GRADE	TARIFF POINTS	GRADE	TARIFF POINTS	GRADE	TARIFF POINTS
Principal Subject		Global Perspectives and Research		Short Course	
D1	TBC	D1	TBC	D1	TBC.
D2	145	D2	140	D2	TBC
D3	130	D3	126	D3	60
M1	115	M1	112	M1	53
M2	101	M2	98	M2	46
M3	87	M3	84	M3	39
P1	73	P1	70	P1	32
P2	59	P2	56	P2	26
P3	46	P3	42	P3	20

21

CERTIFICATE OF PERSONAL EFFECTIVENESS (COPE)

GRADE	TARIFF POINTS
PASS	70

Points are awarded for the Certificate of Personal Effectiveness (CoPE) awarded by ASDAN and CCEA

22

CISI INTRODUCTION TO SECURITIES AND INVESTMENT

GRADE	TARIFF POINTS
PASS WITH DISTINCTION	60
PASS WITH MERIT	40
PASS	20

23

CITY AND GUILDS LAND BASED SERVICES LEVEL 3 QUALIFICATIONS

GRADE	TARIFF POINTS			
	EXTENDED DIPLOMA	DIPLOMA	SUBSIDIARY DIPLOMA	CERTIFICATE
DISTINCTION*	420	280	140	70
DISTINCTION	360	240	120	60
MERIT	240	160	80	40
PASS	120	80	40	20

24

GRADED DANCE AND VOCATIONAL GRADED DANCE

GRADE	TARIFF POINTS	GRADE	TARIFF POINTS	GRADE	TARIFF POINTS
Graded Dance					
Grade 8		Grade 7		Grade 6	
DISTINCTION	65	DISTINCTION	55	DISTINCTION	40
MERIT	55	MERIT	45	MERIT	35
PASS	45	PASS	35	PASS	30
Vocational Graded Dance					
Advanced Foundation		Intermediate			
DISTINCTION	70	DISTINCTION	65		
MERIT	55	MERIT	50		
PASS	45	PASS	40		

25

DIPLOMA IN FASHION RETAIL

GRADE	TARIFF POINTS
DISTINCTION	160
MERIT	120
PASS	80

Applies to the NQF and QCF versions of the qualifications awarded by ABC Awards

UCAS TARIFF TABLES

26

DIPLOMA IN FOUNDATION STUDIES (ART & DESIGN AND ART, DESIGN & MEDIA)	
GRADE	TARIFF POINTS
DISTINCTION	285
MERIT	225
PASS	165

Awarded by ABC, Edexcel, UAL and WJEC

27

EDI LEVEL 3 CERTIFICATE IN ACCOUNTING, CERTIFICATE IN ACCOUNTING (IAS)	
GRADE	TARIFF POINTS
DISTINCTION	120
MERIT	90
PASS	70

28

ESSENTIAL SKILLS (NORTHERN IRELAND)	
GRADE	TARIFF POINTS
LEVEL 2	10

Only allocated at level 2 if studied as part of a wider composite qualification such as 14-19 Diploma or Welsh Baccalaureate

29

ESSENTIAL SKILLS WALES	
GRADE	TARIFF POINTS
LEVEL 4	30
LEVEL 3	20
LEVEL 2	10

Only allocated at level 2 if studied as part of a wider composite qualification such as 14-19 Diploma or Welsh Baccalaureate

30

EXTENDED PROJECT (STAND ALONE)	
GRADE	TARIFF POINTS
A*	70
A	60
B	50
C	40
D	30
E	20

Points for the Extended Project cannot be counted if taken as part of Progression/Advanced Diploma

31

FREE-STANDING MATHEMATICS	
GRADE	TARIFF POINTS
A	20
B	17
C	13
D	10
E	7

Covers free-standing Mathematics - Additional Maths, Using and Applying Statistics, Working with Algebraic and Graphical Techniques, Modelling with Calculus

32

FUNCTIONAL SKILLS	
GRADE	TARIFF POINTS
LEVEL 2	10

Only allocated if studied as part of a wider composite qualification such as 14-19 Diploma or Welsh Baccalaureate

33

GCE AND VCE									
GRADE	TARIFF POINTS	GRADE	TARIFF POINTS	GRADE	TARIFF POINTS	GRADE	TARIFF POINTS	GRADE	TARIFF POINTS
GCE & AVCE Double Award		GCE A level with additional AS (9 units)		GCE A level & AVCE		GCE AS Double Award		GCE AS & AS VCE	
A*A*	280	A*A	200	A*	140	AA	120	A	60
A*A	260	AA	180	A	120	AB	110	B	50
AA	240	AB	170	B	100	BB	100	C	40
AB	220	BB	150	C	80	BC	90	D	30
BB	200	BC	140	D	60	CC	80	E	20
BC	180	CC	120	E	40	CD	70		
CC	160	CD	110			DD	60		
CD	140	DD	90			DE	50		
DD	120	DE	80			EE	40		
DE	100	EE	60						
EE	80								

34

HONG KONG DIPLOMA OF SECONDARY EDUCATION					
GRADE	TARIFF POINTS	GRADE	TARIFF POINTS	GRADE	TARIFF POINTS
All subjects except mathematics		Mathematics compulsory component		Mathematics optional components	
5**	No value	5**	No value	5**	No value
5*	130	5*	60	5*	70
5	120	5	45	5	60
4	80	4	35	4	50
3	40	3	25	3	40

No value for 5** pending receipt of candidate evidence (post 2012)

UCAS TARIFF TABLES

35

IFS SCHOOL OF FINANCE (NQF & QCF)			
GRADE	TARIFF POINTS	GRADE	TARIFF POINTS
Certificate in Financial Studies (CeFS)		Diploma in Financial Studies (DipFS)	
A	60	A	120
B	50	B	100
C	40	C	80
D	30	D	60
E	20	E	40

Applicants with the ifs Diploma cannot also count points allocated to the ifs Certificate. Completion of both qualifications will result in a maximum of 120 UCAS Tariff points

36

LEVEL 3 CERTIFICATE / DIPLOMA FOR iMEDIA USERS (iMEDIA)	
GRADE	TARIFF POINTS
DIPLOMA	66
CERTIFICATE	40

Awarded by OCR

37

INTERNATIONAL BACCALAUREATE (IB) DIPLOMA			
GRADE	TARIFF POINTS	GRADE	TARIFF POINTS
45	720	34	479
44	698	33	457
43	676	32	435
42	654	31	413
41	632	30	392
40	611	29	370
39	589	28	348
38	567	27	326
37	545	26	304
36	523	25	282
35	501	24	260

38

INTERNATIONAL BACCALAUREATE (IB) CERTIFICATE					
GRADE	TARIFF POINTS	GRADE	TARIFF POINTS	GRADE	TARIFF POINTS
Higher Level		Standard Level		Core	
7	130	7	70	3	120
6	110	6	59	2	80
5	80	5	43	1	40
4	50	4	27	0	10
3	20	3	11		

39

IRISH LEAVING CERTIFICATE			
GRADE	TARIFF POINTS	GRADE	TARIFF POINTS
Higher		Ordinary	
A1	90	A1	39
A2	77	A2	26
B1	71	B1	20
B2	64	B2	14
B3	58	B3	7
C1	52		
C2	45		
C3	39		
D1	33		
D2	26		
D3	20		

40

IT PROFESSIONALS (iPRO)	
GRADE	TARIFF POINTS
DIPLOMA	100
CERTIFICATE	80

Awarded by OCR

41

KEY SKILLS	
GRADE	TARIFF POINTS
LEVEL 4	30
LEVEL 3	20
LEVEL 2	10

Only allocated at level 2 if studied as part of a wider composite qualification such as 14-19 Diploma or Welsh Baccalaureate

UCAS TARIFF TABLES

42

MUSIC EXAMINATIONS

GRADE	TARIFF POINTS	GRADE	TARIFF POINTS	GRADE	TARIFF POINTS
Practical					
Grade 8		Grade 7		Grade 6	
DISTINCTION	75	DISTINCTION	60	DISTINCTION	45
MERIT	70	MERIT	55	MERIT	40
PASS	55	PASS	40	PASS	25
Theory					
Grade 8		Grade 7		Grade 6	
DISTINCTION	30	DISTINCTION	20	DISTINCTION	15
MERIT	25	MERIT	15	MERIT	10
PASS	20	PASS	10	PASS	5

Points shown are for the ABRSM, LCMM/University of West London, Rockschool and Trinity Guildhall/Trinity College London Advanced Level music examinations

43

OCR LEVEL 3 CERTIFICATE IN MATHEMATICS FOR ENGINEERING

GRADE	TARIFF POINTS
A*	TBC
A	90
B	75
C	60
D	45
E	30

44

OCR LEVEL 3 CERTIFICATE FOR YOUNG ENTERPRISE

GRADE	TARIFF POINTS
DISTINCTION	40
MERIT	30
PASS	20

45

OCR NATIONALS

GRADE	TARIFF POINTS	GRADE	TARIFF POINTS	GRADE	TARIFF POINTS
National Extended Diploma		National Diploma		National Certificate	
D1	360	D	240	D	120
D2/M1	320	M1	200	M	80
M2	280	M2/P1	160	P	40
M3	240	P2	120		
P1	200	P3	80		
P2	160				
P3	120				

46

PRINCIPAL LEARNING WALES

GRADE	TARIFF POINTS
A*	210
A	180
B	150
C	120
D	90
E	60

47

PROGRESSION DIPLOMA

GRADE	TARIFF POINTS
A*	350
A	300
B	250
C	200
D	150
E	100

Advanced Diploma = Progression Diploma plus Additional & Specialist Learning (ASL). Please see the appropriate qualification to calculate the ASL score

48

GRADE	TARIFF POINTS				
	Extended Diploma	Diploma	Subsidiary Diploma	Extended Certificate	Certificate
DISTINCTION	240	180	120	60	30
MERIT	160	120	80	40	20
PASS	80	60	40	20	10

ROCKSCHOOL MUSIC PRACTITIONERS QUALIFICATIONS

49

SCOTTISH QUALIFICATIONS

GRADE	TARIFF POINTS	GRADE	TARIFF POINTS	GRADE	TARIFF POINTS	GROUP	TARIFF POINTS
Advanced Higher		Higher		Scottish Interdisciplinary Project		Scottish National Certificates	
A	130	A	80	A	65	C	125
B	110	B	65	B	55	B	100
C	90	C	50	C	45	A	75
D	72	D	36				
Ungraded Higher		NPA PC Passport					
PASS	45	PASS	45				
		Core Skills					
		HIGHER	20				

Details of the subjects covered by each Scottish National Certificate can be found at www.ucas.com/students/ucas_tariff/tarifftables

50

SPEECH AND DRAMA EXAMINATIONS

GRADE	TARIFF POINTS	GRADE	TARIFF POINTS	GRADE	TARIFF POINTS	GRADE	TARIFF POINTS
PCertLAM		Grade 8		Grade 7		Grade 6	
DISTINCTION	90	DISTINCTION	65	DISTINCTION	55	DISTINCTION	40
MERIT	80	MERIT	60	MERIT	50	MERIT	35
PASS	60	PASS	45	PASS	35	PASS	20

Details of the Speech and Drama Qualifications covered by the Tariff can be found at www.ucas.com/students/ucas_tariff/tarifftables

51

SPORTS LEADERS UK	
GRADE	TARIFF POINTS
PASS	30

These points are awarded to Higher Sports Leader Award and Level 3 Certificate in Higher Sports Leadership (QCF)

52

WELSH BACCALAUREATE ADVANCED DIPLOMA (CORE)	
GRADE	TARIFF POINTS
PASS	120

These points are awarded only when a candidate achieves the Welsh Baccalaureate Advanced Diploma

Results

4

Step 4 – Results

You should arrange your holidays so that you are at home when your exam results are published because, if there are any issues to discuss, admissions tutors will want to speak to you in person.

We receive many exam results direct from the exam boards – check the list at **www.ucas.com**.

If your qualification is listed, we send your results to the universities and colleges that you have accepted as your firm and insurance choices. If your qualification is not listed, you must send your exam results to the universities and colleges where you are holding offers.

After you have received your exam results check Track to find out if you have a place on your chosen course.

If you have met all the conditions for your firm choice, the university or college will confirm that you have a place. Occasionally, they may still confirm you have a place even if you have not quite met all the offer conditions; or they may offer you a place on a similar course.

If you have not met the conditions of your firm choice and the university or college has not confirmed your place, but you have met all the conditions of your insurance or second offer, your insurance university or college will confirm that you have a place.

When a university or college tells us that you have a place, we send you confirmation by letter.

RE-MARKED EXAMS

If you ask for any of your exams to be re-marked, you must tell the universities and colleges where you're holding offers. If a university or college cannot confirm your place based on the initial results, you should ask them if they would be able to reconsider their decision after the re-mark. They are under no obligation to reconsider their position even if your re-mark results in higher grades. Don't forget that re-marks may also result in lower grades.

The exam boards tell us about any re-marks that result in grade changes. We then send the revised grades to the universities and colleges where you're holding offers. As soon as you know about any grade changes, you should also tell these universities and colleges.

'CASHING IN' A LEVEL RESULTS

If you have taken A levels, your school or college must certificate or 'cash in' all your unit scores before the exam board can award final grades. If when you collect your A level results you have to add up your unit scores to find out your final grades, this means your school or college has not 'cashed in' your results.

We receive only cashed in results from the exam boards, so if your school or college has not cashed in your results, you must ask them to send a 'cash in' request to the exam board. You also need to tell the universities and colleges where you're holding offers that there'll be a delay in receiving your results and call our Customer Service Unit to find out when your results have been received.

When we receive your 'cashed in' results from the exam board we send them straight away to the universities and colleges where you're holding offers.

WHAT IF YOU DON'T HAVE A PLACE?

If you have not met the conditions of either your firm or insurance choice, and your chosen universities or colleges have not confirmed your place, you are eligible for Clearing. In Clearing you can apply for any courses that still have vacancies (but remember that admissions tutors will still be reading your original personal statement). Clearing operates from mid-July to late September 2013 (page 134).

BETTER RESULTS THAN EXPECTED?

If you obtain exam results that meet and exceed the conditions of the offer for your firm choice, you can for a short period use a process called adjustment to look for an alternative place, whilst still keeping your original firm choice. See page 135 for information about Adjustment.

Next steps

5

Step 5 – Next steps

You might find yourself with different exam results than you were expecting, or you may change your mind about what you want to do. If so, there may be other options open to you.

CLEARING

Clearing is a service that helps people without a place find suitable course vacancies. It runs from mid-July until the end of September, but most people use it after the exam results are published in August.

You could consider related or alternative subjects or perhaps combining your original choice of subject with another. Your teachers or careers adviser, or the universities and colleges themselves, can provide useful guidance.

Course vacancies are listed at **www.ucas.com** and in the national media following the publication of exam results in August. **Once you have your exam results**, if you're in Clearing you need to look at the vacancy listings and then contact any university or college you are interested in.

Talk to the institutions; don't be afraid to call them. Make sure you have your Personal ID and Clearing Number ready and prepare notes on what you will say to them about:

- why you want to study the course
- why you want to study at their university or college
- any relevant employment or activities you have done that relate to the course
- your grades.

Accepting an offer - you can contact as many universities and colleges as you like through Clearing, and you may informally be offered more than one place. If this happens, you will need to decide which offer you want to accept. If you're offered a place you want to be formally considered for, you enter the course details in Track, and the university or college will then let you know if they're accepting you.

ADJUSTMENT

If you receive better results than expected, and meet and exceed the conditions of your conditional firm choice, you have the opportunity to reconsider what and where you want to study. This process is called Adjustment.

Adjustment runs from A level results day on 15 August 2013 until the end of August. Your individual Adjustment period starts on A level results day or when your conditional firm choice changes to unconditional firm, whichever is the later. You then have a maximum of five calendar days to register and secure an alternative course, if you decide you want to do this. If you want to try to find an alternative course you must register in Track to use Adjustment, so universities and colleges can view your application.

There are no vacancy listings for Adjustment, so you'll need to talk to the institutions. When you contact a university or college make it clear that you are applying through Adjustment, not Clearing. If they want to consider you they will ask for your Personal ID, so they can view your application.

If you don't find an alternative place then you remain accepted at your original firm choice.

Adjustment is entirely optional; remember that nothing really beats the careful research you carried out to find the right courses before you made your UCAS application. Talk to a careers adviser at your school, college or local careers office, as they can help you decide if registering to use Adjustment is right for you.

More information about Adjustment and Clearing is available at **www.ucas.com**. You can also view UCAStv video guides on how to use Adjustment and Clearing at **www.ucas.tv**.

IF YOU ARE STILL WITHOUT A PLACE TO STUDY

If you haven't found a suitable place, or changed your mind about what you want to do, there are lots of other options. Ask for advice from your school, college or careers office. Here are some suggestions you might want to consider:

- studying a part-time course (there's a part-time course search at **www.ucas.com** from July until September)
- studying a foundation degree
- re-sit your exams
- getting some work experience
- studying in another country
- reapplying next year to university or college through UCAS
- taking a gap year
- doing an apprenticeship (you'll find a vacancy search on the National Apprenticeship Service (NAS) website at **www.apprenticeships.org.uk**)
- finding a job
- starting a business.

More advice and links to other organisations can be found on the UCAS website at **www.ucas.com/students/extsteps/advice**.

Starting university
or college

Step 6 – Starting university or college

Congratulations! Now that you have confirmed your place at university or college you will need to finalise your plans on how to get there, where to live and how to finance it. Make lists of things to do with deadlines and start contacting people whose help you can call on. Will you travel independently or ask your parents or relatives to help with transport? If you are keeping a car at uni, have you checked out parking facilities and told your insurance company?

Make sure you have everything organised, including travel arrangements, essential documents and paperwork, books and equipment required for the course. The university will send you joining information – contact the Admissions Office or the Students' Union if you have questions about anything to do with starting your course.

Freshers week will help you to settle in and make friends, but don't forget you are there to study. You may find the teaching methods rather alien at first, but remember there are plenty of sources of help, including your tutors, other students or student mentors, and the Students Union.

Where to live - unless you are planning to live at home, your university or college will usually be able to provide you with guidance on finding somewhere to live. The earlier you contact them the better your chance of finding a suitable range of options, from hall to private landlords. Find out what facilities are available at the different types of accommodation and check whether it fits within your budget. Check what you need to bring with you and what is supplied. Don't leave it all to the last minute – especially things like arranging a bank account, checking what proof of identity you might need, gathering together a few essentials like a mug and supplies of coffee, insurance cover, TV licence etc.

Student finance - you will need to budget for living costs, accommodation, travel, and books (and tuition fees if you are paying them up front). Learn about budgeting by visiting **www.ucas.com** where you will find further links to useful resources to help you manage your money. Remember that if you do get into financial difficulties the welfare office at the university will help you change tack and manage better in future, but it is always better to live within your means from the outset.

Useful contacts

CONNECTING WITH UCAS

You can follow UCAS on Twitter at **www.twitter.com/ ucas_online**, and ask a question or see what others are asking on Facebook at **www.facebook.com/ ucasonline**. You can also watch videos of UCAS advisers answering frequently asked questions on YouTube at **www.youtube.com/ucasonline**.

There are many UCAStv video guides to help with your journey into higher education, such as *How to choose your courses*, *Attending events*, *Open Days* and *How to apply*. These can all be viewed at **www.ucas.tv** or in the relevant section of **www.ucas.com**.

If you need to speak to UCAS, please contact the Customer Service Unit on 0871 468 0 468 or 0044 871 468 0 468 from outside the UK. Calls from BT landlines within the UK will cost no more than 9p per minute. The cost of calls from mobiles and other networks may vary.

If you have hearing difficulties, you can call the Text Relay service on 18001 0871 468 0 468 (outside the UK 0044 151 494 1260). Calls are charged at normal rates.

CAREERS ADVICE

The Directgov Careers Helpline for Young People is for you if you live in England, are aged 13 to 19 and want advice on getting to where you want to be in life.

Careers advisers can give you information, advice and practical help with all sorts of things, like choosing subjects at school or mapping out your future career options. They can help you with anything that might be affecting you at school, college, work or in your personal or family life.

Contact a careers adviser at **www.gov.uk/en/YoungPeople/index.htm**.

Skills Development Scotland provides a starting point for anyone looking for careers information, advice or guidance.
www.myworldofwork.co.uk.

Careers Wales – Wales' national all-age careers guidance service.
www.careerswales.com or **www.gyrfacymru.com**.

Northern Ireland Careers Service website for the all-age careers guidance service in Northern Ireland.
www.nidirect.gov.uk/careers.

If you're not sure what job you want or you need to help to decide which course to do, give learndirect a call on 0800 101 901 or visit **www.learndirect.co.uk**.

GENERAL HIGHER EDUCATION ADVICE

National Union of Students (NUS) is the national voice of students, helping them to campaign, get cheap student discounts and provide advice on living student life to the full – **www.nus.org.uk**.

STUDENTS WITH DISABILITIES

If you have a disability or specific learning difficulty, you are strongly encouraged to make early direct contact with individual institutions before submitting your application. Most universities and colleges have disability coordinators or advisers. You can find their contact details and further advice on the Disability Rights UK website – **www.disabilityalliance.org**.

There is financial help for students with disabilities, known as Disabled Students' Allowances (DSAs). More information is available on the Directgov website at **www.direct.gov.uk/disabledstudents**.

YEAR OUT

For useful information on taking a year out, see **www.gap-year.com**.

The Year Out Group website is packed with information and guidance for young people and their parents and advisers. **www.yearoutgroup.org**.

Essential reading

UCAS has brought together the best books and resources you need to make the important decisions regarding entry to higher education. With guidance on choosing courses, finding the right institution, information about student finance, admissions tests, gap years and lots more, you can find the most trusted guides at **www.ucasbooks.com**.

The publications listed on the following pages and many others are available through **www.ucasbooks.com** or from UCAS Publication Services unless otherwise stated.

UCAS PUBLICATION SERVICES

UCAS Publication Services
PO Box 130, Cheltenham, Gloucestershire GL52 3ZF

f: 01242 544 806
e: publicationservices@ucas.ac.uk
// www.ucasbooks.com

ENTIRE RESEARCH AND APPLICATION PROCESS EXPLAINED

The UCAS Guide to getting into University and College

This guide contains advice and up-to-date information about the entire research and application process, and brings together the expertise of UCAS staff, along with insights and tips from well known universities including Oxford and Cambridge, and students who are involved with or have experienced the process first-hand.

The book clearly sets out the information you need in an easy-to-read format, with myth busters, tips from students, checklists and much more; this book will be a companion for applicants throughout their entire journey into higher education.
Published by UCAS
Price £11.99
Publication date January 2011

NEED HELP COMPLETING YOUR APPLICATION?

How to Complete your UCAS Application 2013
A must for anyone applying through UCAS. Contains advice on the preparation needed, a step-by-step guide to filling out the UCAS application, information on the UCAS process and useful tips for completing the personal statement.
Published by Trotman
Price £12.99
Publication date May 2012

Insider's Guide to Applying to University
Full of honest insights, this is a thorough guide to the application process. It reveals advice from careers advisers and current students, guidance on making sense of university information and choosing courses. Also includes tips for the personal statement, interviews, admissions tests, UCAS Extra and Clearing.
Published by Trotman
Price £12.99
Publication date June 2011

How to Write a Winning UCAS Personal Statement
The personal statement is your chance to stand out from the crowd. Based on information from admissions tutors, this book will help you sell yourself. It includes specific guidance for over 30 popular subjects, common mistakes to avoid, information on what admissions tutors look for, and much more.
Published by Trotman
Price £12.99
Publication date March 2010

CHOOSING COURSES

Progression Series 2013 entry
The 'UCAS guide to getting into…' titles are designed to help you access good quality, useful information on some of the most competitive subject areas. The books cover advice on applying through UCAS, routes to qualifications, course details, job prospects, case studies and career advice.

New for 2013: information on the pros and cons of league tables and how to read them.

The UCAS Guide to getting into…
Art and Design
Economics, Finance and Accountancy
Engineering and Mathematics
Journalism, Broadcasting, Media Production and
  Performing Arts
Law
Medicine, Dentistry and Optometry
Nursing, Healthcare and Social Work
Psychology
Sports Science and Physiotherapy
Teaching and Education
Published by UCAS
Price £15.99 each
Publication date: June 2012

UCAS Parent Guide
Free of charge.
Order online at **www.ucas.com/parents**.
Publication date February 2012

Open Days 2012

Attending open days, taster courses and higher education conventions is an important part of the application process. This publication makes planning attendance at these events quick and easy.
Published annually by UCAS.
Price £3.50
Publication date January 2012

Heap 2013: University Degree Course Offers

An independent, reliable guide to selecting university degree courses in the UK.

The guide lists degree courses available at universities and colleges throughout the UK and the grades, UCAS points or equivalent that you need to achieve to get on to each course listed.
Published by Trotman
Price £32.99
Publication date May 2012

ESSENTIAL READING

Choosing Your Degree Course & University

With so many universities and courses to choose from, it is not an easy decision for students embarking on their journey to higher education. This guide will offer expert guidance on the questions students need to ask when considering the opportunities available.
Published by Trotman
Price £24.99
Publication date April 2012

Degree Course Descriptions

Providing details of the nature of degree courses, the descriptions in this book are written by heads of departments and senior lecturers at major universities. Each description contains an overview of the course area, details of course structures, career opportunities and more.
Published by COA
Price £12.99
Publication date September 2011

CHOOSING WHERE TO STUDY

The Virgin Guide to British Universities

An insider's guide to choosing a university or college. Written by students and using independent statistics, this guide evaluates what you get from a higher education institution.
Published by Virgin
Price £15.99
Publication date May 2011

Times Good University Guide 2013

How do you find the best university for the subject you wish to study? You need a guide that evaluates the quality of what is available, giving facts, figures and comparative assessments of universities. The rankings provide hard data, analysed, interpreted and presented by a team of experts.
Published by Harper Collins
Price £16.99
Publication date June 2012

A Parent's Guide to Graduate Jobs

A must-have guide for any parent who is worried about their child's job prospects when they graduate.

In this guide, the graduate careers guru, Paul Redmond, advises parents how to help their son or daughter:

- increase their employability
- boost their earning potential
- acquire essential work skills
- use their own contacts to get them ahead
- gain the right work experience.

Published by Trotman
Price £12.99
Publication date January 2012

Which Uni?

One person's perfect uni might be hell for someone else. Picking the right one will give you the best chance of future happiness, academic success and brighter job prospects. This guide is packed with tables from a variety of sources, rating universities on everything from the quality of teaching to the make-up of the student population and much more.
Published by Trotman
Price £14.99
Publication date September 2011

Getting into the UK's Best Universities and Courses

This book is for those who set their goals high and dream of studying on a highly regarded course at a good university. It provides information on selecting the best courses for a subject, the application and personal statement, interviews, results day, timescales for applications and much more.
Published by Trotman
Price £12.99
Publication date June 2011

FINANCIAL INFORMATION

Student Finance - e-book

All students need to know about tuition fees, loans, grants, bursaries and much more. Covering all forms of income and expenditure, this comprehensive guide is produced in association with UCAS and offers great value for money.
Published by Constable Robinson
Price £4.99
Publication date May 2012

CAREERS PLANNING

A-Z of Careers and Jobs

It is vital to be well informed about career decisions and this guide will help you make the right choice. It provides full details of the wide range of opportunities on the market, the personal qualities and skills needed for each job, entry qualifications and training, realistic salary expectations and useful contact details.
Published by Kogan Page
Price £16.99
Publication date March 2012

The Careers Directory

An indispensable resource for anyone seeking careers information, covering over 350 careers. It presents up-to-date information in an innovative double-page format. Ideal for students in years 10 to 13 who are considering their futures and for other careers professionals.
Published by COA
Price £14.99
Publication date September 2011

Careers with a Science Degree

Over 100 jobs and areas of work for graduates of biological, chemical and physical sciences are described in this guide.

Whether you have yet to choose your degree subject and want to know where the various choices could lead, or are struggling for ideas about what to do with your science degree, this book will guide and inspire you. The title includes: nature of the work and potential employers, qualifications required for entry, including personal qualities and skills; training routes and opportunities for career development and postgraduate study options.
Published by Lifetime Publishing
Price £12.99
Publication date September 2010

Careers with an Arts and Humanities Degree

Covers careers and graduate opportunities related to these degrees.

The book describes over 100 jobs and areas of work suitable for graduates from a range of disciplines including: English and modern languages, history and geography, music and the fine arts. The guide highlights: graduate opportunities, training routes, postgraduate study options and entry requirements.
Published by Lifetime Publishing
Price £12.99
Publication date September 2010

'Getting into...' guides

Clear and concise guides to help applicants secure places. They include qualifications required, advice on applying, tests, interviews and case studies. The guides give an honest view and discuss current issues and careers.

Getting into Oxford and Cambridge
Publication date April 2011
Getting into Veterinary School
Publication date February 2011
Published by Trotman
Price £12.99 each

DEFERRING ENTRY

Gap Years: The Essential Guide

The essential book for all young people planning a gap year before continuing with their education. This up-to-date guide provides essential information on specialist gap year programmes, as well as the vast range of jobs and voluntary opportunities available to young people around the world.
Published by Crimson Publishing
Price £9.99
Publication date April 2012

Gap Year Guidebook 2012

This thorough and easy-to-use guide contains everything you need to know before taking a gap year. It includes real-life traveller tips, hundreds of contact details, realistic advice on everything from preparing, learning and working abroad, coping with coming home and much more.
Published by John Catt Education
Price £14.99
Publication date November 2011

Summer Jobs Worldwide 2012

This unique and specialist guide contains over
40,000 jobs for all ages. No other book includes
such a variety and wealth of summer work
opportunities in Britain and aboard. Anything from
horse trainer in Iceland, to a guide for nature walks
in Peru, to a yoga centre helper in Greece, to an
animal keeper for London Zoo, can be found.
Published by Crimson Publishing
Price £14.99
Publication date November 2011

Please note all publications incur a postage and
packing charge. All information was correct at the time
of printing.

For a full list of publications, please visit
www.ucasbooks.com.

Save with UCAS Card

If you're in Year 12, S5 or equivalent and thinking about higher education, sign up for the **FREE** UCAS Card to receive all these benefits:

- information about courses and unis
- expert advice from UCAS
- exclusive discounts for card holders

UCAS

Register today at
www.ucas.com/ucascard

find us on
Facebook

Courses

Courses

Keen to get started on your law career? This section contains details of the various degree courses available at UK institutions.

EXPLAINING THE LIST OF COURSES

The list of courses has been divided into subject categories (see over for list of subjects). We list the universities and colleges by their UCAS institution codes. Within each institution, courses are listed first by award type (such as BA, BSc, FdA, HND, MA and many others), then alphabetically by course title.

You might find some courses showing an award type '(Mod)', which indicates a combined degree that might be modular in design. A small number of courses have award type '(FYr)'. This indicates a 12-month foundation course, after which students can choose to apply for a degree course. In either case, you should contact the university or college for further details.

Generally speaking, when a course comprises two or more subjects, the word used to connect the subjects indicates the make-up of the award: 'Subject A and Subject B' is a joint award, where both subjects carry equal weight; 'Subject A with Subject B' is a major/minor award, where Subject A accounts for at least 60% of your study. If the title shows 'Subject A/Subject B', it may indicate that students can decide on the weighting of the subjects at the end of the first year. You should check with the university or college for full details.

Each entry shows the UCAS course code and the duration of the course. Where known, the entry contains details of the minimum qualification requirements for the course, as supplied to UCAS by the universities and colleges. Bear in mind that possessing the minimum qualifications does not guarantee acceptance to the course: there may be far more applicants than places. You may be asked to attend an interview, present a portfolio or sit an admissions test (see page 96).

Courses with entry requirements that require applicants to disclose information about spent and unspent convictions and may require a Criminal Records Bureau (CRB) check, are marked '**CRB Check:** Required'.

Before applying for any course, you are advised to contact the university or college to check any changes in entry requirements and to see if any new courses have come on stream since the lists were approved for publication. To make this easy, each institution's entry starts with their address, email, phone and fax details, as well as their website address. You will also find it useful to check Course Finder at **www.ucas.com**.

LIST OF SUBJECT CATEGORIES

The list of courses in this section has been divided into the following subject categories.

BUSINESS & MANAGEMENT COMBINATIONS

A20 THE UNIVERSITY OF ABERDEEN
UNIVERSITY OFFICE
KING'S COLLEGE
ABERDEEN AB24 3FX
t: +44 (0) 1224 273504 f: +44 (0) 1224 272034
e: sras@abdn.ac.uk
// www.abdn.ac.uk/sras

M1N2 LLB Law with options in Management Studies
Duration: 3FT/4FT Ord/Hon
Entry Requirements: *GCE:* BBB. *SQAH:* AABB-ABBBB. *SQAAH:* BBB. *IB:* 34.

MN92 MA Legal Studies and Management Studies
Duration: 4FT Hon
Entry Requirements: *GCE:* BBB. *SQAH:* BBBB. *IB:* 30.

A40 ABERYSTWYTH UNIVERSITY
ABERYSTWYTH UNIVERSITY, WELCOME CENTRE
PENGLAIS CAMPUS
ABERYSTWYTH
CEREDIGION SY23 3FB
t: 01970 622021 f: 01970 627410
e: ug-admissions@aber.ac.uk
// www.aber.ac.uk

M1N1 BA Law with Business & Management
Duration: 3FT Hon
Entry Requirements: *GCE:* 340. *IB:* 28.

N1M1 BScEcon Business & Management with Law
Duration: 3FT Hon
Entry Requirements: *GCE:* 280. *IB:* 27.

A80 ASTON UNIVERSITY, BIRMINGHAM
ASTON TRIANGLE
BIRMINGHAM B4 7ET
t: 0121 204 4444 f: 0121 204 3696
e: admissions@aston.ac.uk (automatic response)
// www.aston.ac.uk/prospective-students/ug

M1N2 LLB Law with Management
Duration: 4SW Hon   CRB Check: Required
Entry Requirements: *GCE:* AAB. *SQAH:* AAAAB. *SQAAH:* AAB. *IB:* 34. *OCR NED:* D1

M1NF LLB Law with Management
Duration: 3FT Hon   CRB Check: Required
Entry Requirements: *GCE:* AAB. *SQAH:* AAAAB. *SQAAH:* AAB. *IB:* 34. *OCR NED:* D1

B90 THE UNIVERSITY OF BUCKINGHAM
YEOMANRY HOUSE
HUNTER STREET
BUCKINGHAM MK18 1EG
t: 01280 820313 f: 01280 822245
e: info@buckingham.ac.uk
// www.buckingham.ac.uk

M1N2 LLB Law with Management Studies
Duration: 2FT Hon
Entry Requirements: *GCE:* 300. *SQAH:* ABBB. *SQAAH:* BBB. *IB:* 34. *OCR NED:* M2 Interview required.

C20 CARDIFF METROPOLITAN UNIVERSITY (UWIC)
ADMISSIONS UNIT
LLANDAFF CAMPUS
WESTERN AVENUE
CARDIFF CF5 2YB
t: 029 2041 6070 f: 029 2041 6286
e: admissions@cardiffmet.ac.uk
// www.cardiffmet.ac.uk

N1M1 BA Business & Management Studies with Law
Duration: 3FT/4SW Hon
Entry Requirements: *GCE:* 300. *IB:* 26. *BTEC ExtDip:* DDM. *OCR NED:* M1

C85 COVENTRY UNIVERSITY
THE STUDENT CENTRE
COVENTRY UNIVERSITY
1 GULSON RD
COVENTRY CV1 2JH
t: 024 7615 2222 f: 024 7615 2223
e: studentenquiries@coventry.ac.uk
// www.coventry.ac.uk

MN2F BA Legal Studies and Management
Duration: 3FT Hon
Entry Requirements: *GCE:* 260. *IB:* 28. *BTEC Dip:* DD. *BTEC ExtDip:* MMM. *OCR ND:* D *OCR NED:* M3

MN22 HNC Legal Studies and Management
Duration: 1FT HNC
Entry Requirements: *GCE:* 160. *IB:* 24. *BTEC Dip:* MM. *BTEC ExtDip:* MPP. *OCR ND:* P1 *OCR NED:* P2

22NM HND Legal Studies and Management
Duration: 2FT HND
Entry Requirements: *GCE:* 200. *IB:* 24. *BTEC Dip:* DM. *BTEC ExtDip:* MMP. *OCR ND:* M1 *OCR NED:* P1

D26 DE MONTFORT UNIVERSITY
THE GATEWAY
LEICESTER LE1 9BH
t: 0116 255 1551 f: 0116 250 6204
e: enquiries@dmu.ac.uk
// www.dmu.ac.uk

M1N6 BA Human Resource Management and Law
Duration: 3FT/4SW Hon
Entry Requirements: *GCE:* 280. *IB:* 28. *BTEC Dip:* D*D*. *BTEC ExtDip:* DMM. *OCR NED:* M2 Interview required.

D39 UNIVERSITY OF DERBY
KEDLESTON ROAD
DERBY DE22 1GB
t: 01332 591167 f: 01332 597724
e: askadmissions@derby.ac.uk
// www.derby.ac.uk

MN26 BA Applied Criminology and Human Resources Management
Duration: 3FT Hon
Entry Requirements: *Foundation:* Distinction. *GCE:* 260-300. *IB:* 28. *BTEC Dip:* D*D*. *BTEC ExtDip:* DMM. *OCR NED:* M2

NM21 BA Business Management and Law
Duration: 3FT Hon
Entry Requirements: *Foundation:* Distinction. *GCE:* 260-300. *IB:* 28. *BTEC Dip:* D*D*. *BTEC ExtDip:* DMM. *OCR NED:* M2

NM61 BA Human Resource Management and Law
Duration: 3FT Hon
Entry Requirements: *Foundation:* Distinction. *GCE:* 260-300. *IB:* 28. *BTEC Dip:* D*D*. *BTEC ExtDip:* DMM. *OCR NED:* M2

D86 DURHAM UNIVERSITY
DURHAM UNIVERSITY
UNIVERSITY OFFICE
DURHAM DH1 3HP
t: 0191 334 2000 f: 0191 334 6055
e: admissions@durham.ac.uk
// www.durham.ac.uk

LMV0 BA Combined Honours in Social Sciences option - Management Studies
Duration: 3FT Hon
Entry Requirements: *GCE:* AAA. *SQAH:* AAAAA. *SQAAH:* AAA. *IB:* 38.

E28 UNIVERSITY OF EAST LONDON
DOCKLANDS CAMPUS
UNIVERSITY WAY
LONDON E16 2RD
t: 020 8223 3333 f: 020 8223 2978
e: study@uel.ac.uk
// www.uel.ac.uk

N2MC BA Business Management with Law
Duration: 3FT Hon
Entry Requirements: *GCE:* 240. *IB:* 24.

NM21 BA Business Management/Law
Duration: 3FT Hon
Entry Requirements: *GCE:* 240. *IB:* 24.

N2M1 BSc Health Services Management with Law
Duration: 3FT Hon
Entry Requirements: *GCE:* 240. *IB:* 28.

M1N2 LLB Law with Business Management
Duration: 3FT Hon
Entry Requirements: *GCE:* 240. *IB:* 24.

E42 EDGE HILL UNIVERSITY
ORMSKIRK
LANCASHIRE L39 4QP
t: 01695 657000 f: 01695 584355
e: study@edgehill.ac.uk
// www.edgehill.ac.uk

M1N2 LLB Law with Management
Duration: 3FT Hon
Entry Requirements: *GCE:* 280. *IB:* 26. *OCR ND:* D *OCR NED:* M2

E59 EDINBURGH NAPIER UNIVERSITY
CRAIGLOCKHART CAMPUS
EDINBURGH EH14 1DJ
t: +44 (0)8452 60 60 40 f: 0131 455 6464
e: info@napier.ac.uk
// www.napier.ac.uk

N2M1 BA Business Management with Law
Duration: 3FT/4FT Ord/Hon
Entry Requirements: *GCE:* 230.

M1N1 LLB Law with Business Management
Duration: 3FT/4FT Ord/Hon
Entry Requirements: Contact the institution for details.

G28 UNIVERSITY OF GLASGOW
71 SOUTHPARK AVENUE
UNIVERSITY OF GLASGOW
GLASGOW G12 8QQ
t: 0141 330 6062 f: 0141 330 2961
e: student.recruitment@glasgow.ac.uk
// www.glasgow.ac.uk

MN12 LLB Law/Business Management
Duration: 4FT Hon
Entry Requirements: *GCE:* AAB. *SQAH:* AAAAB. *IB:* 34.
Admissions Test required.

G74 GREENWICH SCHOOL OF MANAGEMENT
MERIDIAN HOUSE
ROYAL HILL
GREENWICH
LONDON SE10 8RD
t: +44(0)20 8516 7800 f: +44(0)20 8516 7801
e: admissions@greenwich-college.ac.uk
// www.greenwich-college.ac.uk/
?utm_source=UCAS&utm_medium=Profil

MCN2 BSc Law with Management (Accelerated with Foundation Year)
Duration: 3FT Hon
Entry Requirements: *OCR ND:* P3 Interview required.

M1N2 BSc Law with Management (Accelerated)
Duration: 2FT Hon
Entry Requirements: *GCE:* 240-300. *IB:* 24. *OCR ND:* D *OCR NED:* M3 Interview required.

H24 HERIOT-WATT UNIVERSITY, EDINBURGH
EDINBURGH CAMPUS
EDINBURGH EH14 4AS
t: 0131 449 5111 f: 0131 451 3630
e: ugadmissions@hw.ac.uk
// www.hw.ac.uk

N2M2 MA Business Management with Business Law
Duration: 4FT Hon
Entry Requirements: *GCE:* BBB. *SQAH:* AAAB-BBBBC. *SQAAH:* BB. *IB:* 29.

K12 KEELE UNIVERSITY
KEELE UNIVERSITY
STAFFORDSHIRE ST5 5BG
t: 01782 734005 f: 01782 632343
e: undergraduate@keele.ac.uk
// www.keele.ac.uk

MNX2 BA Business Management and Criminology
Duration: 3FT Hon
Entry Requirements: *GCE:* ABB.

MN19 BA Business Management and Law
Duration: 3FT Hon
Entry Requirements: *GCE:* ABB.

MN16 BA Human Resource Management and Law
Duration: 3FT Hon
Entry Requirements: *GCE:* ABB.

L34 UNIVERSITY OF LEICESTER
UNIVERSITY ROAD
LEICESTER LE1 7RH
t: 0116 252 5281 f: 0116 252 2447
e: admissions@le.ac.uk
// www.le.ac.uk

MN22 LLB Law with Management
Duration: 3FT Hon
Entry Requirements: Contact the institution for details.

L46 LIVERPOOL HOPE UNIVERSITY
HOPE PARK
LIVERPOOL L16 9JD
t: 0151 291 3331 f: 0151 291 3434
e: administration@hope.ac.uk
// www.hope.ac.uk

NM2C BA Business Management and Law
Duration: 3FT Hon
Entry Requirements: *GCE:* 300-320. *IB:* 25.

L68 LONDON METROPOLITAN UNIVERSITY
166-220 HOLLOWAY ROAD
LONDON N7 8DB
t: 020 7133 4200
e: admissions@londonmet.ac.uk
// www.londonmet.ac.uk

MN2F BA Business Management and Business Law
Duration: 3FT Hon
Entry Requirements: *GCE:* 240. *IB:* 28.

NM62 BA Human Resource Management and Employment Law
Duration: 3FT Hon
Entry Requirements: *GCE:* 240. *IB:* 28.

MN11 BA Law and Business Management
Duration: 3FT Hon
Entry Requirements: *GCE:* 240. *IB:* 28.

M40 THE MANCHESTER METROPOLITAN UNIVERSITY
ADMISSIONS OFFICE
ALL SAINTS (GMS)
ALL SAINTS
MANCHESTER M15 6BH
t: 0161 247 2000
// www.mmu.ac.uk

N2M2 BA Business Management with Legal Studies
Duration: 3FT Hon
Entry Requirements: *GCE:* 280. *IB:* 28. *BTEC Dip:* D*D*. *BTEC ExtDip:* DMM.

MN2P BA Human Resource Management/Legal Studies
Duration: 3FT Hon
Entry Requirements: *GCE:* 280. *IB:* 28. *BTEC Dip:* D*D*. *BTEC ExtDip:* DMM.

N38 UNIVERSITY OF NORTHAMPTON
PARK CAMPUS
BOUGHTON GREEN ROAD
NORTHAMPTON NN2 7AL
t: 0800 358 2232 f: 01604 722083
e: admissions@northampton.ac.uk
// www.northampton.ac.uk

M9NG BA Criminology with Applied Management
Duration: 3FT Hon
Entry Requirements: *GCE:* 260-280. *SQAH:* AAA-BBBB. *IB:* 24. *BTEC Dip:* DD. *BTEC ExtDip:* DMM. *OCR ND:* D *OCR NED:* M2

M9NV BA Criminology/Events Management
Duration: 3FT Hon
Entry Requirements: *GCE:* 260-280. *SQAH:* AAA-BBBB. *IB:* 24. *BTEC Dip:* DD. *BTEC ExtDip:* DMM. *OCR ND:* D *OCR NED:* M2

M9N2 BA Criminology/Management
Duration: 3FT Hon
Entry Requirements: *GCE:* 260-280. *SQAH:* AAA-BBBB. *IB:* 24. *BTEC Dip:* DD. *BTEC ExtDip:* DMM. *OCR ND:* D *OCR NED:* M2

M9FV BA Criminology/Wastes Management
Duration: 3FT Hon
Entry Requirements: *GCE:* 260-280. *SQAH:* AAA-BBBB. *IB:* 24. *BTEC Dip:* DD. *BTEC ExtDip:* DMM. *OCR ND:* D *OCR NED:* M2

N8MX BA Events Management/Criminology
Duration: 3FT Hon
Entry Requirements: *GCE:* 260-280. *SQAH:* AAA-BBBB. *IB:* 24. *BTEC Dip:* DD. *BTEC ExtDip:* DMM. *OCR ND:* D *OCR NED:* M2

N8M1 BA Events Management/Law
Duration: 3FT Hon
Entry Requirements: *GCE:* 260-280. *SQAH:* AAA-BBBB. *IB:* 24. *BTEC Dip:* DD. *BTEC ExtDip:* DMM. *OCR ND:* D *OCR NED:* M2

N6M1 BA Human Resource Management/Law
Duration: 3FT Hon
Entry Requirements: *GCE:* 260-280. *SQAH:* AAA-BBBB. *IB:* 24. *BTEC Dip:* DD. *BTEC ExtDip:* DMM. *OCR ND:* D *OCR NED:* M2

M1NG BA Law with Applied Management
Duration: 3FT Hon
Entry Requirements: *GCE:* 260-280. *SQAH:* AAA-BBBB. *IB:* 24. *BTEC Dip:* DD. *BTEC ExtDip:* DMM. *OCR ND:* D *OCR NED:* M2

M1N8 BA Law/Events Management
Duration: 3FT Hon
Entry Requirements: *GCE:* 260-280. *SQAH:* AAA-BBBB. *IB:* 24. *BTEC Dip:* DD. *BTEC ExtDip:* DMM. *OCR ND:* D *OCR NED:* M2

M1N6 BA Law/Human Resource Management
Duration: 3FT Hon
Entry Requirements: *GCE:* 260-280. *SQAH:* AAA-BBBB. *IB:* 24. *BTEC Dip:* DD. *BTEC ExtDip:* DMM. *OCR ND:* D *OCR NED:* M2

M1N2 BA Law/Management
Duration: 3FT Hon
Entry Requirements: *GCE:* 260-280. *SQAH:* AAA-BBBB. *IB:* 24. *BTEC Dip:* DD. *BTEC ExtDip:* DMM. *OCR ND:* D *OCR NED:* M2

M1FV BA Law/Wastes Management
Duration: 3FT Hon
Entry Requirements: *GCE:* 260-280. *SQAH:* AAA-BBBB. *IB:* 24. *BTEC Dip:* DD. *BTEC ExtDip:* DMM. *OCR ND:* D *OCR NED:* M2

N2M9 BA Management/Criminology
Duration: 3FT Hon
Entry Requirements: *GCE:* 260-280. *SQAH:* AAA-BBBB. *IB:* 24. *BTEC Dip:* DD. *BTEC ExtDip:* DMM. *OCR ND:* D *OCR NED:* M2

F8MX BSc Wastes Management/Criminology
Duration: 3FT Hon
Entry Requirements: *GCE:* 260-280. *SQAH:* AAA-BBBB. *IB:* 24. *BTEC Dip:* DD. *BTEC ExtDip:* DMM. *OCR ND:* D *OCR NED:* M2

F8MC BSc Wastes Management/Law
Duration: 3FT Hon
Entry Requirements: *GCE:* 260-280. *SQAH:* AAA-BBBB. *IB:* 24. *BTEC Dip:* DD. *BTEC ExtDip:* DMM. *OCR ND:* D *OCR NED:* M2

N77 NORTHUMBRIA UNIVERSITY
TRINITY BUILDING
NORTHUMBERLAND ROAD
NEWCASTLE UPON TYNE NE1 8ST
t: 0191 243 7420 f: 0191 227 4561
e: er.admissions@northumbria.ac.uk
// www.northumbria.ac.uk

M1N8 LLB Law with Property Asset Management
Duration: 3FT Hon
Entry Requirements: *GCE:* ABB. *SQAH:* ABBBC. *SQAAH:* ABC. *IB:* 27. *BTEC ExtDip:* DDM. *OCR NED:* D2

R36 ROBERT GORDON UNIVERSITY
ROBERT GORDON UNIVERSITY
SCHOOLHILL
ABERDEEN
SCOTLAND AB10 1FR
t: 01224 26 27 28 f: 01224 26 21 47
e: UGOffice@rgu.ac.uk
// www.rgu.ac.uk

M990 BA Law and Management
Duration: 4FT Hon
Entry Requirements: *GCE:* BCC. *SQAH:* BBBC. *IB:* 27.

S03 THE UNIVERSITY OF SALFORD
SALFORD M5 4WT
t: 0161 295 4545 f: 0161 295 4646
e: ug-admissions@salford.ac.uk
// www.salford.ac.uk

N1M1 BSc Business and Management Studies with Law
Duration: 3FT Hon
Entry Requirements: *GCE:* BBC. *IB:* 29. *BTEC ExtDip:* DMM. *OCR ND:* D *OCR NED:* M2

N1MC BSc Business and Management Studies with Law with Professional Experience
Duration: 4FT Hon
Entry Requirements: Contact the institution for details.

S64 ST MARY'S UNIVERSITY COLLEGE, TWICKENHAM
WALDEGRAVE ROAD
STRAWBERRY HILL
MIDDLESEX TW1 4SX
t: 020 8240 4029 f: 020 8240 2361
e: admit@smuc.ac.uk
// www.smuc.ac.uk

MN22 BA Business Law and Management Studies
Duration: 3FT Hon
Entry Requirements: *GCE:* 220. *IB:* 28. *OCR ND:* M1 *OCR NED:* P1 Interview required.

S75 THE UNIVERSITY OF STIRLING
STUDENT RECRUITMENT & ADMISSIONS SERVICE
UNIVERSITY OF STIRLING
STIRLING
SCOTLAND FK9 4LA
t: 01786 467044 f: 01786 466800
e: admissions@stir.ac.uk
// www.stir.ac.uk

MN16 BA Human Resource Management and Law
Duration: 4FT Hon
Entry Requirements: *GCE:* BBC. *SQAH:* BBBB. *SQAAH:* AAA-CCC. *IB:* 32. *BTEC ExtDip:* DMM.

S78 THE UNIVERSITY OF STRATHCLYDE
GLASGOW G1 1XQ
t: 0141 552 4400 f: 0141 552 0775
// www.strath.ac.uk

NM62 BA Human Resource Management and Business Law
Duration: 4FT Hon
Entry Requirements: *GCE:* AAB. *SQAH:* AAAABB-AAAB. *IB:* 36.

MN16 BA Law and Human Resource Management
Duration: 4FT Hon
Entry Requirements: *GCE:* ABB. *SQAH:* AAABB-AAAB. *IB:* 34.

GM22 BA Management Science and Business Law
Duration: 4FT Hon
Entry Requirements: *GCE:* AAB. *SQAH:* AAAABB-AAAB. *IB:* 36.

S84 UNIVERSITY OF SUNDERLAND
STUDENT HELPLINE
THE STUDENT GATEWAY
CHESTER ROAD
SUNDERLAND SR1 3SD
t: 0191 515 3000 f: 0191 515 3805
e: student.helpline@sunderland.ac.uk
// www.sunderland.ac.uk

NM19 BA Business Management and Criminology
Duration: 3FT Hon
Entry Requirements: *GCE:* 260-360. *IB:* 31. *OCR ND:* D *OCR NED:* M3

NM21 BA Business Management and Law
Duration: 3FT Hon
Entry Requirements: *GCE:* 260-360. *OCR ND:* D *OCR NED:* M3

N1M9 BA Business Management with Criminology
Duration: 3FT Hon
Entry Requirements: *GCE:* 260-360. *IB:* 31. *OCR ND:* D *OCR NED:* M3

MN91 BA Criminology and Business Management
Duration: 3FT Hon
Entry Requirements: *GCE:* 260-360. *OCR ND:* D *OCR NED:* M3

M9N1 BA Criminology with Business Management
Duration: 3FT Hon
Entry Requirements: *GCE:* 260-360. *OCR ND:* D *OCR NED:* M3

S93 SWANSEA UNIVERSITY
SINGLETON PARK
SWANSEA SA2 8PP
t: 01792 295111 f: 01792 295110
e: admissions@swansea.ac.uk
// www.swansea.ac.uk

N2M1 BA Business Management with Law
Duration: 3FT Hon
Entry Requirements: *GCE:* ABB-BBB. *IB:* 33.

U20 UNIVERSITY OF ULSTER
COLERAINE
CO. LONDONDERRY
NORTHERN IRELAND BT52 1SA
t: 028 7012 4221 f: 028 7012 4908
e: online@ulster.ac.uk
// www.ulster.ac.uk

M1N6 LLB Law with Human Resource Management
Duration: 3FT Hon
Entry Requirements: *GCE:* BBB. *SQAH:* AABCC. *SQAAH:* BBB. *IB:* 25.

W50 UNIVERSITY OF WESTMINSTER
2ND FLOOR, CAVENDISH HOUSE
101 NEW CAVENDISH STREET,
LONDON W1W 6XH
t: 020 7915 5511
e: course-enquiries@westminster.ac.uk
// www.westminster.ac.uk

NM22 BA Business Management (Law)
Duration: 3FT/4SW Hon
Entry Requirements: *GCE:* BCC. *IB:* 28.

W75 UNIVERSITY OF WOLVERHAMPTON
ADMISSIONS UNIT
MX207, CAMP STREET
WOLVERHAMPTON
WEST MIDLANDS WV1 1AD
t: 01902 321000 f: 01902 321896
e: admissions@wlv.ac.uk
// www.wlv.ac.uk

NM61 BA Human Resource Management and Law
Duration: 3FT Hon
Entry Requirements: *GCE:* 160-220. *IB:* 28.

W76 UNIVERSITY OF WINCHESTER
WINCHESTER
HANTS SO22 4NR
t: 01962 827234 f: 01962 827288
e: course.enquiries@winchester.ac.uk
// www.winchester.ac.uk

NM81 BA Event Management and Law
Duration: 3FT Hon
Entry Requirements: *GCE:* 260-300. *IB:* 25.

MN12 BA Law and Business Management
Duration: 3FT Hon
Entry Requirements: *Foundation:* Distinction. *GCE:* 260-300. *IB:* 25. *OCR ND:* D *OCR NED:* M2

MN1V BA Law and Sports Management
Duration: 3FT Hon
Entry Requirements: *GCE:* 260-300. *IB:* 24.

BUSINESS LAW

A30 UNIVERSITY OF ABERTAY DUNDEE
BELL STREET
DUNDEE DD1 1HG
t: 01382 308080 f: 01382 308081
e: sro@abertay.ac.uk
// www.abertay.ac.uk

M120 BA European Business Law (Top-Up)
Duration: 2FT Hon
Entry Requirements: HND required.

A40 ABERYSTWYTH UNIVERSITY
ABERYSTWYTH UNIVERSITY, WELCOME CENTRE
PENGLAIS CAMPUS
ABERYSTWYTH
CEREDIGION SY23 3FB
t: 01970 622021 f: 01970 627410
e: ug-admissions@aber.ac.uk
// www.aber.ac.uk

M140 LLB Business Law
Duration: 3FT Hon
Entry Requirements: *GCE:* 340. *IB:* 34.

B06 BANGOR UNIVERSITY
BANGOR UNIVERSITY
BANGOR
GWYNEDD LL57 2DG
t: 01248 388484 f: 01248 370451
e: admissions@bangor.ac.uk
// www.bangor.ac.uk

NM11 BA Business and Law
Duration: 3FT Hon
Entry Requirements: Contact the institution for details.

M1N1 LLB Law with Business Studies
Duration: 3FT Hon
Entry Requirements: *GCE:* 280. *IB:* 28.

B25 BIRMINGHAM CITY UNIVERSITY
PERRY BARR
BIRMINGHAM B42 2SU
t: 0121 331 5595 f: 0121 331 7994
// www.bcu.ac.uk

M1MG LLB Law with Business Law
Duration: 3FT Hon
Entry Requirements: *GCE:* 280. *IB:* 28. *OCR ND:* D

B32 THE UNIVERSITY OF BIRMINGHAM
EDGBASTON
BIRMINGHAM B15 2TT
t: 0121 415 8900 f: 0121 414 7159
e: admissions@bham.ac.uk
// www.birmingham.ac.uk

M1N1 LLB Law with Business Studies
Duration: 3FT Hon
Entry Requirements: *GCE:* A*AB-AAA. *SQAAH:* AAA. *IB:* 36. *BTEC SubDip:* D. *BTEC Dip:* D*D*. *BTEC ExtDip:* D*D*D. Admissions Test required.

B54 BPP UNIVERSITY COLLEGE OF PROFESSIONAL STUDIES LIMITED
142-144 UXBRIDGE ROAD
LONDON W12 8AW
t: 02031 312 298
e: admissions@bpp.com
// undergraduate.bpp.com/

M221 LLB Business Law
Duration: 3FT Hon
Entry Requirements: *GCE:* 300.

M225 LLB Business Law (Accelerated)
Duration: 2FT Hon
Entry Requirements: *GCE:* 300.

B56 THE UNIVERSITY OF BRADFORD
RICHMOND ROAD
BRADFORD
WEST YORKSHIRE BD7 1DP
t: 0800 073 1225 f: 01274 235585
e: course-enquiries@bradford.ac.uk
// www.bradford.ac.uk

NM11 BA Business Studies and Law
Duration: 3FT Hon
Entry Requirements: *GCE:* 300. *IB:* 25.

NM21 BA Business Studies and Law (4 years)
Duration: 4SW Hon
Entry Requirements: *GCE:* 300. *IB:* 25.

B72 UNIVERSITY OF BRIGHTON
MITHRAS HOUSE 211
LEWES ROAD
BRIGHTON BN2 4AT
t: 01273 644644 f: 01273 642607
e: admissions@brighton.ac.uk
// www.brighton.ac.uk

M1NC LLB Law with Business
Duration: 3FT/4SW Hon
Entry Requirements: *GCE:* BBB. *IB:* 30.

B80 UNIVERSITY OF THE WEST OF ENGLAND, BRISTOL
FRENCHAY CAMPUS
COLDHARBOUR LANE
BRISTOL BS16 1QY
t: +44 (0)117 32 83333 f: +44 (0)117 32 82810
e: admissions@uwe.ac.uk
// www.uwe.ac.uk

NM11 BA Business and Law
Duration: 3FT/4SW Hon
Entry Requirements: *GCE:* 320.

B90 THE UNIVERSITY OF BUCKINGHAM
YEOMANRY HOUSE
HUNTER STREET
BUCKINGHAM MK18 1EG
t: 01280 820313 f: 01280 822245
e: info@buckingham.ac.uk
// www.buckingham.ac.uk

LM11 BSc Economics, Business and Law
Duration: 2FT Hon
Entry Requirements: *GCE:* BBB. *SQAH:* ABBB. *SQAAH:* BBB. *IB:* 34.

M1N3 LLB Law with Business Finance
Duration: 2FT Hon
Entry Requirements: *GCE:* 300. *SQAH:* ABBB. *SQAAH:* BBB. *IB:* 34. *OCR NED:* M2 Interview required.

B94 BUCKINGHAMSHIRE NEW UNIVERSITY
QUEEN ALEXANDRA ROAD
HIGH WYCOMBE
BUCKINGHAMSHIRE HP11 2JZ
t: 0800 0565 660 f: 01494 605 023
e: admissions@bucks.ac.uk
// bucks.ac.uk

M221 LLB Business Law
Duration: 3FT Hon
Entry Requirements: *GCE:* 300-340. *IB:* 25. *OCR ND:* D *OCR NED:* M2

C10 CANTERBURY CHRIST CHURCH UNIVERSITY
NORTH HOLMES ROAD
CANTERBURY
KENT CT1 1QU
t: 01227 782900 f: 01227 782888
e: admissions@canterbury.ac.uk
// www.canterbury.ac.uk

MN91 BA Applied Criminology and Business Studies
Duration: 3FT Hon
Entry Requirements: *GCE:* 240. *IB:* 24.

M9N1 BA Applied Criminology with Business Studies
Duration: 3FT Hon
Entry Requirements: *GCE:* 240. *IB:* 24.

GM52 BA Business Computing and Legal Studies
Duration: 3FT Hon
Entry Requirements: *GCE:* 240. *IB:* 24.

G5M2 BA Business Computing with Legal Studies
Duration: 3FT Hon
Entry Requirements: *GCE:* 240. *IB:* 24.

M2GM BA Legal Studies with Business Computing
Duration: 3FT Hon
Entry Requirements: *GCE:* 240. *IB:* 24.

MN21 BA/BSc Legal Studies and Business Studies
Duration: 3FT Hon
Entry Requirements: *GCE:* 240. *IB:* 24.

M2N1 BA/BSc Legal Studies with Business Studies
Duration: 3FT Hon
Entry Requirements: *GCE:* 240. *IB:* 24.

N1M9 BSc Business Studies with Applied Criminology
Duration: 3FT Hon
Entry Requirements: *GCE:* 240. *IB:* 24.

N1M2 BSc Business Studies with Legal Studies
Duration: 3FT Hon
Entry Requirements: *GCE:* 240. *IB:* 24.

C30 UNIVERSITY OF CENTRAL LANCASHIRE
PRESTON
LANCS PR1 2HE
t: 01772 201201 f: 01772 894954
e: uadmissions@uclan.ac.uk
// www.uclan.ac.uk

MN11 BA Law and Business
Duration: 3FT Hon
Entry Requirements: *GCE:* 260-300. *IB:* 28. *OCR ND:* D *OCR NED:* M2

C55 UNIVERSITY OF CHESTER
PARKGATE ROAD
CHESTER CH1 4BJ
t: 01244 511000 f: 01244 511300
e: enquiries@chester.ac.uk
// www.chester.ac.uk

MN11 BA Law and Business
Duration: 3FT Hon
Entry Requirements: *GCE:* 240-280. *SQAH:* BBBB. *IB:* 26.

D26 DE MONTFORT UNIVERSITY
THE GATEWAY
LEICESTER LE1 9BH
t: 0116 255 1551 f: 0116 250 6204
e: enquiries@dmu.ac.uk
// www.dmu.ac.uk

MN11 BA Business and Law
Duration: 3FT/4SW Hon
Entry Requirements: *GCE:* 280. *IB:* 28. *BTEC Dip:* D*D*. *BTEC ExtDip:* DMM. *OCR NED:* M2 Interview required.

M221 LLB Business Law
Duration: 3FT/3FT Hon/Ord
Entry Requirements: *GCE:* 300. *IB:* 30. *BTEC ExtDip:* DDM. Interview required.

E28 UNIVERSITY OF EAST LONDON
DOCKLANDS CAMPUS
UNIVERSITY WAY
LONDON E16 2RD
t: 020 8223 3333 f: 020 8223 2978
e: study@uel.ac.uk
// www.uel.ac.uk

GM5C BA/BSc Business Information Systems/Law
Duration: 3FT Hon
Entry Requirements: *GCE:* 240. *IB:* 24.

E56 THE UNIVERSITY OF EDINBURGH
STUDENT RECRUITMENT & ADMISSIONS
57 GEORGE SQUARE
EDINBURGH EH8 9JU
t: 0131 650 4360 f: 0131 651 1236
e: sra.enquiries@ed.ac.uk
// www.ed.ac.uk/studying/undergraduate/

MN11 LLB Law and Business Studies
Duration: 4FT Hon
Entry Requirements: *GCE:* AAA-BBB. *SQAH:* AAAA-BBBB. *IB:* 34.

NM11 MA Business Studies and Law
Duration: 4FT Hon
Entry Requirements: *GCE:* AAA-BBB. *SQAH:* AAAA-BBBB. *IB:* 34.

E77 EUROPEAN BUSINESS SCHOOL, LONDON
INNER CIRCLE
REGENT'S PARK
LONDON NW1 4NS
t: +44 (0)20 7487 7505 f: +44 (0)20 7487 7425
e: ebsl@regents.ac.uk
// www.ebslondon.ac.uk

N1M1 BA International Business with Law and one language
Duration: 3FT/4FT Hon
Entry Requirements: *GCE:* 240-300.

N1MC BA International Business with Law and two languages
Duration: 3FT/4FT Hon
Entry Requirements: *GCE:* 240-300.

G14 UNIVERSITY OF GLAMORGAN, CARDIFF AND PONTYPRIDD
ENQUIRIES AND ADMISSIONS UNIT
PONTYPRIDD CF37 1DL
t: 08456 434030 f: 01443 654050
e: enquiries@glam.ac.uk
// www.glam.ac.uk

NM11 BA Business and Law
Duration: 3FT Hon
Entry Requirements: *GCE:* BBC. *IB:* 25. *BTEC SubDip:* M. *BTEC Dip:* D*D*. *BTEC ExtDip:* DMM. *OCR NED:* M2

N1M1 BA Business with Law
Duration: 3FT Hon
Entry Requirements: *GCE:* 240-280. *IB:* 30.

M1N1 LLB Law with Business
Duration: 3FT Hon
Entry Requirements: *GCE:* BBB. *IB:* 26. *BTEC SubDip:* M. *BTEC Dip:* D*D*. *BTEC ExtDip:* DDM.

G28 UNIVERSITY OF GLASGOW
71 SOUTHPARK AVENUE
UNIVERSITY OF GLASGOW
GLASGOW G12 8QQ
t: 0141 330 6062 f: 0141 330 2961
e: student.recruitment@glasgow.ac.uk
// www.glasgow.ac.uk

MN11 LLB Law/Business Economics
Duration: 4FT Hon
Entry Requirements: *GCE:* AAB. *SQAH:* AAAAB. *IB:* 34.
Admissions Test required.

G70 UNIVERSITY OF GREENWICH
GREENWICH CAMPUS
OLD ROYAL NAVAL COLLEGE
PARK ROW
LONDON SE10 9LS
t: 020 8331 9000 f: 020 8331 8145
e: courseinfo@gre.ac.uk
// www.gre.ac.uk

M221 BA Business Law
Duration: 3FT Hon
Entry Requirements: *GCE:* 260. *IB:* 24.

H24 HERIOT-WATT UNIVERSITY, EDINBURGH
EDINBURGH CAMPUS
EDINBURGH EH14 4AS
t: 0131 449 5111 f: 0131 451 3630
e: ugadmissions@hw.ac.uk
// www.hw.ac.uk

NM32 MA Accountancy and Business Law
Duration: 4FT Hon
Entry Requirements: *GCE:* BBB. *SQAH:* AAAB-BBBBC. *SQAAH:* BB. *IB:* 29.

LM12 MA Economics and Business Law
Duration: 4FT Hon
Entry Requirements: *GCE:* BBB. *SQAH:* AAAB-BBBBC. *SQAAH:* BB. *IB:* 29.

NMH2 MA Finance and Business Law
Duration: 4FT Hon
Entry Requirements: *GCE:* BBB. *SQAH:* AAAB-BBBBC. *SQAAH:* BB. *IB:* 29.

H36 UNIVERSITY OF HERTFORDSHIRE
UNIVERSITY ADMISSIONS SERVICE
COLLEGE LANE
HATFIELD
HERTS AL10 9AB
t: 01707 284800
// www.herts.ac.uk

N1M1 BSc Business/Law
Duration: 3FT/4SW Hon
Entry Requirements: *GCE:* 320.

M1N1 BSc Law/Business
Duration: 3FT/4SW Hon
Entry Requirements: *GCE:* 320.

N1MC FdA Business with Law
Duration: 2FT Fdg
Entry Requirements: *GCE:* 120.

H60 THE UNIVERSITY OF HUDDERSFIELD
QUEENSGATE
HUDDERSFIELD HD1 3DH
t: 01484 473969 f: 01484 472765
e: admissionsandrecords@hud.ac.uk
// www.hud.ac.uk

MN11 BA Law and Business
Duration: 3FT/4SW Hon
Entry Requirements: *GCE:* 300.

H72 THE UNIVERSITY OF HULL
THE UNIVERSITY OF HULL
COTTINGHAM ROAD
HULL HU6 7RX
t: 01482 466100 f: 01482 442290
e: admissions@hull.ac.uk
// www.hull.ac.uk

M1N1 LLB Law with Business
Duration: 3FT Hon
Entry Requirements: *GCE:* 320. *IB:* 30. *BTEC ExtDip:* DDM.

K12 KEELE UNIVERSITY
KEELE UNIVERSITY
STAFFORDSHIRE ST5 5BG
t: 01782 734005 f: 01782 632343
e: undergraduate@keele.ac.uk
// www.keele.ac.uk

MN91 BA Criminology and International Business
Duration: 3FT Hon
Entry Requirements: *GCE:* ABB.

NM11 BA International Business and Law
Duration: 3FT Hon
Entry Requirements: *GCE:* ABB.

K24 THE UNIVERSITY OF KENT
RECRUITMENT & ADMISSIONS OFFICE
REGISTRY
UNIVERSITY OF KENT
CANTERBURY, KENT CT2 7NZ
t: 01227 827272 f: 01227 827077
e: information@kent.ac.uk
// www.kent.ac.uk

MN12 BA Law and Business Administration
Duration: 3FT Hon
Entry Requirements: *GCE:* AAB. *SQAH:* AAAAB. *IB:* 33. *OCR ND:* D *OCR NED:* M1

1M1N HND Business (Law)
Duration: 2FT HND
Entry Requirements: *GCE:* 80. *SQAH:* BC. *SQAAH:* C. *IB:* 24. *OCR ND:* M2 *OCR NED:* M3

K84 KINGSTON UNIVERSITY
STUDENT INFORMATION & ADVICE CENTRE
COOPER HOUSE
40-46 SURBITON ROAD
KINGSTON UPON THAMES KT1 2HX
t: 0844 8552177 f: 020 8547 7080
e: aps@kingston.ac.uk
// www.kingston.ac.uk

N1M1 BA Business with Law
Duration: 3FT Hon
Entry Requirements: *GCE:* 280. *SQAH:* BBCCC. *SQAAH:* BCC. *IB:* 25.

N1MC BA Business with Law with industrial placement (4 years)
Duration: 4FT Hon
Entry Requirements: *GCE:* 280. *SQAH:* BBCCC. *SQAAH:* BCC. *IB:* 25.

N1MD BA Business with Law with year abroad (4 years)
Duration: 4FT Hon
Entry Requirements: *GCE:* 280. *SQAH:* BBCCC. *SQAAH:* BCC. *IB:* 25.

M1N1 LLB Law with Business
Duration: 3FT Hon
Entry Requirements: *GCE:* 320. *IB:* 27.

M1ND LLB Law with Business with Industrial Placement
Duration: 4SW Hon
Entry Requirements: *GCE:* 320. *IB:* 27.

L39 UNIVERSITY OF LINCOLN
ADMISSIONS
BRAYFORD POOL
LINCOLN LN6 7TS
t: 01522 886097 f: 01522 886146
e: admissions@lincoln.ac.uk
// www.lincoln.ac.uk

NM11 LLB Law and Business
Duration: 3FT Hon
Entry Requirements: *GCE:* 300.

L41 THE UNIVERSITY OF LIVERPOOL
THE FOUNDATION BUILDING
BROWNLOW HILL
LIVERPOOL L69 7ZX
t: 0151 794 2000 f: 0151 708 6502
e: ugrecruitment@liv.ac.uk
// www.liv.ac.uk

M102 LLB Law with Business Studies
Duration: 3FT Hon
Entry Requirements: *GCE:* AAA. *SQAH:* AAAAA. *SQAAH:* AA. *IB:* 36. *OCR ND:* D *OCR NED:* D2

L62 THE LONDON COLLEGE, UCK
VICTORIA GARDENS
NOTTING HILL GATE
LONDON W11 3PE
t: 020 7243 4000 f: 020 7243 1484
e: admissions@lcuck.ac.uk
// www.lcuck.ac.uk

122M HND Business Law
Duration: 2FT HND
Entry Requirements: Contact the institution for details.

L63 LCA BUSINESS SCHOOL, LONDON
19 CHARTERHOUSE STREET
LONDON EC1N 6RA
t: 020 7400 6789
e: info@lcabusinessschool.com
// www.lcabusinessschool.com

NM11 BSc Business and Law
Duration: 3FT Hon
Entry Requirements: *GCE:* 260. *SQAH:* BBCCC. *IB:* 24. *OCR ND:* D *OCR NED:* M2 Interview required.

L68 LONDON METROPOLITAN UNIVERSITY
166-220 HOLLOWAY ROAD
LONDON N7 8DB
t: 020 7133 4200
e: admissions@londonmet.ac.uk
// www.londonmet.ac.uk

MNF1 BA International Business and Business Law
Duration: 3FT Hon
Entry Requirements: *GCE:* 240. *IB:* 28.

M221 LLB Business Law
Duration: 3FT Hon
Entry Requirements: *GCE:* 320. *IB:* 28.

M40 THE MANCHESTER METROPOLITAN UNIVERSITY
ADMISSIONS OFFICE
ALL SAINTS (GMS)
ALL SAINTS
MANCHESTER M15 6BH
t: 0161 247 2000
// www.mmu.ac.uk

MN2C BA Business/Legal Studies
Duration: 3FT Hon
Entry Requirements: *GCE:* 280. *IB:* 28. *BTEC Dip:* D*D*. *BTEC ExtDip:* DMM.

N37 UNIVERSITY OF WALES, NEWPORT
ADMISSIONS
LODGE ROAD
CAERLEON
NEWPORT NP18 3QT
t: 01633 432030 f: 01633 432850
e: admissions@newport.ac.uk
// www.newport.ac.uk

NM11 BA Business and Law
Duration: 3FT Hon
Entry Requirements: *GCE:* 240. *IB:* 24.

MN11 BA Law and Business (Top-Up)
Duration: 1FT Hon
Entry Requirements: Contact the institution for details.

N38 UNIVERSITY OF NORTHAMPTON
PARK CAMPUS
BOUGHTON GREEN ROAD
NORTHAMPTON NN2 7AL
t: 0800 358 2232 f: 01604 722083
e: admissions@northampton.ac.uk
// www.northampton.ac.uk

N1MC BA Business Entrepreneurship/Law
Duration: 3FT Hon
Entry Requirements: *GCE:* 260-280. *SQAH:* AAA-BBBB. *IB:* 24. *BTEC Dip:* DD. *BTEC ExtDip:* DMM. *OCR ND:* D *OCR NED:* M2

N1M9 BA Business/Criminology
Duration: 3FT Hon
Entry Requirements: *GCE:* 260-280. *SQAH:* AAA-BBBB. *IB:* 24. *BTEC Dip:* DD. *BTEC ExtDip:* DMM. *OCR ND:* D *OCR NED:* M2

N1M1 BA Business/Law
Duration: 3FT Hon
Entry Requirements: *GCE:* 260-280. *SQAH:* AAA-BBBB. *IB:* 24. *BTEC Dip:* DD. *BTEC ExtDip:* DMM. *OCR ND:* D *OCR NED:* M2

M9N1 BA Criminology/Business
Duration: 3FT Hon
Entry Requirements: *GCE:* 260-280. *SQAH:* AAA-BBBB. *IB:* 24. *BTEC Dip:* DD. *BTEC ExtDip:* DMM. *OCR ND:* D *OCR NED:* M2

M9G5 BA Criminology/Business Computing Systems
Duration: 3FT Hon
Entry Requirements: *GCE:* 260-280. *SQAH:* AAA-BBBB. *IB:* 24. *BTEC Dip:* DD. *BTEC ExtDip:* DMM. *OCR ND:* D *OCR NED:* M2

M1N1 BA Law/Business
Duration: 3FT Hon
Entry Requirements: *GCE:* 260-280. *SQAH:* AAA-BBBB. *IB:* 24. *BTEC Dip:* DD. *BTEC ExtDip:* DMM. *OCR ND:* D *OCR NED:* M2

M1G5 BA Law/Business Computing Systems
Duration: 3FT Hon
Entry Requirements: *GCE:* 260-280. *SQAH:* AAA-BBBB. *IB:* 24. *BTEC Dip:* DD. *BTEC ExtDip:* DMM. *OCR ND:* D *OCR NED:* M2

M1NF BA Law/Business Entrepreneurship
Duration: 3FT Hon
Entry Requirements: *GCE:* 260-280. *SQAH:* AAA-BBBB. *IB:* 24. *BTEC Dip:* DD. *BTEC ExtDip:* DMM. *OCR ND:* D *OCR NED:* M2

G5M9 BSc Business Computing Systems/Criminology
Duration: 3FT Hon
Entry Requirements: *GCE:* 260-280. *SQAH:* AAA-BBBB. *IB:* 24. *BTEC Dip:* DD. *BTEC ExtDip:* DMM. *OCR ND:* D *OCR NED:* M2

G5M1 BSc Business Computing Systems/Law
Duration: 3FT Hon
Entry Requirements: *GCE:* 260-280. *SQAH:* AAA-BBBB. *IB:* 24.
BTEC Dip: DD. *BTEC ExtDip:* DMM. *OCR ND:* D *OCR NED:* M2

N77 NORTHUMBRIA UNIVERSITY
TRINITY BUILDING
NORTHUMBERLAND ROAD
NEWCASTLE UPON TYNE NE1 8ST
t: 0191 243 7420 f: 0191 227 4561
e: er.admissions@northumbria.ac.uk
// www.northumbria.ac.uk

M1N1 LLB Law with Business
Duration: 3FT Hon
Entry Requirements: *GCE:* ABB. *SQAH:* ABBBC. *SQAAH:* ABC. *IB:* 27. *BTEC ExtDip:* DDM. *OCR NED:* D2

M1N9 LLB Law with International Business
Duration: 3FT Hon
Entry Requirements: *GCE:* ABB. *SQAH:* ABBBC. *SQAAH:* ABC. *IB:* 27. *BTEC ExtDip:* DDM. *OCR NED:* D2

N91 NOTTINGHAM TRENT UNIVERSITY
DRYDEN BUILDING
BURTON STREET
NOTTINGHAM NG1 4BU
t: +44 (0) 115 848 4200 f: +44 (0) 115 848 8869
e: applications@ntu.ac.uk
// www.ntu.ac.uk

M221 LLB Business Law
Duration: 3FT Hon
Entry Requirements: *GCE:* 300.

P60 PLYMOUTH UNIVERSITY
DRAKE CIRCUS
PLYMOUTH PL4 8AA
t: 01752 585858 f: 01752 588055
e: admissions@plymouth.ac.uk
// www.plymouth.ac.uk

M2ND BA Law with Business
Duration: 3FT Hon
Entry Requirements: Contact the institution for details.

M2N1 BSc Law with Business
Duration: 3FT Hon
Entry Requirements: *GCE:* 300. *IB:* 26.

NM12 BSc Maritime Business and Maritime Law
Duration: 3FT Hon
Entry Requirements: *GCE:* 240. *IB:* 24.

M2NC LLB Law with Business
Duration: 3FT Hon
Entry Requirements: Contact the institution for details.

P80 UNIVERSITY OF PORTSMOUTH
ACADEMIC REGISTRY
UNIVERSITY HOUSE
WINSTON CHURCHILL AVENUE
PORTSMOUTH PO1 2UP
t: 023 9284 8484 f: 023 9284 3082
e: admissions@port.ac.uk
// www.port.ac.uk

M1N1 BA Law with Business Communication
Duration: 3FT Hon
Entry Requirements: Contact the institution for details.

M1NC LLB Law with Business
Duration: 3FT/4SW Hon
Entry Requirements: *GCE:* 280. *IB:* 28. *BTEC SubDip:* D. *BTEC Dip:* D*D*. *BTEC ExtDip:* DMM.

S21 SHEFFIELD HALLAM UNIVERSITY
CITY CAMPUS
HOWARD STREET
SHEFFIELD S1 1WB
t: 0114 225 5555 f: 0114 225 2167
e: admissions@shu.ac.uk
// www.shu.ac.uk

M225 LLB Business Law
Duration: 3FT Hon
Entry Requirements: *GCE:* 300.

S64 ST MARY'S UNIVERSITY COLLEGE, TWICKENHAM
WALDEGRAVE ROAD
STRAWBERRY HILL
MIDDLESEX TW1 4SX
t: 020 8240 4029 f: 020 8240 2361
e: admit@smuc.ac.uk
// www.smuc.ac.uk

MV21 BA Business Law and History
Duration: 3FT Hon
Entry Requirements: *GCE:* 240. *SQAH:* BBBC. *IB:* 28. *OCR ND:* D *OCR NED:* M3 Interview required.

MV25 BA Business Law and Philosophy
Duration: 3FT Hon
Entry Requirements: *GCE:* 240. *SQAH:* BBBC. *IB:* 28. *OCR ND:* D *OCR NED:* M3 Interview required.

M2R4 BA Business Law and Spanish
Duration: 3FT Hon
Entry Requirements: Contact the institution for details.

MN28 BA Business Law and Tourism
Duration: 3FT Hon
Entry Requirements: *GCE:* 220. *IB:* 28. *OCR ND:* M1 *OCR NED:* P1 Interview required.

ML23 BA/BSc Business Law and Sociology
Duration: 3FT Hon
Entry Requirements: *GCE:* 240. *SQAH:* BBBC. *IB:* 28. *OCR ND:* D *OCR NED:* M3 Interview required.

S72 STAFFORDSHIRE UNIVERSITY
COLLEGE ROAD
STOKE ON TRENT ST4 2DE
t: 01782 292753 f: 01782 292740
e: admissions@staffs.ac.uk
// www.staffs.ac.uk

M221 LLB Law (Business Law)
Duration: 3FT Hon
Entry Requirements: *GCE:* 280. *IB:* 26. *OCR NED:* M2

S75 THE UNIVERSITY OF STIRLING
STUDENT RECRUITMENT & ADMISSIONS SERVICE
UNIVERSITY OF STIRLING
STIRLING
SCOTLAND FK9 4LA
t: 01786 467044 f: 01786 466800
e: admissions@stir.ac.uk
// www.stir.ac.uk

M221 BA Business Law
Duration: 4FT Hon
Entry Requirements: *GCE:* BBC. *SQAH:* BBBB. *SQAAH:* AAA-CCC. *IB:* 32. *BTEC ExtDip:* DMM.

MN11 BA Business Studies and Law
Duration: 4FT Hon
Entry Requirements: *GCE:* BBC. *SQAH:* BBBB. *SQAAH:* AAA-CCC. *IB:* 32. *BTEC ExtDip:* DMM.

MN24 BAcc Accountancy and Business Law
Duration: 4FT Hon
Entry Requirements: *GCE:* BBC. *SQAH:* BBBB. *SQAAH:* AAA-CCC. *IB:* 32. *BTEC ExtDip:* DMM.

S78 THE UNIVERSITY OF STRATHCLYDE
GLASGOW G1 1XQ
t: 0141 552 4400 f: 0141 552 0775
// www.strath.ac.uk

NM42 BA Accounting and Business Law
Duration: 4FT Hon
Entry Requirements: *GCE:* AAA. *SQAH:* AAAAAB-AAAA. *IB:* 36.

MN21 BA Business Enterprise and Business Law
Duration: 4FT Hon
Entry Requirements: *GCE:* AAB. *SQAH:* AAAABB-AAAB. *IB:* 36.

MN28 BA Business Law and Hospitality & Tourism
Duration: 4FT Hon
Entry Requirements: *GCE:* AAB. *SQAH:* AAAABB-AAAB. *IB:* 36.

LM12 BA Economics and Business Law
Duration: 4FT Hon
Entry Requirements: *GCE:* AAB. *SQAH:* AAAABB-AAAB. *IB:* 36.

NM32 BA Finance and Business Law
Duration: 4FT Hon
Entry Requirements: *GCE:* AAB. *SQAH:* AAAABB-AAAB. *IB:* 36.

NM52 BA Marketing and Business Law
Duration: 4FT Hon
Entry Requirements: *GCE:* AAB. *SQAH:* AAAABB-AAAB. *IB:* 36.

S84 UNIVERSITY OF SUNDERLAND
STUDENT HELPLINE
THE STUDENT GATEWAY
CHESTER ROAD
SUNDERLAND SR1 3SD
t: 0191 515 3000 f: 0191 515 3805
e: student.helpline@sunderland.ac.uk
// www.sunderland.ac.uk

M221 BA Business Law
Duration: 1FT Hon
Entry Requirements: Contact the institution for details.

S90 UNIVERSITY OF SUSSEX
UNDERGRADUATE ADMISSIONS
SUSSEX HOUSE
UNIVERSITY OF SUSSEX
BRIGHTON BN1 9RH
t: 01273 678416 f: 01273 678545
e: ug.applicants@sussex.ac.uk
// www.sussex.ac.uk

MN11 LLB Law and Business
Duration: 4FT Hon
Entry Requirements: *GCE:* AAA-AAB. *SQAH:* AAAAA-AAABB. *IB:* 35. *BTEC SubDip:* D. *BTEC Dip:* DD. *BTEC ExtDip:* DDD. *OCR ND:* D *OCR NED:* D1

M1N1 LLB Law with Business
Duration: 3FT Hon
Entry Requirements: *GCE:* AAA-AAB. *SQAH:* AAAAA-AAABB. *IB:* 35. *BTEC SubDip:* D. *BTEC Dip:* DD. *BTEC ExtDip:* DDD. *OCR ND:* D *OCR NED:* D1

S93 SWANSEA UNIVERSITY
SINGLETON PARK
SWANSEA SA2 8PP
t: 01792 295111 f: 01792 295110
e: admissions@swansea.ac.uk
// www.swansea.ac.uk

MN11 LLB Law and Business Studies
Duration: 3FT Hon
Entry Requirements: *GCE:* 280-300.

M1N1 LLB Law with Business
Duration: 3FT Hon
Entry Requirements: *GCE:* AAB. *IB:* 34.

T20 TEESSIDE UNIVERSITY
MIDDLESBROUGH TS1 3BA
t: 01642 218121 f: 01642 384201
e: registry@tees.ac.uk
// www.tees.ac.uk

N1M1 BA Business with Law
Duration: 3FT/4SW Hon
Entry Requirements: *GCE:* 240. *IB:* 30. *BTEC SubDip:* D*. *BTEC Dip:* DD. *BTEC ExtDip:* MMM.

W20 THE UNIVERSITY OF WARWICK
COVENTRY CV4 8UW
t: 024 7652 3723 f: 024 7652 4649
e: ugadmissions@warwick.ac.uk
// www.warwick.ac.uk

MN11 BA Law and Business Studies
Duration: 3FT Hon
Entry Requirements: *GCE:* AABc. *SQAAH:* AAB-AB. *IB:* 36. *OCR ND:* D

W75 UNIVERSITY OF WOLVERHAMPTON
ADMISSIONS UNIT
MX207, CAMP STREET
WOLVERHAMPTON
WEST MIDLANDS WV1 1AD
t: 01902 321000 f: 01902 321896
e: admissions@wlv.ac.uk
// www.wlv.ac.uk

NM11 BA Business and Law
Duration: 3FT Hon
Entry Requirements: *GCE:* 160-220. *IB:* 28.

COMMERCIAL LAW

B40 BLACKBURN COLLEGE
FEILDEN STREET
BLACKBURN BB2 1LH
t: 01254 292594 f: 01254 679647
e: he-admissions@blackburn.ac.uk
// www.blackburn.ac.uk

M221 LLB Commercial Law
Duration: 3FT Hon
Entry Requirements: *GCE:* 220. *IB:* 26.

B80 UNIVERSITY OF THE WEST OF ENGLAND, BRISTOL
FRENCHAY CAMPUS
COLDHARBOUR LANE
BRISTOL BS16 1QY
t: +44 (0)117 32 83333 f: +44 (0)117 32 82810
e: admissions@uwe.ac.uk
// www.uwe.ac.uk

M221 LLB Commercial Law
Duration: 3FT Hon
Entry Requirements: *GCE:* 300.

C85 COVENTRY UNIVERSITY
THE STUDENT CENTRE
COVENTRY UNIVERSITY
1 GULSON RD
COVENTRY CV1 2JH
t: 024 7615 2222 f: 024 7615 2223
e: studentenquiries@coventry.ac.uk
// www.coventry.ac.uk

M221 LLB Commercial Law
Duration: 3FT/4SW Hon
Entry Requirements: *GCE:* BBB. *SQAH:* BBBBC. *IB:* 30. *BTEC ExtDip:* DDM. *OCR NED:* M1

M22C LLB Commercial Law
Duration: 2FT/3SW Hon
Entry Requirements: *GCE:* ABB. *SQAH:* BBBBC. *IB:* 31.

H36 UNIVERSITY OF HERTFORDSHIRE
UNIVERSITY ADMISSIONS SERVICE
COLLEGE LANE
HATFIELD
HERTS AL10 9AB
t: 01707 284800
// www.herts.ac.uk

M221 LLB Commercial Law
Duration: 3FT Hon
Entry Requirements: *GCE:* 300.

H72 THE UNIVERSITY OF HULL
THE UNIVERSITY OF HULL
COTTINGHAM ROAD
HULL HU6 7RX
t: 01482 466100 f: 01482 442290
e: admissions@hull.ac.uk
// www.hull.ac.uk

M221 LLB Commercial Law
Duration: 3FT Hon
Entry Requirements: *GCE:* 320. *IB:* 30. *BTEC ExtDip:* DDM.

W05 THE UNIVERSITY OF WEST LONDON
ST MARY'S ROAD
EALING
LONDON W5 5RF
t: 0800 036 8888 f: 020 8566 1353
e: learning.advice@uwl.ac.uk
// www.uwl.ac.uk

M221 LLB Commercial Law
Duration: 3FT Hon
Entry Requirements: *GCE:* 300. *IB:* 28. Interview required.

W50 UNIVERSITY OF WESTMINSTER
2ND FLOOR, CAVENDISH HOUSE
101 NEW CAVENDISH STREET,
LONDON W1W 6XH
t: 020 7915 5511
e: course-enquiries@westminster.ac.uk
// www.westminster.ac.uk

M221 LLB Commercial Law
Duration: 3FT Hon
Entry Requirements: *GCE:* ABB. *SQAH:* AABBB. *SQAAH:* ABB. *IB:* 32. Interview required.

COMPUTING & MATHEMATICS COMBINATIONS

A40 ABERYSTWYTH UNIVERSITY
ABERYSTWYTH UNIVERSITY, WELCOME CENTRE
PENGLAIS CAMPUS
ABERYSTWYTH
CEREDIGION SY23 3FB
t: 01970 622021 f: 01970 627410
e: ug-admissions@aber.ac.uk
// www.aber.ac.uk

M1G1 BA Law with Mathematics
Duration: 3FT Hon
Entry Requirements: *GCE:* 340. *IB:* 28.

C10 CANTERBURY CHRIST CHURCH UNIVERSITY
NORTH HOLMES ROAD
CANTERBURY
KENT CT1 1QU
t: 01227 782900 f: 01227 782888
e: admissions@canterbury.ac.uk
// www.canterbury.ac.uk

GM42 BA Internet Computing and Legal Studies
Duration: 3FT Hon
Entry Requirements: *GCE:* 240. *IB:* 24.

G4MF BA Internet Computing with Legal Studies
Duration: 3FT Hon
Entry Requirements: *GCE:* 240. *IB:* 24.

M2G4 BA Legal Studies with Internet Computing
Duration: 3FT Hon
Entry Requirements: *GCE:* 240. *IB:* 24.

G4M2 BA/BSc Computing with Legal Studies
Duration: 3FT Hon
Entry Requirements: *GCE:* 240. *IB:* 24.

MG24 BA/BSc Legal Studies and Computing
Duration: 3FT Hon
Entry Requirements: *GCE:* 240. *IB:* 24.

M2G5 BA/BSc Legal Studies with Computing
Duration: 3FT Hon
Entry Requirements: *GCE:* 240. *IB:* 24.

D39 UNIVERSITY OF DERBY
KEDLESTON ROAD
DERBY DE22 1GB
t: 01332 591167 f: 01332 597724
e: askadmissions@derby.ac.uk
// www.derby.ac.uk

MG21 BA/BSc Applied Criminology and Mathematics
Duration: 3FT Hon
Entry Requirements: *Foundation:* Distinction. *GCE:* 260-300. *IB:* 28. *BTEC Dip:* D*D*. *BTEC ExtDip:* DMM. *OCR NED:* M2

MG11 BA/BSc Law and Mathematics
Duration: 3FT Hon
Entry Requirements: *Foundation:* Distinction. *GCE:* 260-300. *IB:* 28. *BTEC Dip:* D*D*. *BTEC ExtDip:* DMM. *OCR NED:* M2

E28 UNIVERSITY OF EAST LONDON
DOCKLANDS CAMPUS
UNIVERSITY WAY
LONDON E16 2RD
t: 020 8223 3333 f: 020 8223 2978
e: study@uel.ac.uk
// www.uel.ac.uk

IM11 BA/BSc Computing and Law
Duration: 3FT Hon
Entry Requirements: *GCE:* 240. *IB:* 24.

I1M1 BSc Computing with Law
Duration: 3FT Hon
Entry Requirements: *GCE:* 240. *IB:* 24.

H36 UNIVERSITY OF HERTFORDSHIRE
UNIVERSITY ADMISSIONS SERVICE
COLLEGE LANE
HATFIELD
HERTS AL10 9AB
t: 01707 284800
// www.herts.ac.uk

G4M1 BSc Computing/Law
Duration: 3FT/4SW Hon
Entry Requirements: *GCE:* 320.

M1G4 BSc Law/Computing
Duration: 3FT/4SW Hon
Entry Requirements: *GCE:* 320.

K12 KEELE UNIVERSITY
KEELE UNIVERSITY
STAFFORDSHIRE ST5 5BG
t: 01782 734005 f: 01782 632343
e: undergraduate@keele.ac.uk
// www.keele.ac.uk

GM4X BSc Creative Computing and Criminology
Duration: 3FT Hon
Entry Requirements: *GCE:* BBC.

GM4C BSc Creative Computing and Law
Duration: 3FT Hon
Entry Requirements: *GCE:* ABB.

GM11 BSc Law and Mathematics
Duration: 3FT Hon
Entry Requirements: *GCE:* ABB.

N38 UNIVERSITY OF NORTHAMPTON
PARK CAMPUS
BOUGHTON GREEN ROAD
NORTHAMPTON NN2 7AL
t: 0800 358 2232 f: 01604 722083
e: admissions@northampton.ac.uk
// www.northampton.ac.uk

M9G4 BA Criminology/Computing
Duration: 3FT Hon
Entry Requirements: *GCE:* 260-280. *SQAH:* AAA-BBBB. *IB:* 24.
BTEC Dip: DD. *BTEC ExtDip:* DMM. *OCR ND:* D *OCR NED:* M2

G4M9 BSc Computing/Criminology
Duration: 3FT Hon
Entry Requirements: *GCE:* 260-280. *SQAH:* AAA-BBBB. *IB:* 24.
BTEC Dip: DD. *BTEC ExtDip:* DMM. *OCR ND:* D *OCR NED:* M2

CRIMINAL JUSTICE, CIVIL & COMMUNITY LAW

A40 ABERYSTWYTH UNIVERSITY
ABERYSTWYTH UNIVERSITY, WELCOME CENTRE
PENGLAIS CAMPUS
ABERYSTWYTH
CEREDIGION SY23 3FB
t: 01970 622021 f: 01970 627410
e: ug-admissions@aber.ac.uk
// www.aber.ac.uk

M131 LLB Criminal Law
Duration: 3FT Hon
Entry Requirements: *GCE:* 340. *IB:* 34.

B06 BANGOR UNIVERSITY
BANGOR UNIVERSITY
BANGOR
GWYNEDD LL57 2DG
t: 01248 388484 f: 01248 370451
e: admissions@bangor.ac.uk
// www.bangor.ac.uk

LM3Y BA Cymdeithaseg and Criminology & Criminal Justice
Duration: 3FT Hon
Entry Requirements: Contact the institution for details.

LM4X BA Polisi Cymdeithasol and Criminology & Criminal Justice
Duration: 3FT Hon
Entry Requirements: Contact the institution for details.

B40 BLACKBURN COLLEGE
FEILDEN STREET
BLACKBURN BB2 1LH
t: 01254 292594 f: 01254 679647
e: he-admissions@blackburn.ac.uk
// www.blackburn.ac.uk

LM32 FdA Criminology and Criminal Justice
Duration: 2FT Fdg
Entry Requirements: *GCE:* 80.

M212 LLB Criminal Law
Duration: 3FT Hon
Entry Requirements: *GCE:* 220. *IB:* 26.

B41 BLACKPOOL AND THE FYLDE COLLEGE AN ASSOCIATE COLLEGE OF LANCASTER UNIVERSITY
ASHFIELD ROAD
BISPHAM
BLACKPOOL
LANCS FY2 0HB
t: 01253 504346 f: 01253 504198
e: admissions@blackpool.ac.uk
// www.blackpool.ac.uk

M212 BA Criminology and Criminal Justice (Top-Up)
Duration: 1FT Hon
Entry Requirements: Contact the institution for details.

M211 FdA Criminology and Criminal Justice
Duration: 2FT Fdg
Entry Requirements: *GCE:* 120-360. *IB:* 24.

B56 THE UNIVERSITY OF BRADFORD
RICHMOND ROAD
BRADFORD
WEST YORKSHIRE BD7 1DP
t: 0800 073 1225 f: 01274 235585
e: course-enquiries@bradford.ac.uk
// www.bradford.ac.uk

M211 BA Applied Criminal Justice Studies
Duration: 3FT Hon
Entry Requirements: *GCE:* 240. *IB:* 24.

B80 UNIVERSITY OF THE WEST OF ENGLAND, BRISTOL
FRENCHAY CAMPUS
COLDHARBOUR LANE
BRISTOL BS16 1QY
t: +44 (0)117 32 83333 f: +44 (0)117 32 82810
e: admissions@uwe.ac.uk
// www.uwe.ac.uk

MM92 FdA Criminology and Criminal Justice
Duration: 2FT Fdg
Entry Requirements: *GCE:* 120.

B94 BUCKINGHAMSHIRE NEW UNIVERSITY
QUEEN ALEXANDRA ROAD
HIGH WYCOMBE
BUCKINGHAMSHIRE HP11 2JZ
t: 0800 0565 660 f: 01494 605 023
e: admissions@bucks.ac.uk
// bucks.ac.uk

L4M9 BSc Police Studies with Criminal Investigation
Duration: 3FT Hon
Entry Requirements: *GCE:* 240-280. *IB:* 25. *OCR ND:* D *OCR NED:* M2

C30 UNIVERSITY OF CENTRAL LANCASHIRE
PRESTON
LANCS PR1 2HE
t: 01772 201201 f: 01772 894954
e: uadmissions@uclan.ac.uk
// www.uclan.ac.uk

M930 BA Criminology and Criminal Justice
Duration: 3FT Hon
Entry Requirements: *GCE:* 240-280. *SQAH:* BBBC. *IB:* 28. *OCR ND:* D *OCR NED:* M3

FM42 BSc Forensic Science and Criminal Investigation
Duration: 3FT Hon
Entry Requirements: *GCE:* 280-320. *SQAH:* BBBBC-BBCCC. *IB:* 28. *OCR NED:* M2

FM49 BSc Police and Criminal Investigation
Duration: 3FT Hon
Entry Requirements: *GCE:* 280-320. *SQAH:* BBBBC-BBCCC. *IB:* 28. *OCR NED:* M2

D26 DE MONTFORT UNIVERSITY
THE GATEWAY
LEICESTER LE1 9BH
t: 0116 255 1551 f: 0116 250 6204
e: enquiries@dmu.ac.uk
// www.dmu.ac.uk

M211 LLB Law and Criminal Justice
Duration: 3FT Hon
Entry Requirements: *GCE:* 300. *IB:* 30. *BTEC ExtDip:* DDM. Interview required.

D52 DONCASTER COLLEGE
THE HUB
CHAPPELL DRIVE
SOUTH YORKSHIRE DN1 2RF
t: 01302 553610
e: he@don.ac.uk
// www.don.ac.uk

ML13 BA Criminal Justice
Duration: 3FT Hon
Entry Requirements: *GCE:* 160.

E28 UNIVERSITY OF EAST LONDON
DOCKLANDS CAMPUS
UNIVERSITY WAY
LONDON E16 2RD
t: 020 8223 3333 f: 020 8223 2978
e: study@uel.ac.uk
// www.uel.ac.uk

M930 BA Criminology and Criminal Justice
Duration: 3FT Hon
Entry Requirements: *GCE:* 240. *IB:* 24.

ML95 BA Criminology and Youth & Community Work
Duration: 3FT Hon
Entry Requirements: *GCE:* 240.

M9L5 BA Criminology with Youth & Community Work
Duration: 3FT Hon
Entry Requirements: *GCE:* 240. *IB:* 24.

E42 EDGE HILL UNIVERSITY
ORMSKIRK
LANCASHIRE L39 4QP
t: 01695 657000 f: 01695 584355
e: study@edgehill.ac.uk
// www.edgehill.ac.uk

M900 BA Criminology & Criminal Justice
Duration: 3FT Hon
Entry Requirements: *GCE:* 280. *IB:* 26. *OCR ND:* D *OCR NED:* M2

G14 UNIVERSITY OF GLAMORGAN, CARDIFF AND PONTYPRIDD
ENQUIRIES AND ADMISSIONS UNIT
PONTYPRIDD CF37 1DL
t: 08456 434030 f: 01443 654050
e: enquiries@glam.ac.uk
// www.glam.ac.uk

M901 BSc Criminology and Criminal Justice
Duration: 3FT Hon
Entry Requirements: *GCE:* BBC. *IB:* 25. *BTEC SubDip:* M. *BTEC Dip:* D*D*. *BTEC ExtDip:* DMM.

G53 GLYNDWR UNIVERSITY
PLAS COCH
MOLD ROAD
WREXHAM LL11 2AW
t: 01978 293439 f: 01978 290008
e: sid@glyndwr.ac.uk
// www.glyndwr.ac.uk

M240 BA Criminal Justice
Duration: 3FT Hon
Entry Requirements: *GCE:* 240.

G70 UNIVERSITY OF GREENWICH
GREENWICH CAMPUS
OLD ROYAL NAVAL COLLEGE
PARK ROW
LONDON SE10 9LS
t: 020 8331 9000 f: 020 8331 8145
e: courseinfo@gre.ac.uk
// www.gre.ac.uk

MC98 BSc Criminology and Criminal Psychology
Duration: 3FT Hon
Entry Requirements: *GCE:* 280. *IB:* 24.

K24 THE UNIVERSITY OF KENT
RECRUITMENT & ADMISSIONS OFFICE
REGISTRY
UNIVERSITY OF KENT
CANTERBURY, KENT CT2 7NZ
t: 01227 827272 f: 01227 827077
e: information@kent.ac.uk
// www.kent.ac.uk

M900 BA Criminal Justice Studies
Duration: 3FT Hon
Entry Requirements: *GCE:* BBB. *SQAH:* ABBBB. *SQAAH:* BBB. *IB:* 33. *OCR ND:* D *OCR NED:* M1

L23 UNIVERSITY OF LEEDS
THE UNIVERSITY OF LEEDS
WOODHOUSE LANE
LEEDS LS2 9JT
t: 0113 343 3999
e: admissions@leeds.ac.uk
// www.leeds.ac.uk

MM29 BA Criminal Justice and Criminology
Duration: 3FT Hon
Entry Requirements: *GCE:* AAB. *IB:* 33.

L51 LIVERPOOL JOHN MOORES UNIVERSITY
KINGSWAY HOUSE
HATTON GARDEN
LIVERPOOL L3 2AJ
t: 0151 231 5090 f: 0151 904 6368
e: courses@ljmu.ac.uk
// www.ljmu.ac.uk

M291 BA Criminal Justice
Duration: 3FT Hon
Entry Requirements: *GCE:* 280. *IB:* 28.

CM82 BSc Forensic Psychology and Criminal Justice
Duration: 3FT Hon
Entry Requirements: *GCE:* 300. *IB:* 29.

MM12 LLB Law and Criminal Justice
Duration: 3FT Hon
Entry Requirements: *GCE:* 300. *IB:* 29.

M80 MIDDLESEX UNIVERSITY
MIDDLESEX UNIVERSITY
THE BURROUGHS
LONDON NW4 4BT
t: 020 8411 5555 f: 020 8411 5649
e: enquiries@mdx.ac.uk
// www.mdx.ac.uk

M930 BA Criminal Justice and Criminology
Duration: 3FT/4SW Hon
Entry Requirements: *GCE:* 200-300. *IB:* 28.

N37 UNIVERSITY OF WALES, NEWPORT
ADMISSIONS
LODGE ROAD
CAERLEON
NEWPORT NP18 3QT
t: 01633 432030 f: 01633 432850
e: admissions@newport.ac.uk
// www.newport.ac.uk

LM3F BA Criminology & Criminal Justice
Duration: 3FT Hon
Entry Requirements: *GCE:* 240. *IB:* 24. Interview required.

ML93 BA Criminology & Criminal Justice and Social Studies
Duration: 3FT Hon
Entry Requirements: *GCE:* 240. *IB:* 24. Interview required.

LM3G BA Criminology & Criminal Justice and Youth Justice
Duration: 3FT Hon
Entry Requirements: *GCE:* 240. *IB:* 24. Interview required.

N38 UNIVERSITY OF NORTHAMPTON
PARK CAMPUS
BOUGHTON GREEN ROAD
NORTHAMPTON NN2 7AL
t: 0800 358 2232 f: 01604 722083
e: admissions@northampton.ac.uk
// www.northampton.ac.uk

M211 BA Applied Criminal Justice (top-up)
Duration: 1FT Hon
Entry Requirements: Interview required. HND required.

LM42 FdA Police and Criminal Justice Services
Duration: 2FT Fdg   CRB Check: Required
Entry Requirements: *GCE:* 220-260. *SQAH:* BC-CCC. *IB:* 24.
BTEC Dip: DD. *BTEC ExtDip:* DMM. *OCR ND:* D *OCR NED:* M2
Interview required.

P60 PLYMOUTH UNIVERSITY
DRAKE CIRCUS
PLYMOUTH PL4 8AA
t: 01752 585858 f: 01752 588055
e: admissions@plymouth.ac.uk
// www.plymouth.ac.uk

M214 BSc Criminology & Criminal Justice Studies with Law
Duration: 3FT Hon
Entry Requirements: *GCE:* 260. *IB:* 24.

M9LF BSc Criminology & Criminal Justice Studies with Politics
Duration: 3FT Hon
Entry Requirements: *GCE:* 260. *IB:* 24.

M9CV BSc Criminology & Criminal Justice Studies with Psychology
Duration: 3FT Hon
Entry Requirements: *GCE:* 260. *IB:* 24.

M9LH BSc Criminology & Criminal Justice Studies with Sociology
Duration: 3FT Hon
Entry Requirements: *GCE:* 260. *IB:* 24.

M213 BSc Criminology and Criminal Justice Studies
Duration: 3FT Hon
Entry Requirements: *GCE:* 260. *IB:* 24.

M215 BSc Law with Criminology & Criminal Justice Studies
Duration: 3FT Hon
Entry Requirements: *GCE:* 300. *IB:* 26.

C8MX BSc Psychology with Criminology and Criminal Justice Studies
Duration: 3FT Hon
Entry Requirements: *GCE:* 320. *IB:* 28.

M216 LLB Law with Criminology and Criminal Justice Studies
Duration: 3FT Hon
Entry Requirements: Contact the institution for details.

P80 UNIVERSITY OF PORTSMOUTH
ACADEMIC REGISTRY
UNIVERSITY HOUSE
WINSTON CHURCHILL AVENUE
PORTSMOUTH PO1 2UP
t: 023 9284 8484 f: 023 9284 3082
e: admissions@port.ac.uk
// www.port.ac.uk

M930 BSc Criminology and Criminal Justice
Duration: 3FT Hon
Entry Requirements: *GCE:* 240-300. *BTEC Dip:* DD. *BTEC ExtDip:* DMM.

Q75 QUEEN'S UNIVERSITY BELFAST
UNIVERSITY ROAD
BELFAST BT7 1NN
t: 028 9097 3838 f: 028 9097 5151
e: admissions@qub.ac.uk
// www.qub.ac.uk

M2R1 LLB Common & Civil Law with French
Duration: 4FT Hon
Entry Requirements: *GCE:* AAA-AABa. *SQAH:* AAAAB-AAABB. *SQAAH:* AAA-AAB. *IB:* 36.

M2R4 LLB Common & Civil Law with Spanish
Duration: 4FT Hon
Entry Requirements: *GCE:* AAA-AABa. *SQAH:* AAAAB-AAABB. *SQAAH:* AAA-AAB. *IB:* 36.

S30 SOUTHAMPTON SOLENT UNIVERSITY
EAST PARK TERRACE
SOUTHAMPTON
HAMPSHIRE SO14 0RT
t: +44 (0) 23 8031 9039 f: + 44 (0)23 8022 2259
e: admissions@solent.ac.uk
// www.solent.ac.uk/

C8M9 BSc Psychology (Criminal Behaviour)
Duration: 3FT Hon
Entry Requirements: *Foundation:* Distinction. *GCE:* 240. *SQAAH:* AA-CCD. *IB:* 24. *BTEC ExtDip:* MMM. *OCR ND:* D *OCR NED:* M3

S46 SOUTH NOTTINGHAM COLLEGE
WEST BRIDGFORD CENTRE
GREYTHORN DRIVE
WEST BRIDGFORD
NOTTINGHAM NG2 7GA
t: 0115 914 6400 f: 0115 914 6444
e: enquiries@snc.ac.uk
// www.snc.ac.uk

ML93 FdA Criminal Justice
Duration: 2FT Fdg
Entry Requirements: Contact the institution for details.

S51 ST HELENS COLLEGE
WATER STREET
ST HELENS
MERSEYSIDE WA10 1PP
t: 01744 733766 f: 01744 623400
e: enquiries@sthelens.ac.uk
// www.sthelens.ac.uk

M211 BSc Criminal Justice (Top-Up)
Duration: 1FT Hon
Entry Requirements: Interview required. HND required.

M900 FdA Criminal Justice
Duration: 2FT Fdg
Entry Requirements: *GCE:* 100. *IB:* 18.

S52 SOUTH TYNESIDE COLLEGE
ST GEORGE'S AVENUE
SOUTH SHIELDS
TYNE & WEAR NE34 6ET
t: 0191 427 3900 f: 0191 427 3535
e: info@stc.ac.uk
// www.stc.ac.uk

M211 FdSc Criminal Justice
Duration: 2FT Fdg
Entry Requirements: *GCE:* 200. Interview required.

S72 STAFFORDSHIRE UNIVERSITY
COLLEGE ROAD
STOKE ON TRENT ST4 2DE
t: 01782 292753 f: 01782 292740
e: admissions@staffs.ac.uk
// www.staffs.ac.uk

FM4X BSc Policing and Criminal Investigation
Duration: 3FT Hon
Entry Requirements: *GCE:* 200-280. *IB:* 24.

S93 SWANSEA UNIVERSITY
SINGLETON PARK
SWANSEA SA2 8PP
t: 01792 295111 f: 01792 295110
e: admissions@swansea.ac.uk
// www.swansea.ac.uk

M2L4 BSc Criminology and Criminal Justice
Duration: 3FT Hon
Entry Requirements: *GCE:* BBB. *IB:* 32.

MM12 LLB Law (Crime and Criminal Justice)
Duration: 3FT Hon
Entry Requirements: Contact the institution for details.

U20 UNIVERSITY OF ULSTER
COLERAINE
CO. LONDONDERRY
NORTHERN IRELAND BT52 1SA
t: 028 7012 4221 f: 028 7012 4908
e: online@ulster.ac.uk
// www.ulster.ac.uk

M931 BSc Criminology and Criminal Justice
Duration: 3FT Hon
Entry Requirements: *GCE:* 300-320.

U40 UNIVERSITY OF THE WEST OF SCOTLAND
PAISLEY
RENFREWSHIRE
SCOTLAND PA1 2BE
t: 0141 848 3727 f: 0141 848 3623
e: admissions@uws.ac.uk
// www.uws.ac.uk

M211 BA Criminal Justice
Duration: 3FT/4FT Ord/Hon
Entry Requirements: *GCE:* CD. *SQAH:* BBC.

W50 UNIVERSITY OF WESTMINSTER
2ND FLOOR, CAVENDISH HOUSE
101 NEW CAVENDISH STREET,
LONDON W1W 6XH
t: 020 7915 5511
e: course-enquiries@westminster.ac.uk
// www.westminster.ac.uk

M211 BA Criminal Justice
Duration: 3FT Hon
Entry Requirements: *GCE:* BBC. *SQAH:* AABBB. *SQAAH:* ABB. *IB:* 32. Interview required.

W75 UNIVERSITY OF WOLVERHAMPTON
ADMISSIONS UNIT
MX207, CAMP STREET
WOLVERHAMPTON
WEST MIDLANDS WV1 1AD
t: 01902 321000 f: 01902 321896
e: admissions@wlv.ac.uk
// www.wlv.ac.uk

MM91 BA Criminology & Criminal Justice and Law
Duration: 3FT Hon
Entry Requirements: *GCE:* 160-220. *IB:* 28.

MM92 BA Criminology and Criminal Justice
Duration: 3FT Hon
Entry Requirements: *GCE:* 240.

LM59 BA Social Care and Criminology & Criminal Justice
Duration: 3FT Hon
Entry Requirements: *GCE:* 160-220. *IB:* 26.

LM49 BA Social Policy and Criminology & Criminal Justice
Duration: 3FT Hon
Entry Requirements: *GCE:* 160-220. *IB:* 24.

LM39 BA Sociology and Criminology & Criminal Justice
Duration: 3FT Hon
Entry Requirements: *GCE:* 160-220. *IB:* 24.

W76 UNIVERSITY OF WINCHESTER
WINCHESTER
HANTS SO22 4NR
t: 01962 827234 f: 01962 827288
e: course.enquiries@winchester.ac.uk
// www.winchester.ac.uk

LM51 BA Childhood,Youth & Community Studies and Law
Duration: 3FT Hon
Entry Requirements: *Foundation:* Distinction. *GCE:* 260-300. *IB:* 25. *OCR ND:* D *OCR NED:* M2

LM15 BA Health, Community & Social Care Studies and Law
Duration: 3FT Hon
Entry Requirements: Contact the institution for details.

CRIMINOLOGY

A40 ABERYSTWYTH UNIVERSITY
ABERYSTWYTH UNIVERSITY, WELCOME CENTRE
PENGLAIS CAMPUS
ABERYSTWYTH
CEREDIGION SY23 3FB
t: 01970 622021 f: 01970 627410
e: ug-admissions@aber.ac.uk
// www.aber.ac.uk

M1M9 BA Law with Criminology
Duration: 3FT Hon
Entry Requirements: *GCE:* 340. *IB:* 28.

B06 BANGOR UNIVERSITY
BANGOR UNIVERSITY
BANGOR
GWYNEDD LL57 2DG
t: 01248 388484 f: 01248 370451
e: admissions@bangor.ac.uk
// www.bangor.ac.uk

M1M9 LLB Law with Criminology
Duration: 3FT Hon
Entry Requirements: *GCE:* 280. *IB:* 28.

B25 BIRMINGHAM CITY UNIVERSITY
PERRY BARR
BIRMINGHAM B42 2SU
t: 0121 331 5595 f: 0121 331 7994
// www.bcu.ac.uk

M900 BA Criminology
Duration: 3FT Hon
Entry Requirements: *GCE:* 280. *IB:* 30. *OCR NED:* M2

ML9K BA Criminology and Policing
Duration: 3FT Hon
Entry Requirements: *GCE:* 280. *IB:* 26.

MC98 BA Criminology and Psychology
Duration: 3FT Hon
Entry Requirements: *GCE:* 280. *IB:* 26.

ML94 BA Criminology and Security Studies
Duration: 3FT Hon
Entry Requirements: *GCE:* 280. *IB:* 26.

LM39 BA Sociology and Criminology
Duration: 3FT Hon
Entry Requirements: *GCE:* 280. *IB:* 26. *OCR NED:* M2

M1MF LLB Law with Criminology
Duration: 3FT Hon
Entry Requirements: *GCE:* 280. *IB:* 28.

B40 BLACKBURN COLLEGE
FEILDEN STREET
BLACKBURN BB2 1LH
t: 01254 292594 f: 01254 679647
e: he-admissions@blackburn.ac.uk
// www.blackburn.ac.uk

M900 BA Criminology (Top-Up)
Duration: 2FT Hon
Entry Requirements: Contact the institution for details.

M930 BA Criminology (Top-Up)
Duration: 1FT Hon
Entry Requirements: HND required.

B72 UNIVERSITY OF BRIGHTON
MITHRAS HOUSE 211
LEWES ROAD
BRIGHTON BN2 4AT
t: 01273 644644 f: 01273 642607
e: admissions@brighton.ac.uk
// www.brighton.ac.uk

MC98 BA Applied Psychology and Criminology
Duration: 3FT Hon
Entry Requirements: *GCE:* BBB. *IB:* 30.

LM49 BA Criminology and Social Policy
Duration: 3FT Hon
Entry Requirements: *GCE:* BBB. *IB:* 30.

LM39 BA Criminology and Sociology
Duration: 3FT Hon
Entry Requirements: *GCE:* BBB. *IB:* 30.

B80 UNIVERSITY OF THE WEST OF ENGLAND, BRISTOL
FRENCHAY CAMPUS
COLDHARBOUR LANE
BRISTOL BS16 1QY
t: +44 (0)117 32 83333 f: +44 (0)117 32 82810
e: admissions@uwe.ac.uk
// www.uwe.ac.uk

M900 BA Criminology
Duration: 3FT Hon
Entry Requirements: *GCE:* 320.

MM19 BA Criminology and Law
Duration: 3FT Hon
Entry Requirements: *GCE:* 320.

ML93 BA Criminology and Sociology
Duration: 3FT Hon
Entry Requirements: *GCE:* 320.

M9C8 BSc (Hons) Criminology with Psychology
Duration: 3FT Hon
Entry Requirements: *GCE:* 320.

C8M9 BSc (Hons) Psychology with Criminology
Duration: 3FT/4SW Hon
Entry Requirements: *GCE:* 340.

B94 BUCKINGHAMSHIRE NEW UNIVERSITY
QUEEN ALEXANDRA ROAD
HIGH WYCOMBE
BUCKINGHAMSHIRE HP11 2JZ
t: 0800 0565 660 f: 01494 605 023
e: admissions@bucks.ac.uk
// bucks.ac.uk

M930 BSc Criminology
Duration: 3FT Hon
Entry Requirements: *GCE:* 200-240. *IB:* 24. *OCR ND:* M1 *OCR NED:* M3

LM39 BSc Criminology and Sociology
Duration: 3FT Hon
Entry Requirements: *GCE:* 200-240. *IB:* 24. *OCR ND:* M1 *OCR NED:* M3

CM89 BSc Psychology and Criminology
Duration: 3FT Hon
Entry Requirements: *GCE:* 240-280. *IB:* 25. *OCR ND:* D *OCR NED:* M2

C10 CANTERBURY CHRIST CHURCH UNIVERSITY
NORTH HOLMES ROAD
CANTERBURY
KENT CT1 1QU
t: 01227 782900 f: 01227 782888
e: admissions@canterbury.ac.uk
// www.canterbury.ac.uk

M900 BA Applied Criminology
Duration: 3FT Hon
Entry Requirements: *GCE:* 240. *IB:* 24.

MT97 BA Applied Criminology and American Studies
Duration: 3FT Hon
Entry Requirements: *GCE:* 240. *IB:* 24.

MQ93 BA Applied Criminology and English Literature
Duration: 3FT Hon
Entry Requirements: *GCE:* 240. *IB:* 24.

MP9H BA Applied Criminology and Film, Radio & Television Studies
Duration: 3FT Hon
Entry Requirements: *GCE:* 240. *IB:* 24.

MF94 BA Applied Criminology and Forensic Investigation
Duration: 3FT Hon
Entry Requirements: *GCE:* 240. *IB:* 24.

MF98 BA Applied Criminology and Geography
Duration: 3FT Hon
Entry Requirements: *GCE:* 240. *IB:* 24.

MB99 BA Applied Criminology and Health Studies
Duration: 3FT Hon
Entry Requirements: *GCE:* 240. *IB:* 24.

MC98 BA Applied Criminology and Psychology
Duration: 3FT Hon
Entry Requirements: *GCE:* 260. *IB:* 24.

MV96 BA Applied Criminology and Religious Studies
Duration: 3FT Hon
Entry Requirements: *GCE:* 240. *IB:* 24.

ML93 BA Applied Criminology and Sociology & Social Science
Duration: 3FT Hon
Entry Requirements: *GCE:* 240. *IB:* 24.

CM89 BA Applied Criminology and Sport & Exercise Psychology
Duration: 3FT Hon
Entry Requirements: *GCE:* 240. *IB:* 24.

MC96 BA Applied Criminology and Sport & Exercise Science
Duration: 3FT Hon
Entry Requirements: *GCE:* 240. *IB:* 24.

M9T7 BA Applied Criminology with American Studies
Duration: 3FT Hon
Entry Requirements: *GCE:* 240. *IB:* 24.

M9Q3 BA Applied Criminology with English Literature
Duration: 3FT Hon
Entry Requirements: *GCE:* 240. *IB:* 24.

M9PH BA Applied Criminology with Film, Radio & Television Studies
Duration: 3FT Hon
Entry Requirements: *GCE:* 240. *IB:* 24.

M9F4 BA Applied Criminology with Forensic Investigation
Duration: 3FT Hon
Entry Requirements: *GCE:* 240. *IB:* 24.

M9FK BA Applied Criminology with Forensic Investigation 'International Only'
Duration: 4FT Hon
Entry Requirements: Interview required.

M9F8 BA Applied Criminology with Geography
Duration: 3FT Hon
Entry Requirements: *GCE:* 240. *IB:* 24.

M9B9 BA Applied Criminology with Health Studies
Duration: 3FT Hon
Entry Requirements: *GCE:* 240. *IB:* 24.

M9C8 BA Applied Criminology with Psychology
Duration: 3FT Hon
Entry Requirements: *GCE:* 260. *IB:* 24.

M9CW BA Applied Criminology with Psychology 'International Only'
Duration: 4FT Hon
Entry Requirements: *GCE:* 260. *IB:* 24.

M9V6 BA Applied Criminology with Religious Studies
Duration: 3FT Hon
Entry Requirements: *GCE:* 240. *IB:* 24.

M2M9 BA Legal Studies with Applied Criminology 'International Only'
Duration: 4FT Hon
Entry Requirements: Interview required.

T7M9 BA/BSc American Studies with Applied Criminology
Duration: 3FT Hon
Entry Requirements: *GCE:* 240. *IB:* 24.

M292 BA/BSc Applied Criminology with Legal Studies
Duration: 3FT Hon
Entry Requirements: *GCE:* 240. *IB:* 24.

M9L3 BA/BSc Applied Criminology with Sociology & Social Science
Duration: 3FT Hon
Entry Requirements: *GCE:* 240. *IB:* 24.

M9CV BA/BSc Applied Criminology with Sport & Exercise Psychology
Duration: 3FT Hon
Entry Requirements: *GCE:* 240. *IB:* 24.

M9C6 BA/BSc Applied Criminology with Sport & Exercise Science
Duration: 3FT Hon
Entry Requirements: *GCE:* 240. *IB:* 24.

Q3M9 BA/BSc English Literature with Applied Criminology
Duration: 3FT Hon
Entry Requirements: *GCE:* 240. *IB:* 24.

P3MX BA/BSc Film, Radio & Television Studies with Applied Criminology
Duration: 3FT Hon
Entry Requirements: *GCE:* 240. *IB:* 24.

B9M9 BA/BSc Health Studies with Applied Criminology
Duration: 3FT Hon
Entry Requirements: *GCE:* 240. *IB:* 24.

M290 BA/BSc Legal Studies and Applied Criminology
Duration: 3FT Hon
Entry Requirements: *GCE:* 240. *IB:* 24.

M291 BA/BSc Legal Studies with Applied Criminology
Duration: 3FT Hon
Entry Requirements: *GCE:* 240. *IB:* 24.

C8MX BA/BSc Psychology with Applied Criminology
Duration: 3FT Hon
Entry Requirements: *GCE:* 260. *IB:* 24.

V6M9 BA/BSc Religious Studies with Applied Criminology
Duration: 3FT Hon
Entry Requirements: *GCE:* 240. *IB:* 24.

L3M9 BA/BSc Sociology & Social Science with Applied Criminology
Duration: 3FT Hon
Entry Requirements: *GCE:* 240. *IB:* 24.

C8M9 BA/BSc Sport & Exercise Psychology with Applied Criminology
Duration: 3FT Hon
Entry Requirements: Contact the institution for details.

F4M9 BSc/BA Forensic Investigation with Applied Criminology
Duration: 3FT Hon
Entry Requirements: *GCE:* 240. *IB:* 24.

F8M9 BSc/BA Geography with Applied Criminology
Duration: 3FT Hon
Entry Requirements: *GCE:* 240. *IB:* 24.

C6M9 BSc/BA Sport & Exercise Science with Applied Criminology
Duration: 3FT Hon
Entry Requirements: *GCE:* 240. *IB:* 24.

C15 CARDIFF UNIVERSITY
PO BOX 927
30-36 NEWPORT ROAD
CARDIFF CF24 0DE
t: 029 2087 9999 f: 029 2087 6138
e: admissions@cardiff.ac.uk
// www.cardiff.ac.uk

XM39 BScEcon Education and Criminology
Duration: 3FT Hon
Entry Requirements: *GCE:* BBB. *SQAAH:* BBB. *IB:* 32. *OCR ND:* D *OCR NED:* D1

ML94 BScEcon Social Policy and Criminology
Duration: 3FT Hon
Entry Requirements: *GCE:* BBB. *SQAAH:* BBB. *IB:* 32. *OCR ND:* D *OCR NED:* D1

LM39 BScEcon Sociology and Criminology
Duration: 3FT Hon
Entry Requirements: *GCE:* ABB. *SQAAH:* ABB. *IB:* 34. *OCR ND:* D *OCR NED:* D1

M190 LLB Law and Criminology (Integrated)
Duration: 3FT Hon
Entry Requirements: *GCE:* AAB. *SQAAH:* AAB. *IB:* 34. Interview required.

C30 UNIVERSITY OF CENTRAL LANCASHIRE
PRESTON
LANCS PR1 2HE
t: 01772 201201 f: 01772 894954
e: uadmissions@uclan.ac.uk
// www.uclan.ac.uk

MV95 BA Criminology and Philosophy
Duration: 3FT Hon
Entry Requirements: *GCE:* 260-300. *IB:* 28. *BTEC Dip:* D*D*.
BTEC ExtDip: DMM. *OCR ND:* D *OCR NED:* M2

LM49 BA Criminology and Social Policy
Duration: 3FT Hon
Entry Requirements: *GCE:* 260-300. *SQAH:* ABBCC-BBBB.
SQAAH: BBB-CCC. *IB:* 30.

LM39 BA Criminology and Sociology
Duration: 3FT Hon
Entry Requirements: *GCE:* 260-300. *SQAH:* ABBCC-BBBB.
SQAAH: BBB-CCC. *IB:* 30. *BTEC Dip:* D*D*. *BTEC ExtDip:* DMM.

M190 BA Law and Criminology
Duration: 3FT Hon
Entry Requirements: *GCE:* CCC. *IB:* 24. *OCR ND:* D *OCR NED:* M3

LM31 BA Sociology and Criminology
Duration: 3FT Hon
Entry Requirements: *GCE:* 260-300. *SQAH:* ABBCC-BBBB.
SQAAH: BBB-CCC. *IB:* 30.

CMV9 BSc Psychology and Criminology
Duration: 3FT Hon
Entry Requirements: *Foundation:* Distinction. *GCE:* 260-300.
SQAH: BBBBC-BBCCC. *IB:* 30. *OCR NED:* M2

M191 LLB Law with Criminology
Duration: 3FT Hon
Entry Requirements: *GCE:* BBB. *SQAH:* AAAB. *IB:* 30. *OCR ND:* D
OCR NED: D2

C55 UNIVERSITY OF CHESTER
PARKGATE ROAD
CHESTER CH1 4BJ
t: 01244 511000 f: 01244 511300
e: enquiries@chester.ac.uk
// www.chester.ac.uk

ML9N BA Criminology and Counselling Skills
Duration: 3FT Hon
Entry Requirements: *GCE:* 240-280. *SQAH:* BBBB. *IB:* 26.

MQ93 BA Criminology and English
Duration: 3FT Hon
Entry Requirements: *Foundation:* Merit. *GCE:* 260-300. *SQAH:* BBBB. *IB:* 28.

MR91 BA Criminology and French
Duration: 4FT Hon
Entry Requirements: *GCE:* 240-280. *SQAH:* BBBB. *IB:* 26.

MRX4 BA Criminology and Spanish
Duration: 4FT Hon
Entry Requirements: *GCE:* 240-280. *SQAH:* BBBB. *IB:* 26.

MV96 BA Criminology and Theology & Religious Studies
Duration: 3FT Hon
Entry Requirements: *GCE:* 240-280. *SQAH:* BBBB. *IB:* 26.

MP95 BA Journalism and Criminology
Duration: 3FT Hon
Entry Requirements: *GCE:* 240-280. *SQAH:* BBBB. *IB:* 26.

MM19 BA Law and Criminology
Duration: 3FT Hon
Entry Requirements: *GCE:* 240-280. *SQAH:* BBBB. *IB:* 26.

LM29 BA Politics and Criminology
Duration: 3FT Hon
Entry Requirements: *GCE:* 240-280. *SQAH:* BBBB. *IB:* 26.

M900 BSc Criminology
Duration: 3FT Hon
Entry Requirements: *GCE:* 240-280. *SQAH:* BBBB. *IB:* 26.

MF94 BSc Criminology and Forensic Biology
Duration: 3FT Hon
Entry Requirements: *GCE:* 240-280. *SQAH:* BBBB. *IB:* 26.

MF98 BSc Criminology and Geography
Duration: 3FT Hon
Entry Requirements: *GCE:* 260-300. *SQAH:* BBBB. *IB:* 28.

MC98 BSc Criminology and Psychology
Duration: 3FT Hon
Entry Requirements: *Foundation:* Pass. *GCE:* 260-300. *SQAH:* BBBB. *IB:* 28.

ML93 BSc Criminology and Sociology
Duration: 3FT Hon
Entry Requirements: *GCE:* 240-280. *SQAH:* BBBB. *IB:* 26.

M1LH LLB Law with Criminology
Duration: 3FT Hon
Entry Requirements: *Foundation:* Pass. *GCE:* 260-300. *SQAH:* BBBB. *IB:* 28.

C85 COVENTRY UNIVERSITY
THE STUDENT CENTRE
COVENTRY UNIVERSITY
1 GULSON RD
COVENTRY CV1 2JH
t: 024 7615 2222 f: 024 7615 2223
e: studentenquiries@coventry.ac.uk
// www.coventry.ac.uk

M930 BA Criminology and Law
Duration: 3FT/4SW Hon
Entry Requirements: *GCE:* BCC. *SQAH:* BCCCC. *IB:* 28. *BTEC ExtDip:* DMM. *OCR NED:* M2

CM89 BA Criminology and Psychology
Duration: 3FT/4SW Hon
Entry Requirements: *GCE:* BCC. *SQAH:* BCCCC. *IB:* 28. *BTEC ExtDip:* DMM. *OCR NED:* M2

LM39 BA Sociology and Criminology
Duration: 3FT/4SW Hon
Entry Requirements: *GCE:* BCC. *SQAH:* BCCCC. *IB:* 28. *BTEC ExtDip:* DMM. *OCR NED:* M2

CM82 BSc Psychology and Criminology
Duration: 3FT/4SW Hon
Entry Requirements: *GCE:* BBB. *SQAH:* BBBBC. *IB:* 28. *BTEC ExtDip:* DDM. *OCR NED:* M1

C99 UNIVERSITY OF CUMBRIA
FUSEHILL STREET
CARLISLE
CUMBRIA CA1 2HH
t: 01228 616234 f: 01228 616235
// www.cumbria.ac.uk

LM31 BA Criminology and Law
Duration: 3FT Hon
Entry Requirements: *GCE:* 180-200. *SQAH:* AAAB. *IB:* 30.

LM39 BA Criminology and Social Sciences
Duration: 3FT Hon
Entry Requirements: *Foundation:* Merit. *GCE:* 200. *IB:* 28. *OCR ND:* M1 *OCR NED:* P1

LM49 BSc Policing, Investigation and Criminology
Duration: 3FT Hon
Entry Requirements: *GCE:* 200. *IB:* 24.

MM91 DipHE Criminology and Law
Duration: 2FT Dip
Entry Requirements: Contact the institution for details.

LM3Y DipHE Criminology and Social Sciences
Duration: 2FT Dip
Entry Requirements: *Foundation:* Pass. *GCE:* 80. *IB:* 24.

112M DipHE Policing, Investigation and Criminology
Duration: 2FT Dip
Entry Requirements: Contact the institution for details.

D39 UNIVERSITY OF DERBY
KEDLESTON ROAD
DERBY DE22 1GB
t: 01332 591167 f: 01332 597724
e: askadmissions@derby.ac.uk
// www.derby.ac.uk

NM49 BA Accounting and Applied Criminology
Duration: 3FT Hon
Entry Requirements: *Foundation:* Distinction. *GCE:* 260-300. *IB:* 28. *BTEC Dip:* D*D*. *BTEC ExtDip:* DMM. *OCR NED:* M2

MX23 BA Applied Criminology and Education Studies
Duration: 3FT Hon
Entry Requirements: *Foundation:* Distinction. *GCE:* 260-300. *IB:* 28. *BTEC Dip:* D*D*. *BTEC ExtDip:* DMM. *OCR NED:* M2

MQ23 BA Applied Criminology and English
Duration: 3FT Hon
Entry Requirements: *Foundation:* Distinction. *GCE:* 260-300. *IB:* 28. *BTEC Dip:* D*D*. *BTEC ExtDip:* DMM. *OCR NED:* M2

MP2H BA Applied Criminology and Film & Television Studies
Duration: 3FT Hon
Entry Requirements: *Foundation:* Distinction. *GCE:* 260-300. *IB:* 28. *BTEC Dip:* D*D*. *BTEC ExtDip:* DMM. *OCR NED:* M2

MV21 BA Applied Criminology and History
Duration: 3FT Hon
Entry Requirements: *Foundation:* Distinction. *GCE:* 260-300. *IB:* 28. *BTEC Dip:* D*D*. *BTEC ExtDip:* DMM. *OCR NED:* M2

MM21 BA Applied Criminology and Law
Duration: 3FT Hon
Entry Requirements: *Foundation:* Distinction. *GCE:* 260-300. *IB:* 28. *BTEC Dip:* D*D*. *BTEC ExtDip:* DMM. *OCR NED:* M2

MC28 BA Applied Criminology and Psychology
Duration: 3FT Hon
Entry Requirements: *Foundation:* Distinction. *GCE:* 260-300. *IB:* 28. *BTEC Dip:* D*D*. *BTEC ExtDip:* DMM. *OCR NED:* M2

ML23 BA Applied Criminology and Sociology
Duration: 3FT Hon
Entry Requirements: *Foundation:* Distinction. *GCE:* 260-300. *IB:* 28. *BTEC Dip:* D*D*. *BTEC ExtDip:* DMM. *OCR NED:* M2

MC26 BA Applied Criminology and Sport & Exercise Studies
Duration: 3FT Hon
Entry Requirements: *Foundation:* Distinction. *GCE:* 260-300. *IB:* 28. *BTEC Dip:* D*D*. *BTEC ExtDip:* DMM. *OCR NED:* M2

MW24 BA Applied Criminology and Theatre Studies
Duration: 3FT Hon
Entry Requirements: *Foundation:* Distinction. *GCE:* 260-300. *IB:* 28. *BTEC Dip:* D*D*. *BTEC ExtDip:* DMM. *OCR NED:* M2

KM19 BA Architectural Design and Applied Criminology
Duration: 3FT Hon
Entry Requirements: *Foundation:* Distinction. *GCE:* 260-300. *IB:* 28. *BTEC Dip:* D*D*. *BTEC ExtDip:* DMM. *OCR NED:* M2

PM39 BA Professional Writing and Applied Criminology
Duration: 3FT Hon
Entry Requirements: *Foundation:* Distinction. *GCE:* 260-300. *IB:* 28. *BTEC Dip:* D*D*. *BTEC ExtDip:* DMM. *OCR NED:* M2

ML27 BA/BSc Applied Criminology and Geography
Duration: 3FT Hon
Entry Requirements: *Foundation:* Distinction. *GCE:* 260-300. *IB:* 28. *BTEC Dip:* D*D*. *BTEC ExtDip:* DMM. *OCR NED:* M2

LM99 BA/BSc Third World Development and Applied Criminology
Duration: 3FT Hon
Entry Requirements: *Foundation:* Distinction. *GCE:* 260-300. *IB:* 28. *BTEC Dip:* D*D*. *BTEC ExtDip:* DMM. *OCR NED:* M2

M1M2 LLB Law with Criminology
Duration: 3FT Hon
Entry Requirements: *GCE:* 320. *IB:* 28. *BTEC Dip:* D*D*. *BTEC ExtDip:* DMM. *OCR NED:* D2

E28 UNIVERSITY OF EAST LONDON
DOCKLANDS CAMPUS
UNIVERSITY WAY
LONDON E16 2RD
t: 020 8223 3333 f: 020 8223 2978
e: study@uel.ac.uk
// www.uel.ac.uk

L6M2 BA Anthropology with Criminology
Duration: 3FT Hon
Entry Requirements: *GCE:* 240. *IB:* 24.

WM89 BA Creative & Professional Writing/Criminology
Duration: 3FT Hon
Entry Requirements: *GCE:* 240. *IB:* 24.

M9F4 BA Criminology with Forensic Science
Duration: 3FT Hon
Entry Requirements: *GCE:* 240. *IB:* 24.

M9M1 BA Criminology with Law
Duration: 3FT Hon
Entry Requirements: *GCE:* 240. *IB:* 28.

M9P3 BA Criminology with Media Studies
Duration: 3FT Hon
Entry Requirements: *GCE:* 240. *IB:* 24.

M9C8 BA Criminology with Psychology
Duration: 3FT Hon
Entry Requirements: *GCE:* 240. *IB:* 24.

MC98 BA Criminology with Psychosocial Studies
Duration: 3FT Hon
Entry Requirements: *GCE:* 240. *IB:* 24.

M9LH BA Criminology with Sociology
Duration: 3FT Hon
Entry Requirements: *GCE:* 240. *IB:* 24.

M9B2 BA Criminology with Toxicology
Duration: 3FT Hon
Entry Requirements: *GCE:* 240. *IB:* 28.

MV91 BA Criminology/History
Duration: 3FT Hon
Entry Requirements: *GCE:* 240. *IB:* 24.

ML92 BA Criminology/International Politics
Duration: 3FT Hon
Entry Requirements: *GCE:* 240. *IB:* 24.

MM19 BA Criminology/Law
Duration: 3FT Hon
Entry Requirements: *GCE:* 240. *IB:* 24.

M9CW BA Criminology/Psychosocial Studies
Duration: 3FT Hon
Entry Requirements: *GCE:* 240. *IB:* 24.

M9L3 BA Criminology/Sociology
Duration: 3FT Hon
Entry Requirements: *GCE:* 240. *IB:* 24.

M1M2 BA Law with Criminology
Duration: 3FT Hon
Entry Requirements: *GCE:* 240. *IB:* 24.

MF94 BA/BSc Criminology and Forensic Science
Duration: 3FT Hon
Entry Requirements: *GCE:* 240. *IB:* 28.

F4M9 BSc Forensic Science with Criminology
Duration: 3FT Hon
Entry Requirements: *GCE:* 240. *IB:* 24.

C5M9 BSc Immunology with Criminology
Duration: 3FT Hon
Entry Requirements: *GCE:* 240. *IB:* 24.

B2M9 BSc Pharmacology with Criminology
Duration: 3FT Hon
Entry Requirements: *GCE:* 240. *IB:* 24.

C8M9 BSc Psychology with Criminology
Duration: 3FT Hon
Entry Requirements: *GCE:* 240. *IB:* 24.

B2MX BSc Toxicology with Criminology
Duration: 3FT Hon
Entry Requirements: *GCE:* 240. *IB:* 24.

E42 EDGE HILL UNIVERSITY
ORMSKIRK
LANCASHIRE L39 4QP
t: 01695 657000 f: 01695 584355
e: study@edgehill.ac.uk
// www.edgehill.ac.uk

XM32 BA Childhood & Youth Studies and Criminology
Duration: 3FT Hon
Entry Requirements: *GCE:* 280. *IB:* 26. *OCR ND:* D *OCR NED:* M2

ML93 BA Criminology and Sociology
Duration: 3FT Hon
Entry Requirements: *GCE:* 280. *IB:* 26. *OCR ND:* D *OCR NED:* M2

M9M1 BA Criminology with Law
Duration: 3FT Hon
Entry Requirements: *GCE:* 280. *IB:* 26. *OCR ND:* D *OCR NED:* M2

M1M9 LLB Law with Criminology
Duration: 3FT Hon
Entry Requirements: *GCE:* 280. *IB:* 26. *OCR ND:* D *OCR NED:* M2

E59 EDINBURGH NAPIER UNIVERSITY
CRAIGLOCKHART CAMPUS
EDINBURGH EH14 1DJ
t: +44 (0)8452 60 60 40 f: 0131 455 6464
e: info@napier.ac.uk
// www.napier.ac.uk

M900 BA Criminology
Duration: 3FT/4FT Ord/Hon
Entry Requirements: *GCE:* 230.

E70 THE UNIVERSITY OF ESSEX
WIVENHOE PARK
COLCHESTER
ESSEX CO4 3SQ
t: 01206 873666 f: 01206 874477
e: admit@essex.ac.uk
// www.essex.ac.uk

M900 BA Criminology
Duration: 3FT Hon
Entry Requirements: *GCE:* ABB-BBB. *SQAH:* AAAB-AABB.

MT27 BA Criminology and American (United States) Studies (Including Year Abroad)
Duration: 4FT Hon
Entry Requirements: *GCE:* ABB-BBB. *SQAH:* AAAB-AABB. Interview required.

MT2R BA Criminology and American (United States) Studies (term abroad)
Duration: 3FT Hon
Entry Requirements: *GCE:* ABB-BBB. *SQAH:* AAAB-AABB. Interview required.

MP93 BA Criminology and the Media
Duration: 3FT Hon
Entry Requirements: *GCE:* ABB-BBB. *SQAH:* AAAB-AABB.

MV91 BA History and Criminology
Duration: 3FT Hon
Entry Requirements: *GCE:* ABB-BBB. *SQAH:* AAAB-AABB. *IB:* 32.

MV9C BA History and Criminology (Including Year Abroad)
Duration: 4FT Hon
Entry Requirements: *GCE:* ABB-BBB. *SQAH:* AAAB-AABB. *IB:* 32.

LM39 BA Sociology and Criminology
Duration: 3FT Hon
Entry Requirements: *GCE:* ABB-BBB. *SQAH:* AAAB-AABB.

G14 UNIVERSITY OF GLAMORGAN, CARDIFF AND PONTYPRIDD
ENQUIRIES AND ADMISSIONS UNIT
PONTYPRIDD CF37 1DL
t: 08456 434030 f: 01443 654050
e: enquiries@glam.ac.uk
// www.glam.ac.uk

MM91 BSc Criminology and Law
Duration: 3FT Hon
Entry Requirements: *GCE:* BBC. *IB:* 25. *BTEC SubDip:* M. *BTEC Dip:* D*D*. *BTEC ExtDip:* DMM.

ML93 BSc Criminology and Sociology
Duration: 3FT Hon
Entry Requirements: *GCE:* BBC. *IB:* 25. *BTEC SubDip:* M. *BTEC Dip:* D*D*. *BTEC ExtDip:* DMM.

M9C8 BSc Criminology with Psychology
Duration: 3FT Hon
Entry Requirements: *GCE:* BBC. *IB:* 25. *BTEC SubDip:* M. *BTEC Dip:* D*D*. *BTEC ExtDip:* DMM.

M9L3 BSc Criminology with Sociology
Duration: 3FT Hon
Entry Requirements: *GCE:* BBC. *IB:* 25. *BTEC SubDip:* M. *BTEC Dip:* D*D*. *BTEC ExtDip:* DMM.

F4M9 BSc Forensic Science with Criminology
Duration: 3FT Hon
Entry Requirements: *GCE:* BBC. *IB:* 30. *BTEC Dip:* D*D*. *BTEC ExtDip:* DMM.

C8M9 BSc Psychology with Criminology
Duration: 3FT Hon
Entry Requirements: *GCE:* BBC. *IB:* 25. *BTEC SubDip:* M. *BTEC Dip:* D*D*. *BTEC ExtDip:* DMM.

L3M9 BSc Sociology with Criminology
Duration: 3FT Hon
Entry Requirements: *GCE:* BBC. *IB:* 25. *BTEC SubDip:* M. *BTEC Dip:* D*D*. *BTEC ExtDip:* DMM.

M1M9 LLB Law with Criminology
Duration: 3FT Hon
Entry Requirements: *GCE:* BBB. *IB:* 26. *BTEC SubDip:* M. *BTEC Dip:* D*D*. *BTEC ExtDip:* DDM.

G50 THE UNIVERSITY OF GLOUCESTERSHIRE
PARK CAMPUS
THE PARK
CHELTENHAM GL50 2RH
t: 01242 714501 f: 01242 714869
e: admissions@glos.ac.uk
// www.glos.ac.uk

ML93 BA/BSc Criminology and Sociology
Duration: 3FT Hon
Entry Requirements: *GCE:* 280-300.

M900 BSc Criminology
Duration: 3FT Hon
Entry Requirements: *GCE:* 280-300.

MC98 BSc Criminology and Psychology
Duration: 3FT Hon
Entry Requirements: *GCE:* 280-300.

G70 UNIVERSITY OF GREENWICH
GREENWICH CAMPUS
OLD ROYAL NAVAL COLLEGE
PARK ROW
LONDON SE10 9LS
t: 020 8331 9000 f: 020 8331 8145
e: courseinfo@gre.ac.uk
// www.gre.ac.uk

M211 BA Criminology
Duration: 3FT Hon
Entry Requirements: *GCE:* 240. *IB:* 24.

F4M9 BSc Forensic Science with Criminology
Duration: 3FT Hon
Entry Requirements: *GCE:* 260. *IB:* 24.

H60 THE UNIVERSITY OF HUDDERSFIELD
QUEENSGATE
HUDDERSFIELD HD1 3DH
t: 01484 473969 f: 01484 472765
e: admissionsandrecords@hud.ac.uk
// www.hud.ac.uk

M900 BSc Criminology
Duration: 3FT Hon
Entry Requirements: *GCE:* 280.

M2L2 BSc Criminology and International Politics (Top-up)
Duration: 1FT Hon
Entry Requirements: Contact the institution for details.

ML22 BSc Politics and Criminology
Duration: 3FT Hon
Entry Requirements: *GCE:* 300. *SQAH:* BBBBC.

C8M2 BSc Psychology with Criminology
Duration: 3FT Hon
Entry Requirements: *GCE:* 300.

ML93 BSc Sociology and Criminology
Duration: 3FT Hon
Entry Requirements: *GCE:* 280.

L3M9 BSc Sociology with Criminology
Duration: 3FT Hon
Entry Requirements: *GCE:* 280.

H72 THE UNIVERSITY OF HULL
THE UNIVERSITY OF HULL
COTTINGHAM ROAD
HULL HU6 7RX
t: 01482 466100 f: 01482 442290
e: admissions@hull.ac.uk
// www.hull.ac.uk

M930 BA Criminology
Duration: 3FT Hon
Entry Requirements: *GCE:* 280-320. *IB:* 28. *BTEC ExtDip:* DMM.

LM39 BA Criminology and Sociology
Duration: 3FT Hon
Entry Requirements: *GCE:* 280-320. *IB:* 28. *BTEC ExtDip:* DMM.

ML93 BA Criminology and Sociology (with Foundation Year)
Duration: 4FT Hon
Entry Requirements: Interview required.

M9F4 BA Criminology with Forensic Science
Duration: 3FT Hon
Entry Requirements: *GCE:* 280-320. *IB:* 28. *BTEC ExtDip:* DMM.

M9M1 BA Criminology with Law
Duration: 3FT Hon
Entry Requirements: *GCE:* 280-320. *IB:* 28. *BTEC ExtDip:* DMM.

M9C8 BA Criminology with Psychology
Duration: 3FT Hon
Entry Requirements: *GCE:* 280-320. *IB:* 28. *BTEC ExtDip:* DMM.

F4M9 BSc Forensic Science with Criminology
Duration: 3FT Hon
Entry Requirements: *GCE:* 300. *IB:* 30. *BTEC ExtDip:* DDM.

C8M9 BSc Psychology with Criminology
Duration: 3FT Hon
Entry Requirements: *GCE:* 280. *IB:* 32. *BTEC ExtDip:* DMM.

M1M2 LLB Law with Criminology
Duration: 3FT Hon
Entry Requirements: *GCE:* 320. *IB:* 30. *BTEC ExtDip:* DDM.

H73 HULL COLLEGE
QUEEN'S GARDENS
HULL HU1 3DG
t: 01482 329943 f: 01482 598733
e: info@hull-college.ac.uk
// www.hull-college.ac.uk/higher-education

M9L3 BA Criminology (Top-Up)
Duration: 1FT Hon
Entry Requirements: Contact the institution for details.

K12 KEELE UNIVERSITY
KEELE UNIVERSITY
STAFFORDSHIRE ST5 5BG
t: 01782 734005 f: 01782 632343
e: undergraduate@keele.ac.uk
// www.keele.ac.uk

NM49 BA Accounting and Criminology
Duration: 3FT Hon
Entry Requirements: *GCE:* ABB.

MTX7 BA American Studies and Criminology
Duration: 3FT Hon
Entry Requirements: *GCE:* BBB.

LM19 BA Criminology and Economics
Duration: 3FT Hon
Entry Requirements: *GCE:* ABB.

MXX3 BA Criminology and Educational Studies
Duration: 3FT Hon
Entry Requirements: *GCE:* BBC.

MQ93 BA Criminology and English
Duration: 3FT Hon
Entry Requirements: *GCE:* BBB.

MP93 BA Criminology and Film Studies
Duration: 3FT Hon
Entry Requirements: *GCE:* BBB.

MNX3 BA Criminology and Finance
Duration: 3FT Hon
Entry Requirements: *GCE:* ABB.

LM79 BA Criminology and Geography
Duration: 3FT Hon
Entry Requirements: *GCE:* BBC.

MVX1 BA Criminology and History
Duration: 3FT Hon
Entry Requirements: *GCE:* BBB.

LMR9 BA Criminology and Human Geography
Duration: 3FT Hon
Entry Requirements: *GCE:* BBC.

ML92 BA Criminology and International Relations
Duration: 3FT Hon
Entry Requirements: *GCE:* BBB.

M930 BA Criminology and Law
Duration: 3FT Hon
Entry Requirements: *GCE:* AAB.

MNC5 BA Criminology and Marketing
Duration: 3FT Hon
Entry Requirements: *GCE:* ABB.

PM39 BA Criminology and Media, Communications & Culture
Duration: 3FT Hon
Entry Requirements: *GCE:* BBC.

MWX3 BA Criminology and Music
Duration: 3FT Hon
Entry Requirements: *GCE:* BBC.

MVX5 BA Criminology and Philosophy
Duration: 3FT Hon
Entry Requirements: *GCE:* BBB.

LMH9 BA Criminology and Sociology
Duration: 3FT Hon
Entry Requirements: *GCE:* BBC.

ML93 BA Criminology with Social Science Foundation Year
Duration: 4FT Deg
Entry Requirements: *GCE:* CC.

FM79 BSc Applied Environmental Science and Criminology
Duration: 3FT Hon
Entry Requirements: *GCE:* BBC.

CM8Y BSc Applied Psychology and Criminology
Duration: 4FT Deg
Entry Requirements: *GCE:* BBC.

FM59 BSc Astrophysics and Criminology
Duration: 3FT Hon
Entry Requirements: *GCE:* BBC.

CM19 BSc Biology and Criminology
Duration: 3FT Hon
Entry Requirements: *GCE:* BBC.

FM19 BSc Chemistry and Criminology
Duration: 3FT Hon
Entry Requirements: *GCE:* BBC.

GM49 BSc Computer Science and Criminology
Duration: 3FT Hon
Entry Requirements: *GCE:* BBC.

FM42 BSc Criminology and Forensic Science
Duration: 3FT Hon
Entry Requirements: *GCE:* BBC.

MC91 BSc Criminology and Human Biology
Duration: 3FT Hon
Entry Requirements: *GCE:* BBC.

MG95 BSc Criminology and Information Systems
Duration: 3FT Hon
Entry Requirements: *GCE:* BBC.

FMC9 BSc Criminology and Medicinal Chemistry
Duration: 3FT Hon
Entry Requirements: *GCE:* BBC.

BM19 BSc Criminology and Neuroscience
Duration: 3FT Hon
Entry Requirements: *GCE:* BBC.

FM89 BSc Criminology and Physical Geography
Duration: 3FT Hon
Entry Requirements: *GCE:* BBC.

FM39 BSc Criminology and Physics
Duration: 3FT Hon
Entry Requirements: *GCE:* BBC.

CM81 BSc Criminology and Psychology
Duration: 3FT Hon
Entry Requirements: *GCE:* BBC.

GM79 BSc Smart Systems and Criminology
Duration: 3FT Hon
Entry Requirements: *GCE:* BBC.

M1LH LLB Law with Criminology
Duration: 3FT Hon
Entry Requirements: *GCE:* AAB.

K24 THE UNIVERSITY OF KENT
RECRUITMENT & ADMISSIONS OFFICE
REGISTRY
UNIVERSITY OF KENT
CANTERBURY, KENT CT2 7NZ
t: 01227 827272 f: 01227 827077
e: information@kent.ac.uk
// www.kent.ac.uk

MV99 BA Criminology and Cultural Studies
Duration: 3FT Hon
Entry Requirements: *GCE:* ABB. *SQAH:* AABBB. *SQAAH:* ABB. *IB:* 33. *OCR ND:* D *OCR NED:* D2

LM49 BA Criminology and Social Policy
Duration: 3FT Hon
Entry Requirements: *GCE:* ABB. *SQAH:* AABBB. *SQAAH:* ABB. *IB:* 33. *OCR ND:* D *OCR NED:* D2

LM39 BA Criminology and Sociology
Duration: 3FT Hon
Entry Requirements: *GCE:* ABB. *SQAH:* AABBB. *SQAAH:* ABB. *IB:* 33. *OCR ND:* D *OCR NED:* D2

MM19 BA Law and Criminology
Duration: 3FT Hon
Entry Requirements: *GCE:* AAB. *SQAH:* AAAAB. *IB:* 33. *OCR ND:* D *OCR NED:* M1

K84 KINGSTON UNIVERSITY
STUDENT INFORMATION & ADVICE CENTRE
COOPER HOUSE
40-46 SURBITON ROAD
KINGSTON UPON THAMES KT1 2HX
t: 0844 8552177 f: 020 8547 7080
e: aps@kingston.ac.uk
// www.kingston.ac.uk

LM39 BA Criminology
Duration: 3FT Hon
Entry Requirements: *GCE:* 260. *SQAH:* BBCCC. *SQAAH:* BBC.

M9R1 BA Criminology with French
Duration: 3FT Hon
Entry Requirements: *GCE:* 240-320. *SQAH:* BBCCC. *SQAAH:* BBC.

M9C8 BA Criminology with Psychology
Duration: 3FT Hon
Entry Requirements: *GCE:* 240-320. *SQAH:* BBCCC. *SQAAH:* BBC.

M2R4 BA Criminology with Spanish
Duration: 3FT Hon
Entry Requirements: *GCE:* 240-320. *SQAH:* BBCCC. *SQAAH:* BBC.

L2M9 BA Politics with Criminology
Duration: 3FT Hon
Entry Requirements: *GCE:* 220-360.

C8M9 BA Psychology with Criminology
Duration: 3FT Hon
Entry Requirements: *GCE:* 240-320.

M1M9 LLB Law with Criminology
Duration: 3FT Hon
Entry Requirements: *GCE:* 320. *IB:* 27.

M1MX LLB Law with Criminology with Industrial Placement
Duration: 4SW Hon
Entry Requirements: *GCE:* 320. *IB:* 27.

M1MY LLB Law with Criminology with study abroad
Duration: 4FT Hon
Entry Requirements: *GCE:* 320. *IB:* 27.

L14 LANCASTER UNIVERSITY
THE UNIVERSITY
LANCASTER
LANCASHIRE LA1 4YW
t: 01524 592029 f: 01524 846243
e: ugadmissions@lancaster.ac.uk
// www.lancs.ac.uk

M930 BA Criminology
Duration: 3FT Hon
Entry Requirements: *GCE:* AAB. *SQAH:* ABBBB. *SQAAH:* AAB. *IB:* 35.

LM39 BA Criminology and Sociology
Duration: 3FT Hon
Entry Requirements: *GCE:* AAB. *SQAH:* ABBBB. *SQAAH:* AAB. *IB:* 35.

MM12 LLB Law and Criminology
Duration: 3FT Hon
Entry Requirements: *GCE:* AAA. *SQAH:* AAABB. *SQAAH:* AAA. *IB:* 36.

L27 LEEDS METROPOLITAN UNIVERSITY
COURSE ENQUIRIES OFFICE
CITY CAMPUS
LEEDS LS1 3HE
t: 0113 81 23113 f: 0113 81 23129
// www.leedsmet.ac.uk

M900 BA Criminology
Duration: 3FT Hon
Entry Requirements: *GCE:* 200. *IB:* 24.

MC98 BA Criminology & Psychology
Duration: 3FT Hon
Entry Requirements: *GCE:* 200. *IB:* 24.

ML93 BA Criminology & Sociology
Duration: 3FT Hon
Entry Requirements: *GCE:* 200. *IB:* 24.

M1M9 BA Law with Criminology
Duration: 3FT Hon
Entry Requirements: *GCE:* 260. *IB:* 26.

C8M9 BSc Psychology with Criminology
Duration: 3FT Hon
Entry Requirements: *GCE:* 260. *IB:* 24.

L34 UNIVERSITY OF LEICESTER
UNIVERSITY ROAD
LEICESTER LE1 7RH
t: 0116 252 5281 f: 0116 252 2447
e: admissions@le.ac.uk
// www.le.ac.uk

ML26 LLB Law with Criminology
Duration: 3FT Hon
Entry Requirements: *GCE:* AAA. *SQAH:* AAAAA. *SQAAH:* AAA. *IB:* 36.

L39 UNIVERSITY OF LINCOLN
ADMISSIONS
BRAYFORD POOL
LINCOLN LN6 7TS
t: 01522 886097 f: 01522 886146
e: admissions@lincoln.ac.uk
// www.lincoln.ac.uk

M931 BA Criminology
Duration: 3FT Hon
Entry Requirements: *GCE:* 260.

LMF9 BA/BSc Criminology and International Relations
Duration: 3FT Hon
Entry Requirements: *GCE:* 260.

LMG9 BA/BSc Criminology and Politics
Duration: 3FT Hon
Entry Requirements: *GCE:* 260.

LM49 BA/BSc Criminology and Social Policy
Duration: 3FT Hon
Entry Requirements: *GCE:* 260.

CM89 BA/BSc Psychology and Criminology
Duration: 3FT Hon
Entry Requirements: *GCE:* 300.

FM49 BSc Criminology and Forensic Investigation
Duration: 3FT Hon
Entry Requirements: *GCE:* 280.

M930 LLB Criminology and Law
Duration: 3FT Hon
Entry Requirements: *GCE:* 300.

L41 THE UNIVERSITY OF LIVERPOOL
THE FOUNDATION BUILDING
BROWNLOW HILL
LIVERPOOL L69 7ZX
t: 0151 794 2000 f: 0151 708 6502
e: ugrecruitment@liv.ac.uk
// www.liv.ac.uk

LM39 BA Criminology and Sociology
Duration: 3FT Hon
Entry Requirements: *GCE:* ABB. *SQAH:* AABBB. *SQAAH:* ABB. *IB:*
33. Interview required.

M103 LLB Law with Criminology
Duration: 3FT Hon
Entry Requirements: *GCE:* AAA. *SQAH:* AAAAA. *SQAAH:* AA. *IB:*
36. *OCR ND:* D *OCR NED:* D2

L46 LIVERPOOL HOPE UNIVERSITY
HOPE PARK
LIVERPOOL L16 9JD
t: 0151 291 3331 f: 0151 291 3434
e: administration@hope.ac.uk
// www.hope.ac.uk

M990 BA Criminology
Duration: 3FT Hon
Entry Requirements: *GCE:* 300-320. *IB:* 25.

L6M1 BA Criminology and Law
Duration: 3FT Hon
Entry Requirements: *GCE:* 300-320. *IB:* 25.

ML94 BA Criminology and Social Policy
Duration: 3FT Hon
Entry Requirements: *GCE:* 300-320. *IB:* 25.

L51 LIVERPOOL JOHN MOORES UNIVERSITY
KINGSWAY HOUSE
HATTON GARDEN
LIVERPOOL L3 2AJ
t: 0151 231 5090 f: 0151 904 6368
e: courses@ljmu.ac.uk
// www.ljmu.ac.uk

M212 BA Criminology
Duration: 3FT Hon
Entry Requirements: *GCE:* 280. *IB:* 29.

ML23 BA Criminology and Sociology
Duration: 3FT Hon
Entry Requirements: *GCE:* 260. *IB:* 28.

MC2W BSc Criminology and Psychology
Duration: 3FT Hon
Entry Requirements: *GCE:* 280. *IB:* 29. *OCR ND:* D *OCR NED:* M3

L68 LONDON METROPOLITAN UNIVERSITY
166-220 HOLLOWAY ROAD
LONDON N7 8DB
t: 020 7133 4200
e: admissions@londonmet.ac.uk
// www.londonmet.ac.uk

MM1X BA Criminology and Law
Duration: 3FT Hon
Entry Requirements: *GCE:* 280. *IB:* 28. Interview required.

M930 BSc Criminology
Duration: 3FT Hon
Entry Requirements: *GCE:* 280. *IB:* 28. Interview required.

CM8X BSc Criminology and Psychology
Duration: 3FT Hon
Entry Requirements: *GCE:* 300. *IB:* 28.

ML93 BSc Criminology and Sociology
Duration: 3FT Hon
Entry Requirements: *GCE:* 280. *IB:* 28. Interview required.

ML95 BSc Criminology and Youth Studies
Duration: 3FT Hon
Entry Requirements: *GCE:* 280. *IB:* 28. Interview required.

L72 LONDON SCHOOL OF ECONOMICS AND POLITICAL SCIENCE (UNIVERSITY OF LONDON)
HOUGHTON STREET
LONDON WC2A 2AE
t: 020 7955 7125 f: 020 7955 6001
e: ug.admissions@lse.ac.uk
// www.lse.ac.uk

LM42 BSc Social Policy and Criminology
Duration: 3FT Hon
Entry Requirements: *GCE:* ABB. *SQAH:* AAABB-AABBB. *SQAAH:*
ABB. *IB:* 37.

L75 LONDON SOUTH BANK UNIVERSITY
ADMISSIONS AND RECRUITMENT CENTRE
90 LONDON ROAD
LONDON SE1 6LN
t: 0800 923 8888 f: 020 7815 8273
e: course.enquiry@lsbu.ac.uk
// www.lsbu.ac.uk

M930 BSc Criminology
Duration: 3FT Hon
Entry Requirements: *GCE:* 240. *IB:* 24.

M9M1 BSc Criminology with Law
Duration: 3FT Hon
Entry Requirements: *GCE:* 240. *IB:* 24.

M9C8 BSc Criminology with Psychology
Duration: 3FT Hon
Entry Requirements: *GCE:* 240. *IB:* 24.

F4M9 BSc Forensic Science with Criminology
Duration: 3FT Hon
Entry Requirements: *GCE:* 200. *IB:* 24.

C8M9 BSc (Hons) Psychology with Criminology
Duration: 3FT Hon
Entry Requirements: *GCE:* 260. *IB:* 24.

M1M9 LLB Law with Criminology
Duration: 3FT Hon
Entry Requirements: *GCE:* 260. *IB:* 24.

L79 LOUGHBOROUGH UNIVERSITY
LOUGHBOROUGH
LEICESTERSHIRE LE11 3TU
t: 01509 223522 f: 01509 223905
e: admissions@lboro.ac.uk
// www.lboro.ac.uk

ML24 BSc Criminology and Social Policy
Duration: 3FT Hon
Entry Requirements: *IB:* 32. *BTEC ExtDip:* DDM.

M20 THE UNIVERSITY OF MANCHESTER
RUTHERFORD BUILDING
OXFORD ROAD
MANCHESTER M13 9PL
t: 0161 275 2077 f: 0161 275 2106
e: ug-admissions@manchester.ac.uk
// www.manchester.ac.uk

M901 BA Criminology
Duration: 3FT Hon
Entry Requirements: *GCE:* ABB. *SQAH:* AABBB. *SQAAH:* ABB. *IB:* 33. Interview required.

LM29 BA(SocSci) Politics and Criminology
Duration: 3FT Hon
Entry Requirements: *GCE:* ABB. *SQAH:* ABBBB. *SQAAH:* ABB. *IB:* 34.

LM69 BA(SocSci) Social Anthropology and Criminology
Duration: 3FT Hon
Entry Requirements: *GCE:* ABB. *SQAH:* ABBBB. *SQAAH:* ABB. *IB:* 34.

LM39 BA(SocSci) Sociology and Criminology
Duration: 3FT Hon
Entry Requirements: *GCE:* ABB. *SQAH:* ABBBB. *SQAAH:* ABB. *IB:* 34. *BTEC ExtDip:* DDM.

LM19 BAEcon Economics and Criminology
Duration: 3FT Hon
Entry Requirements: *GCE:* AAB. *SQAH:* AAABB. *SQAAH:* AAB. *IB:* 35.

M1M9 LLB Law with Criminology
Duration: 3FT Hon
Entry Requirements: *GCE:* AAA. *SQAH:* AAAAB. *SQAAH:* AAA. *IB:* 37. Interview required.

M40 THE MANCHESTER METROPOLITAN UNIVERSITY
ADMISSIONS OFFICE
ALL SAINTS (GMS)
ALL SAINTS
MANCHESTER M15 6BH
t: 0161 247 2000
// www.mmu.ac.uk

ML9J BA Criminology
Duration: 3FT Hon
Entry Requirements: *GCE:* BBC-BCC. *SQAAH:* BCC. *OCR NED:* M2

MLX3 BA Criminology and Sociology
Duration: 3FT Hon
Entry Requirements: *GCE:* BBC-BCC. *OCR NED:* M2

ML9F BA Criminology/Politics
Duration: 3FT Hon
Entry Requirements: *GCE:* 240-280. *IB:* 29.

MF94 BA/BSc Criminology/Forensic Science
Duration: 3FT Hon
Entry Requirements: *GCE:* 240-280. *IB:* 29.

MC98 BA/BSc Criminology/Psychology
Duration: 3FT Hon
Entry Requirements: *GCE:* 300. *IB:* 30.

M80 MIDDLESEX UNIVERSITY
MIDDLESEX UNIVERSITY
THE BURROUGHS
LONDON NW4 4BT
t: 020 8411 5555 f: 020 8411 5649
e: enquiries@mdx.ac.uk
// www.mdx.ac.uk

L3MX BA Sociology with Criminology
Duration: 3FT/4SW Hon
Entry Requirements: *GCE:* 200-300. *IB:* 28.

CM89 BSc Psychology with Criminology
Duration: 3FT/4SW Hon
Entry Requirements: *GCE:* 200-300. *IB:* 28.

N38 UNIVERSITY OF NORTHAMPTON
PARK CAMPUS
BOUGHTON GREEN ROAD
NORTHAMPTON NN2 7AL
t: 0800 358 2232 f: 01604 722083
e: admissions@northampton.ac.uk
// www.northampton.ac.uk

W8M9 BA Creative Writing/Criminology
Duration: 3FT Hon
Entry Requirements: *GCE:* 260-280. *SQAH:* AAA-BBBB. *IB:* 24.
BTEC Dip: DD. *BTEC ExtDip:* DMM. *OCR ND:* D *OCR NED:* M2

M930 BA Criminology
Duration: 3FT Hon
Entry Requirements: *GCE:* 260-280. *SQAH:* AAA-BBBB. *IB:* 24.
BTEC Dip: DD. *BTEC ExtDip:* DMM. *OCR ND:* D *OCR NED:* M2

M9D4 BA Criminology with Applied Equine Studies
Duration: 3FT Hon
Entry Requirements: *GCE:* 260-280. *SQAH:* AAA-BBBB. *IB:* 24.
BTEC Dip: DD. *BTEC ExtDip:* DMM. *OCR ND:* D *OCR NED:* M2

M9NM BA Criminology/Advertising
Duration: 3FT Hon
Entry Requirements: *GCE:* 260-280. *SQAH:* AAA-BBBB. *IB:* 24.
BTEC Dip: DD. *BTEC ExtDip:* DMM. *OCR ND:* D *OCR NED:* M2

M9C1 BA Criminology/Biological Conservation
Duration: 3FT Hon
Entry Requirements: *GCE:* 260-280. *SQAH:* AAA-BBBB. *IB:* 24.
BTEC Dip: DD. *BTEC ExtDip:* DMM. *OCR ND:* D *OCR NED:* M2

M9W8 BA Criminology/Creative Writing
Duration: 3FT Hon
Entry Requirements: *GCE:* 260-280. *SQAH:* AAA-BBBB. *IB:* 24.
BTEC Dip: DD. *BTEC ExtDip:* DMM. *OCR ND:* D *OCR NED:* M2

M9W4 BA Criminology/Drama
Duration: 3FT Hon
Entry Requirements: *GCE:* 260-280. *SQAH:* AAA-BBBB. *IB:* 24.
BTEC Dip: DD. *BTEC ExtDip:* DMM. *OCR ND:* D *OCR NED:* M2
Interview required.

M9L1 BA Criminology/Economics
Duration: 3FT Hon
Entry Requirements: *GCE:* 260-280. *SQAH:* AAA-BBBB. *IB:* 24.
BTEC Dip: DD. *BTEC ExtDip:* DMM. *OCR ND:* D *OCR NED:* M2

M9X3 BA Criminology/Education Studies
Duration: 3FT Hon
Entry Requirements: *GCE:* 260-280. *SQAH:* AAA-BBBB. *IB:* 24.
BTEC Dip: DD. *BTEC ExtDip:* DMM. *OCR ND:* D *OCR NED:* M2

M9Q3 BA Criminology/English
Duration: 3FT Hon
Entry Requirements: *GCE:* 260-280. *SQAH:* AAA-BBBB. *IB:* 24.
BTEC Dip: DD. *BTEC ExtDip:* DMM. *OCR ND:* D *OCR NED:* M2

M9W6 BA Criminology/Film & Television Studies
Duration: 3FT Hon
Entry Requirements: *GCE:* 260-280. *SQAH:* AAA-BBBB. *IB:* 24.
BTEC Dip: DD. *BTEC ExtDip:* DMM. *OCR ND:* D *OCR NED:* M2

M9L4 BA Criminology/Health Studies
Duration: 3FT Hon
Entry Requirements: *GCE:* 260-280. *SQAH:* AAA-BBBB. *IB:* 24.
BTEC Dip: DD. *BTEC ExtDip:* DMM. *OCR ND:* D *OCR NED:* M2

M9LX BA Criminology/International Development
Duration: 3FT Hon
Entry Requirements: *GCE:* 260-280. *SQAH:* AAA-BBBB. *IB:* 24.
BTEC Dip: DD. *BTEC ExtDip:* DMM. *OCR ND:* D *OCR NED:* M2

M9M1 BA Criminology/Law
Duration: 3FT Hon
Entry Requirements: *GCE:* 260-280. *SQAH:* AAA-BBBB. *IB:* 24.
BTEC Dip: DD. *BTEC ExtDip:* DMM. *OCR ND:* D *OCR NED:* M2

M9N5 BA Criminology/Marketing
Duration: 3FT Hon
Entry Requirements: *GCE:* 260-280. *SQAH:* AAA-BBBB. *IB:* 24.
BTEC Dip: DD. *BTEC ExtDip:* DMM. *OCR ND:* D *OCR NED:* M2

M9PH BA Criminology/Media Production
Duration: 3FT Hon
Entry Requirements: *GCE:* 260-280. *SQAH:* AAA-BBBB. *IB:* 24.
BTEC Dip: DD. *BTEC ExtDip:* DMM. *OCR ND:* D *OCR NED:* M2

M9F8 BA Criminology/Physical Geography
Duration: 3FT Hon
Entry Requirements: *GCE:* 260-280. *SQAH:* AAA-BBBB. *IB:* 24.
BTEC Dip: DD. *BTEC ExtDip:* DMM. *OCR ND:* D *OCR NED:* M2

M9L2 BA Criminology/Politics
Duration: 3FT Hon
Entry Requirements: *GCE:* 260-280. *SQAH:* AAA-BBBB. *IB:* 24.
BTEC Dip: DD. *BTEC ExtDip:* DMM. *OCR ND:* D *OCR NED:* M2

M9W3 BA Criminology/Popular Music
Duration: 3FT Hon
Entry Requirements: *GCE:* 260-280. *SQAH:* AAA-BBBB. *IB:* 24.
BTEC Dip: DD. *BTEC ExtDip:* DMM. *OCR ND:* D *OCR NED:* M2

M9C8 BA Criminology/Psychology
Duration: 3FT Hon
Entry Requirements: *GCE:* 260-280. *SQAH:* AAA-BBBB. *IB:* 24.
BTEC Dip: DD. *BTEC ExtDip:* DMM. *OCR ND:* D *OCR NED:* M2

M9L3 BA Criminology/Sociology
Duration: 3FT Hon
Entry Requirements: *GCE:* 260-280. *SQAH:* AAA-BBBB. *IB:* 24.
BTEC Dip: DD. *BTEC ExtDip:* DMM. *OCR ND:* D *OCR NED:* M2

M9C6 BA Criminology/Sport Studies
Duration: 3FT Hon
Entry Requirements: *GCE:* 260-280. *SQAH:* AAA-BBBB. *IB:* 24.
BTEC Dip: DD. *BTEC ExtDip:* DMM. *OCR ND:* D *OCR NED:* M2

M9N8 BA Criminology/Tourism
Duration: 3FT Hon
Entry Requirements: *GCE:* 260-280. *SQAH:* AAA-BBBB. *IB:* 24.
BTEC Dip: DD. *BTEC ExtDip:* DMM. *OCR ND:* D *OCR NED:* M2

M9GK BA Criminology/Web Design
Duration: 3FT Hon
Entry Requirements: *GCE:* 260-280. *SQAH:* AAA-BBBB. *IB:* 24.
BTEC Dip: DD. *BTEC ExtDip:* DMM. *OCR ND:* D *OCR NED:* M2

W4M9 BA Drama/Criminology
Duration: 3FT Hon
Entry Requirements: *GCE:* 260-280. *SQAH:* AAA-BBBB. *IB:* 24.
BTEC Dip: DD. *BTEC ExtDip:* DMM. *OCR ND:* D *OCR NED:* M2
Interview required.

L1M9 BA Economics/Criminology
Duration: 3FT Hon
Entry Requirements: *GCE:* 260-280. *SQAH:* AAA-BBBB. *IB:* 24.
BTEC Dip: DD. *BTEC ExtDip:* DMM. *OCR ND:* D *OCR NED:* M2

X3M9 BA Education Studies/Criminology
Duration: 3FT Hon
Entry Requirements: *GCE:* 260-280. *SQAH:* AAA-BBBB. *IB:* 24.
BTEC Dip: DD. *BTEC ExtDip:* DMM. *OCR ND:* D *OCR NED:* M2

Q3M9 BA English/Criminology
Duration: 3FT Hon
Entry Requirements: *GCE:* 260-280. *SQAH:* AAA-BBBB. *IB:* 24.
BTEC Dip: DD. *BTEC ExtDip:* DMM. *OCR ND:* D *OCR NED:* M2

W6M9 BA Film & Television Studies/Criminology
Duration: 3FT Hon
Entry Requirements: *GCE:* 260-280. *SQAH:* AAA-BBBB. *IB:* 24.
BTEC Dip: DD. *BTEC ExtDip:* DMM. *OCR ND:* D *OCR NED:* M2

L4M9 BA Health Studies/Criminology
Duration: 3FT Hon
Entry Requirements: *GCE:* 260-280. *SQAH:* AAA-BBBB. *IB:* 24.
BTEC Dip: DD. *BTEC ExtDip:* DMM. *OCR ND:* D *OCR NED:* M2

L9MX BA International Development/Criminology
Duration: 3FT Hon
Entry Requirements: *GCE:* 260-280. *SQAH:* AAA-BBBB. *IB:* 24.
BTEC Dip: DD. *BTEC ExtDip:* DMM. *OCR ND:* D *OCR NED:* M2

M1M9 BA Law/Criminology
Duration: 3FT Hon
Entry Requirements: *GCE:* 260-280. *SQAH:* AAA-BBBB. *IB:* 24.
BTEC Dip: DD. *BTEC ExtDip:* DMM. *OCR ND:* D *OCR NED:* M2

N5M9 BA Marketing/Criminology
Duration: 3FT Hon
Entry Requirements: *GCE:* 260-280. *SQAH:* AAA-BBBB. *IB:* 24.
BTEC Dip: DD. *BTEC ExtDip:* DMM. *OCR ND:* D *OCR NED:* M2

P3MX BA Media Production/Criminology
Duration: 3FT Hon
Entry Requirements: *GCE:* 260-280. *SQAH:* AAA-BBBB. *IB:* 24.
BTEC Dip: DD. *BTEC ExtDip:* DMM. *OCR ND:* D *OCR NED:* M2

L2M9 BA Politics/Criminology
Duration: 3FT Hon
Entry Requirements: *GCE:* 260-280. *SQAH:* AAA-BBBB. *IB:* 24.
BTEC Dip: DD. *BTEC ExtDip:* DMM. *OCR ND:* D *OCR NED:* M2

W3M9 BA Popular Music/Criminology
Duration: 3FT Hon
Entry Requirements: *GCE:* 260-280. *SQAH:* AAA-BBBB. *IB:* 24.
BTEC Dip: DD. *BTEC ExtDip:* DMM. *OCR ND:* D *OCR NED:* M2

C8M9 BA Psychology/Criminology
Duration: 3FT Hon
Entry Requirements: *GCE:* 260-280. *SQAH:* AAA-BBBB. *IB:* 24.
BTEC Dip: DD. *BTEC ExtDip:* DMM. *OCR ND:* D *OCR NED:* M2

L3M9 BA Sociology/Criminology
Duration: 3FT Hon
Entry Requirements: *GCE:* 260-280. *SQAH:* AAA-BBBB. *IB:* 24.
BTEC Dip: DD. *BTEC ExtDip:* DMM. *OCR ND:* D *OCR NED:* M2

C6M9 BA Sport Studies/Criminology
Duration: 3FT Hon
Entry Requirements: *GCE:* 260-280. *SQAH:* AAA-BBBB. *IB:* 24.
BTEC Dip: DD. *BTEC ExtDip:* DMM. *OCR ND:* D *OCR NED:* M2

N8M9 BA Tourism/Criminology
Duration: 3FT Hon
Entry Requirements: *GCE:* 260-280. *SQAH:* AAA-BBBB. *IB:* 24.
BTEC Dip: DD. *BTEC ExtDip:* DMM. *OCR ND:* D *OCR NED:* M2

N5MX BSc Advertising/Criminology
Duration: 3FT Hon
Entry Requirements: *GCE:* 260-280. *SQAH:* AAA-BBBB. *IB:* 24.
BTEC Dip: DD. *BTEC ExtDip:* DMM. *OCR ND:* D *OCR NED:* M2

C1M9 BSc Biological Conservation/Criminology
Duration: 3FT Hon
Entry Requirements: *GCE:* 260-280. *SQAH:* AAA-BBBB. *IB:* 24.
BTEC Dip: DD. *BTEC ExtDip:* DMM. *OCR ND:* D *OCR NED:* M2

F8M9 BSc Physical Geography/Criminology
Duration: 3FT Hon
Entry Requirements: *GCE:* 260-280. *SQAH:* AAA-BBBB. *IB:* 24.
BTEC Dip: DD. *BTEC ExtDip:* DMM. *OCR ND:* D *OCR NED:* M2

G4MX BSc Web Design/Criminology
Duration: 3FT Hon
Entry Requirements: *GCE:* 260-280. *SQAH:* AAA-BBBB. *IB:* 24.
BTEC Dip: DD. *BTEC ExtDip:* DMM. *OCR ND:* D *OCR NED:* M2

N77 NORTHUMBRIA UNIVERSITY
TRINITY BUILDING
NORTHUMBERLAND ROAD
NEWCASTLE UPON TYNE NE1 8ST
t: 0191 243 7420 f: 0191 227 4561
e: er.admissions@northumbria.ac.uk
// www.northumbria.ac.uk

M900 BSc Criminology
Duration: 3FT Hon
Entry Requirements: *GCE:* 300. *SQAH:* BBBBC. *SQAAH:* BBC. *IB:* 26.

MF94 BSc Criminology and Forensic Science
Duration: 3FT Hon
Entry Requirements: *GCE:* 280. *SQAH:* BBCCC. *SQAAH:* BCC. *IB:* 25. *BTEC Dip:* DM. *BTEC ExtDip:* DMM. *OCR NED:* M1

LM39 BSc Criminology and Sociology
Duration: 3FT Hon
Entry Requirements: *GCE:* 300. *SQAH:* BBBBC. *SQAAH:* BBC. *IB:* 26.

C8M9 BSc Psychology with Criminology
Duration: 3FT Hon
Entry Requirements: *GCE:* 320. *SQAH:* BBBBC. *SQAAH:* BBC. *IB:* 26. *OCR ND:* D *OCR NED:* M2

N91 NOTTINGHAM TRENT UNIVERSITY
DRYDEN BUILDING
BURTON STREET
NOTTINGHAM NG1 4BU
t: +44 (0) 115 848 4200 f: +44 (0) 115 848 8869
e: applications@ntu.ac.uk
// www.ntu.ac.uk

C8M2 BSc Psychology with Criminology
Duration: 3FT Hon
Entry Requirements: *GCE:* 300. *OCR NED:* D2

M1L3 LLB Law with Criminology
Duration: 3FT Hon
Entry Requirements: *GCE:* 280. *OCR NED:* M2

P56 UNIVERSITY CENTRE PETERBOROUGH
PARK CRESCENT
PETERBOROUGH PE1 4DZ
t: 0845 1965750 f: 01733 767986
e: UCPenquiries@anglia.ac.uk
// www.anglia.ac.uk/ucp

M900 BA Criminology
Duration: 3FT Hon
Entry Requirements: *GCE:* 220. Interview required.

P80 UNIVERSITY OF PORTSMOUTH
ACADEMIC REGISTRY
UNIVERSITY HOUSE
WINSTON CHURCHILL AVENUE
PORTSMOUTH PO1 2UP
t: 023 9284 8484 f: 023 9284 3082
e: admissions@port.ac.uk
// www.port.ac.uk

M9C8 BSc Criminology with Psychology
Duration: 3FT Hon
Entry Requirements: *GCE:* 240-300. *BTEC Dip:* DD. *BTEC ExtDip:* DMM.

LM39 BSc Sociology and Criminology
Duration: 3FT Hon
Entry Requirements: *GCE:* 240-300. *BTEC Dip:* DD. *BTEC ExtDip:* DMM.

M1L6 LLB Law with Criminology
Duration: 3FT/4SW Hon
Entry Requirements: *GCE:* 320. *IB:* 30. *BTEC SubDip:* D. *BTEC Dip:* DD. *BTEC ExtDip:* DDM.

Q75 QUEEN'S UNIVERSITY BELFAST
UNIVERSITY ROAD
BELFAST BT7 1NN
t: 028 9097 3838 f: 028 9097 5151
e: admissions@qub.ac.uk
// www.qub.ac.uk

M900 BA Criminology
Duration: 3FT Hon
Entry Requirements: *GCE:* ABB-BBBb. *SQAH:* ABBBB. *SQAAH:* ABB. *IB:* 34.

ML94 BA Criminology and Social Policy
Duration: 3FT Hon
Entry Requirements: *GCE:* ABB-BBBb. *SQAH:* ABBBB. *SQAAH:* ABB. *IB:* 34.

ML93 BA Criminology and Sociology
Duration: 3FT Hon
Entry Requirements: *GCE:* ABB-BBBb. *SQAH:* AABBB. *SQAAH:* ABB. *IB:* 34.

R48 ROEHAMPTON UNIVERSITY
ROEHAMPTON LANE
LONDON SW15 5PU
t: 020 8392 3232 f: 020 8392 3470
e: enquiries@roehampton.ac.uk
// www.roehampton.ac.uk

M900 BA Criminology
Duration: 3FT Hon
Entry Requirements: *Foundation:* Distinction. *GCE:* 280. *IB:* 25.
BTEC Dip: D*D*. *BTEC ExtDip:* DMM. *OCR NED:* M2 Interview required.

MC98 BA Criminology and Psychology
Duration: 3FT Hon
Entry Requirements: *GCE:* 300. *IB:* 26. *BTEC ExtDip:* DDM. *OCR NED:* D2 Interview required.

ML9P BA Criminology and Social Anthropology
Duration: 3FT Hon
Entry Requirements: *Foundation:* Distinction. *GCE:* 280. *IB:* 25.
BTEC Dip: D*D*. *BTEC ExtDip:* DMM. *OCR NED:* M2 Interview required.

ML93 BA Criminology and Sociology
Duration: 3FT Hon
Entry Requirements: *Foundation:* Distinction. *GCE:* 280. *IB:* 25.
BTEC Dip: D*D*. *BTEC ExtDip:* DMM. *OCR NED:* M2 Interview required.

PM52 BA/BSc Journalism and Criminology
Duration: 3FT Hon
Entry Requirements: *GCE:* 300. *IB:* 26. *BTEC ExtDip:* DDM. *OCR NED:* D2 Interview required.

WM69 BA/BSc Photography and Criminology
Duration: 3FT Hon
Entry Requirements: *GCE:* 300. *IB:* 26. *BTEC ExtDip:* DDM. *OCR NED:* D2 Interview required.

R72 ROYAL HOLLOWAY, UNIVERSITY OF LONDON
ROYAL HOLLOWAY, UNIVERSITY OF LONDON
EGHAM
SURREY TW20 0EX
t: 01784 414944 f: 01784 473662
e: Admissions@rhul.ac.uk
// www.rhul.ac.uk

LM39 BSc Criminology and Sociology
Duration: 3FT Hon
Entry Requirements: *GCE:* BBB. *SQAH:* BBBBB. *IB:* 32.

S03 THE UNIVERSITY OF SALFORD
SALFORD M5 4WT
t: 0161 295 4545 f: 0161 295 4646
e: ug-admissions@salford.ac.uk
// www.salford.ac.uk

M900 BSc Criminology
Duration: 3FT Hon
Entry Requirements: *GCE:* 280. *IB:* 31. Interview required.

LM39 BSc Criminology and Sociology
Duration: 3FT Hon
Entry Requirements: *GCE:* 260-280. *IB:* 25. *OCR ND:* D *OCR NED:* M2 Interview required.

CM89 BSc Psychology and Criminology
Duration: 3FT Hon
Entry Requirements: *GCE:* 300. *IB:* 27. *OCR NED:* M1

M1M9 LLB Law with Criminology
Duration: 3FT Hon
Entry Requirements: *GCE:* 300. *IB:* 29. *OCR NED:* M2 Interview required.

S18 THE UNIVERSITY OF SHEFFIELD
THE UNIVERSITY OF SHEFFIELD
LEVEL 2, ARTS TOWER
WESTERN BANK
SHEFFIELD S10 2TN
t: 0114 222 8030 f: 0114 222 8032
// www.sheffield.ac.uk

ML94 BA Social Policy and Criminology
Duration: 3FT Hon
Entry Requirements: *GCE:* ABB. *SQAH:* AABBB. *SQAAH:* B. *IB:* 33.
BTEC ExtDip: DDM.

M930 LLB Law and Criminology
Duration: 3FT Hon
Entry Requirements: *GCE:* AAB. *SQAH:* AAABB. *SQAAH:* A. *IB:* 35.
BTEC ExtDip: DDD.

S21 SHEFFIELD HALLAM UNIVERSITY
CITY CAMPUS
HOWARD STREET
SHEFFIELD S1 1WB
t: 0114 225 5555 f: 0114 225 2167
e: admissions@shu.ac.uk
// www.shu.ac.uk

M931 BA Criminology
Duration: 3FT Hon
Entry Requirements: *GCE:* 280.

ML93 BA Criminology and Sociology
Duration: 3FT Hon
Entry Requirements: *GCE:* 280.

MC98 BSc Criminology and Psychology
Duration: 3FT Hon
Entry Requirements: *GCE:* 280.

M1M9 LLB Law with Criminology
Duration: 3FT Hon
Entry Requirements: *GCE:* 300.

S27 UNIVERSITY OF SOUTHAMPTON
HIGHFIELD
SOUTHAMPTON SO17 1BJ
t: 023 8059 4732 f: 023 8059 3037
e: admissions@soton.ac.uk
// www.southampton.ac.uk

LM39 BSc Applied Social Sciences (Criminology)
Duration: 3FT Hon
Entry Requirements: *GCE:* AAB. *SQAH:* AABBB. *SQAAH:* BB. *IB:* 32.

S30 SOUTHAMPTON SOLENT UNIVERSITY
EAST PARK TERRACE
SOUTHAMPTON
HAMPSHIRE SO14 0RT
t: +44 (0) 23 8031 9039 f: + 44 (0)23 8022 2259
e: admissions@solent.ac.uk
// www.solent.ac.uk/

M930 BA Criminology
Duration: 3FT Hon
Entry Requirements: *Foundation:* Distinction. *GCE:* 240. *SQAAH:* AA-CCD. *IB:* 24. *BTEC ExtDip:* MMM. *OCR ND:* D *OCR NED:* M3

MC98 BA Criminology and Psychology
Duration: 3FT Hon
Entry Requirements: *Foundation:* Distinction. *GCE:* 240. *SQAAH:* AA-CCD. *IB:* 24. *BTEC ExtDip:* MMM. *OCR ND:* D *OCR NED:* M3

S72 STAFFORDSHIRE UNIVERSITY
COLLEGE ROAD
STOKE ON TRENT ST4 2DE
t: 01782 292753 f: 01782 292740
e: admissions@staffs.ac.uk
// www.staffs.ac.uk

FMK9 BSc Forensic Science and Criminology
Duration: 3FT Hon
Entry Requirements: *GCE:* 200-280. *IB:* 24.

CMV1 BSc Psychology and Criminology
Duration: 3FT Hon
Entry Requirements: *GCE:* 200-280. *IB:* 24.

M930 LLB Law (Criminology)
Duration: 3FT Hon
Entry Requirements: *GCE:* 280. *IB:* 26. *OCR NED:* M2

S75 THE UNIVERSITY OF STIRLING
STUDENT RECRUITMENT & ADMISSIONS SERVICE
UNIVERSITY OF STIRLING
STIRLING
SCOTLAND FK9 4LA
t: 01786 467044 f: 01786 466800
e: admissions@stir.ac.uk
// www.stir.ac.uk

MM91 BA Criminology and Law
Duration: 4FT Hon
Entry Requirements: *GCE:* BBC. *SQAH:* BBBB. *SQAAH:* AAA-CCC. *IB:* 32. *BTEC ExtDip:* DMM.

MV95 BA Criminology and Philosophy
Duration: 4FT Hon
Entry Requirements: *GCE:* BBC. *SQAH:* BBBB. *SQAAH:* AAA-CCC. *IB:* 32. *BTEC ExtDip:* DMM.

ML92 BA Criminology and Politics
Duration: 4FT Hon
Entry Requirements: *GCE:* BBC. *SQAH:* BBBB. *SQAAH:* AAA-CCC. *IB:* 32. *BTEC ExtDip:* DMM.

LM39 BA Criminology and Sociology
Duration: 4FT Hon
Entry Requirements: *GCE:* BBC. *SQAH:* BBBB. *SQAAH:* AAA-CCC. *IB:* 32. *BTEC ExtDip:* DMM.

S82 UNIVERSITY CAMPUS SUFFOLK (UCS)
WATERFRONT BUILDING
NEPTUNE QUAY
IPSWICH
SUFFOLK IP4 1QJ
t: 01473 338833 f: 01473 339900
e: info@ucs.ac.uk
// www.ucs.ac.uk

ML95 BSc Criminology and Youth Studies
Duration: 3FT Hon
Entry Requirements: *GCE:* 240-280. *IB:* 28. *BTEC ExtDip:* DMM.

S84 UNIVERSITY OF SUNDERLAND
STUDENT HELPLINE
THE STUDENT GATEWAY
CHESTER ROAD
SUNDERLAND SR1 3SD
t: 0191 515 3000 f: 0191 515 3805
e: student.helpline@sunderland.ac.uk
// www.sunderland.ac.uk

XMH9 BA Childhood Studies and Criminology
Duration: 3FT Hon
Entry Requirements: *GCE:* 260-360.

X3M9 BA Childhood Studies with Criminology
Duration: 3FT Hon
Entry Requirements: *GCE:* 260-360.

M930 BA Criminology
Duration: 3FT Hon
Entry Requirements: *GCE:* 260-360. *SQAH:* AAAA-CCCC.

MW95 BA Criminology and Dance
Duration: 3FT Hon
Entry Requirements: *GCE:* 260-360. *IB:* 31. *OCR ND:* D *OCR NED:* M3

MW94 BA Criminology and Drama
Duration: 3FT Hon
Entry Requirements: *GCE:* 260-360. *OCR ND:* D *OCR NED:* M3

MX93 BA Criminology and Education
Duration: 3FT Hon
Entry Requirements: *GCE:* 260-360. *OCR ND:* D *OCR NED:* M3

MQ91 BA Criminology and English Language/Linguistics
Duration: 3FT Hon
Entry Requirements: *GCE:* 260-360. *OCR ND:* D *OCR NED:* M3

MQ93 BA Criminology and English Studies
Duration: 3FT Hon
Entry Requirements: *GCE:* 260-360. *OCR ND:* D *OCR NED:* M3

MV9C BA Criminology and History
Duration: 3FT Hon
Entry Requirements: *GCE:* 260-360. *OCR ND:* D *OCR NED:* M3

MP95 BA Criminology and Journalism
Duration: 3FT Hon
Entry Requirements: *GCE:* 260-360. *OCR ND:* D *OCR NED:* M3

MP9H BA Criminology and Media Studies
Duration: 3FT Hon
Entry Requirements: *GCE:* 260-360. *OCR ND:* D *OCR NED:* M3

WM69 BA Criminology and Photography
Duration: 3FT Hon
Entry Requirements: *GCE:* 260-360. *OCR ND:* D *OCR NED:* M3

LM29 BA Criminology and Politics
Duration: 3FT Hon
Entry Requirements: *GCE:* 260-360. *OCR ND:* D *OCR NED:* M3

CM89 BA Criminology and Psychology
Duration: 3FT Hon
Entry Requirements: *GCE:* 260-360. *OCR ND:* D *OCR NED:* M3

MP92 BA Criminology and Public Relations
Duration: 3FT Hon
Entry Requirements: *GCE:* 260-360. *OCR ND:* D *OCR NED:* M3

LM39 BA Criminology and Sociology
Duration: 3FT Hon
Entry Requirements: *GCE:* 260-360. *OCR ND:* D *OCR NED:* M3

MX91 BA Criminology and TESOL
Duration: 3FT Hon
Entry Requirements: *GCE:* 260-360. *OCR ND:* D *OCR NED:* M3

M9XH BA Criminology with Childhood Studies
Duration: 3FT Hon
Entry Requirements: *GCE:* 260-360.

M9W5 BA Criminology with Dance
Duration: 3FT Hon
Entry Requirements: *GCE:* 260-360. *IB:* 31. *OCR ND:* D *OCR NED:* M3

M9W4 BA Criminology with Drama
Duration: 3FT Hon
Entry Requirements: *GCE:* 260-360. *OCR ND:* D *OCR NED:* M3

M9X3 BA Criminology with Education
Duration: 3FT Hon
Entry Requirements: *GCE:* 260-360. *OCR ND:* D *OCR NED:* M3

M9Q1 BA Criminology with English Language/Linguistics
Duration: 3FT Hon
Entry Requirements: *GCE:* 260-360. *OCR ND:* D *OCR NED:* M3

M9QH BA Criminology with English Studies
Duration: 3FT Hon
Entry Requirements: *GCE:* 260-360. *OCR ND:* D *OCR NED:* M3

M9V1 BA Criminology with History
Duration: 3FT Hon
Entry Requirements: *GCE:* 260-360. *OCR ND:* D *OCR NED:* M3

M9P5 BA Criminology with Journalism
Duration: 3FT Hon
Entry Requirements: *GCE:* 260-360. *OCR ND:* D *OCR NED:* M3

L3M1 BA Criminology with Law
Duration: 3FT Hon
Entry Requirements: *GCE:* 260-360.

M9R1 BA Criminology with MFL (French)
Duration: 3FT Hon
Entry Requirements: *GCE:* 260-360. *OCR ND:* D *OCR NED:* M3

M9R2 BA Criminology with MFL (German)
Duration: 3FT Hon
Entry Requirements: *GCE:* 260-360. *OCR ND:* D *OCR NED:* M3

M9R4 BA Criminology with MFL (Spanish)
Duration: 3FT Hon
Entry Requirements: *GCE:* 260-360. *OCR ND:* D *OCR NED:* M3

M9P3 BA Criminology with Media Studies
Duration: 3FT Hon
Entry Requirements: *GCE:* 260-360. *OCR ND:* D *OCR NED:* M3

M9W6 BA Criminology with Photography
Duration: 3FT Hon
Entry Requirements: *GCE:* 260-360. *OCR ND:* D *OCR NED:* M3

M9L2 BA Criminology with Politics
Duration: 3FT Hon
Entry Requirements: *GCE:* 260-360. *OCR ND:* D *OCR NED:* M3

M9C8 BA Criminology with Psychology
Duration: 3FT Hon
Entry Requirements: *GCE:* 260-360. *OCR ND:* D *OCR NED:* M3

M9P2 BA Criminology with Public Relations
Duration: 3FT Hon
Entry Requirements: *GCE:* 260-360. *OCR ND:* D *OCR NED:* M3

M9L3 BA Criminology with Sociology
Duration: 3FT Hon
Entry Requirements: *GCE:* 260-360. *OCR ND:* D *OCR NED:* M3

M9C6 BA Criminology with Sport
Duration: 3FT Hon
Entry Requirements: *GCE:* 260-360. *OCR ND:* D *OCR NED:* M3

M9X1 BA Criminology with TESOL
Duration: 3FT Hon
Entry Requirements: *GCE:* 260-360. *OCR ND:* D *OCR NED:* M3

W5M9 BA Dance with Criminology
Duration: 3FT Hon
Entry Requirements: *GCE:* 260-360. *IB:* 31. *OCR ND:* D *OCR NED:* M3

W4M9 BA Drama with Criminology
Duration: 3FT Hon
Entry Requirements: *GCE:* 260-360. *OCR ND:* D *OCR NED:* M3

Q1M9 BA English Language & Linguistics with Criminology
Duration: 3FT Hon
Entry Requirements: *GCE:* 260-360. *OCR ND:* D *OCR NED:* M3

Q3M9 BA English with Criminology
Duration: 3FT Hon
Entry Requirements: *GCE:* 260-360. *IB:* 31. *OCR ND:* D *OCR NED:* M3

ML95 BA Health & Social Care and Criminology
Duration: 3FT Hon
Entry Requirements: *GCE:* 260-360.

L5M9 BA Health & Social Care with Criminology
Duration: 3FT Hon
Entry Requirements: *GCE:* 260-360.

V1M9 BA History with Criminology
Duration: 3FT Hon
Entry Requirements: *GCE:* 260-360. *IB:* 31. *OCR ND:* D *OCR NED:* M3

P5M9 BA Journalism with Criminology
Duration: 3FT Hon
Entry Requirements: *GCE:* 260-360. *IB:* 32. *OCR ND:* D *OCR NED:* M3

MM19 BA Law and Criminology
Duration: 3FT Hon
Entry Requirements: *GCE:* 260-360. *OCR ND:* D *OCR NED:* M3

P3M9 BA Media Studies with Criminology
Duration: 3FT Hon
Entry Requirements: *GCE:* 260-360. *IB:* 32. *OCR ND:* D *OCR NED:* M3

MR91 BA Modern Foreign Languages (French) and Criminology
Duration: 3FT Hon
Entry Requirements: *GCE:* 260-360. *IB:* 31. *OCR ND:* D *OCR NED:* M3

MR92 BA Modern Foreign Languages (German) and Criminology
Duration: 3FT Hon
Entry Requirements: *GCE:* 260-360. *IB:* 31. *OCR ND:* D *OCR NED:* M3

MR94 BA Modern Foreign Languages (Spanish) and Criminology
Duration: 3FT Hon
Entry Requirements: *GCE:* 260-360. *IB:* 31. *OCR ND:* D *OCR NED:* M3

L2M9 BA Politics with Criminology
Duration: 3FT Hon
Entry Requirements: *GCE:* 260-360. *IB:* 31. *OCR ND:* D *OCR NED:* M3

PM29 BA Public Relations and Criminology
Duration: 3FT Hon
Entry Requirements: *GCE:* 260-360. *OCR ND:* D *OCR NED:* M3

P2M9 BA Public Relations with Criminology
Duration: 3FT Hon
Entry Requirements: *GCE:* 260-360. *OCR ND:* D *OCR NED:* M3

L3M9 BA Sociology with Criminology
Duration: 3FT Hon
Entry Requirements: *GCE:* 260-360. *IB:* 31. *OCR ND:* D *OCR NED:* M3

X1M9 BA TESOL with Criminology
Duration: 3FT Hon
Entry Requirements: *GCE:* 260-360. *OCR ND:* D *OCR NED:* M3

NM89 BA Tourism and Criminology
Duration: 3FT Hon
Entry Requirements: *GCE:* 260-360. *IB:* 31. *OCR ND:* D *OCR NED:* M3

N8M9 BA Tourism with Criminology
Duration: 3FT Hon
Entry Requirements: *GCE:* 260-360. *IB:* 31. *OCR ND:* D *OCR NED:* M3

MN98 BA/BSc Criminology and Tourism
Duration: 3FT Hon
Entry Requirements: *GCE:* 260-360. *OCR ND:* D *OCR NED:* M3

CM69 BA/BSc Sport and Criminology
Duration: 3FT Hon
Entry Requirements: *GCE:* 260-360. *OCR ND:* D *OCR NED:* M3

C8M9 BSc Psychology with Criminology
Duration: 3FT Hon
Entry Requirements: *GCE:* 260-360. *IB:* 32. *OCR ND:* D *OCR NED:* M3

C6M9 BSc Sport with Criminology
Duration: 3FT Hon
Entry Requirements: *GCE:* 260-360. *OCR ND:* D *OCR NED:* M3

S85 UNIVERSITY OF SURREY
STAG HILL
GUILDFORD
SURREY GU2 7XH
t: +44(0)1483 689305 f: +44(0)1483 689388
e: ugteam@surrey.ac.uk
// www.surrey.ac.uk

LM39 BSc Criminology and Sociology (3 years)
Duration: 3FT Hon
Entry Requirements: *GCE:* ABB. *SQAH:* BBBB. *IB:* 34.

ML93 BSc Criminology and Sociology (4 years)
Duration: 4SW Hon
Entry Requirements: *GCE:* ABB. *SQAH:* BBBB. *IB:* 34.

M1M9 LLB Law with Criminology
Duration: 3FT/4SW Hon
Entry Requirements: *GCE:* AAB. *SQAH:* AAAAB. *SQAAH:* AAB. *IB:* 35. Interview required.

S93 SWANSEA UNIVERSITY
SINGLETON PARK
SWANSEA SA2 8PP
t: 01792 295111 f: 01792 295110
e: admissions@swansea.ac.uk
// www.swansea.ac.uk

MLF4 BSc Criminology and Social Policy
Duration: 3FT Hon
Entry Requirements: *GCE:* BBB. *IB:* 32.

MM19 LLB Law and Criminology
Duration: 3FT Hon
Entry Requirements: *GCE:* ABB. *IB:* 33.

T20 TEESSIDE UNIVERSITY
MIDDLESBROUGH TS1 3BA
t: 01642 218121 f: 01642 384201
e: registry@tees.ac.uk
// www.tees.ac.uk

M980 BSc Criminology
Duration: 3FT Hon
Entry Requirements: *GCE:* 240.

LM39 BSc Criminology and Sociology
Duration: 3FT Hon
Entry Requirements: *GCE:* 240.

M2M1 BSc Criminology with Law
Duration: 3FT Hon
Entry Requirements: *GCE:* 240.

M9C8 BSc Criminology with Psychology
Duration: 3FT Hon
Entry Requirements: *GCE:* 240.

M9L5 BSc Criminology with Youth Studies
Duration: 3FT Hon
Entry Requirements: *GCE:* 240.

CM89 BSc Psychology and Criminology
Duration: 3FT Hon
Entry Requirements: *GCE:* 260.

U20 UNIVERSITY OF ULSTER
COLERAINE
CO. LONDONDERRY
NORTHERN IRELAND BT52 1SA
t: 028 7012 4221 f: 028 7012 4908
e: online@ulster.ac.uk
// www.ulster.ac.uk

L2M9 BSc Politics with Criminology
Duration: 3FT Hon
Entry Requirements: *GCE:* 260-280. *IB:* 24.

L4M9 BSc Social Policy with Criminology
Duration: 3FT Hon
Entry Requirements: *GCE:* 260. *IB:* 24.

L3M9 BSc Sociology with Criminology
Duration: 3FT Hon
Entry Requirements: *GCE:* 260-280. *IB:* 24.

M1M9 LLB Law with Criminology
Duration: 3FT Hon
Entry Requirements: *GCE:* AAB-ABB. *SQAH:* AAAAB-AAABC.
SQAAH: AAB-ABB.

W05 THE UNIVERSITY OF WEST LONDON
ST MARY'S ROAD
EALING
LONDON W5 5RF
t: 0800 036 8888 f: 020 8566 1353
e: learning.advice@uwl.ac.uk
// www.uwl.ac.uk

M2M1 BA Criminology with Law
Duration: 3FT Hon
Entry Requirements: *GCE:* 260. *IB:* 28. Interview required.

M2C8 BA Criminology with Psychology
Duration: 3FT Hon
Entry Requirements: *GCE:* 260. *IB:* 28. Interview required.

W17 WARRINGTON COLLEGIATE
WINWICK ROAD CAMPUS
WINWICK ROAD
WARRINGTON
CHESHIRE WA2 8QA
t: 01925 494494 f: 01925 418328
e: admissions@warrington.ac.uk
// www.warrington.ac.uk

L4M9 HND Public Services with Criminology
Duration: 2FT HND
Entry Requirements: Contact the institution for details.

W50 UNIVERSITY OF WESTMINSTER
2ND FLOOR, CAVENDISH HOUSE
101 NEW CAVENDISH STREET,
LONDON W1W 6XH
t: 020 7915 5511
e: course-enquiries@westminster.ac.uk
// www.westminster.ac.uk

LM39 BA Sociology and Criminology
Duration: 3FT Hon
Entry Requirements: *GCE:* BCC. *SQAH:* BBCCC. *SQAAH:* BCC. *IB:* 28.

W75 UNIVERSITY OF WOLVERHAMPTON
ADMISSIONS UNIT
MX207, CAMP STREET
WOLVERHAMPTON
WEST MIDLANDS WV1 1AD
t: 01902 321000 f: 01902 321896
e: admissions@wlv.ac.uk
// www.wlv.ac.uk

FM42 BSc Forensic Science and Criminology
Duration: 3FT Hon
Entry Requirements: *GCE:* 200. *IB:* 24. *BTEC Dip:* DM. *BTEC ExtDip:* MMP. Interview required.

W76 UNIVERSITY OF WINCHESTER
WINCHESTER
HANTS SO22 4NR
t: 01962 827234 f: 01962 827288
e: course.enquiries@winchester.ac.uk
// www.winchester.ac.uk

LM31 BA Criminology and Law
Duration: 3FT Hon
Entry Requirements: *Foundation:* Distinction. *GCE:* 260-300. *IB:* 25. *OCR ND:* D *OCR NED:* M2

ECONOMICS, ACCOUNTING & FINANCE COMBINATIONS

A20 THE UNIVERSITY OF ABERDEEN
UNIVERSITY OFFICE
KING'S COLLEGE
ABERDEEN AB24 3FX
t: +44 (0) 1224 273504 f: +44 (0) 1224 272034
e: sras@abdn.ac.uk
// www.abdn.ac.uk/sras

NM49 MA Accountancy and Legal Studies
Duration: 4FT Hon
Entry Requirements: *GCE:* BBB. *SQAH:* BBBB. *IB:* 30.

LM19 MA Economics and Legal Studies
Duration: 4FT Hon
Entry Requirements: *GCE:* BBB. *SQAH:* BBBB. *IB:* 30.

NM31 MA Finance and Legal Studies
Duration: 4FT Hon
Entry Requirements: *GCE:* BBB. *SQAH:* BBBB. *IB:* 30.

A40 ABERYSTWYTH UNIVERSITY
ABERYSTWYTH UNIVERSITY, WELCOME CENTRE
PENGLAIS CAMPUS
ABERYSTWYTH
CEREDIGION SY23 3FB
t: 01970 622021 f: 01970 627410
e: ug-admissions@aber.ac.uk
// www.aber.ac.uk

M1N4 BA Law with Accounting & Finance
Duration: 3FT Hon
Entry Requirements: *GCE:* 340. *IB:* 28.

M1L1 BA Law with Economics
Duration: 3FT Hon
Entry Requirements: *GCE:* 340. *IB:* 28.

N4M1 BScEcon Accounting & Finance with Law
Duration: 3FT Hon
Entry Requirements: *GCE:* 300. *IB:* 27.

L1M1 BScEcon Economics with Law
Duration: 3FT Hon
Entry Requirements: *GCE:* 300. *IB:* 27.

B06 BANGOR UNIVERSITY
BANGOR UNIVERSITY
BANGOR
GWYNEDD LL57 2DG
t: 01248 388484 f: 01248 370451
e: admissions@bangor.ac.uk
// www.bangor.ac.uk

M1N4 LLB Law with Accounting & Finance
Duration: 3FT Hon
Entry Requirements: *GCE:* 280. *IB:* 28.

B50 BOURNEMOUTH UNIVERSITY
TALBOT CAMPUS
FERN BARROW
POOLE
DORSET BH12 5BB
t: 01202 524111
// www.bournemouth.ac.uk

NM41 BA Accounting and Law
Duration: 3FT Hon
Entry Requirements: *GCE:* 320. *IB:* 32. *BTEC SubDip:* D. *BTEC Dip:* DD. *BTEC ExtDip:* DDM.

NM3C BA Finance and Law (Top-up)
Duration: 1FT Hon
Entry Requirements: HND required.

NM31 FdA Finance and Law
Duration: 2FT Fdg
Entry Requirements: *GCE:* 120. *IB:* 24. Interview required.

B60 BRADFORD COLLEGE: AN ASSOCIATE COLLEGE OF LEEDS METROPOLITAN UNIVERSITY
GREAT HORTON ROAD
BRADFORD
WEST YORKSHIRE BD7 1AY
t: 01274 433008 f: 01274 431652
e: heregistry@bradfordcollege.ac.uk
// www.bradfordcollege.ac.uk/
university-centre

NM41 BA Accountancy and Law
Duration: 3FT Hon
Entry Requirements: *GCE:* 240.

B90 THE UNIVERSITY OF BUCKINGHAM
YEOMANRY HOUSE
HUNTER STREET
BUCKINGHAM MK18 1EG
t: 01280 820313 f: 01280 822245
e: info@buckingham.ac.uk
// www.buckingham.ac.uk

L000 BA Politics, Economics and Law
Duration: 2FT Hon
Entry Requirements: *GCE:* BCC. *SQAH:* BBBC. *SQAAH:* BCC. *IB:* 31.

M1L1 LLB Law with Economics
Duration: 2FT Hon
Entry Requirements: *GCE:* 300. *SQAH:* ABBB. *SQAAH:* BBB. *IB:* 34. *OCR NED:* M2 Interview required.

D26 DE MONTFORT UNIVERSITY
THE GATEWAY
LEICESTER LE1 9BH
t: 0116 255 1551 f: 0116 250 6204
e: enquiries@dmu.ac.uk
// www.dmu.ac.uk

ML21 BA Law and Economics
Duration: 3FT Hon
Entry Requirements: *GCE:* 280. *IB:* 28. *BTEC Dip:* D*D*. *BTEC ExtDip:* DMM. *OCR NED:* M2 Interview required.

D39 UNIVERSITY OF DERBY
KEDLESTON ROAD
DERBY DE22 1GB
t: 01332 591167 f: 01332 597724
e: askadmissions@derby.ac.uk
// www.derby.ac.uk

MN1K BA Accounting and Law
Duration: 3FT Hon
Entry Requirements: *Foundation:* Distinction. *GCE:* 260-300. *IB:* 28. *BTEC Dip:* D*D*. *BTEC ExtDip:* DMM. *OCR NED:* M2

E56 THE UNIVERSITY OF EDINBURGH
STUDENT RECRUITMENT & ADMISSIONS
57 GEORGE SQUARE
EDINBURGH EH8 9JU
t: 0131 650 4360 f: 0131 651 1236
e: sra.enquiries@ed.ac.uk
// www.ed.ac.uk/studying/undergraduate/

MN14 LLB Law and Accountancy
Duration: 4FT Hon
Entry Requirements: *GCE:* AAA-BBB. *SQAH:* AAAA-BBBB. *IB:* 34.

ML11 LLB Law and Economics
Duration: 4FT Hon
Entry Requirements: *GCE:* AAA-BBB. *SQAH:* AAAB-BBBB. *IB:* 34.

LM11 MA Economics and Law
Duration: 4FT Hon
Entry Requirements: *GCE:* AAA-BBB. *SQAH:* AAAA-BBBB. *IB:* 34.

E59 EDINBURGH NAPIER UNIVERSITY
CRAIGLOCKHART CAMPUS
EDINBURGH EH14 1DJ
t: +44 (0)8452 60 60 40 f: 0131 455 6464
e: info@napier.ac.uk
// www.napier.ac.uk

N4M1 BA Accounting with Law
Duration: 3FT/4FT Ord/Hon
Entry Requirements: *GCE:* 230.

M1N4 LLB Law with Accounting
Duration: 3FT/4FT Ord/Hon
Entry Requirements: Contact the institution for details.

**G14 UNIVERSITY OF GLAMORGAN,
CARDIFF AND PONTYPRIDD**
ENQUIRIES AND ADMISSIONS UNIT
PONTYPRIDD CF37 1DL
t: 08456 434030 f: 01443 654050
e: enquiries@glam.ac.uk
// www.glam.ac.uk

MN14 BA Accounting and Law
Duration: 3FT Hon
Entry Requirements: *GCE:* 220-260. Interview required.

G28 UNIVERSITY OF GLASGOW
71 SOUTHPARK AVENUE
UNIVERSITY OF GLASGOW
GLASGOW G12 8QQ
t: 0141 330 6062 f: 0141 330 2961
e: student.recruitment@glasgow.ac.uk
// www.glasgow.ac.uk

ML11 LLB Law/Economics
Duration: 4FT Hon
Entry Requirements: *GCE:* AAB. *SQAH:* AAAAB. *IB:* 34.
Admissions Test required.

H36 UNIVERSITY OF HERTFORDSHIRE
UNIVERSITY ADMISSIONS SERVICE
COLLEGE LANE
HATFIELD
HERTS AL10 9AB
t: 01707 284800
// www.herts.ac.uk

L1M1 BSc Economics/Law
Duration: 3FT/4SW Hon
Entry Requirements: *GCE:* 320.

M1L1 BSc Law/Economics
Duration: 3FT/4SW Hon
Entry Requirements: *GCE:* 320.

H60 THE UNIVERSITY OF HUDDERSFIELD
QUEENSGATE
HUDDERSFIELD HD1 3DH
t: 01484 473969 f: 01484 472765
e: admissionsandrecords@hud.ac.uk
// www.hud.ac.uk

N4M1 BA(Hons) Accountancy with Law
Duration: 3FT/4SW Hon
Entry Requirements: *GCE:* 300.

K12 KEELE UNIVERSITY
KEELE UNIVERSITY
STAFFORDSHIRE ST5 5BG
t: 01782 734005 f: 01782 632343
e: undergraduate@keele.ac.uk
// www.keele.ac.uk

NM41 BA Accounting and Law
Duration: 3FT Hon
Entry Requirements: *GCE:* ABB.

LM11 BA Economics and Law
Duration: 3FT Hon
Entry Requirements: *GCE:* ABB.

K24 THE UNIVERSITY OF KENT
RECRUITMENT & ADMISSIONS OFFICE
REGISTRY
UNIVERSITY OF KENT
CANTERBURY, KENT CT2 7NZ
t: 01227 827272 f: 01227 827077
e: information@kent.ac.uk
// www.kent.ac.uk

NM41 BA Law and Accounting & Finance (4 years)
Duration: 4FT Hon
Entry Requirements: *GCE:* AAB. *SQAH:* AAAAB. *IB:* 33. *OCR ND:* D *OCR NED:* M1

ML11 BA Law and Economics
Duration: 3FT Hon
Entry Requirements: *GCE:* AAB. *SQAH:* AAAAB. *IB:* 33. *OCR ND:* D

K84 KINGSTON UNIVERSITY
STUDENT INFORMATION & ADVICE CENTRE
COOPER HOUSE
40-46 SURBITON ROAD
KINGSTON UPON THAMES KT1 2HX
t: 0844 8552177 f: 020 8547 7080
e: aps@kingston.ac.uk
// www.kingston.ac.uk

LM11 BA Economics (Applied) and Law
Duration: 3FT Hon
Entry Requirements: *GCE:* 240-320. *IB:* 25.

L39 UNIVERSITY OF LINCOLN
ADMISSIONS
BRAYFORD POOL
LINCOLN LN6 7TS
t: 01522 886097 f: 01522 886146
e: admissions@lincoln.ac.uk
// www.lincoln.ac.uk

NM31 LLB Law and Finance
Duration: 3FT Hon
Entry Requirements: *GCE:* 300.

L41 THE UNIVERSITY OF LIVERPOOL
THE FOUNDATION BUILDING
BROWNLOW HILL
LIVERPOOL L69 7ZX
t: 0151 794 2000 f: 0151 708 6502
e: ugrecruitment@liv.ac.uk
// www.liv.ac.uk

M101 LLB Law with Accounting and Finance
Duration: 3FT Hon
Entry Requirements: *GCE:* AAA. *SQAH:* AAAAA. *SQAAH:* AA. *IB:* 36. *OCR ND:* D *OCR NED:* D2

L63 LCA BUSINESS SCHOOL, LONDON
19 CHARTERHOUSE STREET
LONDON EC1N 6RA
t: 020 7400 6789
e: info@lcabusinessschool.com
// www.lcabusinessschool.com

NM41 BSc Accounting and Law
Duration: 3FT Hon
Entry Requirements: *GCE:* 260. *SQAH:* BBCCC. *IB:* 24. *OCR ND:* D *OCR NED:* M2 Interview required.

N37 UNIVERSITY OF WALES, NEWPORT
ADMISSIONS
LODGE ROAD
CAERLEON
NEWPORT NP18 3QT
t: 01633 432030 f: 01633 432850
e: admissions@newport.ac.uk
// www.newport.ac.uk

MN14 BSc Accounting and Law
Duration: 3FT Hon
Entry Requirements: *GCE:* 240. *IB:* 24.

LM11 BSc Economics and Law
Duration: 3FT Hon
Entry Requirements: *GCE:* 240. *IB:* 24.

N38 UNIVERSITY OF NORTHAMPTON
PARK CAMPUS
BOUGHTON GREEN ROAD
NORTHAMPTON NN2 7AL
t: 0800 358 2232 f: 01604 722083
e: admissions@northampton.ac.uk
// www.northampton.ac.uk

N4M1 BA Accounting/Law
Duration: 3FT Hon
Entry Requirements: *GCE:* 260-280. *SQAH:* AAA-BBBB. *IB:* 24. *BTEC Dip:* DD. *BTEC ExtDip:* DMM. *OCR ND:* D *OCR NED:* M2

L1M1 BA Economics/Law
Duration: 3FT Hon
Entry Requirements: *GCE:* 260-280. *SQAH:* AAA-BBBB. *IB:* 24.
BTEC Dip: DD. *BTEC ExtDip:* DMM. *OCR ND:* D *OCR NED:* M2

M1N4 BA Law/Accounting
Duration: 3FT Hon
Entry Requirements: *GCE:* 260-280. *SQAH:* AAA-BBBB. *IB:* 24.
BTEC Dip: DD. *BTEC ExtDip:* DMM. *OCR ND:* D *OCR NED:* M2

M1L1 BA Law/Economics
Duration: 3FT Hon
Entry Requirements: *GCE:* 260-280. *SQAH:* AAA-BBBB. *IB:* 24.
BTEC Dip: DD. *BTEC ExtDip:* DMM. *OCR ND:* D *OCR NED:* M2

P60 PLYMOUTH UNIVERSITY
DRAKE CIRCUS
PLYMOUTH PL4 8AA
t: 01752 585858 f: 01752 588055
e: admissions@plymouth.ac.uk
// www.plymouth.ac.uk

L1MG BSc Economics with Law
Duration: 3FT/4SW Hon
Entry Requirements: *GCE:* 240. *IB:* 24.

P80 UNIVERSITY OF PORTSMOUTH
ACADEMIC REGISTRY
UNIVERSITY HOUSE
WINSTON CHURCHILL AVENUE
PORTSMOUTH PO1 2UP
t: 023 9284 8484 f: 023 9284 3082
e: admissions@port.ac.uk
// www.port.ac.uk

L1MF BA Economics with Law
Duration: 3FT/4SW Hon
Entry Requirements: *GCE:* 260-300. *IB:* 27. *BTEC Dip:* D*D.
BTEC ExtDip: DMM.

S03 THE UNIVERSITY OF SALFORD
SALFORD M5 4WT
t: 0161 295 4545 f: 0161 295 4646
e: ug-admissions@salford.ac.uk
// www.salford.ac.uk

M1N3 LLB Law with Finance
Duration: 3FT Hon
Entry Requirements: *GCE:* 300. *IB:* 29. *OCR NED:* M2 Interview required.

S09 SCHOOL OF ORIENTAL AND AFRICAN STUDIES (UNIVERSITY OF LONDON)
THORNHAUGH STREET
RUSSELL SQUARE
LONDON WC1H 0XG
t: 020 7898 4301 f: 020 7898 4039
e: undergradadmissions@soas.ac.uk
// www.soas.ac.uk

LM11 BA Law and Economics
Duration: 3FT Hon
Entry Requirements: *GCE:* AAA.

S78 THE UNIVERSITY OF STRATHCLYDE
GLASGOW G1 1XQ
t: 0141 552 4400 f: 0141 552 0775
// www.strath.ac.uk

ML11 BA Law and Economics
Duration: 4FT Hon
Entry Requirements: *GCE:* ABB. *SQAH:* AAABB-AAAB. *IB:* 34.

S90 UNIVERSITY OF SUSSEX
UNDERGRADUATE ADMISSIONS
SUSSEX HOUSE
UNIVERSITY OF SUSSEX
BRIGHTON BN1 9RH
t: 01273 678416 f: 01273 678545
e: ug.applicants@sussex.ac.uk
// www.sussex.ac.uk

M1L1 LLB Law with Politics
Duration: 3FT Hon
Entry Requirements: *GCE:* AAA-AAB. *SQAH:* AAAAA-AAABB. *IB:* 35. *BTEC SubDip:* D. *BTEC Dip:* DD. *BTEC ExtDip:* DDD. *OCR ND:* D *OCR NED:* D1

S93 SWANSEA UNIVERSITY
SINGLETON PARK
SWANSEA SA2 8PP
t: 01792 295111 f: 01792 295110
e: admissions@swansea.ac.uk
// www.swansea.ac.uk

ML11 LLB Law and Economics
Duration: 3FT Hon
Entry Requirements: *GCE:* AAB. *IB:* 34.

U20 UNIVERSITY OF ULSTER
COLERAINE
CO. LONDONDERRY
NORTHERN IRELAND BT52 1SA
t: 028 7012 4221 f: 028 7012 4908
e: online@ulster.ac.uk
// www.ulster.ac.uk

NM41 BSc Accounting and Law
Duration: 4FT Hon
Entry Requirements: *GCE:* AAA. *SQAH:* AAAAA. *SQAAH:* AAA. *IB:* 39.

M1N4 LLB Law with Accounting
Duration: 3FT Hon
Entry Requirements: *GCE:* BBB. *SQAH:* AABCC. *SQAAH:* BBB. *IB:* 25.

W75 UNIVERSITY OF WOLVERHAMPTON
ADMISSIONS UNIT
MX207, CAMP STREET
WOLVERHAMPTON
WEST MIDLANDS WV1 1AD
t: 01902 321000 f: 01902 321896
e: admissions@wlv.ac.uk
// www.wlv.ac.uk

MN1L BA Accounting and Law
Duration: 3FT Hon
Entry Requirements: *GCE:* 160-220. *IB:* 28.

EUROPEAN LAW/LEGAL STUDIES

A20 THE UNIVERSITY OF ABERDEEN
UNIVERSITY OFFICE
KING'S COLLEGE
ABERDEEN AB24 3FX
t: +44 (0) 1224 273504 f: +44 (0) 1224 272034
e: sras@abdn.ac.uk
// www.abdn.ac.uk/sras

M114 LLB Law
Duration: 3FT/4FT Ord/Hon
Entry Requirements: *GCE:* BBB. *SQAH:* AABB-ABBBB. *SQAAH:* BBB. *IB:* 34.

M115 LLB Law - Accelerated (Graduates only)
Duration: 2FT Hon
Entry Requirements: Contact the institution for details.

M120 LLB Law with Belgian Law
Duration: 4FT/5FT Ord/Hon
Entry Requirements: *GCE:* BBB. *SQAH:* AABB-ABBBB. *SQAAH:* BBB. *IB:* 34.

M127 LLB Law with European Legal Studies
Duration: 4FT/5FT Ord/Hon
Entry Requirements: *GCE:* BBB. *SQAH:* AABB-ABBBB. *SQAAH:* BBB. *IB:* 34.

M121 LLB Law with French Law
Duration: 4FT/5FT Ord/Hon
Entry Requirements: *GCE:* BBB. *SQAH:* AABB-ABBBB. *SQAAH:* BBB. *IB:* 34.

M123 LLB Law with German Law
Duration: 4FT/5FT Ord/Hon
Entry Requirements: *GCE:* BBB. *SQAH:* AABB-ABBBB. *SQAAH:* BBB. *IB:* 34.

M126 LLB Law with Spanish Law
Duration: 4FT/5FT Ord/Hon
Entry Requirements: *GCE:* BBB. *SQAH:* AABB-ABBBB. *SQAAH:* BBB. *IB:* 34.

M1N4 LLB Law with options in Accountancy
Duration: 3FT/4FT Ord/Hon
Entry Requirements: *GCE:* BBB. *SQAH:* AABB-ABBBB. *SQAAH:* BBB. *IB:* 34.

M1L1 LLB Law with options in Economics
Duration: 3FT/4FT Ord/Hon
Entry Requirements: *GCE:* BBB. *SQAH:* AABB-ABBBB. *SQAAH:* BBB. *IB:* 34.

M125 LLB Law with options in French
Duration: 3FT/4FT Ord/Hon
Entry Requirements: *GCE:* BBB. *SQAH:* AABB-ABBBB. *SQAAH:* BBB. *IB:* 34.

M128 LLB Law with options in Gaelic Language
Duration: 3FT/4FT Ord/Hon
Entry Requirements: *GCE:* BBB. *SQAH:* AABB-ABBBB. *SQAAH:* BBB. *IB:* 34.

M124 LLB Law with options in German
Duration: 3FT/4FT Ord/Hon
Entry Requirements: *GCE:* BBB. *SQAH:* AABB-ABBBB. *SQAAH:* BBB. *IB:* 34.

M122 LLB Law with options in Spanish
Duration: 3FT/4FT Ord/Hon
Entry Requirements: *GCE:* BBB. *SQAH:* AABB-ABBBB. *SQAAH:* BBB. *IB:* 34.

A30 UNIVERSITY OF ABERTAY DUNDEE
BELL STREET
DUNDEE DD1 1HG
t: 01382 308080 f: 01382 308081
e: sro@abertay.ac.uk
// www.abertay.ac.uk

M114 LLB Law
Duration: 4FT Hon
Entry Requirements: *GCE:* BBC. *SQAH:* ABBB. *IB:* 26.

A40 ABERYSTWYTH UNIVERSITY
ABERYSTWYTH UNIVERSITY, WELCOME CENTRE
PENGLAIS CAMPUS
ABERYSTWYTH
CEREDIGION SY23 3FB
t: 01970 622021 f: 01970 627410
e: ug-admissions@aber.ac.uk
// www.aber.ac.uk

M120 LLB European Law
Duration: 3FT Hon
Entry Requirements: *GCE:* 340. *IB:* 34.

B80 UNIVERSITY OF THE WEST OF ENGLAND, BRISTOL
FRENCHAY CAMPUS
COLDHARBOUR LANE
BRISTOL BS16 1QY
t: +44 (0)117 32 83333 f: +44 (0)117 32 82810
e: admissions@uwe.ac.uk
// www.uwe.ac.uk

M121 LLB European and International Law
Duration: 3FT Hon
Entry Requirements: *GCE:* 300.

D65 UNIVERSITY OF DUNDEE
NETHERGATE
DUNDEE DD1 4HN
t: 01382 383838 f: 01382 388150
e: contactus@dundee.ac.uk
// www.dundee.ac.uk/admissions/undergraduate/

M111 LLB Law (Eng/NI) option - European Studies
Duration: 3FT Hon
Entry Requirements: *GCE:* ABB. *SQAH:* AABB-ABBBB. *IB:* 32.

M114 LLB Law (Scots) option - European Studies
Duration: 4FT Hon
Entry Requirements: *GCE:* ABB. *SQAH:* AABB-ABBBB. *IB:* 32.

E14 UNIVERSITY OF EAST ANGLIA
NORWICH NR4 7TJ
t: 01603 591515 f: 01603 591523
e: admissions@uea.ac.uk
// www.uea.ac.uk

M120 LLB Law with European Legal Systems (4 years)
Duration: 4FT Hon   CRB Check: Required
Entry Requirements: *GCE:* AAB. *SQAH:* AAAAB. *SQAAH:* AAB. *IB:* 33. *BTEC SubDip:* D. *BTEC Dip:* DD. *BTEC ExtDip:* DDD. *OCR ND:* D *OCR NED:* D1 Interview required.

M121 LLB Law with French Law and Language (4 years)
Duration: 4FT Hon   CRB Check: Required
Entry Requirements: *GCE:* AAB. *SQAH:* AAAAB. *SQAAH:* AAB. *IB:* 33. *BTEC SubDip:* D. *BTEC Dip:* DD. *BTEC ExtDip:* DDD. *OCR ND:* D *OCR NED:* D1 Interview required.

E70 THE UNIVERSITY OF ESSEX
WIVENHOE PARK
COLCHESTER
ESSEX CO4 3SQ
t: 01206 873666 f: 01206 874477
e: admit@essex.ac.uk
// www.essex.ac.uk

M122 LLB English & French Laws (with Maitrise Masters 1)
Duration: 4FT Hon
Entry Requirements: *GCE:* AAB. *SQAH:* AAAA. *IB:* 36. Interview required.

M120 LLB Laws (Including Year Abroad)
Duration: 4FT Hon
Entry Requirements: *GCE:* AAB. *SQAH:* AAAA. *IB:* 36.

E84 UNIVERSITY OF EXETER
LAVER BUILDING
NORTH PARK ROAD
EXETER
DEVON EX4 4QE
t: 01392 723044 f: 01392 722479
e: admissions@exeter.ac.uk
// www.exeter.ac.uk

M120 LLB Law (European) (4 years)
Duration: 4FT Hon
Entry Requirements: *GCE:* AAA-AAB. *SQAH:* AAABB-AABBB. *SQAAH:* AAB-ABB. *BTEC ExtDip:* DDM.

M124 LLB Law with European Study (4 years)
Duration: 4FT Hon
Entry Requirements: *GCE:* AAA-AAB. *SQAH:* AAABB-AABBB. *SQAAH:* AAB-ABB. *BTEC ExtDip:* DDD.

G28 UNIVERSITY OF GLASGOW
71 SOUTHPARK AVENUE
UNIVERSITY OF GLASGOW
GLASGOW G12 8QQ
t: 0141 330 6062 f: 0141 330 2961
e: student.recruitment@glasgow.ac.uk
// www.glasgow.ac.uk

M121 LLB Law with French Legal Studies
Duration: 4FT Hon
Entry Requirements: *GCE:* AAB. *SQAH:* AAAAB. *IB:* 34.
Admissions Test required.

M122 LLB Law with German Legal Studies
Duration: 4FT Hon
Entry Requirements: *GCE:* AAB. *SQAH:* AAAAB. *IB:* 34.
Admissions Test required.

M123 LLB Law with Spanish Legal Studies
Duration: 4FT Hon
Entry Requirements: *GCE:* AAB. *SQAH:* AAAAB. *IB:* 34.
Admissions Test required.

H36 UNIVERSITY OF HERTFORDSHIRE
UNIVERSITY ADMISSIONS SERVICE
COLLEGE LANE
HATFIELD
HERTS AL10 9AB
t: 01707 284800
// www.herts.ac.uk

RM81 BSc European Studies/Law
Duration: 3FT/4SW Hon
Entry Requirements: *GCE:* 320.

M1R8 BSc Law/European Studies
Duration: 3FT/4SW Hon
Entry Requirements: *GCE:* 320.

K24 THE UNIVERSITY OF KENT
RECRUITMENT & ADMISSIONS OFFICE
REGISTRY
UNIVERSITY OF KENT
CANTERBURY, KENT CT2 7NZ
t: 01227 827272 f: 01227 827077
e: information@kent.ac.uk
// www.kent.ac.uk

M121 LLB English and French Law (4 years)
Duration: 4FT Hon
Entry Requirements: *GCE:* AAB. *SQAH:* AAAAB. *SQAAH:* AAB. *IB:* 33. *OCR ND:* D *OCR NED:* M3

M122 LLB English and German Law (4 years)
Duration: 4FT Hon
Entry Requirements: *GCE:* AAB. *SQAH:* AAAAB. *SQAAH:* AAB. *IB:* 33. *OCR ND:* D *OCR NED:* M3

M123 LLB English and Italian Law (4 years)
Duration: 4FT Hon
Entry Requirements: *GCE:* 320. *SQAH:* AAAAB. *SQAAH:* AAB. *IB:* 33. *OCR ND:* D *OCR NED:* M3

M125 LLB English and Spanish Law (4 years)
Duration: 4FT Hon
Entry Requirements: *GCE:* AAB. *SQAH:* AAAAB. *SQAAH:* AAB. *IB:* 33. *OCR ND:* D *OCR NED:* M3

M120 LLB European Legal Studies (4 years)
Duration: 4FT Hon
Entry Requirements: *GCE:* AAB. *SQAH:* AAAAB. *IB:* 33. *OCR ND:* D *OCR NED:* M1

M124 LLB Law with a Language
Duration: 3FT Hon
Entry Requirements: *GCE:* AAB. *SQAH:* AAAAB. *SQAAH:* AAB. *IB:* 33. *OCR ND:* D *OCR NED:* M3

K60 KING'S COLLEGE LONDON (UNIVERSITY OF LONDON)
STRAND
LONDON WC2R 2LS
t: 020 7836 5454 f: 020 7848 7171
e: prospective@kcl.ac.uk
// www.kcl.ac.uk/prospectus

M121 LLB English and French Law
Duration: 4FT Hon
Entry Requirements: *GCE:* A*AAa. *SQAH:* AAA. *SQAAH:* AA. *IB:* 39. Admissions Test required.

M122 LLB Law with German Law
Duration: 4FT Hon
Entry Requirements: *GCE:* A*AAa. *SQAH:* AAA. *SQAAH:* AA. *IB:* 39. Admissions Test required.

L14 LANCASTER UNIVERSITY
THE UNIVERSITY
LANCASTER
LANCASHIRE LA1 4YW
t: 01524 592029 f: 01524 846243
e: ugadmissions@lancaster.ac.uk
// www.lancs.ac.uk

M120 LLB European Legal Studies (4 years)
Duration: 4SW Hon
Entry Requirements: *GCE:* AAA. *SQAH:* AAABB. *SQAAH:* AAA. *IB:* 36.

L34 UNIVERSITY OF LEICESTER
UNIVERSITY ROAD
LEICESTER LE1 7RH
t: 0116 252 5281 f: 0116 252 2447
e: admissions@le.ac.uk
// www.le.ac.uk

M120 LLB English and French Law
Duration: 4FT Hon
Entry Requirements: *GCE:* AAA. *SQAH:* AAAAA. *SQAAH:* AAA. *IB:* 36. Interview required.

O33 OXFORD UNIVERSITY
UNDERGRADUATE ADMISSIONS OFFICE
UNIVERSITY OF OXFORD
WELLINGTON SQUARE
OXFORD OX1 2JD
t: 01865 288000 f: 01865 270212
e: undergraduate.admissions@admin.ox.ac.uk
// www.admissions.ox.ac.uk

M190 BA Law with European Law
Duration: 4FT Hon
Entry Requirements: *GCE:* AAA. *SQAH:* AAAAA-AAAAB. *SQAAH:* AAB. Interview required. Admissions Test required.

M191 BA Law with French Law
Duration: 4FT Hon
Entry Requirements: *GCE:* AAA. *SQAH:* AAAAA-AAAAB. *SQAAH:* AAB. Interview required. Admissions Test required.

M192 BA Law with German Law
Duration: 4FT Hon
Entry Requirements: *GCE:* AAA. *SQAH:* AAAAA-AAAAB. *SQAAH:* AAB. Interview required. Admissions Test required.

M193 BA Law with Italian Law
Duration: 4FT Hon
Entry Requirements: *GCE:* AAA. *SQAH:* AAAAA-AAAAB. *SQAAH:* AAB. Interview required. Admissions Test required.

M194 BA Law with Spanish Law
Duration: 4FT Hon
Entry Requirements: *GCE:* AAA. *SQAH:* AAAAA-AAAAB. *SQAAH:* AAB. Interview required. Admissions Test required.

P80 UNIVERSITY OF PORTSMOUTH
ACADEMIC REGISTRY
UNIVERSITY HOUSE
WINSTON CHURCHILL AVENUE
PORTSMOUTH PO1 2UP
t: 023 9284 8484 f: 023 9284 3082
e: admissions@port.ac.uk
// www.port.ac.uk

M1R8 LLB Law with European Studies
Duration: 3FT/4SW Hon
Entry Requirements: *GCE:* 280. *IB:* 28. *BTEC SubDip:* D. *BTEC Dip:* D*D*. *BTEC ExtDip:* DMM.

Q50 QUEEN MARY, UNIVERSITY OF LONDON
QUEEN MARY, UNIVERSITY OF LONDON
MILE END ROAD
LONDON E1 4NS
t: 020 7882 5555 f: 020 7882 5500
e: admissions@qmul.ac.uk
// www.qmul.ac.uk

M120 LLB English and European Law (4 years)
Duration: 4FT Hon
Entry Requirements: *GCE:* A*AA. *SQAAH:* AAA. *IB:* 36.

R12 THE UNIVERSITY OF READING
THE UNIVERSITY OF READING
PO BOX 217
READING RG6 6AH
t: 0118 378 8619 f: 0118 378 8924
e: student.recruitment@reading.ac.uk
// www.reading.ac.uk

M125 LLB Law with Legal Studies in Europe
Duration: 4FT Hon
Entry Requirements: *GCE:* AAB. *SQAH:* AAABB. *SQAAH:* AAB. *BTEC Dip:* DD. *BTEC ExtDip:* DDD.

S18 THE UNIVERSITY OF SHEFFIELD
THE UNIVERSITY OF SHEFFIELD
LEVEL 2, ARTS TOWER
WESTERN BANK
SHEFFIELD S10 2TN
t: 0114 222 8030 f: 0114 222 8032
// www.sheffield.ac.uk

M120 LLB Law (European and International)
Duration: 4FT Hon
Entry Requirements: *GCE:* AAA. *SQAH:* AAAAB. *SQAAH:* A. *IB:* 37. *BTEC ExtDip:* DDD.

S27 UNIVERSITY OF SOUTHAMPTON
HIGHFIELD
SOUTHAMPTON SO17 1BJ
t: 023 8059 4732 f: 023 8059 3037
e: admissions@soton.ac.uk
// www.southampton.ac.uk

M125 LLB Law (European Legal Studies)
Duration: 4FT Hon
Entry Requirements: *GCE:* AAA-AAB. *SQAAH:* AAA. *IB:* 36.

W20 THE UNIVERSITY OF WARWICK
COVENTRY CV4 8UW
t: 024 7652 3723 f: 024 7652 4649
e: ugadmissions@warwick.ac.uk
// www.warwick.ac.uk

M125 LLB European Law (4 years including year abroad)
Duration: 4FT Hon
Entry Requirements: *GCE:* AAAc. *SQAAH:* AA. *IB:* 38.

W50 UNIVERSITY OF WESTMINSTER
2ND FLOOR, CAVENDISH HOUSE
101 NEW CAVENDISH STREET,
LONDON W1W 6XH
t: 020 7915 5511
e: course-enquiries@westminster.ac.uk
// www.westminster.ac.uk

M125 LLB European Legal Studies (4 years)
Duration: 4FT Hon
Entry Requirements: *GCE:* ABC. *SQAH:* ABBBC. *SQAAH:* ABC. *IB:* 30. Interview required.

HUMAN RIGHTS

A40 ABERYSTWYTH UNIVERSITY
ABERYSTWYTH UNIVERSITY, WELCOME CENTRE
PENGLAIS CAMPUS
ABERYSTWYTH
CEREDIGION SY23 3FB
t: 01970 622021 f: 01970 627410
e: ug-admissions@aber.ac.uk
// www.aber.ac.uk

M990 LLB Human Rights
Duration: 3FT Hon
Entry Requirements: *GCE:* 340. *IB:* 34.

D26 DE MONTFORT UNIVERSITY
THE GATEWAY
LEICESTER LE1 9BH
t: 0116 255 1551 f: 0116 250 6204
e: enquiries@dmu.ac.uk
// www.dmu.ac.uk

M200 LL.B Law, Human Rights and Social Justice
Duration: 3FT Hon
Entry Requirements: *GCE:* 300. *IB:* 30. *BTEC ExtDip:* DDM. Interview required.

E70 THE UNIVERSITY OF ESSEX
WIVENHOE PARK
COLCHESTER
ESSEX CO4 3SQ
t: 01206 873666 f: 01206 874477
e: admit@essex.ac.uk
// www.essex.ac.uk

T7M9 BA Latin American Studies with Human Rights (4 years, with a year in Latin America)
Duration: 4FT Hon
Entry Requirements: *GCE:* ABB-BBB. *SQAH:* AAAB-AABB. *SQAAH:* AAB-ABB. Interview required.

M1M9 BA Law and Human Rights
Duration: 3FT Hon
Entry Requirements: *GCE:* ABB-BBB. *SQAH:* AAAB-AABB. *SQAAH:* AAB-ABB. Interview required.

M102 BA Law and Human Rights (including foundation year)
Duration: 4FT Hon
Entry Requirements: Contact the institution for details.

V5M9 BA Philosophy with Human Rights
Duration: 3FT Hon
Entry Requirements: *GCE:* ABB-BBB. *SQAH:* AAAB-AABB. *SQAAH:* AAB-ABB. Interview required.

V5MX BA Philosophy with Human Rights (Including Year Abroad)
Duration: 4FT Hon
Entry Requirements: *GCE:* ABB-BBB. *SQAH:* AAAB-AABB. *SQAAH:* AAB-ABB. Interview required.

L2M9 BA Politics with Human Rights
Duration: 3FT Hon
Entry Requirements: *GCE:* ABB-BBB. *SQAH:* AAAB-AABB. *SQAAH:* AAB-ABB. Interview required.

LFM9 BA Politics with Human Rights (Including Year Abroad)
Duration: 4FT Hon
Entry Requirements: Contact the institution for details.

L3M9 BA Sociology with Human Rights
Duration: 3FT Hon
Entry Requirements: *GCE:* ABB-BBB. *SQAH:* AAAB-AABB.

LMJ9 BA Sociology with Human Rights (Including Year Abroad)
Duration: 4FT Hon
Entry Requirements: *GCE:* ABB-BBB. *SQAH:* AAAB-AABB.

MM19 LLB Law and Human Rights
Duration: 4FT Hon
Entry Requirements: *GCE:* AAB. *SQAH:* AAAA. *IB:* 36.

H36 UNIVERSITY OF HERTFORDSHIRE
UNIVERSITY ADMISSIONS SERVICE
COLLEGE LANE
HATFIELD
HERTS AL10 9AB
t: 01707 284800
// www.herts.ac.uk

B1M1 BSc Human Biology/Law
Duration: 3FT/4SW Hon
Entry Requirements: *GCE:* 320.

L7M1 BSc Human Geography/Law
Duration: 3FT/4SW Hon
Entry Requirements: *GCE:* 320.

M1B1 BSc Law/Human Biology
Duration: 3FT/4SW Hon
Entry Requirements: *GCE:* 320.

M1L7 BSc Law/Human Geography
Duration: 3FT/4SW Hon
Entry Requirements: *GCE:* 320.

K12 KEELE UNIVERSITY
KEELE UNIVERSITY
STAFFORDSHIRE ST5 5BG
t: 01782 734005 f: 01782 632343
e: undergraduate@keele.ac.uk
// www.keele.ac.uk

CM1C BSc Human Biology and Law
Duration: 3FT Hon
Entry Requirements: *GCE:* ABB.

N38 UNIVERSITY OF NORTHAMPTON
PARK CAMPUS
BOUGHTON GREEN ROAD
NORTHAMPTON NN2 7AL
t: 0800 358 2232 f: 01604 722083
e: admissions@northampton.ac.uk
// www.northampton.ac.uk

L7M1 BA Human Geography/Law
Duration: 3FT Hon
Entry Requirements: *GCE:* 260-280. *SQAH:* AAA-BBBB. *IB:* 24.
BTEC Dip: DD. *BTEC ExtDip:* DMM. *OCR ND:* D *OCR NED:* M2

M1B1 BA Law/Human Bioscience
Duration: 3FT Hon
Entry Requirements: *GCE:* 260-280. *SQAH:* AAA-BBBB. *IB:* 24.
BTEC Dip: DD. *BTEC ExtDip:* DMM. *OCR ND:* D *OCR NED:* M2

M1L7 BA Law/Human Geography
Duration: 3FT Hon
Entry Requirements: *GCE:* 260-280. *SQAH:* AAA-BBBB. *IB:* 24.
BTEC Dip: DD. *BTEC ExtDip:* DMM. *OCR ND:* D *OCR NED:* M2

B1M1 BSc Human Bioscience/Law
Duration: 3FT Hon
Entry Requirements: *GCE:* 260-280. *SQAH:* AAA-BBBB. *IB:* 24.
BTEC Dip: DD. *BTEC ExtDip:* DMM. *OCR ND:* D *OCR NED:* M2

W20 THE UNIVERSITY OF WARWICK
COVENTRY CV4 8UW
t: 024 7652 3723 f: 024 7652 4649
e: ugadmissions@warwick.ac.uk
// www.warwick.ac.uk

MV21 BA Law with Humanities
Duration: 3FT/4FT Hon
Entry Requirements: Contact the institution for details.

INTERNATIONAL LAW

A20 THE UNIVERSITY OF ABERDEEN
UNIVERSITY OFFICE
KING'S COLLEGE
ABERDEEN AB24 3FX
t: +44 (0) 1224 273504 f: +44 (0) 1224 272034
e: sras@abdn.ac.uk
// www.abdn.ac.uk/sras

MLC2 MA International Relations and Legal Studies
Duration: 4FT Hon
Entry Requirements: *GCE:* BBB. *SQAH:* BBBB. *IB:* 30.

A40 ABERYSTWYTH UNIVERSITY
ABERYSTWYTH UNIVERSITY, WELCOME CENTRE
PENGLAIS CAMPUS
ABERYSTWYTH
CEREDIGION SY23 3FB
t: 01970 622021 f: 01970 627410
e: ug-admissions@aber.ac.uk
// www.aber.ac.uk

M1LF BA Law with International Politics
Duration: 3FT Hon
Entry Requirements: *GCE:* 340. *IB:* 28.

L2M1 BScEcon International Politics with Law
Duration: 3FT Hon
Entry Requirements: *GCE:* 300. *IB:* 30.

C10 CANTERBURY CHRIST CHURCH UNIVERSITY
NORTH HOLMES ROAD
CANTERBURY
KENT CT1 1QU
t: 01227 782900 f: 01227 782888
e: admissions@canterbury.ac.uk
// www.canterbury.ac.uk

L2MF BA Politics & Governance with Legal Studies 'International Only'
Duration: 4FT Hon
Entry Requirements: Interview required.

LM2G BA/BSc International Relations and Legal Studies
Duration: 3FT Hon
Entry Requirements: *GCE:* 240. *IB:* 24.

L9M2 BA/BSc International Relations with Legal Studies
Duration: 3FT Hon
Entry Requirements: *GCE:* 240. *IB:* 24.

M2LG BA/BSc Legal Studies with International Relations
Duration: 3FT Hon
Entry Requirements: *GCE:* 240. *IB:* 24.

M101 LLB Law 'International only'
Duration: 4FT Hon
Entry Requirements: Interview required.

C60 CITY UNIVERSITY
NORTHAMPTON SQUARE
LONDON EC1V 0HB
t: 020 7040 5060 f: 020 7040 8995
e: ugadmissions@city.ac.uk
// www.city.ac.uk

M102 Cert International Foundation (Law)
Duration: 1FT FYr
Entry Requirements: Contact the institution for details.

C85 COVENTRY UNIVERSITY
THE STUDENT CENTRE
COVENTRY UNIVERSITY
1 GULSON RD
COVENTRY CV1 2JH
t: 024 7615 2222 f: 024 7615 2223
e: studentenquiries@coventry.ac.uk
// www.coventry.ac.uk

M130 LLB International Law
Duration: 3FT/4SW Hon
Entry Requirements: *GCE:* BBB. *SQAH:* BBBBC. *IB:* 30. *BTEC ExtDip:* DDM. *OCR NED:* M1

M132 LLB International Law
Duration: 2FT/3SW Hon
Entry Requirements: *GCE:* ABB. *SQAH:* BBBBC. *IB:* 31.

D39 UNIVERSITY OF DERBY
KEDLESTON ROAD
DERBY DE22 1GB
t: 01332 591167 f: 01332 597724
e: askadmissions@derby.ac.uk
// www.derby.ac.uk

LM21 BA/BSc International Relations & Global Development and Law
Duration: 3FT Hon
Entry Requirements: *Foundation:* Distinction. *GCE:* 260-300. *IB:* 28. *BTEC Dip:* D*D*. *BTEC ExtDip:* DMM. *OCR NED:* M2

E28 UNIVERSITY OF EAST LONDON
DOCKLANDS CAMPUS
UNIVERSITY WAY
LONDON E16 2RD
t: 020 8223 3333 f: 020 8223 2978
e: study@uel.ac.uk
// www.uel.ac.uk

L2M1 BA International Politics with Law
Duration: 3FT Hon
Entry Requirements: *GCE:* 240. *IB:* 28.

ML12 BA Law / International Politics
Duration: 3FT Hon
Entry Requirements: *GCE:* 240. *IB:* 28.

E56 THE UNIVERSITY OF EDINBURGH
STUDENT RECRUITMENT & ADMISSIONS
57 GEORGE SQUARE
EDINBURGH EH8 9JU
t: 0131 650 4360 f: 0131 651 1236
e: sra.enquiries@ed.ac.uk
// www.ed.ac.uk/studying/undergraduate/

ML1F LLB Law and International Relations
Duration: 4FT Hon
Entry Requirements: *GCE:* AAA-BBB. *SQAH:* AAAA-BBBB. *IB:* 34.

LM29 MA International Relations and Law
Duration: 4FT Hon
Entry Requirements: *GCE:* AAA-BBB. *SQAH:* AAAA-BBBB. *IB:* 34.

H50 HOLBORN COLLEGE
WOOLWICH ROAD
LONDON SE7 8LN
t: 020 8317 6000 f: 020 8317 6001
e: UKAdmissions@kaplan.co.uk
// www.holborncollege.ac.uk

M101 LLB Law (University of London International Programme)
Duration: 3FT Hon
Entry Requirements: *GCE:* 180. *IB:* 24.

H72 THE UNIVERSITY OF HULL
THE UNIVERSITY OF HULL
COTTINGHAM ROAD
HULL HU6 7RX
t: 01482 466100 f: 01482 442290
e: admissions@hull.ac.uk
// www.hull.ac.uk

M130 LLB International Law
Duration: 3FT Hon
Entry Requirements: *GCE:* 320. *IB:* 30. *BTEC ExtDip:* DDM.

K84 KINGSTON UNIVERSITY
STUDENT INFORMATION & ADVICE CENTRE
COOPER HOUSE
40-46 SURBITON ROAD
KINGSTON UPON THAMES KT1 2HX
t: 0844 8552177 f: 020 8547 7080
e: aps@kingston.ac.uk
// www.kingston.ac.uk

LMF1 BA International Relations and Law
Duration: 3FT Hon
Entry Requirements: *GCE:* 280.

M130 LLB International Law
Duration: 3FT Hon
Entry Requirements: *GCE:* 320. *IB:* 27.

M131 LLB International Law with Industrial Placement
Duration: 4SW Hon
Entry Requirements: *GCE:* 320. *IB:* 27.

M132 LLB International Law with study abroad
Duration: 4FT Hon
Entry Requirements: *GCE:* 320. *IB:* 27.

L14 LANCASTER UNIVERSITY
THE UNIVERSITY
LANCASTER
LANCASHIRE LA1 4YW
t: 01524 592029 f: 01524 846243
e: ugadmissions@lancaster.ac.uk
// www.lancs.ac.uk

M101 LLB Law (International)
Duration: 4FT Hon
Entry Requirements: *GCE:* AAA. *SQAH:* AAABB. *SQAAH:* AAA. *IB:* 36.

L46 LIVERPOOL HOPE UNIVERSITY
HOPE PARK
LIVERPOOL L16 9JD
t: 0151 291 3331 f: 0151 291 3434
e: administration@hope.ac.uk
// www.hope.ac.uk

LM2C BA International Relations and Law
Duration: 3FT Hon
Entry Requirements: *GCE:* 300-320. *IB:* 25.

L68 LONDON METROPOLITAN UNIVERSITY
166-220 HOLLOWAY ROAD
LONDON N7 8DB
t: 020 7133 4200
e: admissions@londonmet.ac.uk
// www.londonmet.ac.uk

ML1F BA International Relations and Law
Duration: 3FT Hon
Entry Requirements: *GCE:* 240. *IB:* 28.

M1L2 LLB Law (with International Relations)
Duration: 3FT Hon
Entry Requirements: *GCE:* 320. *IB:* 28.

N91 NOTTINGHAM TRENT UNIVERSITY
DRYDEN BUILDING
BURTON STREET
NOTTINGHAM NG1 4BU
t: +44 (0) 115 848 4200 f: +44 (0) 115 848 8869
e: applications@ntu.ac.uk
// www.ntu.ac.uk

M130 LLB (Hons) International Law
Duration: 3FT Hon
Entry Requirements: *GCE:* 300.

P60 PLYMOUTH UNIVERSITY
DRAKE CIRCUS
PLYMOUTH PL4 8AA
t: 01752 585858 f: 01752 588055
e: admissions@plymouth.ac.uk
// www.plymouth.ac.uk

L2MF BSc International Relations with Law
Duration: 3FT Hon
Entry Requirements: *GCE:* 240. *IB:* 24.

P80 UNIVERSITY OF PORTSMOUTH
ACADEMIC REGISTRY
UNIVERSITY HOUSE
WINSTON CHURCHILL AVENUE
PORTSMOUTH PO1 2UP
t: 023 9284 8484 f: 023 9284 3082
e: admissions@port.ac.uk
// www.port.ac.uk

M1L2 LLB Law with International Relations
Duration: 3FT/4SW Hon
Entry Requirements: *GCE:* 320. *IB:* 30. *BTEC SubDip:* D. *BTEC Dip:* DD. *BTEC ExtDip:* DDM.

S27 UNIVERSITY OF SOUTHAMPTON
HIGHFIELD
SOUTHAMPTON SO17 1BJ
t: 023 8059 4732 f: 023 8059 3037
e: admissions@soton.ac.uk
// www.southampton.ac.uk

M130 LLB Law (International Legal Studies)
Duration: 4FT Hon
Entry Requirements: Contact the institution for details.

S30 SOUTHAMPTON SOLENT UNIVERSITY
EAST PARK TERRACE
SOUTHAMPTON
HAMPSHIRE SO14 0RT
t: +44 (0) 23 8031 9039 f: + 44 (0)23 8022 2259
e: admissions@solent.ac.uk
// www.solent.ac.uk/

M1Q3 LLB Law with International Foundation Year
Duration: 4FT Hon
Entry Requirements: Contact the institution for details.

M102 LLB Law with International Foundation Year (International Only - Jan)
Duration: 4FT Hon
Entry Requirements: Contact the institution for details.

S85 UNIVERSITY OF SURREY
STAG HILL
GUILDFORD
SURREY GU2 7XH
t: +44(0)1483 689305 f: +44(0)1483 689388
e: ugteam@surrey.ac.uk
// www.surrey.ac.uk

M1T9 LLB Law with International Studies (4 years)
Duration: 3FT/4SW Hon
Entry Requirements: *GCE:* AAB. *SQAH:* AAAAB. *SQAAH:* AAB. *IB:* 35. Interview required.

S90 UNIVERSITY OF SUSSEX
UNDERGRADUATE ADMISSIONS
SUSSEX HOUSE
UNIVERSITY OF SUSSEX
BRIGHTON BN1 9RH
t: 01273 678416 f: 01273 678545
e: ug.applicants@sussex.ac.uk
// www.sussex.ac.uk

M1L2 LLB Law with International Relations
Duration: 3FT Hon
Entry Requirements: *GCE:* AAA-AAB. *SQAH:* AAAAA-AAABB. *IB:* 35. *BTEC SubDip:* D. *BTEC Dip:* DD. *BTEC ExtDip:* DDD. *OCR ND:* D *OCR NED:* D1

LANGUAGE COMBINATIONS

A20 THE UNIVERSITY OF ABERDEEN
UNIVERSITY OFFICE
KING'S COLLEGE
ABERDEEN AB24 3FX
t: +44 (0) 1224 273504 f: +44 (0) 1224 272034
e: sras@abdn.ac.uk
// www.abdn.ac.uk/sras

MQ93 MA English and Legal Studies
Duration: 4FT Hon
Entry Requirements: *GCE:* BBB. *SQAH:* BBBB. *IB:* 30.

MR91 MA French and Legal Studies
Duration: 5FT Hon
Entry Requirements: *GCE:* BBB. *SQAH:* BBBB. *IB:* 30.

MRX1 MA French and Legal Studies
Duration: 4FT Hon
Entry Requirements: *GCE:* BBB. *SQAH:* BBBB. *IB:* 30.

MR92 MA German and Legal Studies
Duration: 5FT Hon
Entry Requirements: *GCE:* BBB. *SQAH:* BDDB. *IB:* 30.

MRX2 MA German and Legal Studies
Duration: 4FT Hon
Entry Requirements: *GCE:* BBB. *SQAH:* BBBB. *IB:* 30.

MR94 MA Hispanic Studies and Legal Studies
Duration: 5FT Hon
Entry Requirements: *GCE:* BBB. *SQAH:* BBBB. *IB:* 30.

MRX4 MA Hispanic Studies and Legal Studies
Duration: 4FT Hon
Entry Requirements: *GCE:* BBB. *SQAH:* BBBB. *IB:* 30.

A40 ABERYSTWYTH UNIVERSITY
ABERYSTWYTH UNIVERSITY, WELCOME CENTRE
PENGLAIS CAMPUS
ABERYSTWYTH
CEREDIGION SY23 3FB
t: 01970 622021 f: 01970 627410
e: ug-admissions@aber.ac.uk
// www.aber.ac.uk

M1Q5 BA Law with Cymraeg
Duration: 3FT Hon
Entry Requirements: *GCE:* 340. *IB:* 28.

M1RC BA Law with French (4 years)
Duration: 4FT Hon
Entry Requirements: *GCE:* 340. *IB:* 28.

M1RF BA Law with German (4 years)
Duration: 4FT Hon
Entry Requirements: *GCE:* 340. *IB:* 28.

M1RK BA Law with Spanish (4 years)
Duration: 4FT Hon
Entry Requirements: *GCE:* 340. *IB:* 28.

M1R1 LLB Law with French (4 years)
Duration: 4FT Hon
Entry Requirements: *GCE:* 340. *IB:* 28.

M1R2 LLB Law with German (4 years)
Duration: 4FT Hon
Entry Requirements: *GCE:* 340. *IB:* 28.

M1R4 LLB Law with Spanish (4 years)
Duration: 4FT Hon
Entry Requirements: *GCE:* 340. *IB:* 28.

B06 BANGOR UNIVERSITY
BANGOR UNIVERSITY
BANGOR
GWYNEDD LL57 2DG
t: 01248 388484 f: 01248 370451
e: admissions@bangor.ac.uk
// www.bangor.ac.uk

M1QJ LLB Law with English
Duration: 3FT Hon
Entry Requirements: *GCE:* 280. *IB:* 28.

M1R1 LLB Law with French
Duration: 4FT Hon
Entry Requirements: *GCE:* 280. *IB:* 28.

M1R2 LLB Law with German
Duration: 4FT Hon
Entry Requirements: *GCE:* 280. *IB:* 28.

M1R3 LLB Law with Italian
Duration: 4FT Hon
Entry Requirements: *GCE:* 280. *IB:* 28.

M1QH LLB Law with Professional English
Duration: 3FT Hon
Entry Requirements: *GCE:* 280. *IB:* 28.

M1R4 LLB Law with Spanish
Duration: 4FT Hon
Entry Requirements: *GCE:* 280. *IB:* 28.

M1Q5 LLB Law with Welsh
Duration: 3FT Hon
Entry Requirements: *GCE:* 280. *IB:* 28.

B32 THE UNIVERSITY OF BIRMINGHAM
EDGBASTON
BIRMINGHAM B15 2TT
t: 0121 415 8900 f: 0121 414 7159
e: admissions@bham.ac.uk
// www.birmingham.ac.uk

MR11 LLB Law with French (4 years)
Duration: 4FT Hon
Entry Requirements: *GCE:* A*AB-AAA. *SQAAH:* AAA. *IB:* 36. *BTEC SubDip:* D. *BTEC Dip:* D*D*. *BTEC ExtDip:* D*D*D. Admissions Test required.

MR12 LLB Law with German (4 years)
Duration: 4FT Hon
Entry Requirements: *GCE:* A*AB-AAA. *SQAAH:* AAA. *IB:* 36. *BTEC SubDip:* D. *BTEC Dip:* D*D*. *BTEC ExtDip:* D*D*D. Admissions Test required.

B78 UNIVERSITY OF BRISTOL
UNDERGRADUATE ADMISSIONS OFFICE
SENATE HOUSE
TYNDALL AVENUE
BRISTOL BS8 1TH
t: 0117 928 9000 f: 0117 331 7391
e: ug-admissions@bristol.ac.uk
// www.bristol.ac.uk

MR11 LLB Law and French (4 years)
Duration: 4FT Hon
Entry Requirements: *GCE:* AAA. *SQAH:* AAAAA. *SQAAH:* AA. *IB:* 37. Admissions Test required.

MR12 LLB Law and German (4 years)
Duration: 4FT Hon
Entry Requirements: *GCE:* AAA. *SQAH:* AAAAA. *SQAAH:* AA. *IB:* 37. Admissions Test required.

B90 THE UNIVERSITY OF BUCKINGHAM
YEOMANRY HOUSE
HUNTER STREET
BUCKINGHAM MK18 1EG
t: 01280 820313 f: 01280 822245
e: info@buckingham.ac.uk
// www.buckingham.ac.uk

M1Q3 LLB Law with English Language Studies
Duration: 2FT Hon
Entry Requirements: *GCE:* 300. *SQAH:* ABBB. *SQAAH:* BBB. *IB:* 34. *OCR NED:* M2 Interview required.

M1Q1 LLB Law with English as a Foreign Language
Duration: 2FT Hon
Entry Requirements: *GCE:* 300. *SQAH:* ABBB. *SQAAH:* BBB. *IB:* 34. *OCR NED:* M2 Interview required.

M1R1 LLB Law with French
Duration: 2FT Hon
Entry Requirements: *GCE:* 300. *SQAH:* ABBB. *SQAAH:* BBB. *IB:* 34. *OCR NED:* M2 Interview required.

M1R4 LLB Law with Spanish
Duration: 2FT Hon
Entry Requirements: *GCE:* 300. *SQAH:* ABBB. *SQAAH:* BBB. *IB:* 34. *OCR NED:* M2 Interview required.

C15 CARDIFF UNIVERSITY
PO BOX 927
30-36 NEWPORT ROAD
CARDIFF CF24 0DE
t: 029 2087 9999 f: 029 2087 6138
e: admissions@cardiff.ac.uk
// www.cardiff.ac.uk

RM11 LLB Law and French (Integrated)
Duration: 4FT Hon
Entry Requirements: *GCE:* ABB. *SQAAH:* ABB. *IB:* 32. Interview required.

RM21 LLB Law and German (Integrated)
Duration: 4FT Hon
Entry Requirements: *GCE:* ABB. *SQAAH:* ABB. *IB:* 32. Interview required.

MQ15 LLB Law and Welsh (Integrated)
Duration: 3FT Hon
Entry Requirements: *GCE:* ABB. *IB:* 32. Interview required.

C30 UNIVERSITY OF CENTRAL LANCASHIRE
PRESTON
LANCS PR1 2HE
t: 01772 201201 f: 01772 894954
e: uadmissions@uclan.ac.uk
// www.uclan.ac.uk

M1T6 LLB Law with Arabic
Duration: 4FT Hon
Entry Requirements: *GCE:* BBB. *SQAH:* AAAB. *IB:* 30. *OCR ND:* D *OCR NED:* D2

M1T1 LLB Law with Chinese
Duration: 4FT Hon
Entry Requirements: *GCE:* BBB. *SQAH:* AAAB. *IB:* 30. *OCR ND:* D *OCR NED:* D2

M1T2 LLB Law with Japanese
Duration: 4FT Hon
Entry Requirements: *GCE:* BBB. *SQAH:* AAAB. *IB:* 30. *OCR ND:* D *OCR NED:* D2

C55 UNIVERSITY OF CHESTER
PARKGATE ROAD
CHESTER CH1 4BJ
t: 01244 511000 f: 01244 511300
e: enquiries@chester.ac.uk
// www.chester.ac.uk

MR11 BA Law and French
Duration: 4FT Hon
Entry Requirements: *GCE:* 240-280. *SQAH:* BBBB. *IB:* 26.

MR12 BA Law and German
Duration: 4FT Hon
Entry Requirements: *GCE:* 240-280. *SQAH:* BBBB. *IB:* 26.

MR14 BA Law and Spanish
Duration: 4FT Hon
Entry Requirements: *GCE:* 240-280. *SQAH:* BBBB. *IB:* 26.

D39 UNIVERSITY OF DERBY
KEDLESTON ROAD
DERBY DE22 1GB
t: 01332 591167 f: 01332 597724
e: askadmissions@derby.ac.uk
// www.derby.ac.uk

MT17 BA American Studies and Law
Duration: 3FT Hon
Entry Requirements: *Foundation:* Distinction. *GCE:* 260-300. *IB:* 28. *BTEC Dip:* D*D*. *BTEC ExtDip:* DMM. *OCR NED:* M2

D65 UNIVERSITY OF DUNDEE
NETHERGATE
DUNDEE DD1 4HN
t: 01382 383838 f: 01382 388150
e: contactus@dundee.ac.uk
// www.dundee.ac.uk/admissions/undergraduate/

M1RC LLB Law (Eng/NI) with French
Duration: 3FT Hon
Entry Requirements: *GCE:* ABB. *SQAH:* AABB-ABBBB. *IB:* 32.

M1RF LLB Law (Eng/NI) with German
Duration: 3FT Hon
Entry Requirements: *GCE:* ABB. *SQAH:* AABB-ABBBB. *IB:* 32.

M1RK LLB Law (Eng/NI) with Spanish
Duration: 3FT Hon
Entry Requirements: *GCE:* ABB. *SQAH:* AABB-ABBBB. *IB:* 32.

M1R1 LLB Law (Scots) with French
Duration: 4FT Hon
Entry Requirements: *GCE:* ABB. *SQAH:* AABB-ABBBB. *IB:* 32.

M1R2 LLB Law (Scots) with German
Duration: 4FT Hon
Entry Requirements: *GCE:* ABB. *SQAH:* AABB-ABBBB. *IB:* 32.

M1R4 LLB Law (Scots) with Spanish
Duration: 4FT Hon
Entry Requirements: *GCE:* ABB. *SQAH:* AABB-ABBBB. *IB:* 32.

E28 UNIVERSITY OF EAST LONDON
DOCKLANDS CAMPUS
UNIVERSITY WAY
LONDON E16 2RD
t: 020 8223 3333 f: 020 8223 2978
e: study@uel.ac.uk
// www.uel.ac.uk

Q3MC BA English Literature with Law
Duration: 3FT Hon
Entry Requirements: *GCE:* 240. *IB:* 24.

Q3M1 BA English Literature/Law
Duration: 3FT Hon
Entry Requirements: *GCE:* 240. *IB:* 28.

M1QH BA Law with English Literature
Duration: 3FT Hon
Entry Requirements: *GCE:* 240. *IB:* 28.

E56 THE UNIVERSITY OF EDINBURGH
STUDENT RECRUITMENT & ADMISSIONS
57 GEORGE SQUARE
EDINBURGH EH8 9JU
t: 0131 650 4360 f: 0131 651 1236
e: sra.enquiries@ed.ac.uk
// www.ed.ac.uk/studying/undergraduate/

MQ15 LLB Law and Celtic
Duration: 4FT Hon
Entry Requirements: *GCE:* AAA-BBB. *SQAH:* AAAA-BBBB. *IB:* 34.

MR11 LLB Law and French
Duration: 4FT Hon
Entry Requirements: *GCE:* AAA-BBB. *SQAH:* AAAA-BBBB. *IB:* 34.

MR12 LLB Law and German
Duration: 4FT Hon
Entry Requirements: *GCE:* AAA-BBB. *SQAH:* AAAA-BBBB. *IB:* 34.

MR14 LLB Law and Spanish
Duration: 4FT Hon
Entry Requirements: *GCE:* AAA-BBB. *SQAH:* AAAA-BBBB. *IB:* 34.

G14 UNIVERSITY OF GLAMORGAN, CARDIFF AND PONTYPRIDD
ENQUIRIES AND ADMISSIONS UNIT
PONTYPRIDD CF37 1DL
t: 08456 434030 f: 01443 654050
e: enquiries@glam.ac.uk
// www.glam.ac.uk

Q3M1 BA English with Law
Duration: 3FT Hon
Entry Requirements: *GCE:* BBC. *IB:* 25. *BTEC SubDip:* M. *BTEC Dip:* D*D*. *BTEC ExtDip:* DMM.

M1Q5 LLB Law with Professional Welsh
Duration: 3FT Hon
Entry Requirements: *GCE:* BBB. *IB:* 26. *BTEC SubDip:* M. *BTEC Dip:* D*D*. *BTEC ExtDip:* DDM.

G28 UNIVERSITY OF GLASGOW
71 SOUTHPARK AVENUE
UNIVERSITY OF GLASGOW
GLASGOW G12 8QQ
t: 0141 330 6062 f: 0141 330 2961
e: student.recruitment@glasgow.ac.uk
// www.glasgow.ac.uk

M1R1 LLB Law with French Language
Duration: 4FT Hon
Entry Requirements: *GCE:* AAB. *SQAH:* AAAAB. *IB:* 34.
Admissions Test required.

M1R2 LLB Law with German Language
Duration: 4FT Hon
Entry Requirements: *GCE:* AAB. *SQAH:* AAAAB. *IB:* 34.
Admissions Test required.

M1R3 LLB Law with Italian Language
Duration: 4FT Hon
Entry Requirements: *GCE:* AAB. *SQAH:* AAAAB. *IB:* 34.
Admissions Test required.

M1R4 LLB Law with Spanish Language
Duration: 4FT Hon
Entry Requirements: *GCE:* AAB. *SQAH:* AAAAB. *IB:* 34.
Admissions Test required.

MQ13 LLB Law/English Literature
Duration: 4FT Hon
Entry Requirements: *GCE:* AAB. *SQAH:* AAAAB. *IB:* 34.
Admissions Test required.

MQ15 LLB Law/Gaelic Language
Duration: 4FT Hon
Entry Requirements: *GCE:* AAB. *SQAH:* AAAAB. *IB:* 34.
Admissions Test required.

MR17 LLB Law/Slavonic Studies
Duration: 4FT Hon
Entry Requirements: *GCE:* AAB. *SQAH:* AAAAB. *IB:* 34.
Admissions Test required.

H36 UNIVERSITY OF HERTFORDSHIRE
UNIVERSITY ADMISSIONS SERVICE
COLLEGE LANE
HATFIELD
HERTS AL10 9AB
t: 01707 284800
// www.herts.ac.uk

M1R1 BSc Law/French
Duration: 3FT/4SW Hon
Entry Requirements: *GCE:* 320.

M1R4 BSc Law/Spanish
Duration: 3FT/4SW Hon
Entry Requirements: *GCE:* 320.

H72 THE UNIVERSITY OF HULL
THE UNIVERSITY OF HULL
COTTINGHAM ROAD
HULL HU6 7RX
t: 01482 466100 f: 01482 442290
e: admissions@hull.ac.uk
// www.hull.ac.uk

Q3M1 BA English with Law
Duration: 3FT Hon
Entry Requirements: *GCE:* 280-320. *IB:* 30. *BTEC ExtDip:* DDM.

M1Q3 LLB Law (including Foundation English Language)
Duration: 4FT Hon
Entry Requirements: *GCE:* 320. *IB:* 30.

M1R1 LLB Law with French Law and Language (4 years)
Duration: 4FT Hon
Entry Requirements: *GCE:* 320. *IB:* 30. *BTEC ExtDip:* DDM.

M1R2 LLB Law with German Law and Language (4 years)
Duration: 4FT Hon
Entry Requirements: *GCE:* 320. *IB:* 30. *BTEC ExtDip:* DDM.

M1QH LLB Law with Literature
Duration: 3FT Hon
Entry Requirements: *GCE:* 320. *IB:* 30. *BTEC ExtDip:* DDM.

M1R4 LLB Law with Spanish Law & Language
Duration: 4FT Hon
Entry Requirements: *GCE:* 320. *IB:* 30. *BTEC ExtDip:* DDM.

K12 KEELE UNIVERSITY
KEELE UNIVERSITY
STAFFORDSHIRE ST5 5BG
t: 01782 734005 f: 01782 632343
e: undergraduate@keele.ac.uk
// www.keele.ac.uk

MT17 BA American Studies and Law
Duration: 3FT Hon
Entry Requirements: *GCE:* ABB.

MQ13 BA English and Law
Duration: 3FT Hon
Entry Requirements: *GCE:* ABB.

K24 THE UNIVERSITY OF KENT
RECRUITMENT & ADMISSIONS OFFICE
REGISTRY
UNIVERSITY OF KENT
CANTERBURY, KENT CT2 7NZ
t: 01227 827272 f: 01227 827077
e: information@kent.ac.uk
// www.kent.ac.uk

MQ13 BA Law and English
Duration: 4FT Hon
Entry Requirements: *GCE:* AAB. *SQAH:* AAAAB. *SQAAH:* AAB. *IB:* 33. *OCR ND:* M2 *OCR NED:* M3

M1R1 LLB Law with French and a year in Canada
Duration: 4FT Hon
Entry Requirements: *GCE:* AAB. *SQAH:* AAAAB. *SQAAH:* AAB. *IB:* 33. *OCR ND:* D *OCR NED:* M3

M1R4 LLB Law with Spanish
Duration: 3FT Hon
Entry Requirements: *GCE:* AAB. *SQAH:* AAAAB. *SQAAH:* AAB. *IB:* 33. *OCR ND:* D *OCR NED:* M1

K84 KINGSTON UNIVERSITY
STUDENT INFORMATION & ADVICE CENTRE
COOPER HOUSE
40-46 SURBITON ROAD
KINGSTON UPON THAMES KT1 2HX
t: 0844 8552177 f: 020 8547 7080
e: aps@kingston.ac.uk
// www.kingston.ac.uk

QM31 BA English Literature and Law
Duration: 3FT Hon
Entry Requirements: *GCE:* 280-360.

L23 UNIVERSITY OF LEEDS
THE UNIVERSITY OF LEEDS
WOODHOUSE LANE
LEEDS LS2 9JT
t: 0113 343 3999
e: admissions@leeds.ac.uk
// www.leeds.ac.uk

MR11 LLB Law and French
Duration: 4FT Hon
Entry Requirements: *GCE:* AAA. *SQAAH:* AAA. *IB:* 38.

L34 UNIVERSITY OF LEICESTER
UNIVERSITY ROAD
LEICESTER LE1 7RH
t: 0116 252 5281 f: 0116 252 2447
e: admissions@le.ac.uk
// www.le.ac.uk

M2R9 LLB Law with a Modern Language
Duration: 3FT Hon
Entry Requirements: Contact the institution for details.

L41 THE UNIVERSITY OF LIVERPOOL
THE FOUNDATION BUILDING
BROWNLOW HILL
LIVERPOOL L69 7ZX
t: 0151 794 2000 f: 0151 708 6502
e: ugrecruitment@liv.ac.uk
// www.liv.ac.uk

M104 LLB Law with French
Duration: 4FT Hon
Entry Requirements: *GCE:* AAA. *SQAH:* AAAAA. *SQAAH:* AA. *IB:* 36. *OCR ND:* D *OCR NED:* D2

M105 LLB Law with German
Duration: 4FT Hon
Entry Requirements: *GCE:* AAA. *SQAH:* AAAAA. *SQAAH:* AA. *IB:* 36. *OCR ND:* D *OCR NED:* D2

M106 LLB Law with Italian
Duration: 4FT Hon
Entry Requirements: *GCE:* AAA. *SQAH:* AAAAA. *SQAAH:* AA. *IB:* 36. *OCR ND:* D *OCR NED:* D2

M108 LLB Law with Spanish
Duration: 4FT Hon
Entry Requirements: *GCE:* AAA. *SQAH:* AAAAA. *SQAAH:* AA. *IB:* 36. *OCR ND:* D *OCR NED:* D2

L46 LIVERPOOL HOPE UNIVERSITY
HOPE PARK
LIVERPOOL L16 9JD
t: 0151 291 3331 f: 0151 291 3434
e: administration@hope.ac.uk
// www.hope.ac.uk

QM31 BA English Language and Law
Duration: 3FT Hon
Entry Requirements: *GCE:* 300-320. *IB:* 25.

M40 THE MANCHESTER METROPOLITAN UNIVERSITY
ADMISSIONS OFFICE
ALL SAINTS (GMS)
ALL SAINTS
MANCHESTER M15 6BH
t: 0161 247 2000
// www.mmu.ac.uk

MQ2H BA English/Legal Studies
Duration: 3FT Hon
Entry Requirements: *GCE:* 280. *IB:* 28. *BTEC Dip:* D*D*. *BTEC ExtDip:* DMM.

N38 UNIVERSITY OF NORTHAMPTON
PARK CAMPUS
BOUGHTON GREEN ROAD
NORTHAMPTON NN2 7AL
t: 0800 358 2232 f: 01604 722083
e: admissions@northampton.ac.uk
// www.northampton.ac.uk

R1M1 BA French/Law
Duration: 3FT Hon
Entry Requirements: *GCE:* 260-280. *SQAH:* AAA-BBBB. *IB:* 24. *BTEC Dip:* DD. *BTEC ExtDip:* DMM. *OCR ND:* D *OCR NED:* M2

M1R1 BA Law/French
Duration: 3FT Hon
Entry Requirements: *GCE:* 260-280. *SQAH:* AAA-BBBB. *IB:* 24. *BTEC Dip:* DD. *BTEC ExtDip:* DMM. *OCR ND:* D *OCR NED:* M2

N84 THE UNIVERSITY OF NOTTINGHAM
THE ADMISSIONS OFFICE
THE UNIVERSITY OF NOTTINGHAM
UNIVERSITY PARK
NOTTINGHAM NG7 2RD
t: 0115 951 5151 f: 0115 951 4668
// www.nottingham.ac.uk

M1R1 BA Law with French and French Law
Duration: 4FT Hon   CRB Check: Required
Entry Requirements: *GCE:* AAA. *SQAAH:* AAA. *IB:* 38. Admissions Test required.

M1R2 BA Law with German and German Law
Duration: 4FT Hon   CRB Check: Required
Entry Requirements: *GCE:* AAA. *SQAAH:* AAA. *IB:* 38. Admissions Test required.

M1R4 BA Law with Spanish and Spanish Law
Duration: 4FT Hon   CRB Check: Required
Entry Requirements: *GCE:* AAA. *SQAAH:* AAA. *IB:* 38. Admissions Test required.

P80 UNIVERSITY OF PORTSMOUTH
ACADEMIC REGISTRY
UNIVERSITY HOUSE
WINSTON CHURCHILL AVENUE
PORTSMOUTH PO1 2UP
t: 023 9284 8484 f: 023 9284 3082
e: admissions@port.ac.uk
// www.port.ac.uk

RM81 BA Languages and Law
Duration: 4FT Hon
Entry Requirements: *GCE:* 200-280. *BTEC Dip:* DD. *BTEC ExtDip:* MMM.

S03 THE UNIVERSITY OF SALFORD
SALFORD M5 4WT
t: 0161 295 4545 f: 0161 295 4646
e: ug-admissions@salford.ac.uk
// www.salford.ac.uk

M9R4 LLB Law with Spanish
Duration: 4FT Hon
Entry Requirements: *GCE:* 300. *IB:* 29. *OCR NED:* M2 Interview required.

S09 SCHOOL OF ORIENTAL AND AFRICAN STUDIES (UNIVERSITY OF LONDON)
THORNHAUGH STREET
RUSSELL SQUARE
LONDON WC1H 0XG
t: 020 7898 4301 f: 020 7898 4039
e: undergradadmissions@soas.ac.uk
// www.soas.ac.uk

MT16 BA Law and Arabic
Duration: 4FT Hon
Entry Requirements: *GCE:* AAA.

MTCH BA Law and Burmese
Duration: 3FT Hon
Entry Requirements: *GCE:* AAA.

MT11 BA Law and Chinese
Duration: 4FT Hon
Entry Requirements: *GCE:* AAA.

MT19 BA Law and Georgian
Duration: 3FT Hon
Entry Requirements: *GCE:* AAA.

MTC5 BA Law and Hausa
Duration: 4FT Hon
Entry Requirements: *GCE:* AAA.

MQ14 BA Law and Hebrew
Duration: 4FT Hon
Entry Requirements: *GCE:* AAA.

MTDH BA Law and Indonesian
Duration: 3FT Hon
Entry Requirements: *GCE:* AAA.

MTDL BA Law and Korean
Duration: 4FT Hon
Entry Requirements: *GCE:* AAA.

MQ11 BA Law and Linguistics
Duration: 3FT Hon
Entry Requirements: *GCE:* AAA.

TMJC BA Law and South-East Asian Studies
Duration: 3FT Hon
Entry Requirements: *GCE:* AAA.

TM61 BA Middle Eastern Studies and Law
Duration: 3FT Hon
Entry Requirements: *GCE:* AAA.

MTD6 BA Persian and Law
Duration: 3FT Hon
Entry Requirements: *GCE:* AAA.

TMH1 BA South Asian Studies and Law
Duration: 3FT Hon
Entry Requirements: Contact the institution for details.

TM3C BA South Asian Studies and Law (Including Year Abroad)
Duration: 4FT Hon
Entry Requirements: *GCE:* AAA.

MTD5 BA Swahili and Law
Duration: 4FT Hon
Entry Requirements: *GCE:* AAA.

TM31 BA Thai and Law
Duration: 3FT Hon
Entry Requirements: *GCE:* AAA.

MTC6 BA Turkish and Law
Duration: 4FT Hon
Entry Requirements: *GCE:* AAA.

MT1H BA Vietnamese and Law
Duration: 3FT Hon
Entry Requirements: *GCE:* AAA.

S18 THE UNIVERSITY OF SHEFFIELD
THE UNIVERSITY OF SHEFFIELD
LEVEL 2, ARTS TOWER
WESTERN BANK
SHEFFIELD S10 2TN
t: 0114 222 8030 f: 0114 222 8032
// www.sheffield.ac.uk

M1R1 LLB Law with French
Duration: 4FT Hon
Entry Requirements: *GCE:* AAB. *SQAH:* AAABB. *SQAAH:* B. *IB:* 35.
BTEC ExtDip: DDD.

M1R2 LLB Law with German
Duration: 4FT Hon
Entry Requirements: *GCE:* AAB. *SQAH:* AAABB. *SQAAH:* B. *IB:* 35.
BTEC ExtDip: DDD.

M1R4 LLB Law with Spanish
Duration: 4FT Hon
Entry Requirements: *GCE:* AAB. *SQAH:* AAABB. *SQAAH:* B. *IB:* 35.
BTEC ExtDip: DDD.

S75 THE UNIVERSITY OF STIRLING
STUDENT RECRUITMENT & ADMISSIONS SERVICE
UNIVERSITY OF STIRLING
STIRLING
SCOTLAND FK9 4LA
t: 01786 467044 f: 01786 466800
e: admissions@stir.ac.uk
// www.stir.ac.uk

RM11 BA French and Law
Duration: 4FT Hon
Entry Requirements: *GCE:* BBC. *SQAH:* BBBB. *SQAAH:* AAA-CCC.
IB: 32. *BTEC ExtDip:* DMM.

MR14 BA Law and Spanish
Duration: 4FT Hon
Entry Requirements: *GCE:* BBC. *SQAH:* BBBB. *SQAAH:* AAA-CCC.
IB: 32. *BTEC ExtDip:* DMM.

S78 THE UNIVERSITY OF STRATHCLYDE
GLASGOW G1 1XQ
t: 0141 552 4400 f: 0141 552 0775
// www.strath.ac.uk

QM31 BA English and Law
Duration: 4FT Hon
Entry Requirements: *GCE:* ABB. *SQAH:* AAABB-AAAB. *IB:* 34.

RM11 BA French and Law
Duration: 5FT Hon
Entry Requirements: *GCE:* ABB. *SQAH:* AAABB-AAAB. *IB:* 34.

RM31 BA Italian and Law
Duration: 5FT Hon
Entry Requirements: *GCE:* ABB. *SQAH:* AAABB-AAAB. *IB:* 34.

MR14 BA Law and Spanish
Duration: 5FT Hon
Entry Requirements: *GCE:* ABB. *SQAH:* AAABB-AAAB. *IB:* 34.

M1R1 LLB Law (Scots) with French
Duration: 5FT Hon   CRB Check: Required
Entry Requirements *GCE:* AAB. *SQAH:* AAAAB. *IB:* 38.

M1R3 LLB Law(Scots) with Italian
Duration: 5FT Hon   CRB Check: Required
Entry Requirements: *GCE:* AAB. *SQAH:* AAAAB. *IB:* 38.

M1R4 LLB Law(Scots) with Spanish
Duration: 5FT Hon   CRB Check: Required
Entry Requirements: *GCE:* AAB. *SQAH:* AAAAB. *IB:* 38.

S84 UNIVERSITY OF SUNDERLAND
STUDENT HELPLINE
THE STUDENT GATEWAY
CHESTER ROAD
SUNDERLAND SR1 3SD
t: 0191 515 3000 f: 0191 515 3805
e: student.helpline@sunderland.ac.uk
// www.sunderland.ac.uk

Q1M1 BA English Language & Linguistics with Law
Duration: 3FT Hon
Entry Requirements: *GCE:* 260-360. *OCR ND:* D *OCR NED:* M3

MQ13 BA Law and English
Duration: 3FT Hon
Entry Requirements: *GCE:* 260-360. *OCR ND:* D *OCR NED:* M3

RM11 BA Modern Foreign Languages (French) and Law
Duration: 3FT Hon
Entry Requirements: *GCE:* 260-360. *IB:* 31. *OCR ND:* D *OCR NED:* M3

MR12 BA Modern Foreign Languages (German) and Law
Duration: 3FT Hon
Entry Requirements: *GCE:* 260-360. *IB:* 31. *OCR ND:* D *OCR NED:* M3

MR14 BA Modern Foreign Languages (Spanish) and Law
Duration: 3FT Hon
Entry Requirements: *GCE:* 260-360. *IB:* 31. *OCR ND:* D *OCR NED:* M3

MQ11 BA/BSc Law and English Language/Linguistics
Duration: 3FT Hon
Entry Requirements: *GCE:* 260-360. *OCR ND:* D *OCR NED:* M3

S90 UNIVERSITY OF SUSSEX
UNDERGRADUATE ADMISSIONS
SUSSEX HOUSE
UNIVERSITY OF SUSSEX
BRIGHTON BN1 9RH
t: 01273 678416 f: 01273 678545
e: ug.applicants@sussex.ac.uk
// www.sussex.ac.uk

M1RY LLB Law (with a study abroad year)
Duration: 4FT Hon
Entry Requirements: *GCE:* AAA-AAB. *SQAH:* AAAAA-AAABB. *SQAAH:* AAB. *IB:* 35. *BTEC SubDip:* D. *BTEC Dip:* DD. *BTEC ExtDip:* DDD. *OCR ND:* D *OCR NED:* D1

M1TP LLB Law with American Studies
Duration: 4FT Hon
Entry Requirements: *GCE:* AAA-AAB. *SQAH:* AAAAA-AAABB. *IB:* 35. *BTEC SubDip:* D. *BTEC Dip:* DD. *BTEC ExtDip:* DDD. *OCR ND:* D *OCR NED:* D1

M1TT LLB Law with American Studies
Duration: 3FT Hon
Entry Requirements: *GCE:* AAA-AAB. *SQAH:* AAAAA-AAABB. *IB:* 35. *BTEC SubDip:* D. *BTEC Dip:* DD. *BTEC ExtDip:* DDD. *OCR ND:* D *OCR NED:* D1

S93 SWANSEA UNIVERSITY
SINGLETON PARK
SWANSEA SA2 8PP
t: 01792 295111 f: 01792 295110
e: admissions@swansea.ac.uk
// www.swansea.ac.uk

R1M9 BA French with Legal Studies (4 years)
Duration: 4FT Hon
Entry Requirements: *GCE:* BBB. *IB:* 32.

R2M9 BA German with Legal Studies
Duration: 4FT Hon
Entry Requirements: *GCE:* BBB. *IB:* 32.

R4M9 BA Spanish with Legal Studies
Duration: 4FT Hon
Entry Requirements: *GCE:* BBB. *IB:* 32.

Q5M9 BA Welsh with Legal Studies
Duration: 3FT Hon
Entry Requirements: *GCE:* BBB. *IB:* 32.

MT17 LLB Law and American Studies
Duration: 3FT Hon
Entry Requirements: *GCE:* AAB. *IB:* 34.

MT1R LLB Law and American Studies (with an Intercalary Year)
Duration: 4FT Hon
Entry Requirements: *GCE:* AAB. *IB:* 34.

MR11 LLB Law and French
Duration: 4FT Hon
Entry Requirements: *GCE:* AAB. *IB:* 34.

MR12 LLB Law and German
Duration: 4FT Hon
Entry Requirements: *GCE:* AAB. *IB:* 34.

MR13 LLB Law and Italian
Duration: 4FT Hon
Entry Requirements: *GCE:* AAB. *IB:* 34.

MR14 LLB Law and Spanish
Duration: 4FT Hon
Entry Requirements: *GCE:* AAB. *IB:* 34.

MQ15 LLB Law and Welsh
Duration: 4FT Hon
Entry Requirements: *GCE:* AAB. *IB:* 34.

U20 UNIVERSITY OF ULSTER
COLERAINE
CO. LONDONDERRY
NORTHERN IRELAND BT52 1SA
t: 028 7012 4221 f: 028 7012 4908
e: online@ulster.ac.uk
// www.ulster.ac.uk

M1Q5 LLB Law with Irish
Duration: 3FT Hon
Entry Requirements: *GCE:* BBB. *SQAH:* AABCC. *SQAAH:* BBB. *IB:* 25.

W50 UNIVERSITY OF WESTMINSTER
2ND FLOOR, CAVENDISH HOUSE
101 NEW CAVENDISH STREET,
LONDON W1W 6XH
t: 020 7915 5511
e: course-enquiries@westminster.ac.uk
// www.westminster.ac.uk

M1R1 LLB Law with French
Duration: 4FT Hon
Entry Requirements: *GCE:* ABC. *SQAH:* ABBBC. *SQAAH:* ABC. *IB:* 30. Interview required.

W76 UNIVERSITY OF WINCHESTER
WINCHESTER
HANTS SO22 4NR
t: 01962 827234 f: 01962 827288
e: course.enquiries@winchester.ac.uk
// www.winchester.ac.uk

QM3C BA English Language Studies and Law
Duration: 3FT Hon
Entry Requirements: *Foundation:* Distinction. *GCE:* 260-300. *IB:* 25. *OCR ND:* D *OCR NED:* M2

MQ13 BA Law and English
Duration: 3FT Hon
Entry Requirements: *Foundation:* Distinction. *GCE:* 260-300. *IB:* 25. *OCR ND:* D *OCR NED:* M2

LAW

A40 ABERYSTWYTH UNIVERSITY
ABERYSTWYTH UNIVERSITY, WELCOME CENTRE
PENGLAIS CAMPUS
ABERYSTWYTH
CEREDIGION SY23 3FB
t: 01970 622021 f: 01970 627410
e: ug-admissions@aber.ac.uk
// www.aber.ac.uk

M103 BA Law
Duration: 3FT Hon
Entry Requirements: *GCE:* 340. *IB:* 28.

M100 LLB Law
Duration: 3FT Hon
Entry Requirements: *GCE:* 340. *IB:* 34.

M101 LLB Law (2 years)
Duration: 2FT Hon
Entry Requirements: Contact the institution for details.

A60 ANGLIA RUSKIN UNIVERSITY
BISHOP HALL LANE
CHELMSFORD
ESSEX CM1 1SQ
t: 0845 271 3333 f: 01245 251789
e: answers@anglia.ac.uk
// www.anglia.ac.uk

M100 LLB Law
Duration: 3FT Hon
Entry Requirements: *GCE:* 240-280. *SQAH:* AABC. *SQAAH:* AB. *IB:* 30.

B06 BANGOR UNIVERSITY
BANGOR UNIVERSITY
BANGOR
GWYNEDD LL57 2DG
t: 01248 388484 f: 01248 370451
e: admissions@bangor.ac.uk
// www.bangor.ac.uk

M100 LLB Law
Duration: 3FT Hon
Entry Requirements: *GCE:* 280. *IB:* 28.

M101 LLB Law (2 year programme)
Duration: 2FT Hon
Entry Requirements: *GCE:* 280. *IB:* 28.

B22 UNIVERSITY OF BEDFORDSHIRE
PARK SQUARE
LUTON
BEDS LU1 3JU
t: 0844 8482234 f: 01582 489323
e: admissions@beds.ac.uk
// www.beds.ac.uk

M100 LLB Law
Duration: 3FT Hon
Entry Requirements: *Foundation:* Pass. *GCE:* 200. *SQAH:* BCC.
SQAAH: BCC. *IB:* 24. *OCR ND:* M1 *OCR NED:* P1

B24 BIRKBECK, UNIVERSITY OF LONDON
MALET STREET
LONDON WC1E 7HX
t: 020 7631 6316
e: webform: www.bbk.ac.uk/ask
// www.bbk.ac.uk/ask

M100 LLB Law
Duration: 3FT Hon
Entry Requirements: *GCE:* AAB. *SQAH:* AAAA-AABB. *IB:* 28.
Interview required.

B25 BIRMINGHAM CITY UNIVERSITY
PERRY BARR
BIRMINGHAM B42 2SU
t: 0121 331 5595 f: 0121 331 7994
// www.bcu.ac.uk

M100 LLB Law
Duration: 3FT Hon
Entry Requirements: *GCE:* 280. *IB:* 28.

B32 THE UNIVERSITY OF BIRMINGHAM
EDGBASTON
BIRMINGHAM B15 2TT
t: 0121 415 8900 f: 0121 414 7159
e: admissions@bham.ac.uk
// www.birmingham.ac.uk

M100 LLB Law
Duration: 3FT Hon
Entry Requirements: *GCE:* A*AB-AAA. *SQAAH:* AAA. *IB:* 36. *BTEC
SubDip:* D. *BTEC Dip:* D*D*. *BTEC ExtDip:* D*D*D. Admissions
Test required.

B40 BLACKBURN COLLEGE
FEILDEN STREET
BLACKBURN BB2 1LH
t: 01254 292594 f: 01254 679647
e: he-admissions@blackburn.ac.uk
// www.blackburn.ac.uk

M101 LLB Law (Accelerated Route)
Duration: 2FT Hon
Entry Requirements: Contact the institution for details.

M102 LLB Law Fast Track (Top-Up)
Duration: 2FT Hon
Entry Requirements: HND required.

M100 LLB Law: Multimode (3 years)
Duration: 3FT Hon
Entry Requirements: *GCE:* 220. *IB:* 26.

B44 UNIVERSITY OF BOLTON
DEANE ROAD
BOLTON BL3 5AB
t: 01204 903903 f: 01204 399074
e: enquiries@bolton.ac.uk
// www.bolton.ac.uk

M100 LLB Law
Duration: 3FT Hon
Entry Requirements: *GCE:* 300. Interview required.

B50 BOURNEMOUTH UNIVERSITY
TALBOT CAMPUS
FERN BARROW
POOLE
DORSET BH12 5BB
t: 01202 524111
// www.bournemouth.ac.uk

M100 LLB Law
Duration: 4SW Hon
Entry Requirements: *GCE:* 320. *IB:* 32. *BTEC SubDip:* D. *BTEC
Dip:* DD. *BTEC ExtDip:* DDM.

B54 BPP UNIVERSITY COLLEGE OF PROFESSIONAL STUDIES LIMITED
142-144 UXBRIDGE ROAD
LONDON W12 8AW
t: 02031 312 298
e: admissions@bpp.com
// undergraduate.bpp.com/

M100 LLB Law
Duration: 3FT Hon
Entry Requirements: *GCE:* 300.

M101 LLB Law (Accelerated)
Duration: 2FT Hon
Entry Requirements: *GCE:* 300.

B56 THE UNIVERSITY OF BRADFORD
RICHMOND ROAD
BRADFORD
WEST YORKSHIRE BD7 1DP
t: 0800 073 1225 f: 01274 235585
e: course-enquiries@bradford.ac.uk
// www.bradford.ac.uk

M100 LLB Law
Duration: 3FT Hon
Entry Requirements: *GCE:* 300. *IB:* 25.

B60 BRADFORD COLLEGE: AN ASSOCIATE COLLEGE OF LEEDS METROPOLITAN UNIVERSITY
GREAT HORTON ROAD
BRADFORD
WEST YORKSHIRE BD7 1AY
t: 01274 433008 f: 01274 431652
e: heregistry@bradfordcollege.ac.uk
// www.bradfordcollege.ac.uk/
university-centre

M100 LLB Law
Duration: 3FT Hon
Entry Requirements: *GCE:* 240. *IB:* 24.

B78 UNIVERSITY OF BRISTOL
UNDERGRADUATE ADMISSIONS OFFICE
SENATE HOUSE
TYNDALL AVENUE
BRISTOL BS8 1TH
t: 0117 928 9000 f: 0117 331 7391
e: ug-admissions@bristol.ac.uk
// www.bristol.ac.uk

M100 LLB Law
Duration: 3FT Hon
Entry Requirements: *GCE:* AAA. *SQAH:* AAAAA. *SQAAH:* AA. *IB:* 37. Admissions Test required.

B80 UNIVERSITY OF THE WEST OF ENGLAND, BRISTOL
FRENCHAY CAMPUS
COLDHARBOUR LANE
BRISTOL BS16 1QY
t: +44 (0)117 32 83333 f: +44 (0)117 32 82810
e: admissions@uwe.ac.uk
// www.uwe.ac.uk

M100 LLB Law
Duration: 3FT Hon
Entry Requirements: *GCE:* 340.

B84 BRUNEL UNIVERSITY
UXBRIDGE
MIDDLESEX UB8 3PH
t: 01895 265265 f: 01895 269790
e: admissions@brunel.ac.uk
// www.brunel.ac.uk

M103 LLB Law
Duration: 3FT Hon
Entry Requirements: *GCE:* AAB. *SQAAH:* AAB. *IB:* 35. *BTEC ExtDip:* D*D*D.

M101 LLB Law (4 year Thick SW)
Duration: 4SW Hon
Entry Requirements: *GCE:* AAB. *SQAAH:* AAB. *IB:* 35. *BTEC ExtDip:* D*D*D.

B90 THE UNIVERSITY OF BUCKINGHAM
YEOMANRY HOUSE
HUNTER STREET
BUCKINGHAM MK18 1EG
t: 01280 820313 f: 01280 822245
e: info@buckingham.ac.uk
// www.buckingham.ac.uk

M100 LLB Law
Duration: 2FT Hon
Entry Requirements: *GCE:* 300. *SQAH:* ABBB. *SQAAH:* BBB. *IB:* 34. *OCR NED:* M2 Interview required.

B94 BUCKINGHAMSHIRE NEW UNIVERSITY
QUEEN ALEXANDRA ROAD
HIGH WYCOMBE
BUCKINGHAMSHIRE HP11 2JZ
t: 0800 0565 660 f: 01494 605 023
e: admissions@bucks.ac.uk
// bucks.ac.uk

M100 LLB Law
Duration: 3FT Hon
Entry Requirements: *GCE:* 300-340. *IB:* 25. *OCR ND:* D *OCR NED:* M2

C05 UNIVERSITY OF CAMBRIDGE
CAMBRIDGE ADMISSIONS OFFICE
FITZWILLIAM HOUSE
32 TRUMPINGTON STREET
CAMBRIDGE CB2 1QY
t: 01223 333 308 f: 01223 746 868
e: admissions@cam.ac.uk
// www.study.cam.ac.uk/undergraduate/

M100 BA Law
Duration: 3FT Hon
Entry Requirements: *GCE:* A*AA. *SQAAH:* AAA-AAB. Interview required. Admissions Test required.

C10 CANTERBURY CHRIST CHURCH UNIVERSITY
NORTH HOLMES ROAD
CANTERBURY
KENT CT1 1QU
t: 01227 782900 f: 01227 782888
e: admissions@canterbury.ac.uk
// www.canterbury.ac.uk

M102 BA Law
Duration: 3FT Hon
Entry Requirements: *GCE:* 260. *IB:* 24.

M100 LLB Law
Duration: 3FT Hon   CRB Check: Required
Entry Requirements: *GCE:* 260. *IB:* 24. Interview required.

C15 CARDIFF UNIVERSITY
PO BOX 927
30-36 NEWPORT ROAD
CARDIFF CF24 0DE
t: 029 2087 9999 f: 029 2087 6138
e: admissions@cardiff.ac.uk
// www.cardiff.ac.uk

M100 LLB Law
Duration: 3FT Hon
Entry Requirements: *GCE:* AAA. *SQAAH:* AAA. *IB:* 36. Interview required.

M101 LLB Law (Graduate entry)
Duration: 2FT Hon
Entry Requirements: Interview required.

C30 UNIVERSITY OF CENTRAL LANCASHIRE
PRESTON
LANCS PR1 2HE
t: 01772 201201 f: 01772 894954
e: uadmissions@uclan.ac.uk
// www.uclan.ac.uk

M101 BA Law (Foundation Entry)
Duration: 4FT Hon
Entry Requirements: Contact the institution for details.

M100 LLB Law
Duration: 3FT Hon
Entry Requirements: *GCE:* BBB. *IB:* 32. *OCR ND:* D *OCR NED:* D2

M102 LLB Senior Status
Duration: 2FT Hon
Entry Requirements: Contact the institution for details.

M110 MLaw Law
Duration: 4FT Hon
Entry Requirements: Contact the institution for details.

C55 UNIVERSITY OF CHESTER
PARKGATE ROAD
CHESTER CH1 4BJ
t: 01244 511000 f: 01244 511300
e: enquiries@chester.ac.uk
// www.chester.ac.uk

M100 LLB Law
Duration: 3FT Hon
Entry Requirements: *Foundation:* Pass. *GCE:* 260-300. *SQAH:* BBBB. *IB:* 28.

C60 CITY UNIVERSITY
NORTHAMPTON SQUARE
LONDON EC1V 0HB
t: 020 7040 5060 f: 020 7040 8995
e: ugadmissions@city.ac.uk
// www.city.ac.uk

M100 LLB Law
Duration: 3FT Hon
Entry Requirements: *GCE:* A*AA. *SQAH:* ABBBB. *IB:* 35.

C85 COVENTRY UNIVERSITY
THE STUDENT CENTRE
COVENTRY UNIVERSITY
1 GULSON RD
COVENTRY CV1 2JH
t: 024 7615 2222 f: 024 7615 2223
e: studentenquiries@coventry.ac.uk
// www.coventry.ac.uk

M100 LLB Law
Duration: 3FT/4SW Hon
Entry Requirements: *GCE:* BBB. *SQAH:* BBBBC. *IB:* 30. *BTEC ExtDip:* DDM. *OCR NED:* M1

M102 LLB Law
Duration: 2FT/3SW Hon
Entry Requirements: *GCE:* ABB. *SQAH:* BBBBC. *IB:* 31.

C92 CROYDON COLLEGE
COLLEGE ROAD
CROYDON CR9 1DX
t: 020 8760 5934 f: 020 8760 5880
e: admissions@croydon.ac.uk
// www.croydon.ac.uk

M100 LLB Law
Duration: 3FT Hon
Entry Requirements: *GCE:* 80-100. Interview required.

C99 UNIVERSITY OF CUMBRIA
FUSEHILL STREET
CARLISLE
CUMBRIA CA1 2HH
t: 01228 616234 f: 01228 616235
// www.cumbria.ac.uk

M100 LLB Law
Duration: 3FT Hon
Entry Requirements: *GCE:* BBC. *SQAH:* AAAB. *IB:* 30.

D26 DE MONTFORT UNIVERSITY
THE GATEWAY
LEICESTER LE1 9BH
t: 0116 255 1551 f: 0116 250 6204
e: enquiries@dmu.ac.uk
// www.dmu.ac.uk

M100 LLB Law
Duration: 3FT Hon
Entry Requirements: *GCE:* 320. *IB:* 30. *BTEC ExtDip:* DDM. *OCR NED:* D2 Interview required.

D39 UNIVERSITY OF DERBY
KEDLESTON ROAD
DERBY DE22 1GB
t: 01332 591167 f: 01332 597724
e: askadmissions@derby.ac.uk
// www.derby.ac.uk

M100 LLB Law
Duration: 3FT Hon
Entry Requirements: *GCE:* 320. *IB:* 28. *BTEC Dip:* D*D*. *BTEC ExtDip:* DMM. *OCR NED:* D2

D86 DURHAM UNIVERSITY
DURHAM UNIVERSITY
UNIVERSITY OFFICE
DURHAM DH1 3HP
t: 0191 334 2000 f: 0191 334 6055
e: admissions@durham.ac.uk
// www.durham.ac.uk

M101 LLB Law
Duration: 3FT Hon
Entry Requirements: *GCE:* A*AA. *SQAH:* AAAAA. *SQAAH:* AAA. *IB:* 38. Admissions Test required.

M102 LLB Law with Foundation
Duration: 4FT Hon
Entry Requirements: Contact the institution for details.

E14 UNIVERSITY OF EAST ANGLIA
NORWICH NR4 7TJ
t: 01603 591515 f: 01603 591523
e: admissions@uea.ac.uk
// www.uea.ac.uk

M100 LLB Law
Duration: 3FT Hon   CRB Check: Required
Entry Requirements: *GCE:* AAB. *SQAH:* AAAAB. *SQAAH:* AAB. *IB:* 33. *BTEC SubDip:* D. *BTEC Dip:* DD. *BTEC ExtDip:* DDD. *OCR ND:* D *OCR NED:* D1 Interview required.

E28 UNIVERSITY OF EAST LONDON
DOCKLANDS CAMPUS
UNIVERSITY WAY
LONDON E16 2RD
t: 020 8223 3333 f: 020 8223 2978
e: study@uel.ac.uk
// www.uel.ac.uk

M100 LLB Law
Duration: 3FT Hon
Entry Requirements: *GCE:* 240. *IB:* 24.

E42 EDGE HILL UNIVERSITY
ORMSKIRK
LANCASHIRE L39 4QP
t: 01695 657000 f: 01695 584355
e: study@edgehill.ac.uk
// www.edgehill.ac.uk

M100 LLB Law
Duration: 3FT Hon
Entry Requirements: *GCE:* 280. *IB:* 26. *OCR ND:* D *OCR NED:* M2

E59 EDINBURGH NAPIER UNIVERSITY
CRAIGLOCKHART CAMPUS
EDINBURGH EH14 1DJ
t: +44 (0)8452 60 60 40 f: 0131 455 6464
e: info@napier.ac.uk
// www.napier.ac.uk

M100 LLB Law (Accelerated)
Duration: 2FT Ord
Entry Requirements: Contact the institution for details.

E70 THE UNIVERSITY OF ESSEX
WIVENHOE PARK
COLCHESTER
ESSEX CO4 3SQ
t: 01206 873666 f: 01206 874477
e: admit@essex.ac.uk
// www.essex.ac.uk

M100 LLB Law
Duration: 3FT Hon
Entry Requirements: *GCE:* AAB. *SQAH:* AAAA. *IB:* 36.

M101 LLB Law (including foundation year)
Duration: 4FT Hon
Entry Requirements: Contact the institution for details.

E84 UNIVERSITY OF EXETER
LAVER BUILDING
NORTH PARK ROAD
EXETER
DEVON EX4 4QE
t: 01392 723044 f: 01392 722479
e: admissions@exeter.ac.uk
// www.exeter.ac.uk

M106 LLB Graduate Entry LLB (2 years)
Duration: 2FT Hon
Entry Requirements: Contact the institution for details.

M103 LLB Law
Duration: 3FT Hon
Entry Requirements: *GCE:* AAA-AAB. *SQAH:* AAABB-AABBB.
SQAAH: AAB-ABB. *BTEC ExtDip:* DDD.

G14 UNIVERSITY OF GLAMORGAN, CARDIFF AND PONTYPRIDD
ENQUIRIES AND ADMISSIONS UNIT
PONTYPRIDD CF37 1DL
t: 08456 434030 f: 01443 654050
e: enquiries@glam.ac.uk
// www.glam.ac.uk

M100 LLB Law
Duration: 3FT Hon
Entry Requirements: *GCE:* BBB. *IB:* 26. *BTEC SubDip:* M. *BTEC Dip:* D*D*. *BTEC ExtDip:* DDM.

M101 LLB Law (Accelerated Route)
Duration: 2FT Hon
Entry Requirements: Contact the institution for details.

M102 MLaw Law
Duration: 4FT Hon
Entry Requirements: *GCE:* BBB. *IB:* 26. *BTEC SubDip:* M. *BTEC Dip:* D*D*. *BTEC ExtDip:* DDM.

G50 THE UNIVERSITY OF GLOUCESTERSHIRE
PARK CAMPUS
THE PARK
CHELTENHAM GL50 2RH
t: 01242 714501 f: 01242 714869
e: admissions@glos.ac.uk
// www.glos.ac.uk

M100 LLB Law
Duration: 3FT Hon
Entry Requirements: *GCE:* 280-300.

M101 LLB Law
Duration: 2FT Hon
Entry Requirements: *GCE:* 280-300.

G70 UNIVERSITY OF GREENWICH
GREENWICH CAMPUS
OLD ROYAL NAVAL COLLEGE
PARK ROW
LONDON SE10 9LS
t: 020 8331 9000 f: 020 8331 8145
e: courseinfo@gre.ac.uk
// www.gre.ac.uk

M100 LLB Law
Duration: 3FT Hon
Entry Requirements: *GCE:* 320. *IB:* 30.

G74 GREENWICH SCHOOL OF MANAGEMENT
MERIDIAN HOUSE
ROYAL HILL
GREENWICH
LONDON SE10 8RD
t: +44(0)20 8516 7800 f: +44(0)20 8516 7801
e: admissions@greenwich-college.ac.uk
// www.greenwich-college.ac.uk/
?utm_source=UCAS&utm_medium=Profil

M101 LLB Law (Accelerated with Foundation Year)
Duration: 3FT Hon
Entry Requirements: *OCR ND:* P3 Interview required.

M100 LLB Law (Accelerated)
Duration: 2FT Hon
Entry Requirements: *GCE:* 240-300. *IB:* 24. *OCR ND:* D *OCR NED:* M3 Interview required.

H36 UNIVERSITY OF HERTFORDSHIRE
UNIVERSITY ADMISSIONS SERVICE
COLLEGE LANE
HATFIELD
HERTS AL10 9AB
t: 01707 284800
// www.herts.ac.uk

M100 LLB Law
Duration: 3FT Hon
Entry Requirements: *GCE:* 320.

M101 LLB Hons Law
Duration: 2FT Hon
Entry Requirements: *GCE:* 340.

H50 HOLBORN COLLEGE
WOOLWICH ROAD
LONDON SE7 8LN
t: 020 8317 6000 f: 020 8317 6001
e: UKAdmissions@kaplan.co.uk
// www.holborncollege.ac.uk

M103 LLB Law
Duration: 3FT Hon
Entry Requirements: *GCE:* 180. *IB:* 24.

M100 LLB Law (with Foundation Year)
Duration: 4FT Hon
Entry Requirements: Contact the institution for details.

H60 THE UNIVERSITY OF HUDDERSFIELD
QUEENSGATE
HUDDERSFIELD HD1 3DH
t: 01484 473969 f: 01484 472765
e: admissionsandrecords@hud.ac.uk
// www.hud.ac.uk

M102 BA Law (Top-up)
Duration: 1FT Hon
Entry Requirements: HND required.

M100 LLB/MLP Law (Exempting)
Duration: 3FT/4FT Hon
Entry Requirements: *GCE:* 360. Interview required.

H72 THE UNIVERSITY OF HULL
THE UNIVERSITY OF HULL
COTTINGHAM ROAD
HULL HU6 7RX
t: 01482 466100 f: 01482 442290
e: admissions@hull.ac.uk
// www.hull.ac.uk

M100 LLB Law
Duration: 3FT Hon
Entry Requirements: *GCE:* 320. *IB:* 30. *BTEC ExtDip:* DDM.

M101 LLB Law Senior Status
Duration: 2FT Hon
Entry Requirements: Contact the institution for details.

K12 KEELE UNIVERSITY
KEELE UNIVERSITY
STAFFORDSHIRE ST5 5BG
t: 01782 734005 f: 01782 632343
e: undergraduate@keele.ac.uk
// www.keele.ac.uk

M100 LLB Law (Single Honours)
Duration: 3FT Hon
Entry Requirements: *GCE:* AAB.

K24 THE UNIVERSITY OF KENT
RECRUITMENT & ADMISSIONS OFFICE
REGISTRY
UNIVERSITY OF KENT
CANTERBURY, KENT CT2 7NZ
t: 01227 827272 f: 01227 827077
e: information@kent.ac.uk
// www.kent.ac.uk

M105 CertHE Law
Duration: 1FT Cer
Entry Requirements: *IB:* 33. Interview required. Admissions Test required.

M100 LLB Law
Duration: 3FT Hon
Entry Requirements: *GCE:* AAB. *SQAH:* AAAAB. *IB:* 33. *OCR ND:* D *OCR NED:* M1

M103 LLB Law with a Year in China
Duration: 4FT Hon
Entry Requirements: *GCE:* AAA. *SQAH:* AAAAB. *IB:* 33. *OCR ND:* D *OCR NED:* M1

M104 LLB Law with a Year in the Hong Kong Special Administrative Region (China)
Duration: 4FT Hon
Entry Requirements: *GCE:* AAA. *SQAH:* AAAAB. *IB:* 33. *OCR ND:* D *OCR NED:* M1

K60 KING'S COLLEGE LONDON (UNIVERSITY OF LONDON)
STRAND
LONDON WC2R 2LS
t: 020 7836 5454 f: 020 7848 7171
e: prospective@kcl.ac.uk
// www.kcl.ac.uk/prospectus

M100 LLB Law
Duration: 3FT Hon
Entry Requirements: *GCE:* A*AAa. *SQAH:* AAAAA. *SQAAH:* AA. *IB:* 39. Admissions Test required.

K84 KINGSTON UNIVERSITY
STUDENT INFORMATION & ADVICE CENTRE
COOPER HOUSE
40-46 SURBITON ROAD
KINGSTON UPON THAMES KT1 2HX
t: 0844 8552177 f: 020 8547 7080
e: aps@kingston.ac.uk
// www.kingston.ac.uk

M104 BA Law with industrial placement
Duration: 4SW Hon
Entry Requirements: *GCE:* 280. *SQAH:* BBCCC. *SQAAH:* BCC. *IB:* 25.

M105 BA Law with year abroad
Duration: 4FT Hon
Entry Requirements: *GCE:* 280. *IB:* 25.

M100 LLB Law
Duration: 3FT Hon
Entry Requirements: *GCE:* 320. *IB:* 27.

M101 LLB Law (Senior Status)
Duration: 2FT Hon
Entry Requirements: Contact the institution for details.

M102 LLB Law with Industrial Placement
Duration: 4SW Hon
Entry Requirements: *GCE:* 320. *IB:* 27.

M103 LLB Law with study abroad
Duration: 4FT Hon
Entry Requirements: *GCE:* 320. *IB:* 27.

L14 LANCASTER UNIVERSITY
THE UNIVERSITY
LANCASTER
LANCASHIRE LA1 4YW
t: 01524 592029 f: 01524 846243
e: ugadmissions@lancaster.ac.uk
// www.lancs.ac.uk

M100 LLB Law
Duration: 3FT Hon
Entry Requirements: *GCE:* AAA. *SQAH:* AAABB. *SQAAH:* AAA. *IB:* 36.

L17 THE COLLEGE OF LAW
LONDON, BIRMINGHAM, CHESTER ,GUILDFORD
ADMINISTRATION ADDRESS: BRABOEUF MANOR
ST CATHERINES, PORTSMOUTH RD.
GUILDFORD GU3 1HA
t: 01483 216000
e: admissions@lawcol.co.uk
// www.college-of-law.co.uk/degree/

M100 LLB Law
Duration: 2FT Hon
Entry Requirements: *GCE:* ABB. *IB:* 33. Interview required.

L23 UNIVERSITY OF LEEDS
THE UNIVERSITY OF LEEDS
WOODHOUSE LANE
LEEDS LS2 9JT
t: 0113 343 3999
e: admissions@leeds.ac.uk
// www.leeds.ac.uk

M100 LLB Law
Duration: 3FT Hon
Entry Requirements: *GCE:* AAA. *SQAH:* AAAAA. *SQAAH:* AAA. *IB:* 38.

M101 LLB Law (graduate programme)
Duration: 2FT Hon
Entry Requirements: Contact the institution for details.

L27 LEEDS METROPOLITAN UNIVERSITY
COURSE ENQUIRIES OFFICE
CITY CAMPUS
LEEDS LS1 3HE
t: 0113 81 23113 f: 0113 81 23129
// www.leedsmet.ac.uk

M100 LLB Law
Duration: 3FT Hon
Entry Requirements: *GCE:* 260. *IB:* 26.

L34 UNIVERSITY OF LEICESTER
UNIVERSITY ROAD
LEICESTER LE1 7RH
t: 0116 252 5281 f: 0116 252 2447
e: admissions@le.ac.uk
// www.le.ac.uk

M100 LLB Law
Duration: 3FT Hon
Entry Requirements: *GCE:* AAA. *SQAH:* AAAAA. *SQAAH:* AAA. *IB:* 36.

M101 LLB Law (Senior Status)
Duration: 2FT Hon
Entry Requirements: Contact the institution for details.

L39 UNIVERSITY OF LINCOLN
ADMISSIONS
BRAYFORD POOL
LINCOLN LN6 7TS
t: 01522 886097 f: 01522 886146
e: admissions@lincoln.ac.uk
// www.lincoln.ac.uk

M100 LLB Law
Duration: 3FT Hon
Entry Requirements: *GCE:* 300.

L41 THE UNIVERSITY OF LIVERPOOL
THE FOUNDATION BUILDING
BROWNLOW HILL
LIVERPOOL L69 7ZX
t: 0151 794 2000 f: 0151 708 6502
e: ugrecruitment@liv.ac.uk
// www.liv.ac.uk

M100 LLB Law
Duration: 3FT Hon
Entry Requirements: *GCE:* AAA. *SQAH:* AAAAA. *SQAAH:* AA. *IB:* 36. *OCR ND:* D *OCR NED:* D2

L51 LIVERPOOL JOHN MOORES UNIVERSITY
KINGSWAY HOUSE
HATTON GARDEN
LIVERPOOL L3 2AJ
t: 0151 231 5090 f: 0151 904 6368
e: courses@ljmu.ac.uk
// www.ljmu.ac.uk

M100 LLB Law
Duration: 3FT Hon
Entry Requirements: *GCE:* 300. *IB:* 29.

L62 THE LONDON COLLEGE, UCK
VICTORIA GARDENS
NOTTING HILL GATE
LONDON W11 3PE
t: 020 7243 4000 f: 020 7243 1484
e: admissions@lcuck.ac.uk
// www.lcuck.ac.uk

M100 Dip Paralegal Studies
Duration: 1FT Dip
Entry Requirements: Contact the institution for details.

L68 LONDON METROPOLITAN UNIVERSITY
166-220 HOLLOWAY ROAD
LONDON N7 8DB
t: 020 7133 4200
e: admissions@londonmet.ac.uk
// www.londonmet.ac.uk

M104 BA Diplomacy and Law
Duration: 3FT Hon
Entry Requirements: Contact the institution for details.

M101 BA Law
Duration: 3FT Hon
Entry Requirements: *GCE:* 240. *IB:* 28.

M100 LLB Law
Duration: 3FT Hon
Entry Requirements: *GCE:* 320. *IB:* 28.

L72 LONDON SCHOOL OF ECONOMICS AND POLITICAL SCIENCE (UNIVERSITY OF LONDON)
HOUGHTON STREET
LONDON WC2A 2AE
t: 020 7955 7125 f: 020 7955 6001
e: ug.admissions@lse.ac.uk
// www.lse.ac.uk

M100 LLB Law (Bachelor of Laws)
Duration: 3FT Hon
Entry Requirements: *GCE:* A*AA. *SQAH:* AAAAA. *SQAAH:* AAA. *IB:* 38.

L75 LONDON SOUTH BANK UNIVERSITY
ADMISSIONS AND RECRUITMENT CENTRE
90 LONDON ROAD
LONDON SE1 6LN
t: 0800 923 8888 f: 020 7815 8273
e: course.enquiry@lsbu.ac.uk
// www.lsbu.ac.uk

M100 LLB Law
Duration: 3FT Hon
Entry Requirements: *GCE:* 260. *IB:* 24.

M20 THE UNIVERSITY OF MANCHESTER
RUTHERFORD BUILDING
OXFORD ROAD
MANCHESTER M13 9PL
t: 0161 275 2077 f: 0161 275 2106
e: ug-admissions@manchester.ac.uk
// www.manchester.ac.uk

M100 LLB Law
Duration: 3FT Hon
Entry Requirements: *GCE:* AAA. *SQAH:* AAAAB. *SQAAH:* AAA. *IB:* 37. Interview required.

M40 THE MANCHESTER METROPOLITAN UNIVERSITY
ADMISSIONS OFFICE
ALL SAINTS (GMS)
ALL SAINTS
MANCHESTER M15 6BH
t: 0161 247 2000
// www.mmu.ac.uk

M102 BA Economics (Foundation)
Duration: 4FT Hon
Entry Requirements: *GCE:* 160. *IB:* 24. *BTEC Dip:* MM. *BTEC ExtDip:* MPP.

M100 LLB Law
Duration: 3FT Hon
Entry Requirements: *GCE:* ABB. *IB:* 30. *OCR ND:* D Interview required.

M101 LLB Law (Foundation)
Duration: 4FT Hon
Entry Requirements: *GCE:* 200. *IB:* 25. *BTEC Dip:* DM. *BTEC ExtDip:* MMP.

M80 MIDDLESEX UNIVERSITY
MIDDLESEX UNIVERSITY
THE BURROUGHS
LONDON NW4 4BT
t: 020 8411 5555 f: 020 8411 5649
e: enquiries@mdx.ac.uk
// www.mdx.ac.uk

M101 BA Law
Duration: 3FT Hon
Entry Requirements: *GCE:* 200-300. *IB:* 28.

M100 LLB Law
Duration: 3FT Hon
Entry Requirements: *GCE:* 200-360. *IB:* 28.

N21 NEWCASTLE UNIVERSITY
KING'S GATE
NEWCASTLE UPON TYNE NE1 7RU
t: 01912083333
// www.ncl.ac.uk

M101 LLB Law
Duration: 3FT/4SW Hon
Entry Requirements: *GCE:* AAA. *IB:* 36.

N30 NEW COLLEGE NOTTINGHAM
ADAMS BUILDING
STONEY STREET
THE LACE MARKET
NOTTINGHAM NG1 1NG
t: 0115 910 0100 f: 0115 953 4349
e: he.team@ncn.ac.uk
// www.ncn.ac.uk

M100 FdA Law
Duration: 2FT Fdg
Entry Requirements: *GCE:* 160-240.

N38 UNIVERSITY OF NORTHAMPTON
PARK CAMPUS
BOUGHTON GREEN ROAD
NORTHAMPTON NN2 7AL
t: 0800 358 2232 f: 01604 722083
e: admissions@northampton.ac.uk
// www.northampton.ac.uk

M100 LLB Law
Duration: 3FT Hon
Entry Requirements: *GCE:* 280-320. *SQAH:* AABB. *IB:* 26. *BTEC Dip:* DD. *BTEC ExtDip:* DMM. *OCR ND:* D *OCR NED:* M2

M101 LLB Law (2 year fast track)
Duration: 2FT Hon
Entry Requirements: *GCE:* 280-320. *SQAH:* AABB. *IB:* 26. *BTEC Dip:* DD. *BTEC ExtDip:* DMM. *OCR ND:* D *OCR NED:* M2

N77 NORTHUMBRIA UNIVERSITY
TRINITY BUILDING
NORTHUMBERLAND ROAD
NEWCASTLE UPON TYNE NE1 8ST
t: 0191 243 7420 f: 0191 227 4561
e: er.admissions@northumbria.ac.uk
// www.northumbria.ac.uk

M100 MLaw Law (Exempting)
Duration: 4FT Hon
Entry Requirements: *GCE:* ABB. *SQAH:* ABBBC. *SQAAH:* ABC. *IB:* 27. *BTEC ExtDip:* DDM. *OCR NED:* D2

N84 THE UNIVERSITY OF NOTTINGHAM
THE ADMISSIONS OFFICE
THE UNIVERSITY OF NOTTINGHAM
UNIVERSITY PARK
NOTTINGHAM NG7 2RD
t: 0115 951 5151 f: 0115 951 4668
// www.nottingham.ac.uk

M100 BA Law
Duration: 3FT Hon   CRB Check: Required
Entry Requirements: *GCE:* A*AA. *SQAAH:* AAA. *IB:* 38.
Admissions Test required.

M101 LLB Law (Senior Status)
Duration: 2FT Hon   CRB Check: Required
Entry Requirements: Admissions Test required.

N91 NOTTINGHAM TRENT UNIVERSITY
DRYDEN BUILDING
BURTON STREET
NOTTINGHAM NG1 4BU
t: +44 (0) 115 848 4200 f: +44 (0) 115 848 8869
e: applications@ntu.ac.uk
// www.ntu.ac.uk

M100 LLB Law
Duration: 3FT Hon
Entry Requirements: *GCE:* 300.

M101 LLB Law
Duration: 4SW Hon
Entry Requirements: *GCE:* 320.

O33 OXFORD UNIVERSITY
UNDERGRADUATE ADMISSIONS OFFICE
UNIVERSITY OF OXFORD
WELLINGTON SQUARE
OXFORD OX1 2JD
t: 01865 288000 f: 01865 270212
e: undergraduate.admissions@admin.ox.ac.uk
// www.admissions.ox.ac.uk

M100 BA Law
Duration: 3FT Hon
Entry Requirements: *GCE:* AAA. *SQAH:* AAAAA-AAAAB. *SQAAH:*
AAB. Interview required. Admissions Test required.

O66 OXFORD BROOKES UNIVERSITY
ADMISSIONS OFFICE
HEADINGTON CAMPUS
GIPSY LANE
OXFORD OX3 0BP
t: 01865 483040 f: 01865 483983
e: admissions@brookes.ac.uk
// www.brookes.ac.uk

M100 LLB Law
Duration: 3FT Hon
Entry Requirements: *GCE:* ABB.

P60 PLYMOUTH UNIVERSITY
DRAKE CIRCUS
PLYMOUTH PL4 8AA
t: 01752 585858 f: 01752 588055
e: admissions@plymouth.ac.uk
// www.plymouth.ac.uk

M100 ML Law
Duration: 3FT Hon
Entry Requirements: Contact the institution for details.

P80 UNIVERSITY OF PORTSMOUTH
ACADEMIC REGISTRY
UNIVERSITY HOUSE
WINSTON CHURCHILL AVENUE
PORTSMOUTH PO1 2UP
t: 023 9284 8484 f: 023 9284 3082
e: admissions@port.ac.uk
// www.port.ac.uk

M100 LLB Law
Duration: 3FT/4SW Hon
Entry Requirements: *GCE:* 320. *IB:* 30. *BTEC SubDip:* D. *BTEC
Dip:* DD. *BTEC ExtDip:* DDM.

Q50 QUEEN MARY, UNIVERSITY OF LONDON
QUEEN MARY, UNIVERSITY OF LONDON
MILE END ROAD
LONDON E1 4NS
t: 020 7882 5555 f: 020 7882 5500
e: admissions@qmul.ac.uk
// www.qmul.ac.uk

M100 LLB Law
Duration: 3FT Hon
Entry Requirements: *GCE:* A*AA. *SQAAH:* AAA. *IB:* 36.

M101 LLB Law (Senior Status)
Duration: 2FT Hon
Entry Requirements: Contact the institution for details.

Q75 QUEEN'S UNIVERSITY BELFAST
UNIVERSITY ROAD
BELFAST BT7 1NN
t: 028 9097 3838 f: 028 9097 5151
e: admissions@qub.ac.uk
// www.qub.ac.uk

M100 LLB Law
Duration: 3FT Hon
Entry Requirements: *GCE:* AAA-AABa. *SQAH:* AAAAB. *SQAAH:*
AAA. *IB:* 36.

R12 THE UNIVERSITY OF READING
THE UNIVERSITY OF READING
PO BOX 217
READING RG6 6AH
t: 0118 378 8619 f: 0118 378 8924
e: student.recruitment@reading.ac.uk
// www.reading.ac.uk

M100 LLB Law
Duration: 3FT Hon
Entry Requirements: *GCE:* AAB. *SQAH:* AAABB. *SQAAH:* AAB.
BTEC Dip: DD. *BTEC ExtDip:* DDD.

R90 RUSKIN COLLEGE OXFORD
WALTON STREET
OXFORD OX1 2HE
t: 01865 759604 f: 01865 759640
e: admissions@ruskin.ac.uk
// www.ruskin.ac.uk

M100 CertHE Law
Duration: 1FT Cer
Entry Requirements: Interview required.

S03 THE UNIVERSITY OF SALFORD
SALFORD M5 4WT
t: 0161 295 4545 f: 0161 295 4646
e: ug-admissions@salford.ac.uk
// www.salford.ac.uk

M100 LLB Law
Duration: 3FT Hon
Entry Requirements: *IB:* 30. Interview required.

S09 SCHOOL OF ORIENTAL AND AFRICAN STUDIES (UNIVERSITY OF LONDON)
THORNHAUGH STREET
RUSSELL SQUARE
LONDON WC1H 0XG
t: 020 7898 4301 f: 020 7898 4039
e: undergradadmissions@soas.ac.uk
// www.soas.ac.uk

M100 LLB Law
Duration: 3FT Hon
Entry Requirements: *GCE:* AAA.

S18 THE UNIVERSITY OF SHEFFIELD
THE UNIVERSITY OF SHEFFIELD
LEVEL 2, ARTS TOWER
WESTERN BANK
SHEFFIELD S10 2TN
t: 0114 222 8030 f: 0114 222 8032
// www.sheffield.ac.uk

M100 LLB Law
Duration: 3FT Hon
Entry Requirements: *GCE:* AAA. *SQAH:* AAAAB. *SQAAH:* A. *IB:* 37.
BTEC ExtDip: DDD.

S21 SHEFFIELD HALLAM UNIVERSITY
CITY CAMPUS
HOWARD STREET
SHEFFIELD S1 1WB
t: 0114 225 5555 f: 0114 225 2167
e: admissions@shu.ac.uk
// www.shu.ac.uk

M100 LLB Law
Duration: 3FT Hon
Entry Requirements: *GCE:* 300.

M101 LLB Law plus Maitrise en Droit Francais
Duration: 3FT Hon
Entry Requirements: *GCE:* 300.

S27 UNIVERSITY OF SOUTHAMPTON
HIGHFIELD
SOUTHAMPTON SO17 1BJ
t: 023 8059 4732 f: 023 8059 3037
e: admissions@soton.ac.uk
// www.southampton.ac.uk

M100 LLB Law
Duration: 3FT Hon
Entry Requirements: *GCE:* AAA-AAB. *SQAAH:* AAA. *IB:* 36.

M101 LLB Law (Accelerated Programme)
Duration: 2FT Hon
Entry Requirements: *GCE:* AAA-AAB. *SQAAH:* AAA. *IB:* 36.

S30 SOUTHAMPTON SOLENT UNIVERSITY
EAST PARK TERRACE
SOUTHAMPTON
HAMPSHIRE SO14 0RT
t: +44 (0) 23 8031 9039 f: + 44 (0)23 8022 2259
e: admissions@solent.ac.uk
// www.solent.ac.uk/

M100 LLB Law
Duration: 3FT Hon
Entry Requirements: *GCE:* 220. *IB:* 32.

S32 SOUTH DEVON COLLEGE
LONG ROAD
PAIGNTON
DEVON TQ4 7EJ
t: 08000 213181 f: 01803 540541
e: university@southdevon.ac.uk
// www.southdevon.ac.uk/
welcome-to-university-level

M100 FdSc Law
Duration: 2FT Fdg
Entry Requirements: Contact the institution for details.

S64 ST MARY'S UNIVERSITY COLLEGE, TWICKENHAM
WALDEGRAVE ROAD
STRAWBERRY HILL
MIDDLESEX TW1 4SX
t: 020 8240 4029 f: 020 8240 2361
e: admit@smuc.ac.uk
// www.smuc.ac.uk

M100 LLB Law
Duration: 3FT Hon
Entry Requirements: Contact the institution for details.

S72 STAFFORDSHIRE UNIVERSITY
COLLEGE ROAD
STOKE ON TRENT ST4 2DE
t: 01782 292753 f: 01782 292740
e: admissions@staffs.ac.uk
// www.staffs.ac.uk

001M HND Law
Duration: 2FT HND
Entry Requirements: Contact the institution for details.

M100 LLB Law
Duration: 3FT Hon
Entry Requirements: *GCE:* 280. *IB:* 26. *OCR NED:* M2

M101 LLB Law (Fast-Track)
Duration: 2FT Hon
Entry Requirements: *GCE:* 320. *SQAAH:* ABB-BB. *IB:* 26. *BTEC ExtDip:* DDM. *OCR ND:* D Interview required.

S84 UNIVERSITY OF SUNDERLAND
STUDENT HELPLINE
THE STUDENT GATEWAY
CHESTER ROAD
SUNDERLAND SR1 3SD
t: 0191 515 3000 f: 0191 515 3805
e: student.helpline@sunderland.ac.uk
// www.sunderland.ac.uk

M100 LLB Law (Qualifying)
Duration: 3FT Hon
Entry Requirements: *GCE:* 260-360. *IB:* 33. *OCR ND:* D *OCR NED:* M2

S85 UNIVERSITY OF SURREY
STAG HILL
GUILDFORD
SURREY GU2 7XH
t: +44(0)1483 689305 f: +44(0)1483 689388
e: ugteam@surrey.ac.uk
// www.surrey.ac.uk

M100 LLB Law (3 or 4 years)
Duration: 3FT/4SW Hon
Entry Requirements: *GCE:* AAB. *SQAH:* AAAAB. *SQAAH:* AAB. *IB:* 35. Interview required.

S90 UNIVERSITY OF SUSSEX
UNDERGRADUATE ADMISSIONS
SUSSEX HOUSE
UNIVERSITY OF SUSSEX
BRIGHTON BN1 9RH
t: 01273 678416 f: 01273 678545
e: ug.applicants@sussex.ac.uk
// www.sussex.ac.uk

M101 LLB Graduate Entry LLB (2 years)
Duration: 2FT Hon
Entry Requirements: Contact the institution for details.

M100 LLB Law
Duration: 3FT Hon
Entry Requirements: *GCE:* AAA-AAB. *SQAH:* AAAAA-AAABB. *IB:* 35. *BTEC SubDip:* D. *BTEC Dip:* DD. *BTEC ExtDip:* DDD. *OCR ND:* D *OCR NED:* D1

S93 SWANSEA UNIVERSITY
SINGLETON PARK
SWANSEA SA2 8PP
t: 01792 295111 f: 01792 295110
e: admissions@swansea.ac.uk
// www.swansea.ac.uk

M100 LLB Law
Duration: 3FT Hon
Entry Requirements: *GCE:* AAB. *IB:* 34.

T20 TEESSIDE UNIVERSITY
MIDDLESBROUGH TS1 3BA
t: 01642 218121 f: 01642 384201
e: registry@tees.ac.uk
// www.tees.ac.uk

M100 LLB Law
Duration: 3FT Hon
Entry Requirements: *GCE:* 260.

U20 UNIVERSITY OF ULSTER
COLERAINE
CO. LONDONDERRY
NORTHERN IRELAND BT52 1SA
t: 028 7012 4221 f: 028 7012 4908
e: online@ulster.ac.uk
// www.ulster.ac.uk

M100 LLB Law
Duration: 3FT Hon
Entry Requirements: *GCE:* AAB-ABB. *SQAH:* AAAAB-AAABC.

U40 UNIVERSITY OF THE WEST OF SCOTLAND
PAISLEY
RENFREWSHIRE
SCOTLAND PA1 2BE
t: 0141 848 3727 f: 0141 848 3623
e: admissions@uws.ac.uk
// www.uws.ac.uk

M100 BA Law
Duration: 3FT/4FT/5SW Ord/Hon
Entry Requirements: *GCE:* CCC. *SQAH:* BBBC.

U80 UNIVERSITY COLLEGE LONDON (UNIVERSITY OF LONDON)
GOWER STREET
LONDON WC1E 6BT
t: 020 7679 3000 f: 020 7679 3001
// www.ucl.ac.uk

M100 LLB Law
Duration: 3FT Hon
Entry Requirements: *GCE:* A*AAe. *SQAAH:* AAA. *IB:* 39. Interview required. Admissions Test required.

M101 LLB Law with Advanced Studies (4 years)
Duration: 4FT Hon
Entry Requirements: *GCE:* A*AAe. *SQAAH:* AAA. *IB:* 39. Interview required. Admissions Test required.

M102 LLB Law with Another Legal System (4 years)
Duration: 4FT Hon
Entry Requirements: *GCE:* A*AAe. *SQAAH:* AAA. *IB:* 39. Interview required. Admissions Test required.

W05 THE UNIVERSITY OF WEST LONDON
ST MARY'S ROAD
EALING
LONDON W5 5RF
t: 0800 036 8888 f: 020 8566 1353
e: learning.advice@uwl.ac.uk
// www.uwl.ac.uk

M101 LLB Law
Duration: 3FT Hon
Entry Requirements: *GCE:* 300. *IB:* 28. Interview required.

M100 LLB Law (with foundation year)
Duration: 4FT Hon
Entry Requirements: *GCE:* 200. *IB:* 28. Interview required.

W20 THE UNIVERSITY OF WARWICK
COVENTRY CV4 8UW
t: 024 7652 3723 f: 024 7652 4649
e: ugadmissions@warwick.ac.uk
// www.warwick.ac.uk

M100 LLB Law
Duration: 3FT Hon
Entry Requirements: *GCE:* AAAc. *SQAH:* AAA. *SQAAH:* AA. *IB:* 38. *OCR ND:* D

M101 LLB Law
Duration: 4FT Hon
Entry Requirements: *GCE:* AAAc. *SQAAH:* AA. *IB:* 38. *OCR ND:* D

M108 LLB Law (with Study Abroad in English)
Duration: 4FT Hon
Entry Requirements: *GCE:* AAAc. *SQAAH:* AA. *IB:* 38. *OCR ND:* D

W50 UNIVERSITY OF WESTMINSTER
2ND FLOOR, CAVENDISH HOUSE
101 NEW CAVENDISH STREET,
LONDON W1W 6XH
t: 020 7915 5511
e: course-enquiries@westminster.ac.uk
// www.westminster.ac.uk

M100 LLB Law
Duration: 3FT Hon
Entry Requirements: *GCE:* ABB. *SQAH:* AABBB. *SQAAH:* ABB. *IB:* 32. Interview required.

W75 UNIVERSITY OF WOLVERHAMPTON
ADMISSIONS UNIT
MX207, CAMP STREET
WOLVERHAMPTON
WEST MIDLANDS WV1 1AD
t: 01902 321000 f: 01902 321896
e: admissions@wlv.ac.uk
// www.wlv.ac.uk

M100 LLB Law
Duration: 3FT Hon
Entry Requirements: *GCE:* 160-220. *IB:* 28.

W76 UNIVERSITY OF WINCHESTER
WINCHESTER
HANTS SO22 4NR
t: 01962 827234 f: 01962 827288
e: course.enquiries@winchester.ac.uk
// www.winchester.ac.uk

M100 LLB Law
Duration: 3FT Hon
Entry Requirements: *Foundation:* Distinction. *GCE:* 260-300. *IB:* 25. *OCR ND:* D

W81 WORCESTER COLLEGE OF TECHNOLOGY
DEANSWAY
WORCESTER WR1 2JF
t: 01905 725555 f: 01905 28906
// www.wortech.ac.uk

M100 LLB Law
Duration: 4FT Hon
Entry Requirements: Contact the institution for details.

Y50 THE UNIVERSITY OF YORK
STUDENT RECRUITMENT AND ADMISSIONS
UNIVERSITY OF YORK
HESLINGTON
YORK YO10 5DD
t: 01904 324000 f: 01904 323538
e: ug-admissions@york.ac.uk
// www.york.ac.uk

M100 LLB Law
Duration: 3FT Hon
Entry Requirements: *GCE:* AAA. *SQAH:* AAAAA. *SQAAH:* AA. *IB:* 36. *BTEC ExtDip:* DDD. Interview required.

LEGAL STUDIES

A20 THE UNIVERSITY OF ABERDEEN
UNIVERSITY OFFICE
KING'S COLLEGE
ABERDEEN AB24 3FX
t: +44 (0) 1224 273504 f: +44 (0) 1224 272034
e: sras@abdn.ac.uk
// www.abdn.ac.uk/sras

LM69 MA Anthropology and Legal Studies
Duration: 4FT Hon
Entry Requirements: *GCE:* BBB. *SQAH:* BBBB. *IB:* 30.

MV96 MA Divinity and Legal Studies
Duration: 4FT Hon
Entry Requirements: *GCE:* BBB. *SQAH:* BBBB. *IB:* 30.

VM12 MA History and Legal Studies
Duration: 4FT Hon
Entry Requirements: *GCE:* BBB. *SQAH:* BBBB. *IB:* 30.

VM51 MA Legal Studies and Philosophy
Duration: 4FT Hon
Entry Requirements: *GCE:* BBB. *SQAH:* BBBB. *IB:* 30.

ML12 MA Legal Studies and Politics
Duration: 4FT Hon
Entry Requirements: *GCE:* BBB. *SQAH:* BBBB. *IB:* 30.

CM89 MA Legal Studies and Psychology
Duration: 4FT Hon
Entry Requirements: *GCE:* BBB. *SQAH:* BBBB. *IB:* 30.

ML13 MA Legal Studies and Sociology
Duration: 4FT Hon
Entry Requirements: *GCE:* BBB. *SQAH:* BBBB. *IB:* 30.

B25 BIRMINGHAM CITY UNIVERSITY
PERRY BARR
BIRMINGHAM B42 2SU
t: 0121 331 5595 f: 0121 331 7994
// www.bcu.ac.uk

039M HND Legal Studies
Duration: 2FT HND
Entry Requirements: *GCE:* 160. *IB:* 24.

M130 LLB Law with American Legal Studies
Duration: 3FT Hon
Entry Requirements: *GCE:* 280. *IB:* 28.

B40 BLACKBURN COLLEGE
FEILDEN STREET
BLACKBURN BB2 1LH
t: 01254 292594 f: 01254 679647
e: he-admissions@blackburn.ac.uk
// www.blackburn.ac.uk

009M HND Legal Studies
Duration: 2FT HND
Entry Requirements: *GCE:* 120.

C10 CANTERBURY CHRIST CHURCH UNIVERSITY
NORTH HOLMES ROAD
CANTERBURY
KENT CT1 1QU
t: 01227 782900 f: 01227 782888
e: admissions@canterbury.ac.uk
// www.canterbury.ac.uk

LM2F BA Global Politics and Legal Studies
Duration: 3FT Hon
Entry Requirements: *GCE:* 240. *IB:* 24.

L2MG BA Global Politics with Legal Studies
Duration: 3FT Hon
Entry Requirements: *GCE:* 240. *IB:* 24.

M2LF BA Legal Studies with Global Politics
Duration: 3FT Hon
Entry Requirements: *GCE:* 240. *IB:* 24.

M2L2 BA Legal Studies with Politics & Governance
Duration: 3FT Hon
Entry Requirements: *GCE:* 240. *IB:* 24.

LM22 BA Politics & Governance and Legal Studies
Duration: 3FT Hon
Entry Requirements: *GCE:* 240. *IB:* 24.

L2M2 BA Politics & Governance with Legal Studies
Duration: 3FT Hon
Entry Requirements: *GCE:* 240. *IB:* 24.

X3M2 BA/BSc Early Childhood Studies with Legal Studies
Duration: 3FT Hon   CRB Check: Required
Entry Requirements: *GCE:* 240. *IB:* 24.

F4M2 BA/BSc Forensic Investigation with Legal Studies
Duration: 3FT Hon
Entry Requirements: *GCE:* 240. *IB:* 24.

B9M2 BA/BSc Health Studies with Legal Studies
Duration: 3FT Hon
Entry Requirements: *GCE:* 240. *IB:* 24.

V1M2 BA/BSc History with Legal Studies
Duration: 3FT Hon
Entry Requirements: *GCE:* 240. *IB:* 24.

MC21 BA/BSc Legal Studies and Biosciences
Duration: 3FT Hon
Entry Requirements: *GCE:* 240. *IB:* 24.

MX23 BA/BSc Legal Studies and Early Childhood Studies
Duration: 3FT Hon   CRB Check: Required
Entry Requirements: *GCE:* 240. *IB:* 24.

FM42 BA/BSc Legal Studies and Forensic Investigation
Duration: 3FT Hon
Entry Requirements: *GCE:* 240. *IB:* 24.

MV21 BA/BSc Legal Studies and History
Duration: 3FT Hon
Entry Requirements: *GCE:* 240. *IB:* 24.

MN25 BA/BSc Legal Studies and Marketing
Duration: 3FT Hon
Entry Requirements: *GCE:* 240. *IB:* 24.

MP23 BA/BSc Legal Studies and Media and Communications
Duration: 3FT Hon
Entry Requirements: *GCE:* 240. *IB:* 24.

MW23 BA/BSc Legal Studies and Music
Duration: 3FT Hon
Entry Requirements: *GCE:* 240. *IB:* 24. Interview required.

MC28 BA/BSc Legal Studies and Sport & Exercise Psychology
Duration: 3FT Hon
Entry Requirements: *GCE:* 240. *IB:* 24.

MC26 BA/BSc Legal Studies and Sport & Exercise Science
Duration: 3FT Hon
Entry Requirements: *GCE:* 240. *IB:* 24.

MN28 BA/BSc Legal Studies and Tourism & Leisure Studies
Duration: 3FT Hon
Entry Requirements: *GCE:* 240. *IB:* 24.

M2C1 BA/BSc Legal Studies with Biosciences
Duration: 3FT Hon
Entry Requirements: *GCE:* 240. *IB:* 24.

MWX3 BA/BSc Legal Studies with Early Childhood Studies
Duration: 3FT Hon   CRB Check: Required
Entry Requirements: *GCE:* 240. *IB:* 24.

M2F4 BA/BSc Legal Studies with Forensic Investigation
Duration: 3FT Hon
Entry Requirements: *GCE:* 240. *IB:* 24.

M2B9 BA/BSc Legal Studies with Health Studies
Duration: 3FT Hon
Entry Requirements: *GCE:* 240. *IB:* 24.

M2V1 BA/BSc Legal Studies with History
Duration: 3FT Hon
Entry Requirements: *GCE:* 240. *IB:* 24.

M2N5 BA/BSc Legal Studies with Marketing
Duration: 3FT Hon
Entry Requirements: *GCE:* 240. *IB:* 24.

M2PH BA/BSc Legal Studies with Media and Communications
Duration: 3FT Hon
Entry Requirements: *GCE:* 240. *IB:* 24.

M2W3 BA/BSc Legal Studies with Music
Duration: 3FT Hon
Entry Requirements: *GCE:* 240. *IB:* 24.

M2C8 BA/BSc Legal Studies with Sport & Exercise Psychology
Duration: 3FT Hon
Entry Requirements: *GCE:* 240. *IB:* 24.

M2C6 BA/BSc Legal Studies with Sport & Exercise Science
Duration: 3FT Hon
Entry Requirements: *GCE:* 240. *IB:* 24.

M2N8 BA/BSc Legal Studies with Tourism & Leisure Studies
Duration: 3FT Hon
Entry Requirements: *GCE:* 240. *IB:* 24.

P3M2 BA/BSc Media and Communications with Legal Studies
Duration: 3FT Hon
Entry Requirements: *GCE:* 240. *IB:* 24.

W3M2 BA/BSc Music with Legal Studies
Duration: 3FT Hon
Entry Requirements: *GCE:* 240. *IB:* 24.

C8M2 BA/BSc Sport & Exercise Psychology with Legal Studies
Duration: 3FT Hon
Entry Requirements: Contact the institution for details.

C6M2 BA/BSc Sport & Exercise Science with Legal Studies
Duration: 3FT Hon
Entry Requirements: *GCE:* 240. *IB:* 24.

N8M2 BA/BSc Tourism & Leisure Studies with Legal Studies
Duration: 3FT Hon
Entry Requirements: *GCE:* 240. *IB:* 24.

BM92 BSc Health Studies and Legal Studies
Duration: 3FT Hon
Entry Requirements: *GCE:* 240. *IB:* 24.

N5M2 BSc Marketing with Legal Studies
Duration: 3FT Hon
Entry Requirements: *GCE:* 240. *IB:* 24.

C1M2 BSc/BA Biosciences with Legal Studies
Duration: 3FT Hon
Entry Requirements: *GCE:* 240. *IB:* 24.

C85 COVENTRY UNIVERSITY
THE STUDENT CENTRE
COVENTRY UNIVERSITY
1 GULSON RD
COVENTRY CV1 2JH
t: 024 7615 2222 f: 024 7615 2223
e: studentenquiries@coventry.ac.uk
// www.coventry.ac.uk

M250 BA Legal Studies
Duration: 3FT Hon
Entry Requirements: *GCE:* 260. *IB:* 28. *BTEC Dip:* DD. *BTEC ExtDip:* MMM. *OCR ND:* D *OCR NED:* M3

152M HNC Legal Studies
Duration: 1FT HNC
Entry Requirements: *GCE:* 160. *IB:* 24. *BTEC Dip:* MM. *BTEC ExtDip:* MPP. *OCR ND:* P1 *OCR NED:* P2

052M HND Legal Studies
Duration: 2FT HND
Entry Requirements: *GCE:* 200. *IB:* 24. *BTEC Dip:* DM. *BTEC ExtDip:* MMP. *OCR ND:* M1 *OCR NED:* P1

D39 UNIVERSITY OF DERBY
KEDLESTON ROAD
DERBY DE22 1GB
t: 01332 591167 f: 01332 597724
e: askadmissions@derby.ac.uk
// www.derby.ac.uk

XM31 BA Education Studies and Law
Duration: 3FT Hon
Entry Requirements: *Foundation:* Distinction. *GCE:* 260-300. *IB:* 28. *BTEC Dip:* D*D*. *BTEC ExtDip:* DMM. *OCR NED:* M2

MP13 BA Film & Television Studies and Law
Duration: 3FT Hon
Entry Requirements: *Foundation:* Distinction. *GCE:* 260-300. *IB:* 28. *BTEC Dip:* D*D*. *BTEC ExtDip:* DMM. *OCR NED:* M2

MW14 BA Law and Theatre Studies
Duration: 3FT Hon
Entry Requirements: *Foundation:* Distinction. *GCE:* 260-300. *IB:* 28. *BTEC Dip:* D*D*. *BTEC ExtDip:* DMM. *OCR NED:* M2

PMH1 BA Media Studies and Law
Duration: 3FT Hon
Entry Requirements: *Foundation:* Distinction. *GCE:* 260-300. *IB:* 28. *BTEC Dip:* D*D*. *BTEC ExtDip:* DMM. *OCR NED:* M2

CM61 BA Sport & Exercise Studies and Law
Duration: 3FT Hon
Entry Requirements: *Foundation:* Distinction. *GCE:* 260-300. *IB:* 28. *BTEC Dip:* D*D*. *BTEC ExtDip:* DMM. *OCR NED:* M2

E28 UNIVERSITY OF EAST LONDON
DOCKLANDS CAMPUS
UNIVERSITY WAY
LONDON E16 2RD
t: 020 8223 3333 f: 020 8223 2978
e: study@uel.ac.uk
// www.uel.ac.uk

XHM1 BA Education Studies with Law
Duration: 3FT Hon
Entry Requirements: *GCE:* 240. *IB:* 28.

M1W4 BA Law with Theatre Studies
Duration: 3FT Hon
Entry Requirements: *GCE:* 240. *IB:* 28.

CM81 BA Law/Psychosocial Studies
Duration: 3FT Hon
Entry Requirements: *GCE:* 240. *IB:* 28.

G14 UNIVERSITY OF GLAMORGAN, CARDIFF AND PONTYPRIDD
ENQUIRIES AND ADMISSIONS UNIT
PONTYPRIDD CF37 1DL
t: 08456 434030 f: 01443 654050
e: enquiries@glam.ac.uk
// www.glam.ac.uk

M250 FdA Paralegal Studies
Duration: 2FT Fdg
Entry Requirements: Contact the institution for details.

G28 UNIVERSITY OF GLASGOW
71 SOUTHPARK AVENUE
UNIVERSITY OF GLASGOW
GLASGOW G12 8QQ
t: 0141 330 6062 f: 0141 330 2961
e: student.recruitment@glasgow.ac.uk
// www.glasgow.ac.uk

M1M9 LLB Law with Italian Legal Studies
Duration: 4FT Hon
Entry Requirements: *GCE:* AAB. *SQAH:* AAAAB. *IB:* 34.
Admissions Test required.

G80 GRIMSBY INSTITUTE OF FURTHER AND HIGHER EDUCATION
NUNS CORNER
GRIMSBY
NE LINCOLNSHIRE DN34 5BQ
t: 0800 328 3631
e: headmissions@grimsby.ac.uk
// www.grimsby.ac.uk

M900 BA Criminological Studies
Duration: 3FT Hon   CRB Check: Required
Entry Requirements: Contact the institution for details.

H36 UNIVERSITY OF HERTFORDSHIRE
UNIVERSITY ADMISSIONS SERVICE
COLLEGE LANE
HATFIELD
HERTS AL10 9AB
t: 01707 284800
// www.herts.ac.uk

F9M1 BSc Environmental Studies/Law
Duration: 3FT/4SW Hon
Entry Requirements: *GCE:* 320.

B9M1 BSc Health Studies/Law
Duration: 3FT/4SW Hon
Entry Requirements: *GCE:* 320.

M1F9 BSc Law/Environmental Studies
Duration: 3FT/4SW Hon
Entry Requirements: *GCE:* 320.

M1B9 BSc Law/Health Studies
Duration: 3FT/4SW Hon
Entry Requirements: *GCE:* 320.

H72 THE UNIVERSITY OF HULL
THE UNIVERSITY OF HULL
COTTINGHAM ROAD
HULL HU6 7RX
t: 01482 466100 f: 01482 442290
e: admissions@hull.ac.uk
// www.hull.ac.uk

ML12 LLB Law and Legislative Studies
Duration: 4FT Hon
Entry Requirements: *GCE:* 340. *IB:* 30. *BTEC ExtDip:* DDM.
Interview required.

K12 KEELE UNIVERSITY
KEELE UNIVERSITY
STAFFORDSHIRE ST5 5BG
t: 01782 734005 f: 01782 632343
e: undergraduate@keele.ac.uk
// www.keele.ac.uk

MX13 BA Educational Studies and Law
Duration: 3FT Hon
Entry Requirements: *GCE:* ABB.

K84 KINGSTON UNIVERSITY
STUDENT INFORMATION & ADVICE CENTRE
COOPER HOUSE
40-46 SURBITON ROAD
KINGSTON UPON THAMES KT1 2HX
t: 0844 8552177 f: 020 8547 7080
e: aps@kingston.ac.uk
// www.kingston.ac.uk

PM31 BA Film Studies and Law
Duration: 3FT Hon
Entry Requirements: *GCE:* 280.

L21 LEEDS CITY COLLEGE
TECHNOLOGY CAMPUS
COOKRIDGE STREET
LEEDS LS2 8BL
t: 0113 216 2406 f: 0113 216 2401
e: helen.middleton@leedscitycollege.ac.uk
// www.leedscitycollege.ac.uk

M990 FdA Legal Studies
Duration: 2FT Fdg
Entry Requirements: *GCE:* E.

L39 UNIVERSITY OF LINCOLN
ADMISSIONS
BRAYFORD POOL
LINCOLN LN6 7TS
t: 01522 886097 f: 01522 886146
e: admissions@lincoln.ac.uk
// www.lincoln.ac.uk

M250 BA Legal Studies
Duration: 1FT Hon
Entry Requirements: Contact the institution for details.

M40 THE MANCHESTER METROPOLITAN UNIVERSITY
ADMISSIONS OFFICE
ALL SAINTS (GMS)
ALL SAINTS
MANCHESTER M15 6BH
t: 0161 247 2000
// www.mmu.ac.uk

LM52 BA Abuse Studies/Legal Studies
Duration: 3FT Hon
Entry Requirements: *GCE:* 280. *IB:* 28. *BTEC Dip:* D*D*. *BTEC ExtDip:* DMM.

ML25 BA Childhood & Youth Studies/Legal Studies
Duration: 3FT Hon
Entry Requirements: *GCE:* 280. *IB:* 28. *BTEC Dip:* D*D*. *BTEC ExtDip:* DMM.

MLG3 BA Crime Studies/Legal Studies
Duration: 3FT Hon
Entry Requirements: *GCE:* 280. *IB:* 28. *BTEC Dip:* D*D*. *BTEC ExtDip:* DMM.

MW2K BA Drama/Legal Studies
Duration: 3FT Hon
Entry Requirements: *GCE:* 280. *IB:* 28. *BTEC Dip:* D*D*. *BTEC ExtDip:* DMM. Interview required.

MV2M BA Legal Studies/Philosophy
Duration: 3FT Hon
Entry Requirements: *GCE:* 280. *IB:* 28. *BTEC Dip:* D*D*. *BTEC ExtDip:* DMM.

MLFJ BA Legal Studies/Sociology
Duration: 3FT Hon
Entry Requirements: *GCE:* 280. *IB:* 28. *BTEC Dip:* D*D*. *BTEC ExtDip:* DMM.

MC2P BA/BSc Legal Studies/Sport
Duration: 3FT Hon
Entry Requirements: *GCE:* 280. *IB:* 28. *BTEC Dip:* D*D*. *BTEC ExtDip:* DMM.

N37 UNIVERSITY OF WALES, NEWPORT
ADMISSIONS
LODGE ROAD
CAERLEON
NEWPORT NP18 3QT
t: 01633 432030 f: 01633 432850
e: admissions@newport.ac.uk
// www.newport.ac.uk

BM92 BA Counselling Studies and Youth Justice
Duration: 3FT Hon
Entry Requirements: *GCE:* 240. *IB:* 24. Interview required.

LMH2 BA Social Studies and Youth Justice
Duration: 3FT Hon
Entry Requirements: *GCE:* 240. *IB:* 24. Interview required.

N38 UNIVERSITY OF NORTHAMPTON
PARK CAMPUS
BOUGHTON GREEN ROAD
NORTHAMPTON NN2 7AL
t: 0800 358 2232 f: 01604 722083
e: admissions@northampton.ac.uk
// www.northampton.ac.uk

X3M1 BA Education Studies/Law
Duration: 3FT Hon
Entry Requirements: *GCE:* 260-280. *SQAH:* AAA-BBBB. *IB:* 24.
BTEC Dip: DD. *BTEC ExtDip:* DMM. *OCR ND:* D *OCR NED:* M2

W6M1 BA Film & Television Studies/Law
Duration: 3FT Hon
Entry Requirements: *GCE:* 260-280. *SQAH:* AAA-BBBB. *IB:* 24.
BTEC Dip: DD. *BTEC ExtDip:* DMM. *OCR ND:* D *OCR NED:* M2

L4M1 BA Health Studies/Law
Duration: 3FT Hon
Entry Requirements: *GCE:* 260-280. *SQAH:* AAA-BBBB. *IB:* 24.
BTEC Dip: DD. *BTEC ExtDip:* DMM. *OCR ND:* D *OCR NED:* M2

M1D4 BA Law with Applied Equine Studies
Duration: 3FT Hon
Entry Requirements: *GCE:* 260-280. *SQAH:* AAA-BBBB. *IB:* 24.
BTEC Dip: DD. *BTEC ExtDip:* DMM. *OCR ND:* D *OCR NED:* M2

M1X3 BA Law/Education Studies
Duration: 3FT Hon
Entry Requirements: *GCE:* 260-280. *SQAH:* AAA-BBBB. *IB:* 24.
BTEC Dip: DD. *BTEC ExtDip:* DMM. *OCR ND:* D *OCR NED:* M2

M1W6 BA Law/Film & Television Studies
Duration: 3FT Hon
Entry Requirements: *GCE:* 260-280. *SQAH:* AAA-BBBB. *IB:* 24.
BTEC Dip: DD. *BTEC ExtDip:* DMM. *OCR ND:* D *OCR NED:* M2

M1L4 BA Law/Health Studies
Duration: 3FT Hon
Entry Requirements: *GCE:* 260-280. *SQAH:* AAA-BBBB. *IB:* 24.
BTEC Dip: DD. *BTEC ExtDip:* DMM. *OCR ND:* D *OCR NED:* M2

S09 SCHOOL OF ORIENTAL AND AFRICAN STUDIES (UNIVERSITY OF LONDON)
THORNHAUGH STREET
RUSSELL SQUARE
LONDON WC1H 0XG
t: 020 7898 4301 f: 020 7898 4039
e: undergradadmissions@soas.ac.uk
// www.soas.ac.uk

LM91 BA Law and Development Studies
Duration: 3FT Hon
Entry Requirements: *GCE:* AAA.

S84 UNIVERSITY OF SUNDERLAND
STUDENT HELPLINE
THE STUDENT GATEWAY
CHESTER ROAD
SUNDERLAND SR1 3SD
t: 0191 515 3000 f: 0191 515 3805
e: student.helpline@sunderland.ac.uk
// www.sunderland.ac.uk

XMH1 BA Childhood Studies and Law
Duration: 3FT Hon
Entry Requirements: *GCE:* 260-360.

X3M1 BA Childhood Studies with Law
Duration: 3FT Hon
Entry Requirements: *GCE:* 260-360.

MP13 BA Law and Media Studies
Duration: 3FT Hon
Entry Requirements: *GCE:* 260-360. *OCR ND:* D *OCR NED:* M3

W75 UNIVERSITY OF WOLVERHAMPTON
ADMISSIONS UNIT
MX207, CAMP STREET
WOLVERHAMPTON
WEST MIDLANDS WV1 1AD
t: 01902 321000 f: 01902 321896
e: admissions@wlv.ac.uk
// www.wlv.ac.uk

ML91 BA Law, Social Science and Communication Studies (with Foundation Year)
Duration: 4FT Hon
Entry Requirements: Contact the institution for details.

W76 UNIVERSITY OF WINCHESTER
WINCHESTER
HANTS SO22 4NR
t: 01962 827234 f: 01962 827288
e: course.enquiries@winchester.ac.uk
// www.winchester.ac.uk

MP15 BA Journalism Studies and Law
Duration: 3FT Hon
Entry Requirements: *Foundation:* Distinction. *GCE:* 260-300. *IB:* 25. *OCR ND:* D *OCR NED:* M2

MX13 BA Law and Education Studies
Duration: 3FT Hon
Entry Requirements: *Foundation:* Distinction. *GCE:* 260-300. *IB:* 25. *OCR ND:* D *OCR NED:* M2

MX1H BA Law and Education Studies (Early Childhood)
Duration: 3FT Hon
Entry Requirements: *Foundation:* Distinction. *GCE:* 260-300. *IB:* 25. *OCR ND:* D *OCR NED:* M2

MP13 BA Law and Film Studies
Duration: 3FT Hon
Entry Requirements: *Foundation:* Distinction. *GCE:* 260-300. *IB:* 25. *OCR ND:* D *OCR NED:* M2

MPC3 BA Law and Media Studies
Duration: 3FT Hon
Entry Requirements: *Foundation:* Distinction. *GCE:* 260-300. *IB:* 25. *OCR ND:* D *OCR NED:* M2

ML12 BA Law and Politics & Global Studies
Duration: 3FT Hon
Entry Requirements: *Foundation:* Distinction. *GCE:* 260-300. *IB:* 25. *OCR ND:* D *OCR NED:* M2

MC16 BA Law and Sports Studies
Duration: 3FT Hon
Entry Requirements: *Foundation:* Merit. *GCE:* 260-300. *IB:* 24.

MW1H BA Law and Vocal & Choral Studies
Duration: 3FT Hon
Entry Requirements: *Foundation:* Distinction. *GCE:* 260-300. *IB:* 25. *OCR ND:* D *OCR NED:* M2

SCOTTISH LAW

D65 UNIVERSITY OF DUNDEE
NETHERGATE
DUNDEE DD1 4HN
t: 01382 383838 f: 01382 388150
e: contactus@dundee.ac.uk
// www.dundee.ac.uk/admissions/undergraduate/

M190 LLB Law (Scots and English) Dual Qualifying
Duration: 4FT Hon
Entry Requirements: *GCE:* ABB. *SQAH:* AABB-ABBBB. *IB:* 32.

M114 LLB Law (Scots) option - Politics
Duration: 4FT Hon
Entry Requirements: *GCE:* ABB. *SQAH:* AABB-ABBBB. *IB:* 32.

M114 LLB Law (Scots) option - Philosophy
Duration: 4FT Hon
Entry Requirements: *GCE:* ABB. *SQAH:* AABB-ABBBB. *IB:* 32.

M114 LLB Law (Scots)
Duration: 4FT Hon
Entry Requirements: *GCE:* ABB. *SQAH:* AABB-ABBBB. *IB:* 32.

M114 LLB Law (Scots) option - History
Duration: 4FT Hon
Entry Requirements: *GCE:* ABB. *SQAH:* AABB-ABBBB. *IB:* 32.

M104 LLB Law (Scots) - Accelerated
Duration: 2FT Ord
Entry Requirements: Contact the institution for details.

E56 THE UNIVERSITY OF EDINBURGH
STUDENT RECRUITMENT & ADMISSIONS
57 GEORGE SQUARE
EDINBURGH EH8 9JU
t: 0131 650 4360 f: 0131 651 1236
e: sra.enquiries@ed.ac.uk
// www.ed.ac.uk/studying/undergraduate/

M114 LLB Law
Duration: 4FT Hon
Entry Requirements: *GCE:* AAA-BBB. *SQAH:* AAAA-BBBB. *IB:* 34.

M115 LLB Law (Graduate Entry)
Duration: 2FT Deg
Entry Requirements: Contact the institution for details.

E59 EDINBURGH NAPIER UNIVERSITY
CRAIGLOCKHART CAMPUS
EDINBURGH EH14 1DJ
t: +44 (0)8452 60 60 40 f: 0131 455 6464
e: info@napier.ac.uk
// www.napier.ac.uk

M114 LLB Law
Duration: 3FT/4FT Ord/Hon
Entry Requirements: *GCE:* 260.

G28 UNIVERSITY OF GLASGOW
71 SOUTHPARK AVENUE
UNIVERSITY OF GLASGOW
GLASGOW G12 8QQ
t: 0141 330 6062 f: 0141 330 2961
e: student.recruitment@glasgow.ac.uk
// www.glasgow.ac.uk

M114 LLB Law
Duration: 4FT Hon
Entry Requirements: *GCE:* AAB. *SQAH:* AAAAB. *IB:* 34.
Admissions Test required.

M115 LLB Law (Fast-track) (Graduates Only)
Duration: 2FT Hon
Entry Requirements: Contact the institution for details.

G42 GLASGOW CALEDONIAN UNIVERSITY
STUDENT RECRUITMENT & ADMISSIONS SERVICE
CITY CAMPUS
COWCADDENS ROAD
GLASGOW G4 0BA
t: 0141 331 3000 f: 0141 331 8676
e: undergraduate@gcu.ac.uk
// www.gcu.ac.uk

M114 LLB Law
Duration: 4FT Hon
Entry Requirements: *GCE:* AAB. *SQAH:* AABBB-AABBC.

R36 ROBERT GORDON UNIVERSITY
ROBERT GORDON UNIVERSITY
SCHOOLHILL
ABERDEEN
SCOTLAND AB10 1FR
t: 01224 26 27 28 f: 01224 26 21 47
e: UGOffice@rgu.ac.uk
// www.rgu.ac.uk

M114 LLB Law
Duration: 4FT Hon
Entry Requirements: *GCE:* BBC. *SQAH:* ABBB. *IB:* 28.

S75 THE UNIVERSITY OF STIRLING
STUDENT RECRUITMENT & ADMISSIONS SERVICE
UNIVERSITY OF STIRLING
STIRLING
SCOTLAND FK9 4LA
t: 01786 467044 f: 01786 466800
e: admissions@stir.ac.uk
// www.stir.ac.uk

M114 LLB Law
Duration: 4FT Hon
Entry Requirements: *GCE:* ABB. *SQAH:* AABB. *IB:* 36. *BTEC ExtDip:* DDD.

S78 THE UNIVERSITY OF STRATHCLYDE
GLASGOW G1 1XQ
t: 0141 552 4400 f: 0141 552 0775
// www.strath.ac.uk

M114 LLB Law(Scots)
Duration: 4FT Deg   CRB Check: Required
Entry Requirements: *GCE:* AAB. *SQAH:* AAAAB. *IB:* 38.

M115 LLB Law(Scots) - Accelerated (for Graduates)
Duration: 2FT Ord   CRB Check: Required
Entry Requirements: *GCE:* AAB. *SQAH:* AAAAB. *IB:* 38.

SOCIOLOGY & ANTHROPOLOGY
COMBINATIONS

B06 BANGOR UNIVERSITY
BANGOR UNIVERSITY
BANGOR
GWYNEDD LL57 2DG
t: 01248 388484 f: 01248 370451
e: admissions@bangor.ac.uk
// www.bangor.ac.uk

M1L4 LLB Law with Social Policy
Duration: 3FT Hon
Entry Requirements: *GCE:* 280. *IB:* 28.

B60 BRADFORD COLLEGE: AN ASSOCIATE COLLEGE OF LEEDS METROPOLITAN UNIVERSITY
GREAT HORTON ROAD
BRADFORD
WEST YORKSHIRE BD7 1AY
t: 01274 433008 f: 01274 431652
e: heregistry@bradfordcollege.ac.uk
// www.bradfordcollege.ac.uk/
university-centre

ML14 BA Law and Social Welfare
Duration: 3FT Hon
Entry Requirements: *GCE:* 240.

C15 CARDIFF UNIVERSITY
PO BOX 927
30-36 NEWPORT ROAD
CARDIFF CF24 0DE
t: 029 2087 9999 f: 029 2087 6138
e: admissions@cardiff.ac.uk
// www.cardiff.ac.uk

ML13 LLB Law and Sociology (Integrated)
Duration: 3FT Hon
Entry Requirements: *GCE:* AAB. *SQAAH:* AAB. *IB:* 34. Interview required.

D39 UNIVERSITY OF DERBY
KEDLESTON ROAD
DERBY DE22 1GB
t: 01332 591167 f: 01332 597724
e: askadmissions@derby.ac.uk
// www.derby.ac.uk

LM31 BA Law and Sociology
Duration: 3FT Hon
Entry Requirements: *Foundation:* Distinction. *GCE:* 260-300. *IB:* 28. *BTEC Dip:* D*D*. *BTEC ExtDip:* DMM. *OCR NED:* M2

D86 DURHAM UNIVERSITY
DURHAM UNIVERSITY
UNIVERSITY OFFICE
DURHAM DH1 3HP
t: 0191 334 2000 f: 0191 334 6055
e: admissions@durham.ac.uk
// www.durham.ac.uk

LMV0 BA Combined Honours in Social Sciences option - History
Duration: 3FT Hon
Entry Requirements: *GCE:* AAA. *SQAH:* AAAAA. *SQAAH:* AAA. *IB:* 38.

LMV0 BA Combined Honours in Social Sciences
Duration: 3FT Hon
Entry Requirements: *GCE:* A*AA. *SQAH:* AAAAA. *SQAAH:* AAA. *IB:* 38.

LMV0 BA Combined Honours in Social Sciences option - Anthropology
Duration: 3FT Hon
Entry Requirements: *GCE:* AAA. *SQAH:* AAAAA. *SQAAH:* AAA. *IB:* 38.

LMV0 BA Combined Honours in Social Sciences option - Archaeology
Duration: 3FT Hon
Entry Requirements: *GCE:* AAA. *SQAH:* AAAAA. *SQAAH:* AAA. *IB:* 38.

LMV0 BA Combined Honours in Social Sciences option - Education
Duration: 3FT Hon
Entry Requirements: *GCE:* AAA. *SQAH:* AAAAA. *SQAAH:* AAA. *IB:* 38.

LMV0 BA Combined Honours in Social Sciences option - Psychology
Duration: 3FT Hon
Entry Requirements: *GCE:* AAA. *SQAH:* AAAAA. *SQAAH:* AAA. *IB:* 38.

LMV0 BA Combined Honours in Social Sciences option - Sport
Duration: 3FT Hon
Entry Requirements: *GCE:* AAA. *SQAH:* AAAAA. *SQAAH:* AAA. *IB:* 38.

LMV0 BA Combined Honours in Social Sciences option - Sociology & Social Policy
Duration: 3FT Hon
Entry Requirements: *GCE:* AAA. *SQAH:* AAAAA. *SQAAH:* AAA. *IB:* 38.

LMV0 BA Combined Honours in Social Sciences option - Economics
Duration: 3FT Hon
Entry Requirements: *GCE:* AAA. *SQAH:* AAAAA. *SQAAH:* AAA. *IB:* 38.

LMV0 BA Combined Honours in Social Sciences option - Politics
Duration: 3FT Hon
Entry Requirements: *GCE:* AAA. *SQAH:* AAAAA. *SQAAH:* AAA. *IB:* 38.

LMV0 BA Combined Honours in Social Sciences option - Geography
Duration: 3FT Hon
Entry Requirements: *GCE:* AAA. *SQAH:* AAAAA. *SQAAH:* AAA. *IB:* 38.

L3M1 BA Sociology with Law
Duration: 3FT Hon
Entry Requirements: *GCE:* AAB. *SQAH:* AAB. *SQAAH:* AAABB. *IB:* 36.

E28 UNIVERSITY OF EAST LONDON
DOCKLANDS CAMPUS
UNIVERSITY WAY
LONDON E16 2RD
t: 020 8223 3333 f: 020 8223 2978
e: study@uel.ac.uk
// www.uel.ac.uk

LM31 BA Law/Sociology
Duration: 3FT Hon
Entry Requirements: *GCE:* 240. *IB:* 28.

L3M1 BSc Sociology (Professional Development) with Law
Duration: 3FT Hon
Entry Requirements: *GCE:* 240. *IB:* 24.

E56 THE UNIVERSITY OF EDINBURGH
STUDENT RECRUITMENT & ADMISSIONS
57 GEORGE SQUARE
EDINBURGH EH8 9JU
t: 0131 650 4360 f: 0131 651 1236
e: sra.enquiries@ed.ac.uk
// www.ed.ac.uk/studying/undergraduate/

M1L6 LLB Law and Social Anthropology
Duration: 4FT Hon
Entry Requirements: *GCE:* AAA-BBB. *SQAH:* AAAA-BBBB. *IB:* 34.

ML14 LLB Law and Social Policy
Duration: 4FT Hon
Entry Requirements: *GCE:* AAA-BBB. *SQAH:* AAAB-BBBB. *IB:* 34.

ML13 LLB Law and Sociology
Duration: 4FT Hon
Entry Requirements: *GCE:* AAA-BBB. *SQAH:* AAAA-BBBB. *IB:* 34.

LM41 MA Social Policy and Law
Duration: 4FT Hon
Entry Requirements: *GCE:* AAA-BBB. *SQAH:* AAAA-BBBB. *IB:* 34.

G14 UNIVERSITY OF GLAMORGAN, CARDIFF AND PONTYPRIDD
ENQUIRIES AND ADMISSIONS UNIT
PONTYPRIDD CF37 1DL
t: 08456 434030 f: 01443 654050
e: enquiries@glam.ac.uk
// www.glam.ac.uk

L3M1 BSc Sociology with Law
Duration: 3FT Hon
Entry Requirements: *GCE:* BBC. *IB:* 25. *BTEC SubDip:* M. *BTEC Dip:* D*D*. *BTEC ExtDip:* DMM.

G28 UNIVERSITY OF GLASGOW
71 SOUTHPARK AVENUE
UNIVERSITY OF GLASGOW
GLASGOW G12 8QQ
t: 0141 330 6062 f: 0141 330 2961
e: student.recruitment@glasgow.ac.uk
// www.glasgow.ac.uk

MV13 LLB Law/Economic and Social History
Duration: 4FT Hon
Entry Requirements: *GCE:* AAB. *SQAH:* AAAAB. *IB:* 34.
Admissions Test required.

K12 KEELE UNIVERSITY
KEELE UNIVERSITY
STAFFORDSHIRE ST5 5BG
t: 01782 734005 f: 01782 632343
e: undergraduate@keele.ac.uk
// www.keele.ac.uk

LM31 BA Law and Sociology
Duration: 3FT Hon
Entry Requirements: *GCE:* ABB.

M1L3 LLB Law with Social Science Foundation Year
Duration: 4FT Hon
Entry Requirements: *GCE:* 160. Interview required.

K24 THE UNIVERSITY OF KENT
RECRUITMENT & ADMISSIONS OFFICE
REGISTRY
UNIVERSITY OF KENT
CANTERBURY, KENT CT2 7NZ
t: 01227 827272 f: 01227 827077
e: information@kent.ac.uk
// www.kent.ac.uk

ML16 BA Law and Social Anthropology
Duration: 3FT Hon
Entry Requirements: *GCE:* AAB. *SQAH:* AAAAB. *IB:* 33. *OCR ND:* D *OCR NED:* M1

LM31 BA Law and Sociology
Duration: 3FT Hon
Entry Requirements: *GCE:* AAB. *SQAH:* AAAAB. *IB:* 33. *OCR ND:*
D *OCR NED:* M1

K84 KINGSTON UNIVERSITY
STUDENT INFORMATION & ADVICE CENTRE
COOPER HOUSE
40-46 SURBITON ROAD
KINGSTON UPON THAMES KT1 2HX
t: 0844 8552177 f: 020 8547 7080
e: aps@kingston.ac.uk
// www.kingston.ac.uk

MLC3 BSc Law and Sociology
Duration: 3FT Hon
Entry Requirements: *GCE:* 280.

L46 LIVERPOOL HOPE UNIVERSITY
HOPE PARK
LIVERPOOL L16 9JD
t: 0151 291 3331 f: 0151 291 3434
e: administration@hope.ac.uk
// www.hope.ac.uk

ML14 BA Law and Social Policy
Duration: 3FT Hon
Entry Requirements: *GCE:* 300-320. *IB:* 25.

L72 LONDON SCHOOL OF ECONOMICS AND POLITICAL SCIENCE (UNIVERSITY OF LONDON)
HOUGHTON STREET
LONDON WC2A 2AE
t: 020 7955 7125 f: 020 7955 6001
e: ug.admissions@lse.ac.uk
// www.lse.ac.uk

ML16 BA Anthropology and Law
Duration: 3FT Hon
Entry Requirements: *GCE:* AAB. *SQAH:* AAAAA-AAABB. *SQAAH:* AAA-AAB. *IB:* 37.

L75 LONDON SOUTH BANK UNIVERSITY
ADMISSIONS AND RECRUITMENT CENTRE
90 LONDON ROAD
LONDON SE1 6LN
t: 0800 923 8888 f: 020 7815 8273
e: course.enquiry@lsbu.ac.uk
// www.lsbu.ac.uk

M1L3 LLB Law with Sociology
Duration: 3FT Hon
Entry Requirements: *GCE:* 260. *IB:* 24.

N38 UNIVERSITY OF NORTHAMPTON
PARK CAMPUS
BOUGHTON GREEN ROAD
NORTHAMPTON NN2 7AL
t: 0800 358 2232 f: 01604 722083
e: admissions@northampton.ac.uk
// www.northampton.ac.uk

M1L5 BA Law/Social Care
Duration: 3FT Hon
Entry Requirements: *GCE:* 260-280. *SQAH:* AAA-BBBB. *IB:* 24.
BTEC Dip: DD. *BTEC ExtDip:* DMM. *OCR ND:* D *OCR NED:* M2

M1L3 BA Law/Sociology
Duration: 3FT Hon
Entry Requirements: *GCE:* 260-280. *SQAH:* AAA-BBBB. *IB:* 24.
BTEC Dip: DD. *BTEC ExtDip:* DMM. *OCR ND:* D *OCR NED:* M2

L5M1 BA Social Care/Law
Duration: 3FT Hon
Entry Requirements: *GCE:* 260-280. *SQAH:* AAA-BBBB. *IB:* 24.
BTEC Dip: DD. *BTEC ExtDip:* DMM. *OCR ND:* D *OCR NED:* M2

L3M1 BA Sociology/Law
Duration: 3FT Hon
Entry Requirements: *GCE:* 260-280. *SQAH:* AAA-BBBB. *IB:* 24.
BTEC Dip: DD. *BTEC ExtDip:* DMM. *OCR ND:* D *OCR NED:* M2

S09 SCHOOL OF ORIENTAL AND AFRICAN STUDIES (UNIVERSITY OF LONDON)
THORNHAUGH STREET
RUSSELL SQUARE
LONDON WC1H 0XG
t: 020 7898 4301 f: 020 7898 4039
e: undergradadmissions@soas.ac.uk
// www.soas.ac.uk

LM61 BA Social Anthropology and Law
Duration: 3FT Hon
Entry Requirements: *GCE:* AAA.

S84 UNIVERSITY OF SUNDERLAND
STUDENT HELPLINE
THE STUDENT GATEWAY
CHESTER ROAD
SUNDERLAND SR1 3SD
t: 0191 515 3000 f: 0191 515 3805
e: student.helpline@sunderland.ac.uk
// www.sunderland.ac.uk

LM51 BA Health & Social Care and Law
Duration: 3FT Hon
Entry Requirements: *GCE:* 260-360.

LM31 BA Law and Sociology
Duration: 3FT Hon
Entry Requirements: *GCE:* 260-360. *OCR ND:* D *OCR NED:* M3

U20 UNIVERSITY OF ULSTER
COLERAINE
CO. LONDONDERRY
NORTHERN IRELAND BT52 1SA
t: 028 7012 4221 f: 028 7012 4908
e: online@ulster.ac.uk
// www.ulster.ac.uk

M1L3 LLB Law with Sociology
Duration: 3FT Hon
Entry Requirements: *GCE:* BBB. *SQAH:* AABCC. *SQAAH:* BBB. *IB:* 25.

W20 THE UNIVERSITY OF WARWICK
COVENTRY CV4 8UW
t: 024 7652 3723 f: 024 7652 4649
e: ugadmissions@warwick.ac.uk
// www.warwick.ac.uk

ML13 BA Law and Sociology
Duration: 4FT Hon
Entry Requirements: *GCE:* AABc. *SQAH:* BBB. *SQAAH:* AA. *IB:* 36. *OCR ND:* D

ML23 BA Law with Social Sciences
Duration: 3FT/4FT Hon
Entry Requirements: Contact the institution for details.

W75 UNIVERSITY OF WOLVERHAMPTON
ADMISSIONS UNIT
MX207, CAMP STREET
WOLVERHAMPTON
WEST MIDLANDS WV1 1AD
t: 01902 321000 f: 01902 321896
e: admissions@wlv.ac.uk
// www.wlv.ac.uk

LM41 BA Social Policy and Law
Duration: 3FT Hon
Entry Requirements: Contact the institution for details.

W76 UNIVERSITY OF WINCHESTER
WINCHESTER
HANTS SO22 4NR
t: 01962 827234 f: 01962 827288
e: course.enquiries@winchester.ac.uk
// www.winchester.ac.uk

ML13 BA Law and Sociology
Duration: 3FT Hon
Entry Requirements: *Foundation:* Distinction. *GCE:* 260-300. *IB:* 25. *OCR ND:* D *OCR NED:* M2

OTHER LAW COMBINATIONS

A20 THE UNIVERSITY OF ABERDEEN
UNIVERSITY OFFICE
KING'S COLLEGE
ABERDEEN AB24 3FX
t: +44 (0) 1224 273504 f: +44 (0) 1224 272034
e: sras@abdn.ac.uk
// www.abdn.ac.uk/sras

M1W3 LLB Law with options in Music
Duration: 4FT Hon
Entry Requirements: *GCE:* BBB. *SQAH:* AABB-ABBBB. *SQAAH:* BBB. *IB:* 34.

A40 ABERYSTWYTH UNIVERSITY
ABERYSTWYTH UNIVERSITY, WELCOME CENTRE
PENGLAIS CAMPUS
ABERYSTWYTH
CEREDIGION SY23 3FB
t: 01970 622021 f: 01970 627410
e: ug-admissions@aber.ac.uk
// www.aber.ac.uk

M1N5 BA Law with Marketing
Duration: 3FT Hon
Entry Requirements: *GCE:* 340. *IB:* 28.

M1L2 BA Law with Politics
Duration: 3FT Hon
Entry Requirements: *GCE:* 340. *IB:* 28.

N5M1 BScEcon Marketing with Law
Duration: 3FT Hon
Entry Requirements: *GCE:* 280. *IB:* 27.

L2MC BScEcon Politics with Law
Duration: 3FT Hon
Entry Requirements: *GCE:* 300. *IB:* 30.

B32 THE UNIVERSITY OF BIRMINGHAM
EDGBASTON
BIRMINGHAM B15 2TT
t: 0121 415 8900 f: 0121 414 7159
e: admissions@bham.ac.uk
// www.birmingham.ac.uk

M990 LLB Law (Graduate Entry)
Duration: 2FT Hon
Entry Requirements: Contact the institution for details.

B50 BOURNEMOUTH UNIVERSITY
TALBOT CAMPUS
FERN BARROW
POOLE
DORSET BH12 5BB
t: 01202 524111
// www.bournemouth.ac.uk

M296 LLB Law and Taxation
Duration: 3FT/4SW Hon
Entry Requirements: *GCE:* 320. *IB:* 32. *BTEC SubDip:* D. *BTEC Dip:* DD. *BTEC ExtDip:* DDM.

B54 BPP UNIVERSITY COLLEGE OF PROFESSIONAL STUDIES LIMITED
142-144 UXBRIDGE ROAD
LONDON W12 8AW
t: 02031 312 298
e: admissions@bpp.com
// undergraduate.bpp.com/

MC18 LLB Law with Psychology
Duration: 3FT Hon
Entry Requirements: Contact the institution for details.

MCC8 LLB Law with Psychology (Accelerated)
Duration: 2FT Hon
Entry Requirements: Contact the institution for details.

B60 BRADFORD COLLEGE: AN ASSOCIATE COLLEGE OF LEEDS METROPOLITAN UNIVERSITY
GREAT HORTON ROAD
BRADFORD
WEST YORKSHIRE BD7 1AY
t: 01274 433008 f: 01274 431652
e: heregistry@bradfordcollege.ac.uk
// www.bradfordcollege.ac.uk/university-centre

M190 BA Law IPOS
Duration: 3FT Hon
Entry Requirements: *GCE:* 240.

MN15 BA Marketing and Law
Duration: 3FT Hon
Entry Requirements: *GCE:* 240.

MM12 FdA Law & Legal Practice
Duration: 2FT Fdg
Entry Requirements: *GCE:* 120.

B80 UNIVERSITY OF THE WEST OF ENGLAND, BRISTOL
FRENCHAY CAMPUS
COLDHARBOUR LANE
BRISTOL BS16 1QY
t: +44 (0)117 32 83333 f: +44 (0)117 32 82810
e: admissions@uwe.ac.uk
// www.uwe.ac.uk

C8M1 BSc (Hons) Psychology with Law
Duration: 3FT Hon
Entry Requirements: *GCE:* 340.

M1C8 LLB (Hons) Law with Psychology
Duration: 3FT Hon
Entry Requirements: Contact the institution for details.

B90 THE UNIVERSITY OF BUCKINGHAM
YEOMANRY HOUSE
HUNTER STREET
BUCKINGHAM MK18 1EG
t: 01280 820313 f: 01280 822245
e: info@buckingham.ac.uk
// www.buckingham.ac.uk

M1L2 LLB Law with Politics
Duration: 2FT Hon
Entry Requirements: *GCE:* 300. *SQAH:* ABBB. *SQAAH:* BBB. *IB:* 34. *OCR NED:* M2 Interview required.

C15 CARDIFF UNIVERSITY
PO BOX 927
30-36 NEWPORT ROAD
CARDIFF CF24 0DE
t: 029 2087 9999 f: 029 2087 6138
e: admissions@cardiff.ac.uk
// www.cardiff.ac.uk

ML12 LLB Law and Politics (Integrated)
Duration: 3FT Hon
Entry Requirements: *GCE:* AAB. *SQAAH:* AAB. *IB:* 34. Interview required.

C30 UNIVERSITY OF CENTRAL LANCASHIRE
PRESTON
LANCS PR1 2HE
t: 01772 201201 f: 01772 894954
e: uadmissions@uclan.ac.uk
// www.uclan.ac.uk

ML12 BA Politics and Law
Duration: 3FT Hon
Entry Requirements: *GCE:* 260-300. *IB:* 28. *BTEC Dip:* D*D*. *BTEC ExtDip:* DMM. *OCR ND:* D *OCR NED:* M2

C55 UNIVERSITY OF CHESTER
PARKGATE ROAD
CHESTER CH1 4BJ
t: 01244 511000 f: 01244 511300
e: enquiries@chester.ac.uk
// www.chester.ac.uk

MV11 BA Law and History
Duration: 3FT Hon
Entry Requirements: *GCE:* 260-300. *SQAH:* BBBB. *IB:* 28.

MP15 BA Law and Journalism
Duration: 3FT Hon
Entry Requirements: *GCE:* 240-280. *SQAH:* BBBB. *IB:* 26.

MC18 BA Law and Psychology
Duration: 3FT Hon
Entry Requirements: *Foundation:* Pass. *GCE:* 260-300. *SQAH:* BBBB. *IB:* 28.

LM21 BA Politics and Law
Duration: 3FT Hon
Entry Requirements: *GCE:* 240-280. *SQAH:* BBBB. *IB:* 26.

C60 CITY UNIVERSITY
NORTHAMPTON SQUARE
LONDON EC1V 0HB
t: 020 7040 5060 f: 020 7040 8995
e: ugadmissions@city.ac.uk
// www.city.ac.uk

M110 LLB Graduate Entry LLB (2 years)
Duration: 2FT Hon
Entry Requirements: Contact the institution for details.

C85 COVENTRY UNIVERSITY
THE STUDENT CENTRE
COVENTRY UNIVERSITY
1 GULSON RD
COVENTRY CV1 2JH
t: 024 7615 2222 f: 024 7615 2223
e: studentenquiries@coventry.ac.uk
// www.coventry.ac.uk

MM12 FYr Law and Practice (Foundation Year)
Duration: 1FT FYr
Entry Requirements: *GCE:* 100. *IB:* 24. *BTEC Dip:* MP. *BTEC ExtDip:* PPP. *OCR ND:* P2 *OCR NED:* P3

D26 DE MONTFORT UNIVERSITY
THE GATEWAY
LEICESTER LE1 9BH
t: 0116 255 1551 f: 0116 250 6204
e: enquiries@dmu.ac.uk
// www.dmu.ac.uk

M1N5 BA Law and Marketing
Duration: 3FT/4SW Hon
Entry Requirements: *GCE:* 280. *IB:* 28. *BTEC Dip:* D*D*. *BTEC ExtDip:* DMM. *OCR NED:* M2 Interview required.

CM81 BA Law and Psychology
Duration: 3FT Hon
Entry Requirements: *GCE:* 280. *IB:* 28. *BTEC Dip:* D*D*. *BTEC ExtDip:* DMM. *OCR NED:* M2 Interview required.

D39 UNIVERSITY OF DERBY
KEDLESTON ROAD
DERBY DE22 1GB
t: 01332 591167 f: 01332 597724
e: askadmissions@derby.ac.uk
// www.derby.ac.uk

KM11 BA Architectural Design and Law
Duration: 3FT Hon
Entry Requirements: *Foundation:* Distinction. *GCE:* 260-300. *IB:* 28. *BTEC Dip:* D*D*. *BTEC ExtDip:* DMM. *OCR NED:* M2

WM81 BA Creative Writing and Law
Duration: 3FT Hon
Entry Requirements: *Foundation:* Distinction. *GCE:* 260-300. *IB:* 28. *BTEC Dip:* D*D*. *BTEC ExtDip:* DMM. *OCR NED:* M2

MV11 BA History and Law
Duration: 3FT Hon
Entry Requirements: *Foundation:* Distinction. *GCE:* 260-300. *IB:* 28. *BTEC Dip:* D*D*. *BTEC ExtDip:* DMM. *OCR NED:* M2

MN15 BA Law and Marketing
Duration: 3FT Hon
Entry Requirements: *Foundation:* Distinction. *GCE:* 260-300. *IB:* 28. *BTEC Dip:* D*D*. *BTEC ExtDip:* DMM. *OCR NED:* M2

MW18 BA Law and Professional Writing
Duration: 3FT Hon
Entry Requirements: *Foundation:* Distinction. *GCE:* 260-300. *IB:* 28. *BTEC Dip:* D*D*. *BTEC ExtDip:* DMM. *OCR NED:* M2

CM81 BA Law and Psychology
Duration: 3FT Hon
Entry Requirements: *Foundation:* Distinction. *GCE:* 260-300. *IB:* 28. *BTEC Dip:* D*D*. *BTEC ExtDip:* DMM. *OCR NED:* M2

KM2C BA Property Development and Law
Duration: 3FT Hon
Entry Requirements: *Foundation:* Distinction. *GCE:* 260-300. *IB:* 28. *BTEC Dip:* D*D*. *BTEC ExtDip:* DMM. *OCR NED:* M2

CM1C BSc Biology and Law
Duration: 3FT Hon
Entry Requirements: *Foundation:* Distinction. *GCE:* 260-300. *IB:* 28. *BTEC Dip:* D*D*. *BTEC ExtDip:* DMM. *OCR NED:* M2

FM71 BSc Environmental Hazards and Law
Duration: 3FT Hon
Entry Requirements: *Foundation:* Distinction. *GCE:* 260-300. *IB:* 28. *BTEC Dip:* D*D*. *BTEC ExtDip:* DMM. *OCR NED:* M2

FM8C BSc Geography and Law
Duration: 3FT Hon
Entry Requirements: *Foundation:* Distinction. *GCE:* 260-300. *IB:* 28. *BTEC Dip:* D*D*. *BTEC ExtDip:* DMM. *OCR NED:* M2

D65 UNIVERSITY OF DUNDEE
NETHERGATE
DUNDEE DD1 4HN
t: 01382 383838 f: 01382 388150
e: contactus@dundee.ac.uk
// www.dundee.ac.uk/admissions/
undergraduate/

M111 LLB Law (Eng/NI) option - Philosophy
Duration: 3FT Hon
Entry Requirements: *GCE:* ABB. *SQAH:* AABB-ABBBB. *IB:* 32.

M111 LLB Law (Eng/NI) option - Politics
Duration: 3FT Hon
Entry Requirements: *GCE:* ABB. *SQAH:* AABB-ABBBB. *IB:* 32.

M111 LLB Law (Eng/NI) option - History
Duration: 3FT Hon
Entry Requirements: *GCE:* ABB. *SQAH:* AABB-ABBBB. *IB:* 32.

M111 LLB Law (Eng/NI)
Duration: 3FT Hon
Entry Requirements: *GCE:* ABB. *SQAH:* AABB-ABBBB. *IB:* 32.

M101 LLB Law (Eng/NI) - Accelerated
Duration: 2FT Ord
Entry Requirements: Contact the institution for details.

E14 UNIVERSITY OF EAST ANGLIA
NORWICH NR4 7TJ
t: 01603 591515 f: 01603 591523
e: admissions@uea.ac.uk
// www.uea.ac.uk

M123 LLB Law with American Law
Duration: 4FT Hon   CRB Check: Required
Entry Requirements: *GCE:* AAA. *SQAH:* AAAAB. *SQAAH:* AAB. *IB:* 34. *BTEC SubDip:* D. *BTEC Dip:* DD. *BTEC ExtDip:* DDD. *OCR ND:* D *OCR NED:* D1 Interview required.

E28 UNIVERSITY OF EAST LONDON
DOCKLANDS CAMPUS
UNIVERSITY WAY
LONDON E16 2RD
t: 020 8223 3333 f: 020 8223 2978
e: study@uel.ac.uk
// www.uel.ac.uk

V1M1 BA History with Law
Duration: 3FT Hon
Entry Requirements: *GCE:* 240. *IB:* 28.

M1V1 BA Law with History
Duration: 3FT Hon
Entry Requirements: *GCE:* 240. *IB:* 28.

X3M1 BA Special Needs and Inclusive Education with Law
Duration: 3FT Hon
Entry Requirements: *GCE:* 240. *IB:* 24.

FM41 BA/BSc Forensic Science/Law
Duration: 3FT Hon
Entry Requirements: *GCE:* 240. *IB:* 28.

G4M1 BSc Computer Networks with Law
Duration: 3FT Hon
Entry Requirements: *GCE:* 240. *IB:* 24.

F4M1 BSc Forensic Science with Law
Duration: 3FT Hon
Entry Requirements: *GCE:* 240. *IB:* 24.

B2M1 BSc Toxicology with Law
Duration: 3FT Hon
Entry Requirements: *GCE:* 240. *IB:* 24.

M1W8 LLB Law with Creative and Professional Writing
Duration: 3FT Hon
Entry Requirements: *GCE:* 240. *IB:* 24.

E56 THE UNIVERSITY OF EDINBURGH
STUDENT RECRUITMENT & ADMISSIONS
57 GEORGE SQUARE
EDINBURGH EH8 9JU
t: 0131 650 4360 f: 0131 651 1236
e: sra.enquiries@ed.ac.uk
// www.ed.ac.uk/studying/undergraduate/

MV11 LLB Law and History
Duration: 4FT Hon
Entry Requirements: *GCE:* AAA-BBB. *SQAH:* AAAA-BBBB. *IB:* 34.

ML12 LLB Law and Politics
Duration: 4FT Hon
Entry Requirements: *GCE:* AAA-BBB. *SQAH:* AAAA-BBBB. *IB:* 34.

E59 EDINBURGH NAPIER UNIVERSITY
CRAIGLOCKHART CAMPUS
EDINBURGH EH14 1DJ
t: +44 (0)8452 60 60 40 f: 0131 455 6464
e: info@napier.ac.uk
// www.napier.ac.uk

MCN1 LLB Law with Entrepreneurship
Duration: 3FT/4FT Ord/Hon
Entry Requirements: Contact the institution for details.

E70 THE UNIVERSITY OF ESSEX
WIVENHOE PARK
COLCHESTER
ESSEX CO4 3SQ
t: 01206 873666 f: 01206 874477
e: admit@essex.ac.uk
// www.essex.ac.uk

MVC5 BA Philosophy and Law
Duration: 3FT Hon
Entry Requirements: *GCE:* ABB-BBB. *SQAH:* AAAB-AABB. *BTEC ExtDip:* DDM.

VM51 BA Philosophy and Law (Including Year Abroad)
Duration: 4FT Hon
Entry Requirements: *GCE:* ABB-BBB. *SQAH:* AAAB-AABB. *BTEC ExtDip:* DDM.

LM21 BA Politics and Law
Duration: 3FT Hon
Entry Requirements: *GCE:* AAB-ABB. *SQAH:* AAAA-AAAB. *BTEC ExtDip:* DDM.

LM2C BA Politics and Law (Including Year Abroad)
Duration: 4FT Hon
Entry Requirements: *GCE:* AAB-ABB. *SQAH:* AAAA-AAAB. *BTEC ExtDip:* DDM.

MV15 LLB Law and Philosophy
Duration: 4FT Hon
Entry Requirements: *GCE:* AAB. *SQAH:* AAAA. *IB:* 36.

ML12 LLB Law and Politics
Duration: 4FT Hon
Entry Requirements: *GCE:* AAB. *SQAH:* AAAA. *IB:* 36.

G28 UNIVERSITY OF GLASGOW
71 SOUTHPARK AVENUE
UNIVERSITY OF GLASGOW
GLASGOW G12 8QQ
t: 0141 330 6062 f: 0141 330 2961
e: student.recruitment@glasgow.ac.uk
// www.glasgow.ac.uk

ML17 LLB Law/Geography
Duration: 4FT Hon
Entry Requirements: *GCE:* AAB. *SQAH:* AAAAB. *IB:* 34. Admissions Test required.

MV11 LLB Law/History
Duration: 4FT Hon
Entry Requirements: *GCE:* AAB. *SQAH:* AAAAB. *IB:* 34. Admissions Test required.

MV15 LLB Law/Philosophy
Duration: 4FT Hon
Entry Requirements: *GCE:* AAB. *SQAH:* AAAAB. *IB:* 34. Admissions Test required.

ML12 LLB Law/Politics
Duration: 4FT Hon
Entry Requirements: *GCE:* AAB. *SQAH:* AAAAB. *IB:* 34. Admissions Test required.

G42 GLASGOW CALEDONIAN UNIVERSITY
STUDENT RECRUITMENT & ADMISSIONS SERVICE
CITY CAMPUS
COWCADDENS ROAD
GLASGOW G4 0BA
t: 0141 331 3000 f: 0141 331 8676
e: undergraduate@gcu.ac.uk
// www.gcu.ac.uk

M115 LLB Law (Fast-Track)
Duration: 2FT Hon
Entry Requirements: Contact the institution for details.

H36 UNIVERSITY OF HERTFORDSHIRE
UNIVERSITY ADMISSIONS SERVICE
COLLEGE LANE
HATFIELD
HERTS AL10 9AB
t: 01707 284800
// www.herts.ac.uk

P5M1 BSc Journalism & Media Cultures/Law
Duration: 3FT/4SW Hon
Entry Requirements: *GCE:* 320.

M1P5 BSc Law/Journalism & Media Cultures
Duration: 3FT/4SW Hon
Entry Requirements: *GCE:* 320.

M1V5 BSc Law/Philosophy
Duration: 3FT/4SW Hon
Entry Requirements: *GCE:* 320.

M1C8 BSc Law/Psychology
Duration: 3FT/4SW Hon
Entry Requirements: *GCE:* 320.

V5M1 BSc Philosophy/Law
Duration: 3FT/4SW Hon
Entry Requirements: *GCE:* 320.

C8M1 BSc Psychology/Law
Duration: 3FT/4SW Hon
Entry Requirements: *GCE:* 320.

M190 LLB Government & Politics
Duration: 3FT Hon
Entry Requirements: *GCE:* 300.

H60 THE UNIVERSITY OF HUDDERSFIELD
QUEENSGATE
HUDDERSFIELD HD1 3DH
t: 01484 473969 f: 01484 472765
e: admissionsandrecords@hud.ac.uk
// www.hud.ac.uk

M251 LLB(Hons) Legal Executive Pathway
Duration: 3FT Hon
Entry Requirements: *GCE:* 280. Interview required.

H72 THE UNIVERSITY OF HULL
THE UNIVERSITY OF HULL
COTTINGHAM ROAD
HULL HU6 7RX
t: 01482 466100 f: 01482 442290
e: admissions@hull.ac.uk
// www.hull.ac.uk

LVM0 BA Politics, Philosophy and Law
Duration: 3FT Hon
Entry Requirements: *GCE:* 300-340. *IB:* 30. *BTEC ExtDip:* DDM.

VLM0 BA Politics, Philosophy and Law (including Foundation English Language)
Duration: 4FT Hon
Entry Requirements: *GCE:* 300-340. *IB:* 30.

M1V5 LLB Law with Philosophy
Duration: 3FT Hon
Entry Requirements: *GCE:* 320. *IB:* 30. *BTEC ExtDip:* DDM.

M1L2 LLB Law with Politics
Duration: 3FT Hon
Entry Requirements: *GCE:* 320. *IB:* 30. *BTEC ExtDip:* DDM.

K12 KEELE UNIVERSITY
KEELE UNIVERSITY
STAFFORDSHIRE ST5 5BG
t: 01782 734005 f: 01782 632343
e: undergraduate@keele.ac.uk
// www.keele.ac.uk

MV11 BA History and Law
Duration: 3FT Hon
Entry Requirements: *GCE:* ABB.

MN15 BA Law and Marketing
Duration: 3FT Hon
Entry Requirements: *GCE:* ABB.

PM31 BA Law and Media, Communications & Culture
Duration: 3FT Hon
Entry Requirements: *GCE:* ABB.

MW13 BA Law and Music
Duration: 3FT Hon
Entry Requirements: *GCE:* ABB.

MWD3 BA Law and Music Technology
Duration: 3FT Hon
Entry Requirements: *GCE:* ABB.

MV15 BA Law and Philosophy
Duration: 3FT Hon
Entry Requirements: *GCE:* ABB.

LM21 BA Law and Politics
Duration: 3FT Hon
Entry Requirements: *GCE:* AAB.

FMX1 BSc Applied Environmental Science and Law
Duration: 3FT Hon
Entry Requirements: *GCE:* ABB.

CM71 BSc Biochemistry and Law
Duration: 3FT Hon
Entry Requirements: *GCE:* ABB.

CM11 BSc Biology and Law
Duration: 3FT Hon
Entry Requirements: *GCE:* ABB.

FM11 BSc Chemistry and Law
Duration: 3FT Hon
Entry Requirements: *GCE:* ABB.

GM41 BSc Computer Science and Law
Duration: 3FT Hon
Entry Requirements: *GCE:* ABB.

FM61 BSc Geology and Law
Duration: 3FT Hon
Entry Requirements: *GCE:* ABB.

MG14 BSc Information Systems and Law
Duration: 3FT Hon
Entry Requirements: *GCE:* ABB.

FMCC BSc Law and Medicinal Chemistry
Duration: 3FT Hon
Entry Requirements: *GCE:* ABB.

BM11 BSc Law and Neuroscience
Duration: 3FT Hon
Entry Requirements: *GCE:* ABB.

GM71 BSc Smart Systems and Law
Duration: 3FT Hon
Entry Requirements: *GCE:* ABB.

M1L2 LLB Law with Politics
Duration: 3FT Hon
Entry Requirements: *GCE:* AAB.

K24 THE UNIVERSITY OF KENT
RECRUITMENT & ADMISSIONS OFFICE
REGISTRY
UNIVERSITY OF KENT
CANTERBURY, KENT CT2 7NZ
t: 01227 827272 f: 01227 827077
e: information@kent.ac.uk
// www.kent.ac.uk

VM1C BA Law and History
Duration: 3FT Hon
Entry Requirements: *GCE:* AAB. *SQAH:* AAAAB. *SQAAH:* AAB. *IB:* 33. *OCR ND:* D *OCR NED:* M1

MV15 BA Law and Philosophy
Duration: 3FT Hon
Entry Requirements: *GCE:* AAB. *SQAH:* AAAAB. *SQAAH:* AAB. *IB:* 33. *OCR ND:* D *OCR NED:* M1

ML14 BA Law and Welfare
Duration: 3FT Hon
Entry Requirements: *GCE:* AAB. *SQAH:* AAAAB. *IB:* 33. *OCR ND:* D *OCR NED:* M1

LM21 BA Politics and Law
Duration: 3FT Hon
Entry Requirements: *GCE:* ABB. *SQAH:* AABBB. *SQAAH:* ABB. *IB:* 33. *OCR ND:* D *OCR NED:* D2

CM81 BSc Psychology and Law (4 years)
Duration: 4FT Hon
Entry Requirements: *GCE:* AAB. *SQAH:* AAAAB. *SQAAH:* AAB. *IB:* 33. *OCR ND:* D *OCR NED:* D1

K60 KING'S COLLEGE LONDON (UNIVERSITY OF LONDON)
STRAND
LONDON WC2R 2LS
t: 020 7836 5454 f: 020 7848 7171
e: prospective@kcl.ac.uk
// www.kcl.ac.uk/prospectus

M190 LLB English Law and Hong Kong Law
Duration: 5FT Hon
Entry Requirements: *GCE:* A*AAa. *SQAH:* AAA. *SQAAH:* AA. *IB:* 39. Admissions Test required.

LM21 LLB Politics, Philosophy and Law
Duration: 4FT Hon
Entry Requirements: *GCE:* A*AA. *IB:* 39. Admissions Test required.

K84 KINGSTON UNIVERSITY
STUDENT INFORMATION & ADVICE CENTRE
COOPER HOUSE
40-46 SURBITON ROAD
KINGSTON UPON THAMES KT1 2HX
t: 0844 8552177 f: 020 8547 7080
e: aps@kingston.ac.uk
// www.kingston.ac.uk

WM81 BA Creative Writing and Law
Duration: 3FT Hon
Entry Requirements: *GCE:* 280.

M990 BA Law
Duration: 3FT Hon
Entry Requirements: *GCE:* 280. *SQAH:* BBCCC. *SQAAH:* BCC. *IB:* 25.

ML12 BA Law and Politics
Duration: 3FT Hon
Entry Requirements: *GCE:* 280.

MPC3 BA Law and Television & New Broadcasting Media
Duration: 3FT Hon
Entry Requirements: *GCE:* 280.

L14 LANCASTER UNIVERSITY
THE UNIVERSITY
LANCASTER
LANCASHIRE LA1 4YW
t: 01524 592029 f: 01524 846243
e: ugadmissions@lancaster.ac.uk
// www.lancs.ac.uk

M1L2 LLB Law and Politics
Duration: 3FT Hon
Entry Requirements: *GCE:* AAA. *SQAH:* AAABB. *SQAAH:* AAA. *IB:* 36.

L34 UNIVERSITY OF LEICESTER
UNIVERSITY ROAD
LEICESTER LE1 7RH
t: 0116 252 5281 f: 0116 252 2447
e: admissions@le.ac.uk
// www.le.ac.uk

M2L2 LLB Law with Politics
Duration: 3FT Hon
Entry Requirements: *GCE:* AAA. *SQAH:* AAAAA. *SQAAH:* AAA. *IB:* 36.

L39 UNIVERSITY OF LINCOLN
ADMISSIONS
BRAYFORD POOL
LINCOLN LN6 7TS
t: 01522 886097 f: 01522 886146
e: admissions@lincoln.ac.uk
// www.lincoln.ac.uk

ML12 LLB Law and Politics
Duration: 3FT Hon
Entry Requirements: *GCE:* 300.

L41 THE UNIVERSITY OF LIVERPOOL
THE FOUNDATION BUILDING
BROWNLOW HILL
LIVERPOOL L69 7ZX
t: 0151 794 2000 f: 0151 708 6502
e: ugrecruitment@liv.ac.uk
// www.liv.ac.uk

M107 LLB Law with Philosophy
Duration: 3FT Hon
Entry Requirements: *GCE:* AAA. *SQAH:* AAAAA. *SQAAH:* AA. *IB:* 36. *OCR ND:* D *OCR NED:* D2

L46 LIVERPOOL HOPE UNIVERSITY
HOPE PARK
LIVERPOOL L16 9JD
t: 0151 291 3331 f: 0151 291 3434
e: administration@hope.ac.uk
// www.hope.ac.uk

V3M1 BA Art & Design History and Law
Duration: 3FT Hon
Entry Requirements: *GCE:* 300-320. *IB:* 25.

VM61 BA Christian Theology and Law
Duration: 3FT Hon
Entry Requirements: *GCE:* 300-320. *IB:* 25.

XM3C BA Education and Law
Duration: 3FT Hon   CRB Check: Required
Entry Requirements: *GCE:* 300-320. *IB:* 25.

MG15 BA Information Technology and Law
Duration: 3FT Hon
Entry Requirements: *GCE:* 300-320. *IB:* 25.

MP13 BA Law and Media & Communication
Duration: 3FT Hon
Entry Requirements: *GCE:* 300-320. *IB:* 25.

MV15 BA Law and Philosophy & Ethics
Duration: 3FT Hon
Entry Requirements: *GCE:* 300-320. *IB:* 25.

LM21 BA Law and Politics
Duration: 3FT Hon
Entry Requirements: *GCE:* 300-320. *IB:* 25.

MC18 BA Law and Psychology
Duration: 3FT Hon
Entry Requirements: *GCE:* 300-320. *IB:* 25.

MN18 BA Law and Tourism
Duration: 3FT Hon
Entry Requirements: *GCE:* 300-320. *IB:* 25.

MV1P BA Law and World Religions
Duration: 3FT Hon
Entry Requirements: *GCE:* 300-320. *IB:* 25.

L62 THE LONDON COLLEGE, UCK
VICTORIA GARDENS
NOTTING HILL GATE
LONDON W11 3PE
t: 020 7243 4000 f: 020 7243 1484
e: admissions@lcuck.ac.uk
// www.lcuck.ac.uk

002M Dip Law
Duration: 1FT Oth
Entry Requirements: Contact the institution for details.

L75 LONDON SOUTH BANK UNIVERSITY
ADMISSIONS AND RECRUITMENT CENTRE
90 LONDON ROAD
LONDON SE1 6LN
t: 0800 923 8888 f: 020 7815 8273
e: course.enquiry@lsbu.ac.uk
// www.lsbu.ac.uk

M1C8 LLB Law with Psychology
Duration: 3FT Hon
Entry Requirements: *GCE:* 260. *IB:* 24.

M20 THE UNIVERSITY OF MANCHESTER
RUTHERFORD BUILDING
OXFORD ROAD
MANCHESTER M13 9PL
t: 0161 275 2077 f: 0161 275 2106
e: ug-admissions@manchester.ac.uk
// www.manchester.ac.uk

M1L2 BA Law with Politics
Duration: 3FT Hon
Entry Requirements: *GCE:* AAB. *SQAH:* AAABB. *SQAAH:* AAB. *IB:*
35. Interview required.

LM21 LLB Law with Politics
Duration: 3FT Hon
Entry Requirements: *GCE:* AAB. *SQAH:* AAABB. *SQAAH:* AAB. *IB:*
35. Interview required.

M80 MIDDLESEX UNIVERSITY
MIDDLESEX UNIVERSITY
THE BURROUGHS
LONDON NW4 4BT
t: 020 8411 5555 f: 020 8411 5649
e: enquiries@mdx.ac.uk
// www.mdx.ac.uk

LM32 BA Youth Justice
Duration: 3FT Hon
Entry Requirements: *GCE:* 200-300. *IB:* 28.

N37 UNIVERSITY OF WALES, NEWPORT
ADMISSIONS
LODGE ROAD
CAERLEON
NEWPORT NP18 3QT
t: 01633 432030 f: 01633 432850
e: admissions@newport.ac.uk
// www.newport.ac.uk

CM62 BA/BSc Sport and Youth Justice
Duration: 3FT Hon   CRB Check: Required
Entry Requirements: *GCE:* 240. *IB:* 24. Interview required.

M110 FdA Law
Duration: 2FT Fdg
Entry Requirements: *GCE:* 120. *IB:* 24.

N38 UNIVERSITY OF NORTHAMPTON
PARK CAMPUS
BOUGHTON GREEN ROAD
NORTHAMPTON NN2 7AL
t: 0800 358 2232 f: 01604 722083
e: admissions@northampton.ac.uk
// www.northampton.ac.uk

W8M1 BA Creative Writing/Law
Duration: 3FT Hon
Entry Requirements: *GCE:* 260-280. *SQAH:* AAA-BBBB. *IB:* 24.
BTEC Dip: DD. *BTEC ExtDip:* DMM. *OCR ND:* D *OCR NED:* M2

W5M1 BA Dance/Law
Duration: 3FT Hon
Entry Requirements: *GCE:* 260-280. *SQAH:* AAA-BBBB. *IB:* 24.
BTEC Dip: DD. *BTEC ExtDip:* DMM. *OCR ND:* D *OCR NED:* M2
Interview required.

W4M1 BA Drama/Law
Duration: 3FT Hon
Entry Requirements: *GCE:* 260-280. *SQAH:* AAA-BBBB. *IB:* 24.
BTEC Dip: DD. *BTEC ExtDip:* DMM. *OCR ND:* D *OCR NED:* M2
Interview required.

W1M1 BA Fine Art Painting & Drawing/Law
Duration: 3FT Hon
Entry Requirements: *GCE:* 260-280. *SQAH:* AAA-BBBB. *IB:* 24.
BTEC Dip: DD. *BTEC ExtDip:* DMM. *OCR ND:* D *OCR NED:* M2

V1M1 BA History/Law
Duration: 3FT Hon
Entry Requirements: *GCE:* 260-280. *SQAH:* AAA-BBBB. *IB:* 24.
BTEC Dip: DD. *BTEC ExtDip:* DMM. *OCR ND:* D *OCR NED:* M2

P5M1 BA Journalism/Law
Duration: 3FT Hon
Entry Requirements: *GCE:* 260-280. *SQAH:* AAA-BBBB. *IB:* 24.
BTEC Dip: DD. *BTEC ExtDip:* DMM. *OCR ND:* D *OCR NED:* M2

M1C1 BA Law/Biological Conservation
Duration: 3FT Hon
Entry Requirements: *GCE:* 260-280. *SQAH:* AAA-BBBB. *IB:* 24.
BTEC Dip: DD. *BTEC ExtDip:* DMM. *OCR ND:* D *OCR NED:* M2

M1W8 BA Law/Creative Writing
Duration: 3FT Hon
Entry Requirements: *GCE:* 260-280. *SQAH:* AAA-BBBB. *IB:* 24.
BTEC Dip: DD. *BTEC ExtDip:* DMM. *OCR ND:* D *OCR NED:* M2

M1W5 BA Law/Dance
Duration: 3FT Hon
Entry Requirements: *GCE:* 260-280. *SQAH:* AAA-BBBB. *IB:* 24.
BTEC Dip: DD. *BTEC ExtDip:* DMM. *OCR ND:* D *OCR NED:* M2
Interview required.

M1W4 BA Law/Drama
Duration: 3FT Hon
Entry Requirements: **GCE:** 260-280. **SQAH:** AAA-BBBB. **IB:** 24.
BTEC Dip: DD. **BTEC ExtDip:** DMM. **OCR ND:** D **OCR NED:** M2
Interview required.

M1V1 BA Law/History
Duration: 3FT Hon
Entry Requirements: **GCE:** 260-280. **SQAH:** AAA-BBBB. **IB:** 24.
BTEC Dip: DD. **BTEC ExtDip:** DMM. **OCR ND:** D **OCR NED:** M2

M1P5 BA Law/Journalism
Duration: 3FT Hon
Entry Requirements: **GCE:** 260-280. **SQAH:** AAA-BBBB. **IB:** 24.
BTEC Dip: DD. **BTEC ExtDip:** DMM. **OCR ND:** D **OCR NED:** M2

M1F8 BA Law/Physical Geography
Duration: 3FT Hon
Entry Requirements: **GCE:** 260-280. **SQAH:** AAA-BBBB. **IB:** 24.
BTEC Dip: DD. **BTEC ExtDip:** DMM. **OCR ND:** D **OCR NED:** M2

M1L2 BA Law/Politics
Duration: 3FT Hon
Entry Requirements: **GCE:** 260-280. **SQAH:** AAA-BBBB. **IB:** 24.
BTEC Dip: DD. **BTEC ExtDip:** DMM. **OCR ND:** D **OCR NED:** M2

M1W3 BA Law/Popular Music
Duration: 3FT Hon
Entry Requirements: **GCE:** 260-280. **SQAH:** AAA-BBBB. **IB:** 24.
BTEC Dip: DD. **BTEC ExtDip:** DMM. **OCR ND:** D **OCR NED:** M2

M1C8 BA Law/Psychology
Duration: 3FT Hon
Entry Requirements: **GCE:** 260-280. **SQAH:** AAA-BBBB. **IB:** 24.
BTEC Dip: DD. **BTEC ExtDip:** DMM. **OCR ND:** D **OCR NED:** M2

M1G4 BA Law/Web Design
Duration: 3FT Hon
Entry Requirements: **GCE:** 260-280. **SQAH:** AAA-BBBB. **IB:** 24.
BTEC Dip: DD. **BTEC ExtDip:** DMM. **OCR ND:** D **OCR NED:** M2

L2M1 BA Politics/Law
Duration: 3FT Hon
Entry Requirements: **GCE:** 260-280. **SQAH:** AAA-BBBB. **IB:** 24.
BTEC Dip: DD. **BTEC ExtDip:** DMM. **OCR ND:** D **OCR NED:** M2

W3M1 BA Popular Music/Law
Duration: 3FT Hon
Entry Requirements: **GCE:** 260-280. **SQAH:** AAA-BBBB. **IB:** 24.
BTEC Dip: DD. **BTEC ExtDip:** DMM. **OCR ND:** D **OCR NED:** M2

C8M1 BA Psychology/Law
Duration: 3FT Hon
Entry Requirements: **GCE:** 260-280. **SQAH:** AAA-BBBB. **IB:** 24.
BTEC Dip: DD. **BTEC ExtDip:** DMM. **OCR ND:** D **OCR NED:** M2

X3M2 BA Special Educational Needs & Inclusion/Law
Duration: 3FT Hon
Entry Requirements: **GCE:** 260-280. **SQAH:** AAA-BBBB. **IB:** 24.
BTEC Dip: DD. **BTEC ExtDip:** DMM. **OCR ND:** D **OCR NED:** M2

C1M1 BSc Biological Conservation/Law
Duration: 3FT Hon
Entry Requirements: **GCE:** 260-280. **SQAH:** AAA-BBBB. **IB:** 24.
BTEC Dip: DD. **BTEC ExtDip:** DMM. **OCR ND:** D **OCR NED:** M2

F8M1 BSc Physical Geography/Law
Duration: 3FT Hon
Entry Requirements: **GCE:** 260-280. **SQAH:** AAA-BBBB. **IB:** 24.
BTEC Dip: DD. **BTEC ExtDip:** DMM. **OCR ND:** D **OCR NED:** M2

G4M1 BSc Web Design/Law
Duration: 3FT Hon
Entry Requirements: **GCE:** 260-280. **SQAH:** AAA-BBBB. **IB:** 24.
BTEC Dip: DD. **BTEC ExtDip:** DMM. **OCR ND:** D **OCR NED:** M2

N77 NORTHUMBRIA UNIVERSITY
TRINITY BUILDING
NORTHUMBERLAND ROAD
NEWCASTLE UPON TYNE NE1 8ST
t: 0191 243 7420 f: 0191 227 4561
e: er.admissions@northumbria.ac.uk
// www.northumbria.ac.uk

M1D4 LLB Law with Environment
Duration: 3FT Hon
Entry Requirements: **GCE:** ABB. **SQAH:** ABBBC. **SQAAH:** ABC. **IB:** 27. **BTEC ExtDip:** DDM. **OCR NED:** D2

N91 NOTTINGHAM TRENT UNIVERSITY
DRYDEN BUILDING
BURTON STREET
NOTTINGHAM NG1 4BU
t: +44 (0) 115 848 4200 f: +44 (0) 115 848 8869
e: applications@ntu.ac.uk
// www.ntu.ac.uk

M200 LLB Law and Legal Practice
Duration: 3FT Hon
Entry Requirements: **GCE:** 340. **OCR NED:** D1

M1C8 LLB Law with Psychology
Duration: 3FT Hon
Entry Requirements: **GCE:** 280. **OCR NED:** M2

P60 PLYMOUTH UNIVERSITY
DRAKE CIRCUS
PLYMOUTH PL4 8AA
t: 01752 585858 f: 01752 588055
e: admissions@plymouth.ac.uk
// www.plymouth.ac.uk

C8M2 BSc Psychology with Law
Duration: 3FT Hon
Entry Requirements: *GCE:* 320. *IB:* 28.

M200 LLB Law
Duration: 3FT Hon
Entry Requirements: *GCE:* 300. *IB:* 26.

Q50 QUEEN MARY, UNIVERSITY OF LONDON
QUEEN MARY, UNIVERSITY OF LONDON
MILE END ROAD
LONDON E1 4NS
t: 020 7882 5555 f: 020 7882 5500
e: admissions@qmul.ac.uk
// www.qmul.ac.uk

ML12 BA Law and Politics
Duration: 3FT Hon
Entry Requirements: *GCE:* AAA. *SQAAH:* AAA. *IB:* 36.

Q75 QUEEN'S UNIVERSITY BELFAST
UNIVERSITY ROAD
BELFAST BT7 1NN
t: 028 9097 3838 f: 028 9097 5151
e: admissions@qub.ac.uk
// www.qub.ac.uk

M1L2 LLB Law with Politics
Duration: 3FT Hon
Entry Requirements: *GCE:* AAA-AABa. *SQAH:* AAAAB. *SQAAH:* AAA. *IB:* 36.

S09 SCHOOL OF ORIENTAL AND AFRICAN STUDIES (UNIVERSITY OF LONDON)
THORNHAUGH STREET
RUSSELL SQUARE
LONDON WC1H 0XG
t: 020 7898 4301 f: 020 7898 4039
e: undergradadmissions@soas.ac.uk
// www.soas.ac.uk

VM31 BA History of Art/Archaeology and Law
Duration: 3FT Hon
Entry Requirements: *GCE:* AAA.

LM71 BA Law and Geography
Duration: 3FT Hon
Entry Requirements: *GCE:* AAA.

MV11 BA Law and History
Duration: 3FT Hon
Entry Requirements: *GCE:* AAA.

LM21 BA Politics and Law
Duration: 3FT Hon
Entry Requirements: *GCE:* AAA.

MV16 BA Study of Religions and Law
Duration: 3FT Hon
Entry Requirements: *GCE:* AAA.

S27 UNIVERSITY OF SOUTHAMPTON
HIGHFIELD
SOUTHAMPTON SO17 1BJ
t: 023 8059 4732 f: 023 8059 3037
e: admissions@soton.ac.uk
// www.southampton.ac.uk

M1M2 LLB Law (Maritime Law)
Duration: 3FT Hon
Entry Requirements: Contact the institution for details.

S30 SOUTHAMPTON SOLENT UNIVERSITY
EAST PARK TERRACE
SOUTHAMPTON
HAMPSHIRE SO14 0RT
t: +44 (0) 23 8031 9039 f: + 44 (0)23 8022 2259
e: admissions@solent.ac.uk
// www.solent.ac.uk/

M111 LLB Law (with Law Foundation Year)
Duration: 4FT Hon
Entry Requirements: Contact the institution for details.

S72 STAFFORDSHIRE UNIVERSITY
COLLEGE ROAD
STOKE ON TRENT ST4 2DE
t: 01782 292753 f: 01782 292740
e: admissions@staffs.ac.uk
// www.staffs.ac.uk

LM39 BA Crime, Deviance and Society
Duration: 3FT Hon
Entry Requirements: *GCE:* 200-240. *IB:* 24. *BTEC Dip:* DD. *BTEC ExtDip:* MMM.

MNC2 BA/BSc Law with Internet Commerce
Duration: 3FT Hon
Entry Requirements: *GCE:* 200-320. *IB:* 26. *OCR ND:* D

M290 LLB Law (Advice Work)
Duration: 3FT Hon
Entry Requirements: *GCE:* 180-240. *IB:* 24.

M111 LLB Law with a Foundation Year
Duration: 4FT Hon
Entry Requirements: *GCE:* 100-120. *SQAH:* C. *SQAAH:* D. *IB:* 24.
Interview required.

S75 THE UNIVERSITY OF STIRLING
STUDENT RECRUITMENT & ADMISSIONS SERVICE
UNIVERSITY OF STIRLING
STIRLING
SCOTLAND FK9 4LA
t: 01786 467044 f: 01786 466800
e: admissions@stir.ac.uk
// www.stir.ac.uk

MV11 BA History and Law
Duration: 4FT Hon
Entry Requirements: *GCE:* BBC. *SQAH:* BBBB. *SQAAH:* AAA-CCC.
IB: 32. *BTEC ExtDip:* DMM.

M110 BA Law
Duration: 4FT Hon
Entry Requirements: *GCE:* BBC. *SQAH:* BBBB. *SQAAH:* AAA-CCC.
IB: 32. *BTEC ExtDip:* DMM.

MN15 BA Law and Marketing
Duration: 4FT Hon
Entry Requirements: *GCE:* BBC. *SQAH:* BBBB. *SQAAH:* AAA-CCC.
IB: 32. *BTEC ExtDip:* DMM.

ML12 BA Law and Politics
Duration: 4FT Hon
Entry Requirements: *GCE:* BBC. *SQAH:* BBBB. *SQAAH:* AAA-CCC.
IB: 32. *BTEC ExtDip:* DMM.

M115 LLB Law Accelerated Entry (graduates only)
Duration: 2FT Deg
Entry Requirements: Contact the institution for details.

S78 THE UNIVERSITY OF STRATHCLYDE
GLASGOW G1 1XQ
t: 0141 552 4400 f: 0141 552 0775
// www.strath.ac.uk

VM11 BA History and Law
Duration: 4FT Hon
Entry Requirements: *GCE:* ABB. *SQAH:* AAABB-AAAB. *IB:* 34.

PM51 BA Journalism & Creative Writing and Law
Duration: 4FT Hon
Entry Requirements: *GCE:* ABB. *SQAH:* AAABB-AAAB. *IB:* 34.
Portfolio required.

MX13 BA Law and Education
Duration: 4FT Hon
Entry Requirements: Contact the institution for details.

ML12 BA Law and Politics
Duration: 4FT Hon
Entry Requirements: *GCE:* ABB. *SQAH:* AAABB-AAAB. *IB:* 34.

MC18 BA Law and Psychology
Duration: 4FT Hon
Entry Requirements: *GCE:* ABB. *SQAH:* AAABB-AAAB. *IB:* 34.

G4M1 BSc Computer Science with Law
Duration: 4FT Hon
Entry Requirements: *GCE:* ABB. *SQAH:* AABB-ABBBB. *IB:* 34.

S84 UNIVERSITY OF SUNDERLAND
STUDENT HELPLINE
THE STUDENT GATEWAY
CHESTER ROAD
SUNDERLAND SR1 3SD
t: 0191 515 3000 f: 0191 515 3805
e: student.helpline@sunderland.ac.uk
// www.sunderland.ac.uk

W4M1 BA Drama with Law
Duration: 3FT Hon
Entry Requirements: *GCE:* 260-360. *OCR ND:* D *OCR NED:* M3

P5M1 BA Journalism with Law
Duration: 3FT Hon
Entry Requirements: *GCE:* 260-360. *OCR ND:* D *OCR NED:* M3

MW15 BA Law and Dance
Duration: 3FT Hon
Entry Requirements: *GCE:* 260-360. *OCR ND:* D *OCR NED:* M3

MW14 BA Law and Drama
Duration: 3FT Hon
Entry Requirements: *GCE:* 260-360. *OCR ND:* D *OCR NED:* M3

MX13 BA Law and Education
Duration: 3FT Hon
Entry Requirements: *GCE:* 260-360. *OCR ND:* D *OCR NED:* M3

MV11 BA Law and History
Duration: 3FT Hon
Entry Requirements: *GCE:* 260-360. *OCR ND:* D *OCR NED:* M3

MP15 BA Law and Journalism
Duration: 3FT Hon
Entry Requirements: *GCE:* 260-360. *OCR ND:* D *OCR NED:* M3

LM21 BA Law and Politics
Duration: 3FT Hon
Entry Requirements: *GCE:* 260-360. *OCR ND:* D *OCR NED:* M3

MP12 BA Law and Public Relations
Duration: 3FT Hon
Entry Requirements: *GCE:* 260-360. *OCR ND:* D *OCR NED:* M3

MX11 BA Law and TESOL
Duration: 3FT Hon
Entry Requirements: *GCE:* 260-360. *OCR ND:* D *OCR NED:* M3

N8M1 BA Tourism with Law
Duration: 3FT Hon
Entry Requirements: Contact the institution for details.

CM81 BA/BSc Law and Psychology
Duration: 3FT Hon
Entry Requirements: *GCE:* 260-360. *OCR ND:* D *OCR NED:* M3

MN18 BA/BSc Law and Tourism
Duration: 3FT Hon
Entry Requirements: *GCE:* 260-360. *OCR ND:* D *OCR NED:* M3

CM61 BSc Sport and Law
Duration: 3FT Hon
Entry Requirements: *GCE:* 260-360. *OCR ND:* D *OCR NED:* M3

M200 FdA Law
Duration: 2FT Fdg
Entry Requirements: *GCE:* 100-240. *OCR ND:* P2 *OCR NED:* P3

S93 SWANSEA UNIVERSITY
SINGLETON PARK
SWANSEA SA2 8PP
t: 01792 295111 f: 01792 295110
e: admissions@swansea.ac.uk
// www.swansea.ac.uk

VLM5 BA Philosophy, Politics and Law
Duration: 3FT Hon
Entry Requirements: *GCE:* AAB. *IB:* 34.

MVC1 LLB Law and History
Duration: 3FT Hon
Entry Requirements: *GCE:* AAB. *IB:* 34.

LM21 LLB Law and Politics
Duration: 3FT Hon
Entry Requirements: *GCE:* AAB. *IB:* 34.

T20 TEESSIDE UNIVERSITY
MIDDLESBROUGH TS1 3BA
t: 01642 218121 f: 01642 384201
e: registry@tees.ac.uk
// www.tees.ac.uk

FM49 BSc Crime and Investigation
Duration: 3FT Hon
Entry Requirements: *GCE:* 240.

T85 TRURO AND PENWITH COLLEGE
TRURO COLLEGE
COLLEGE ROAD
TRURO
CORNWALL TR1 3XX
t: 01872 267122 f: 01872 267526
e: heinfo@trurocollege.ac.uk
// www.truro-penwith.ac.uk

M201 FdSc Law
Duration: 2FT Fdg
Entry Requirements: *GCE:* 60. *IB:* 24. *BTEC Dip:* MP. *BTEC ExtDip:* PPP. Interview required.

U20 UNIVERSITY OF ULSTER
COLERAINE
CO. LONDONDERRY
NORTHERN IRELAND BT52 1SA
t: 028 7012 4221 f: 028 7012 4908
e: online@ulster.ac.uk
// www.ulster.ac.uk

M1N5 LLB Law with Marketing
Duration: 3FT Hon
Entry Requirements: *GCE:* BBB. *SQAH:* AABCC. *SQAAH:* BBB. *IB:* 25.

M1LG LLB Law with Politics
Duration: 3FT Hon
Entry Requirements: *GCE:* AAB-ABB. *SQAH:* AAAAB-AAABC. *SQAAH:* AAB-ABB.

U80 UNIVERSITY COLLEGE LONDON (UNIVERSITY OF LONDON)
GOWER STREET
LONDON WC1E 6BT
t: 020 7679 3000 f: 020 7679 3001
// www.ucl.ac.uk

M146 LLB English and German Law (4 years)
Duration: 4FT Hon
Entry Requirements: *GCE:* A*AAe. *SQAAH:* AAA. *IB:* 39. Interview required. Admissions Test required.

M141 LLB Law with French Law (4 years)
Duration: 4FT Hon
Entry Requirements: *GCE:* A*AAe. *SQAAH:* AAA. *IB:* 39. Interview required. Admissions Test required.

M142 LLB Law with German Law (4 years)
Duration: 4FT Hon
Entry Requirements: *GCE:* A*AAe. *SQAAH:* AAA. *IB:* 39. Interview required. Admissions Test required.

M144 LLB Law with Hispanic Law (4 years)
Duration: 4FT Hon
Entry Requirements: *GCE:* A*AAe. *SQAAH:* AAA. *IB:* 39. Interview required. Admissions Test required.

W50 UNIVERSITY OF WESTMINSTER
2ND FLOOR, CAVENDISH HOUSE
101 NEW CAVENDISH STREET,
LONDON W1W 6XH
t: 020 7915 5511
e: course-enquiries@westminster.ac.uk
// www.westminster.ac.uk

M190 LLB Law (Solicitor's Exempting)
Duration: 4FT Hon
Entry Requirements: *GCE:* AAB. *SQAH:* AAABB. *SQAAH:* AAB.
Interview required.

W75 UNIVERSITY OF WOLVERHAMPTON
ADMISSIONS UNIT
MX207, CAMP STREET
WOLVERHAMPTON
WEST MIDLANDS WV1 1AD
t: 01902 321000 f: 01902 321896
e: admissions@wlv.ac.uk
// www.wlv.ac.uk

MV15 BA Law and Philosophy
Duration: 3FT Hon
Entry Requirements: *GCE:* 240.

W76 UNIVERSITY OF WINCHESTER
WINCHESTER
HANTS SO22 4NR
t: 01962 827234 f: 01962 827288
e: course.enquiries@winchester.ac.uk
// www.winchester.ac.uk

WM61 BA Film & Cinema Technologies and Law
Duration: 3FT Hon
Entry Requirements: *Foundation:* Distinction. *GCE:* 260-300. *IB:* 25. *OCR ND:* D *OCR NED:* M2

MV14 BA Law and Archaeology
Duration: 3FT Hon
Entry Requirements: *Foundation:* Distinction. *GCE:* 260-300. *IB:* 25. *OCR ND:* D *OCR NED:* M2

MW18 BA Law and Creative Writing
Duration: 3FT Hon
Entry Requirements: *Foundation:* Distinction. *GCE:* 260-300. *IB:* 25. *OCR ND:* D *OCR NED:* M2

MW14 BA Law and Drama
Duration: 3FT Hon
Entry Requirements: *Foundation:* Distinction. *GCE:* 260-300. *IB:* 25. *OCR ND:* D *OCR NED:* M2

MV11 BA Law and History
Duration: 3FT Hon
Entry Requirements: *Foundation:* Distinction. *GCE:* 260-300. *IB:* 25. *OCR ND:* D *OCR NED:* M2

MP1H BA Law and Media Production
Duration: 3FT Hon
Entry Requirements: *Foundation:* Distinction. *GCE:* 260-300. *IB:* 25. *OCR ND:* D *OCR NED:* M2

MW1X BA Law and Modern Liberal Arts
Duration: 3FT Hon
Entry Requirements: *Foundation:* Distinction. *GCE:* 260-300. *IB:* 25. *OCR ND:* D *OCR NED:* M2

MW1K BA Law and Performing Arts (Contemporary Performance)
Duration: 3FT Hon
Entry Requirements: *Foundation:* Distinction. *GCE:* 260-300. *IB:* 25. *OCR ND:* D *OCR NED:* M2

MC18 BA Law and Psychology
Duration: 3FT Hon
Entry Requirements: *Foundation:* Distinction. *GCE:* 260-300. *IB:* 25. *OCR ND:* D *OCR NED:* M2

W81 WORCESTER COLLEGE OF TECHNOLOGY
DEANSWAY
WORCESTER WR1 2JF
t: 01905 725555 f: 01905 28906
// www.wortech.ac.uk

M990 FdA Paralegal Skills
Duration: 2FT Hon
Entry Requirements: Contact the institution for details.

PS